AGRICULTURAL
SCIENCE

JOHN BREEN
GEORGE MULLEN

FOLENS

AGRICULTURAL SCIENCE

Editor

Anna O'Donovan

Design & Layout

Philip Ryan

Illustration

Michael Phillips

© 1992 Folens Publishers,
Hibernian Industrial Estate,
Greenhills Road,
Tallaght,
Dublin 24.

Produced in Ireland by Folens Publishers

ISBN 0 86121 339 4

Contents

SI Units

The internationally recognised system of units is Système International d'Unités (SI for short). In this book you will meet the following units:

Unit	Used to measure	Symbol
metre	length	m
kilogram	mass	kg
second	time	s
joule	energy	J
pascal	pressure	Pa
hertz	frequency	Hz
volt	potential difference	v

Note
- The Unit name always begins with a small letter
- The symbol (abbreviation) is a capital letter if it is named after a person; otherwise it is a small letter also.

Units are combined with prefixes which have multiplication factors.

Multiplication factor		Prefix	Symbol
1 000 000.0	10^6	mega	M
1 000.0	10^3	kilo	k
100.0	10^2	hecto	h
0.1	10^{-1}	deci	d
0.01	10^{-2}	centi	c
0.001	10^{-3}	milli	m
0.000 001	10^{-6}	micro	μ
0.000 000 001	10^{-9}	nano	n

Note
- Symbols are both singular and plural, e.g. km not kms
- No full stops in symbols e.g. not km. but km
- Group digits in threes around the decimal point. Do not use commas, e.g. 1 234 567.987 65 not 1,234,567.987,65

Non SI Units: A few non SI Units are accepted for everyday usage:

litre (l) = 1 dm^3; 1 millilitre = 1 ml or mL = $1cm^3$

hectare (ha) = 10 000 m^2

degree celsius (°C) (SI uses the Kelvin scale)

tonne = 1 000 kg or 1 Mg

minutes, hour, day, week, month, year

Calculation: You should convince yourself how easy the SI system makes some calculations; e.g. fertilizer applied at 1 g per m^2 = 10 kg per hectare. Compare this with "3 to 4 ounces per square yard" – approximately 100 g per square metre or 1 000 kg (1 tonne) per hectare.

This is much easier in metric. 1 cm rainfall = 10 litres per square metre.

Old terms: Avoid old terms: foot, yard, pound, ounce, acre etc. Think metric!

introduction

What Is Agricultural Science?

Agricultural science involves the application of known scientific principles to the production of food and fibre for human use. The basic agricultural resource, soil, is farmed to produce these commodities. This is done either directly (as with wheat, potatoes, forest products) or indirectly (as with meat, milk, wool).

Agricultural science has been known and practised for very many years. One of the earliest instances of its use was the selection and breeding of barley from wild grass-like plants in southern Turkey in the seventh century BC. At present, agricultural science faces possibly its greatest challenge ever, with many underdeveloped countries striving to cope with crop failures and famine while in developed countries over-production has led to food surpluses and pollution of the environment.

Agriculture in Ireland

Agriculture has always been of great economic and social importance in Ireland. The trend towards industrialisation and away from farming has been less pronounced here than in many other developed countries. This is due to the fact that Ireland has developed as an exporter of agricultural produce. Some other countries, in contrast, produce only enough for their own use and still others do not produce even this much and have to rely on imported food.

The twelve EC countries can be divided into "agricultural exporters" and "agricultural importers". This is done in *Table 1*, which also gives information on agricultural employment and exports.

Table 1: Agricultural employment and exports as percentages of total employment and exports in EC countries 1990

Countries		Employment as% of total employment	Forestry & fisheries exports as % of total exports
Agricultural exporters (exports exceed imports)	Ireland	13.5	28.0
	France	7.8	18.1
	Netherlands	4.9	23.7
	Denmark	8.4	34.3
Agricultural importers (imports exceed exports)	Germany	5.4	6.0
	Italy	12.1	7.3
	Belgium	2.9	11.3
	Luxembourg	4.8	4.3
	UK	2.7	7.6
	Greece	28.5	35.1
	Spain	17.9	16.6
	Portugal	23.1	14.1

Recent Changes in Employment and Production in Agriculture

The following figures for agricultural employment and production show how the importance of agriculture in the national economy has declined in the last 60 years:

	1926	1990
Percentage of work force in agriculture	53.0	13.5
Percentage of exports from agriculture	75.0	28.0

Industrialisation and urbanisation partly explain these figures. However, changes in mechanisation and technology are important also. For example, the number of tractors in Ireland increased from 500 in 1926 to 150 000 in 1990, thus reducing manpower needs. Increased knowledge of soils, fertilizers, and the principles of crop and animal production have led to increased production potential. The combination of these two factors, mechanisation and improved technology, mean that one labour unit (one man) can produce 30 tonnes of potatoes or 17 500 kg of milk per hectare (ha) per annum, now compared to 18 tonnes and 10 000 kg respectively in 1926.

At present, therefore, we have in Ireland a small labour force in agriculture producing large quantities of food and fibre for domestic use and export. The level of technology used varies from very advanced (in pig and poultry production) to relatively backward (in beef production).

The numbers employed in agriculture will continue to fall as industrialisation increases and farming becomes more mechanised and technical. However, they will never approach the very low level of the United Kingdom *(see Table 1)* as long as Ireland remains an agricultural exporting nation. Instead, they are likely to eventually reach a stable figure of about 6 – 7% (comparable to that of the other agricultural exporters).

Land Use Within Agriculture

The total land area of the Republic of Ireland is 6.89 million ha, of which 4.85 million ha (70.4%) is agricultural land. The remainder is made up of mountains, rivers, lakes, roads and urban areas and is collectively termed "non-agricultural land".

The use to which the agricultural land is put is shown in *Table 2*. It can be seen that the ratio of grassland to other crops is

Table 2: Area and percentage of agricultural land devoted to different crops, 1990

	Area (ha)	Percentage
Permanent grassland	2.93 million	60%
Hay and silage	1.24 million	25.6%
Tillage crops	0.51 million	10.5%
Forest crops	0.17 million	3.5%

approximately 6 : 1. This grassland is used almost exclusively by cows, beef cattle and sheep, so the statement once made that "the agricultural economy of Ireland stands on a cloven hoof" is still accurate.

Grassland and Its Utilisation

The utilisation of grassland is the key to Ireland's agricultural economy. Eighty per cent of the beef produced annually is exported, as is 65 per cent of dairy products and about 55 per cent of sheepmeat. All these products are produced mainly from grass, either grazed or fed in winter as silage or hay.

At present we have a total grazing animal population of 16.25 million, comprising 7.1 million cows and cattle, 9.1 million sheep and 0.05 million horses. To obtain information on how intensively we utilise our grassland, these livestock numbers must be converted to *livestock units* (LU), using the conversion data in *Table 3*. (A livestock unit is defined as "the amount of farm livestock which consumes a quantity of food equivalent to that consumed by a mature (550 kg liveweight), productive cow".)

Table 3: Livestock Unit values (conversion factors) of grazing animals

Grazing animals	LU value (conversion factor)
Bulls, cows, heifers-in-calf	1.00
Other cattle, 2 years old and over	1.00
Other cattle, 1-2 years	0.67
Other cattle, < 1 year	0.33
Rams, ewes	0.20
Other sheep, 1 year old and over	0.16
Other sheep, < 1 year	0.10
Working horses	1.50
Other horses	1.00

When this is done, it is found that we have about 6.0 million LU. This represents a more intensive level of utilisation than in the past. *Fig. 1* shows the changes in LU since the 1920s. The sharp increase from 1960 onwards was due to improved agricultural technology (particularly fertilizer usage and grass species development) and increased emphasis nationally on agriculture.

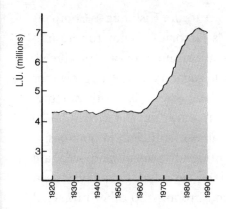

Fig. 1. Livestock Unit (LU) numbers in Ireland, 1922 – 1990

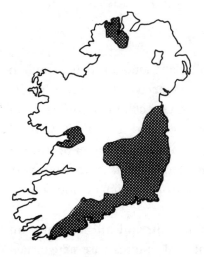

Fig. 2. Location of land devoted largely to tillage crops

Fig. 3 Use of arable land, 1990

We could, however, stock our land even more intensively if we further increased fertilizer use and drained and improved our grassland by replacing old pastures with young, more productive ones (reseeding). This would make our livestock farming more efficient and profitable. It would also release land for other purposes (e.g., tillage crops for human or animal use, use for leisure, forestry production).

Tillage Land and Its Utilisation

While grass grows very well in Ireland due to a favourable climate, tillage crops do not fare so well. This is because our high frequency of rainfall and moderate temperatures lead to moist soil conditions for most of the year. Such conditions favour the growth of grass, but not that of tillage crops, which require periods of dryness for seed-bed preparation and seed sowing and for ripening and harvesting of the crop.

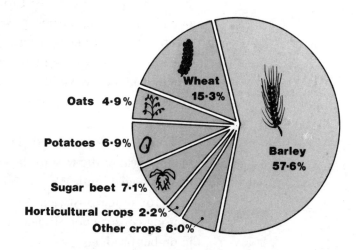

Tillage crops are concentrated mainly in the east, south-east and south of the country *(Fig. 2)*. In these areas rain falls less frequently than elsewhere and the soils are relatively free-draining. This leads to soil conditions moderately suited to tillage production.

Crops grown include barley, wheat, oats, sugar beet, potatoes and horticultural crops. The percentages of these are shown in *Fig. 3*.

Barley, our most important crop, is used for animal feeding (75 per cent) and malting (25 per cent). Ireland is about 60 per cent self-sufficient in animal feedstuffs. Wheat is used for both human and animal consumption. Winter wheat has a very high yield potential and the area devoted to it is increasing rapidly. Oats are grown on a limited scale, mainly for human consumption (porridge meal) and for feeding to thoroughbred horses.

Sugar beet is grown under contract to the Irish Sugar Company and is processed at the company's factories. Sugar for human consumption and molasses for animal consumption are produced. Ireland is 100 per cent self-sufficient in sugar. Potatoes are grown for human consumption. Ireland has a long association with potatoes and is the biggest per capita consumer in the world (110 kg/person/annum). Ireland is normally self-sufficient in potatoes.

Horticultural crops, while accounting for a small land area, are very intensively grown and of considerable value. Crops produced include field vegetables, tomatoes, mushrooms and other protected crops as well as honey, apples and soft fruits. There is scope for major expansion in horticulture especially in the area of fresh vegetables and protected crops.

Forestry and Its Utilisation

At present, the area under forests in Ireland amounts to 0.40 million ha or 5.8 per cent of the total land area. This is the lowest percentage among European countries. Our cultivated forests are of recent origin, 64 per cent having been planted since 1902. Many of these have been planted since 1950 and the trees have not yet reached maturity. Yields from harvested forests have been very good, however, reflecting the suitability of our climate and soil for forestry.

Forestry is located mostly in mountain and hill land and on blanket peat in the west of the country. Most forests are state-owned and managed, and 95% of trees are conifers. Harvested timber is used for fence posts, chip-board manufacture, pallet-wood and housing construction. Ireland is at present about 60% self-sufficient in timber products.

The small extent of current involvement in forestry in Ireland is explained partly by the indiscriminate harvesting, without replanting, in the 17th, 18th and 19th centuries. Planting since 1900 has been restricted by our strong tradition in livestock farming. The present position in the EC is that there are surpluses in most agricultural products, while large quantities of timber are being imported. This is likely to lead to an increased emphasis on forestry in European countries, including Ireland.

Section 1
Soils

1 – Parent Materials

Soil may be defined as:

> *"the unconsolidated mineral and organic material on the immediate surface of the earth that serves as a natural medium for the growth of land plants".*

Soil is developed from the underlying material (the "parent material") by a weathering and ageing process. The nature of the parent material and of the weathering and ageing process strongly influences the properties and usefulness of individual soils.

Parent materials are classified as residual, transported or cumulose. *Residual* materials are rock deposits which weather *in situ* long enough for soils to develop from them.

Transported materials are broken-down rock which has been transported some distance by natural forces such as wind, water, ice or gravity. Soil then develops from these transported materials in their new locations. In Ireland, ice is the main transporting agent and glacial drift – rock debris deposited by melting glaciers – is a widely-occurring parent material.

Cumulose materials are organic materials derived from preserved plant remains. They give rise to peat soils.

1.1 Rock Types

Rocks are divided into three groups, depending on their mode of origin. These are igneous, sedimentary and metamorphic. All of these rock types are commonly found in Ireland.

A. Igneous rocks

All rocks which are formed by the solidification of molten rock material *(magma)* are described as *igneous*. These rocks contain a number of minerals (a *mineral* is any inorganic substance of definite chemical composition which occurs naturally). The most important are quartz, felspar and micas.

Quartz (silicon oxide, SiO_2) is like colourless glass with irregular surfaces. Quartz is acid-forming and igneous rocks high in quartz tend to be acidic and to give rise to acid soils. *Felspar* (silicates of Al, K, Na and Ca) is a mineral which is porcelain-like in appearance and displays white, pink and grey colours normally. *Micas* (hydrated silicates of Al, K, Mg and Fe) are minerals with flat shining surfaces which flake easily into thin sheets. There is a clear form known as white mica or *muscovite* and a black form known as black mica or *biotite*.

When the magma solidifies due to slow cooling near but beneath the earth's surface the minerals form as large crystals which are easily identified *(Fig. 1.1a)*. Granite is the best example of this type of rock. When cooling is fast, as is the case with lava from volcanic eruptions, the resultant mineral crystals are very small and sometimes can only be seen using a microscope *(Fig. 1.1b)*. Basalt, which is solidified lava, is an example.

Fig. 1.1 Photo of (a) Granite; (b) Basalt

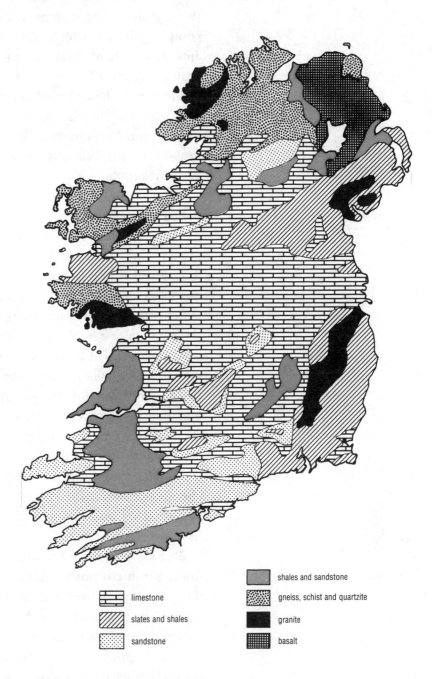

limestone		shales and sandstone
slates and shales		gneiss, schist and quartzite
sandstone		granite
		basalt

Fig. 1.2. Principal rock types of Ireland

Granite is therefore a coarse-grained rock and since it contains a lot of quartz it is acid. Soils derived from granite tend to be coarse-grained and acid also. Basalt, on the other hand, is fine-grained and contains very little quartz, felspars being the main constituent. Soils derived from basalt, therefore, tend to be fine-grained and much less acid than those derived from granite.

Granite is found in counties Dublin, Wicklow, Carlow and Kilkenny (Leinster granite); Galway (Galway granite); Donegal (Donegal granite); Armagh and Down (Newry and Mourne granites), as well as in other isolated locations (*Fig. 1.2*). Each of these granites has its own distinctive appearance and chemical composition. Leinster granite, for example, has a silvery/grey appearance, whereas Galway granite has a pinkish colour imparted by its pink felspar.

Most of the basalt found in Ireland is in Northern Ireland where the huge Antrim plateau covers almost the entire county and extends into Derry as well. There are some small isolated outcrops in the rest of the country, mainly in counties Limerick, Waterford, Wexford and Kildare.

B. Sedimentary rocks

All rocks are subject to weathering and breakdown due to the forces of rain, wind, frost, ice, rivers and sea. The materials resulting from this activity – gravel, sand and clay – eventually form sediments which accumulate at the bottom of the sea or lakes. There, over millions of years, they are converted to solid rock by compaction, cementation or a combination of these processes.

The particles of which sedimentary rocks are composed are very varied in composition. Some have the same chemical composition as the minerals which make up igneous rocks (quartz, felspar and mica) since they were formed by physical disintegration of the igneous rock. Others, however, have new mineral substances formed by chemical weathering of the minerals in the igneous rock. *Clay minerals* fall into this category. These are materials of very complex chemical composition formed by the chemical weathering of felspars. They have an important role to play in the soils developed from sedimentary rocks.

The vast majority of sedimentary rocks are formed on the sea floor. Sediment washed into the sea from rivers is sorted into different particle sizes, the small clay particles, for instance, being carried further out to sea than sand grains. Rocks derived from cemented sand particles are called *sandstones*. The sand is mostly quartz as quartz is the hardest and most durable of the rock minerals. Since it contains so much quartz, sandstone is an acid rock and tends to produce acid soils.

Rocks derived from clay particles are called *shales*. They contain little quartz and are very fine-grained. Soils developed from shales tend to have high clay contents and to be less acid than those developed from sandstone.

The third and final main category of sedimentary rocks is *limestone*. This rock, as the name suggests, contains lime (calcium carbonate, $CaCO_3$) either as the main constituent or as the material cementing particles together. The lime came from the shells of dead shell-fish. Limestone is an alkaline rock and tends to form alkaline soils. The texture of limestone is intermediate between that of sandstone (sandy) and shale (clayey). Soils derived from limestone have correspondingly intermediate textures.

Sedimentary rocks are the most common rock type occurring in Ireland. The centre of the country, which was once a shallow sea, is occupied by limestone. This area stretches from Dublin to parts of Clare, Galway and Mayo and from south Donegal and Fermanagh to north Cork *(Fig. 1.2)*. There are large areas of sandstone in the Waterford/Cork/Kerry region, and in mountain and hill areas of the midlands. Shales are found in the north Kerry/ west Limerick/ west Clare region and in parts of Leitrim, Fermanagh and Kilkenny, giving rise to clayey, poorly-drained soils in these areas.

C. Metamorphic rocks

Metamorphic rocks are formed by the action of intense heat or pressure on igneous or sedimentary rocks. Heat results from close contact with magma and metamorphic rock is usually found at the outer margins of a granite or basalt area. Pressure results from movements of the earth's crust. Sometimes heat and pressure operate simultaneously.

New minerals may be formed during the metamorphic process and the nature of the rock altered. The gross chemical composition remains unchanged, however, despite changes in mineral type and grain size. This is because metamorphism occurs in a confined situation, where there is no chance of loss or addition of chemical elements.

Thus, when limestone is changed into *marble* due to intense heat the two rocks, while very different in appearance and crystal structure, have the same chemical composition, $CaCO_3$. Another example of metamorphism is the conversion of shale to *slate* by intense pressure. *Gneiss* and *schist* are formed from granite and shale by a combination of heat and pressure and *quartzite* is metamorphosed sandstone. The acidity and texture of soils derived from metamorphic rocks depend on the acidity and texture of the rock. Quartzite, for example, gives rise to acid, sandy soils, whereas slate gives rise to clayey soils of lower acidity.

Metamorphic rocks widely occurring in Ireland are found in Connemara and northwest Mayo where schist, gneiss and quartzite form dramatic mountain scenery and in Donegal/Tyrone/Derry, where the same three rock types predominate. An area of the northeast and east midlands (Down, Armagh, Monaghan, Cavan, north Meath and Louth) contains slate mixed with shale. A similar combination of rocks is found in Wicklow, Wexford and east Kildare, in areas east and west of the Leinster Granite *(Fig. 1.2)*. Finally, slate forms the core of the Comeragh, Galtee, Silvermines, Slieve Bloom, Slieve Bearnagh and Slieve Aughty mountain ranges.

The distribution of rock types in the country is shown in *Fig. 1.2*. It can be seen that the low-lying central plain is underlain by limestone in a vast sheet which extends north and south into lowland areas of Ulster and north Munster. Mountains projecting from this sheet are made up of slate and sandstone. Sandstones dominate the south and south-west, including the mountainous regions of west Cork and Kerry, where Old Red Sandstone was folded into mountain ranges millions of years after its initial formation. A mixture of shale and sandstone is found in north Kerry, west Limerick and west Clare. Elsewhere, the limestone is bounded by the mountains and hills of the west, north and east, each area containing its own combination of igneous and metamorphic rocks.

1.2 Glacial Deposits

Glaciation occurs when snow and ice accumulate in mountain river-valleys and move slowly downwards under the influence of gravity. When glaciers reach lowland areas, they coalesce to form larger *piedmont glaciers*. In turn, these coalesce to form giant *ice sheets*. These sheets may cover many thousands of square kilometers and continue to move slowly, being driven onwards by the mountain glaciers and by small differences in elevation.

The outermost extremes of glaciers and ice sheets consist of melting *ice fronts*. If the rate of forward movement of the ice exceeds the wastage by melting at the fronts, then glaciation is said to be *advancing*. If wastage exceeds forward movement, glaciation is said to be *retreating*. Advances and retreats of ice sheets have occurred repeatedly in the past in Ireland and other parts of northern Europe. These events occurred in response to long-term changes in climate. At present, northern Europe is considered to be in an inter-glacial period.

When glaciers and ice sheets move forward, they scrape all soil and loose rock from the underlying surfaces. These materials become intimately mixed in the lower layers of ice and are

Fig. 1.3 (a) Soil development on rock

Fig. 1.3 (b) Soil development on glacial drift

deposited as *glacial drift* back onto the bedrock some distance away. Glacial drift consists of soil particles, pulverised rock and stones of all sizes up to boulders weighing many tonnes. These materials are mixed together without any tendency towards stratification. The stones and boulders are usually rounded and have smooth surfaces as a result of their rubbing against each other repeatedly. Glacial drift can vary in depth from less than a metre to many metres. After glaciation ends, it serves as the parent material for future soil formation.

Ireland was subjected to three successive periods of glaciation, the last period ending about 12 000 years ago. This final glaciation terminated and disrupted any soil formation which had occurred previously and so most of our soils have been formed since this glaciation. This means that they are young soils compared with soils of unglaciated regions of the world, some of which are millions of years old.

Most of the country has a cover of glacial drift and it is from this material that our soils have been formed. The only soils derived directly from residual parent materials are those formed at elevations greater than 200 m (i.e. above the ice-sheet) and those formed from rock from which the glacial drift cover was eroded. Soil development on rock and glacial drift is shown in *Fig. 1.3*.

1.3 Organic Parent Materials

Organic parent materials are made up of partially decomposed plants which have accumulated under very wet soil conditions or in lakes. The wet conditions prevent full decomposition of the plant remains by oxidation. Such materials are referred to as *peat parent materials* and they give rise to *peat soils*. Ireland has an abundance of such materials and they occupy about 11 per cent of the country. They are of recent origin, being only about 2 500 years old.

Peats are of two basically different types, *blanket peat* and *basin peat*. Blanket peat accumulates under conditions of high rainfall and humidity. Such conditions are found in areas in the western counties (Kerry, Clare, Galway, Mayo and Donegal) as well as in the upper parts of mountain ranges. In these areas, the wet weather conditions and low levels of evaporation lead to water-logged soil conditions and a build-up of peat to a depth of 1-2 m normally. The peat soils developed in these areas are wet, acid, infertile and of very limited agricultural use.

Basin peat accumulates in landscape depressions such as lake basins, hollows and river valleys. In lakes, dead remains of vegetation growing around the edges of the lakes and on the surfaces accumulate in an undecomposed state on the lake bottoms. In time, this build-up of organic material, together with encroachment of the vegetation around the edges, causes the lakes to close over completely and become land. In hollows and river valleys, peat accumulation occurs under the influence of waterlogged and flooded conditions. Further development of basin peat gives rise to *raised bogs*, so called because they are raised above the level of the surrounding land. Basin peat is drier and of more agricultural value than blanket peat. The development of basin peat is shown in *Fig. 1.4.*

Fig. 1.4 Stages of development of basin peat. (a) – (d) shows the accumulation of vegetation remains, causing the lake to close over completely. Further peat development gives rise to a raised bog (e)

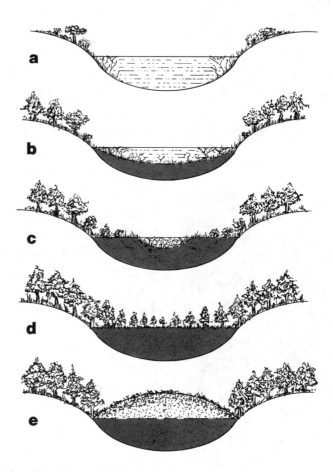

1.4 Weathering Processes

The manner in which bare rock or transported rock fragments are transformed into soil is slow and complex. It involves two processes, weathering and soil formation. Weathering is described now, while soil formation (including peat formation) will be described later in chapter 4.

Weathering of rock material occurs by *physical* and *chemical* agencies.

1.4.1 Physical weathering

The most important kind of physical weathering is *frost action*. Water enters the pores and fissures of rock and, on freezing to ice, expands by 9%. This can exert great pressure (approximately 150 kg cm^{-2}) on the rock, causing it to shatter. As rock shatters the depth of rock fissures, together with wetting, freezing and further shattering, increases. This leads to progressive disintegration of the rock.

Heating and cooling, without the effect of ice action, can also cause shattering due to rock minerals swelling and contracting at different rates. This type of weathering occurs to only a limited extent in Ireland due to our temperate climate.

When rock or soil particles are moved by wind or water or gravity, a certain amount of disintegration is caused by *grinding* action. Falling rock particles on a hillside, the beating effect of heavy rainfall, and sand washed in streams and rivers are examples of this type of weathering.

When plants begin to grow on disintegrated rock, the effects of *plant and animal action* are seen. Growing plant roots are capable of splitting the hardest rocks, while constant digging by animals promotes further disintegration.

1.4.2 Chemical weathering

A range of chemical reactions occurs during the weathering process resulting in both the decomposition and chemical transformation of rock minerals. Some of these are:

1. *Solution* - this is the dissolving of a solid in a liquid which changes solid materials into separate ions. Almost all the minerals in rocks are subject to solution by percolating rainwater, with Ca, Na and K compounds being most soluble and Fe and Al compounds being least soluble.

2. *Hydrolysis* - this is the process of minerals reacting with water to form hydroxides, which are usually more soluble than the original mineral. The action of water on orthoclase felspar, commonly found in granite and basalt, is an example:

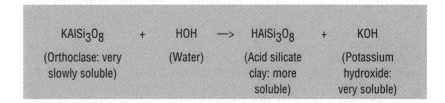

$$KAlSi_3O_8 \quad + \quad HOH \quad \longrightarrow \quad HAlSi_3O_8 \quad + \quad KOH$$

(Orthoclase: very slowly soluble)   (Water)   (Acid silicate clay: more soluble)   (Potassium hydroxide: very soluble)

3. *Carbonation* - this is the reaction of a compound with carbonic acid (H_2CO_3), a weak acid produced when carbon dioxide is dissolved in water. The carbon dioxide comes both from the atmosphere and from plant respiration and decomposition when plant growth exists. Carbonic acid dissolves minerals more readily than water alone. The formation of carbonic acid and its action on limestone are shown as an example of carbonation:

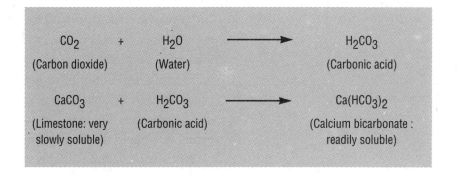

4. *Hydration* - this is the combination of a solid chemical, such as a mineral or salt, with water. One example is:

$$2Fe_2O_3 \quad + \quad 3H_2O \longrightarrow 2Fe_2O_3.3H_2O$$

(Haematite: a red-coloured cement of Old Red Sandstone)   (Water)   (Limonite: yellow in colour, softer and more easily decomposed than haematite)

5. *Oxidation/Reduction* - these reactions involve the addition of oxygen to a chemical compound (oxidation) and its removal (reduction). Either reaction transforms the compound and makes it more easily decomposed. An example of both processes is:

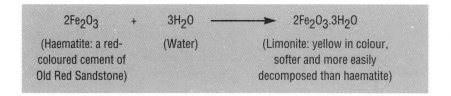

In this reaction, oxidation occurs in dryish, well-aerated conditions. Reduction occurs in wet, stagnant conditions.

Exercises

Exercise 1: Examination and testing of rocks

Materials needed

1. Samples of:

Granite	Marble
Basalt	Schist
Sandstone	Gneiss
Shale	Quartzite
Limestone	

2. Hydrochloric acid (HCl), dilute
3. Hand lens (Magnification : x10)
4. Scalpel blade or penknife

Procedure

1. Examine granite and basalt samples. Compare the grain-size (texture). Identify quartz, felspar and mica in the granite. Peel off flakes of mica using the scalpel blade or penknife.
2. Examine sandstone, shale and limestone samples. Look for signs of stratification (this is seen as parallel lines in the sample and shows where different layers of sediment were deposited successively). Compare the grain- size of the samples.
3. Test sandstone, shale and limestone with dilute HCl. Frothing indicates the presence of $CaCO_3$ (CO_2 is given off).
4. Examine marble, schist, gneiss and quartzite. Test marble with dilute HCl.

Results

Note the results of your examination and tests.

2 – SOIL COMPOSITION

In the definition of soil already given (p.14), attention was drawn to the presence of organic material and to soil's role as a medium for plant growth. Thus, the physical and chemical weathering processes described in *Chapter 1* are only the beginning of soil formation. They merely provide an exposed surface more conducive to trapping water and dust particles than that of bare rock or highly compacted glacial drift.

The trapping of water and dust creates suitable conditions for the growth of simple organisms such as bacteria, fungi and lichens. When these die they provide the embryonic soil with its first supply of organic matter and soil formation has commenced.

Fig. 2.1 Ideal composition of soil

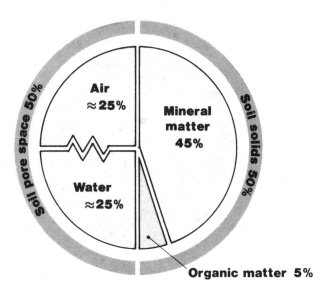

The ideal composition of fully-developed soil is shown in *Fig. 2.1*. The mineral matter is derived from the parent material and the organic matter from the remains of the vegetation growing on the soil. The jagged line separating air and water indicates that the amount of each is *dynamic* or constantly changing. After prolonged rainfall, the water content might rise to 30 - 35% and the air content might fall to 15 - 20%. After a prolonged dry spell, the reverse might happen with air content increasing and water content decreasing. The soil *pore space* should remain constant at 50%, however.

2.1 The Soil Solids

2.1.1 Properties of mineral matter

Mineral matter is composed of mineral particles of different sizes. A number of systems have been used to describe these. The first system was devised by the International Society of Soil Science

matter. Thus, large organic matter particles have little or no chemical activity. They contribute only to the size of soil pores and the drainage of the soil. As particle size decreases, the weathered humus becomes a better source of plant nutrients. In addition, its chemical activity increases dramatically and humus particles are very active in cation exchange.

The smallest particles, *colloidal humus*, have cation exchange rates two to three times greater than those of colloidal clay. This is due to the fact that humus has both *internal* and *external* surfaces engaging in cation exchange. Clay particles usually have external surfaces only. The term *soil colloids* is often used to describe the chemically active constituents in soil. Soil colloids include colloidal clay and colloidal humus. The properties of the soil solids are summarised in *Table 2.2*.

Table 2.2 The properties/activities of the different fractions of the soil solids

Particle size	Soil solids		Property / Activity
	Mineral	**Organic**	
Large	Gravel Coarse sand Fine sand	Plant and animal debris	Creates large soil pores Improves drainage Chemically inactive
Intermediate	Silt	Partially decomposed organic matter	Has little effect on drainage Provides some nutrients Slightly active chemically
Small	Clay Colloidal clay	Humus Colloidal humus	Very active chemically Acts as nutrient source Retains nutrients against leaching. Retains water

2.2 The Soil Pores

Properties of soil air and water

The air and water in soil are held in the soil pores. Soil air has almost the same composition as atmospheric air, the difference being its slightly increased carbon dioxide content and slightly reduced oxygen content.

The comparison is:

	% O_2	% CO_2	% N_2
Atmospheric air	20.97	0.03	79.00
Soil air	20.65	0.25	79.10

The lowered oxygen and raised carbon dioxide levels of soil air are explained by its role in *plant root respiration.*

Roots respire, i.e. they take in oxygen and give out carbon dioxide. Thus, soil air is continually being depleted in oxygen and enriched in carbon dioxide. If the soil pore space is satisfactory and there is a continuous system of pores from the surface down to the roots, then carbon dioxide *diffuses* up to the atmosphere and oxygen *diffuses* down to the roots. (Diffusion is a process by which molecules in a gas move from an area of high concentration to an area of low concentration in an attempt to establish equilibrium.) This diffusion prevents serious soil air composition changes, which could lead to carbon dioxide poisoning or oxygen deficiency.

Water is held in soil by *capillary forces*. *Fig. 2.3* shows water rise in glass tubes of different size. In tubes with very large internal diameters (A) water is not held at all while in very fine tubes (C) a lot of water is held. Soil pore space can be regarded as a collection

Fig. 2.3 Water rise in glass capillary tubes

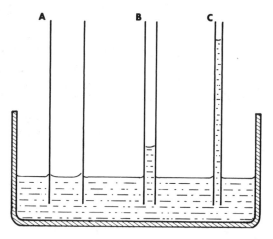

of capillary tubes of different sizes. The largest pores or cracks in soil correspond to tube A and do not hold water at all but let it pass downwards as drainage water. The smaller pores correspond to tubes B and C and they hold water in the soil. It is from these pores that plant roots withdraw water for growth.

Soil water contains plant nutrients in solution. These have come from clay and humus particles and from certain compounds in the soil. These nutrients are taken up by plant roots for growth purposes. Because of this, soil water is often referred to as the *soil solution*.

2.3 Physical Properties of Soils

2.3.1 Soil texture
Soil texture may be defined as:

"the relative proportions of the various-sized mineral particles in a soil".

The mineral particles have already been defined as gravel, coarse and fine sand, silt and clay. For the purpose of soil texture classification, only particles less than 2 mm in diameter are considered. This is because these particles are known to be of greatest practical importance in relation to soil properties and plant growth. Some textural descriptions are: sandy (sand dominant); silty (silt dominant); clay or clayey (clay dominant) and loam (similar amounts of sand, silt and clay).

Texture is probably the single most important physical soil property for two reasons. Firstly, it strongly influences a number of other important properties such as drainage, water storage, ease of tilling, aeration status and natural fertility. Secondly, texture is a fixed soil property, almost impossible to alter. The soils of the Golden Vale in counties Limerick and Tipperary, for example, are clayey and retain a lot of water. This has made them unsuited to tillage, although they are excellent soils for grassland and dairy production. Thus, these soils have a permanent limitation on their use due to their texture.

Determination of soil texture

Soil texture can be estimated by the "feel" method or by more accurate laboratory methods. The feel method is the most commonly used field method and, with a little practice, can be reliable and accurate. It involves (a) feeling the soil between the thumb and forefinger in both the wet and dry states and (b) estimating plasticity by moulding the soil into ribbons and threads. Grittiness and lack of plasticity indicate sandy textures while highly plastic soil is likely to be clayey. The procedure used is shown in *Exercise 2.*

In the accurate laboratory method for determining soil texture, the organic matter is first oxidised using hydrogen peroxide and removed. The amounts of sand, silt and clay are then determined by a combination of sieving and sedimentation techniques. The data obtained can be used to assess the *textural class* of a soil using a *soil texture triangle.* The procedure used is shown in *Exercise 3.*

A simple, but not very accurate, estimation of soil texture may be made by the sedimentation method given in *Exercise 4.*

Properties of soil textural classes

Some of the properties of sand, silt and clay have been given earlier *(see Section 2.1).* The properties of soils of different soil textural class are obviously related to these properties and are summarised in *Table 2.3.* Before examining the table, it should be pointed out that the plastic properties of clay tend to make soils containing large amounts of it unsuited to tillage. This is because, unless the soil is very dry, tillage operations tend to mould the soil into clods instead of breaking it up into a seedbed.

It can be seen from *Table 2.3* that loams and associated textures have the greatest number of desirable properties and the least number of undesirable properties. They are, therefore, the best textural classes overall.

Textural class	Desirable properties	Undesirable properties
Sand Loamy sand	Very easily tilled ("light") Free-draining, well aerated Warms up easily in spring	Prone to nutrient leaching Prone to drought Low interent fertility
Loam Sandy loam Silt loam Clay loam	Easily tilled Good drainage Good aeration Moderately retentive of water (not subject to drought), moderate/good inherent fertility.	None
Silt	Retains some water in periods of drought	Low inherent fertility. Easily waterlogged
Clay Silty clay Silty clay loam	Retains nutrients (inherently fertile) Retains much water in periods of drought	Plastic and sticky, not suited to tillage Easily waterlogged . "Cold" in springtime Susceptible to damage by grazing animals

Table 2.3 *Properties of soils of contrasting textural class*

2.3.2 Soil structure

Soil structure can be defined as:

> *"the coming together of the primary soil particles (sand, silt, clay) into larger, separable units".*

When structure formation occurs, the amount of pore space in the soil automatically increases *(Fig. 2.4)*. This increase improves soil permeability and aeration. Structure formation is of greatest importance in clay soils where the natural pore space is small in amount, causing soft, waterlogged conditions.

Fig 2.4 Cross-sectional views through structureless and structured soil

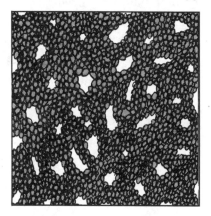 

Structureless
- Pores between primary soil particles only
- Pore space: 20%

Structured
- Pores between primary particles
- Pores between structural units (soil aggregates)
- Pore space 50%

Structure formation: flocculation and aggregation
The structural units in soil are called *aggregates* or *peds*. In the aggregation process, sand and silt particles are held together by clay,

organic cements and *inorganic cements*. All of these cementing particles are colloidal in size and the first step in structure formation is *flocculation*. This is a phenomenon by which colloidal particles come together into *floccules* or small clusters.

Flocculation occurs when the negative charges on the cementing particles *(see page 43)* are satisfied by *polyvalent* cations. These cause the particles to be linked together by bridges of *polarised water molecules*. Floccules are formed. Floccules are further linked together into a sponge-like matrix as shown in *Fig. 2.5*. This matrix physically traps the sand and silt particles into aggregates.

Fig. 2.5 Flocculated clay particles trapping a silt particle

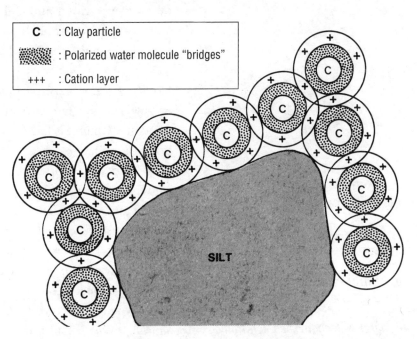

Cations exhibit the following order of effectiveness in promoting flocculation:

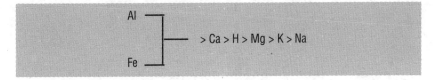

Fortunately, the effective ions (Fe, Al, H, Ca) are abundant in Irish soils. As a result, our soils show a high degree of structural development.

Exercise 5 demonstrates flocculation in a colloidal clay suspension. This demonstration works equally well with colloidal suspensions of humus or inorganic cements.

Structure development in the field

In practice, structure development in the field is accomplished by two processes which proceed simultaneously. These are cementation and separation.

Cementation of silt and sand is enhanced by a number of factors which push particles and cements closer together.

Separation of cemented materials into aggregates is encouraged by any factor which develops cracks and lines of weakness in the soil mass. The factors which accomplish these two processes are:

1. *Wetting and drying:* drying causes shrinkage and pushes particles together. Wetting/drying cycles cause cracks and break-up of the soil mass;

2. *Freezing and thawing:* swelling and shrinkage cause aggregation as above. Ploughing of land in the autumn causes a "frost tilth" to develop over winter and makes spring cultivations easier;

3. *Activity of roots:* small roots ramify the soil and increase particle/cement contact. Large roots crack and break up the soil;

4. *Activity of earthworms:* particles and cements are mixed in the earthworm gut. Earthworm *"casts"* have greatly enhanced soil structure. Channels left by worms promote cracking and break-up of the soil;

5. *Tillage operations:* properly carried out tillage operations promote aggregation by breaking up large soil clods and exposing soil for drying and shrinkage;

The poorest structure formation is usually found deep in the soil where there is little organic matter, root or earthworm activity, or swelling or shrinkage. Poor structures are also often found in bare surface soils subject to compaction (gateways, farm paths or tracks). The best type of structure formation is usually found in topsoils in *permanent grassland.* This is due to high levels of organic matter, root activity and earthworm activity. Examples of these kinds of structure formation are shown in *Fig. 2.6.*

Fig. 2.6 Three contrasting levels of structure formation:

(a, left) structureless soil from a deep subsoil;

(b, centre) weakly-structured soil from a compacted field path;

(c, right) well-aggregated soil from surface layers of permanent grassland.

2.3.3 Soil aeration

The amount of air in soil under ideal conditions is 25% *(Fig. 2.1)*. This amount of air ensures that there are sufficient large pores in the soil to allow diffusion of oxygen down to the roots and carbon dioxide away from the roots. If the soil structure is poor, the amount of *air-filled pores* may be less than this. Then crop growth is impeded due to a combination of oxygen starvation and carbon dioxide toxicity. Experiments have shown that many crops will fail when the level of air-filled pores falls below 8-10%. Crops which need a lot of air, e.g. sugar beet, may fail at higher levels.

Where problems of poor aeration are caused by *soil compaction*, a *subsoiler* or *ripper* may be used to break up compacted layers and let more air into the soil. A subsoiler is a heavy-duty implement pulled by a tractor through the soil; its use will be described in *Chapter 14* .

2.3.4 Soil water

Water is held in soil by *adsorbtion* and *capillary* forces. Adsorbed water is tightly bound to the surfaces of soil particles by chemical attraction between the negative charges on the particles and the positive charges of *polarised* water molecules *(Fig. 2.7)*.

Fig. 2.7 Adsorbed soil water

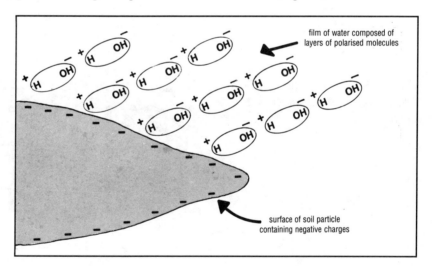

Fig. 2.8 Gravitational, capillary and adsorbed (hygroscopic) water in soil

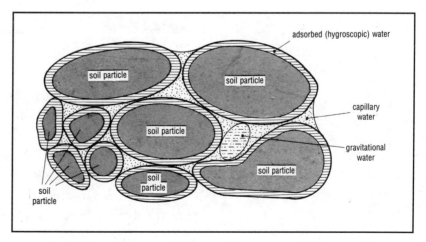

Adsorbed water is so tightly held in the soil that plant roots are not able to remove it. It is also referred to as *hygroscopic water (Fig. 2.8)*.

Capillary water is held in the spaces between the soil particles and aggregates *(Fig. 2.8)*. Some capillary water is *available* to plants. This is the water held in large pores by small capillary forces which are easily overcome by the roots. Other water held in small pores by large capillary forces is *unavailable* to plants.

Gravitational water is found in very large soil pores and in structural cracks *(Fig. 2.8)*. It is transitory in nature, being present only for short periods during and following heavy rainfall. After it has drained away under the influence of gravity (hence its name), it is replaced in the soil by air, which normally occupies such pores. Gravitational water is available to plants for the short periods in which it is found in soil.

Available water capacity

During heavy rainfall when the large pores are full of gravitational water the soil is said to be *saturated*. When the gravitational water has drained away the soil is at *field capacity (Fig. 2.9)*. This is the condition when all the capillary pores are full and the large pores contain air only. Most Irish soils are at field capacity for most of the time, due to our high frequency of rainfall.

Fig. 2.9 Soil at (a) saturation; (b) field capacity; (c) permanent wilting point

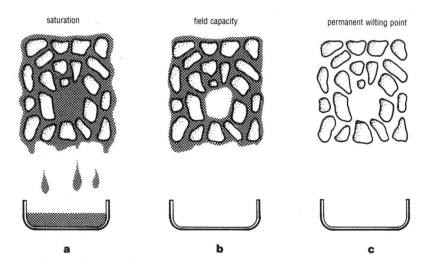

saturation   field capacity   permanent wilting point

a   b   c

Uptake of water by plant roots causes the soil moisture content to fall below the field capacity level. If no water is added to the soil by rainfall or irrigation, the soil becomes progressively drier as the capillary water is used up. Eventually, plants growing on the soil wilt and die of drought. The soil is now at *permanent wilting point.*

The water extracted by crops between field capacity and permanent wilting point is referred to as the *available water capacity* of the soil. This is a very important measurement as it gives an indication of how well the soil will support crop growth during a dry spell of weather.

The available water capacity values for a range of soil textures are shown in *Table 2.4*. It can be seen that loam and clay loam soils have the greatest amounts of available water. It is interesting to note that clay soils still contain 19% water when crops have wilted and died. This water is held in very small capillary pores as well as in the adsorbed form. It may also be noted that gravitational water is not included in the available water capacity. This is because, although it is physically available to plant roots, it is normally present in the root zone for such short periods of time that it is not of much practical importance.

Soil texture	% water at field capacity (A)	% water at permanent wilting point (B)	Available water capacity, % (A-B)
Sand	8	3	5
Sandy loam	16	8	8
Loam	22	11	11
Clay loam	28	14	14
Clay	28	19	9

Table 2.4 *Field capacity, permanent wilting point and available water capacity for a range of soil textures*

Water availability and crop growth

Not all of the water in the available water capacity range is equally available to crops. When the soil is at or near field capacity, the crop can withdraw water quite easily from the largest capillary pores. As the soil dries out, the pores still holding water become smaller in size and the force with which the water is held increases. Consequently, the force that the crop roots have to exert to remove this water increases.

This puts the crop under *moisture stress*. Crop growth can be severely restricted by moisture stress long before permanent wilting point is reached. For this reason, field capacity is the optimum water content for crop growth. Where irrigation is practised, farmers try to keep the soil at field capacity for as much of the time as possible.

Water movement in soil

When gravitational water moves downward in soil, it eventually reaches a depth below which the soil is fully saturated. This depth is known as the *water-table depth* and the upper surface of the saturated soil is referred to as the *water table*.

Water movement in soil can be of two kinds:
1. *unsaturated flow* or movement above the water table and
2. *saturated flow* or movement below the water table.

1. Unsaturated flow occurs within capillary pores *(Fig. 2.10)* and is *very slow*. This is because of the capillary force's tendency to keep the water stationary in the pores. Water moves from moist areas to drier areas, but movement is so slow that unless root development is very extensive, crop water shortage will occur.

   The *capillary fringe* is wetter than the rest of the soil above the water table. If the water table is near the surface with a large capillary fringe (as, for example, in clay soils), the root zone becomes very wet. Poor aeration leads to bad crop growth and invasion by rushes and other water-loving species in grassland. If downward flow of gravitational water is impeded by soil compaction or some other means a *perched water table* results *(Fig. 2.11)*.

Fig. 2.10 Section through soil showing water table with saturated and unsaturated zones

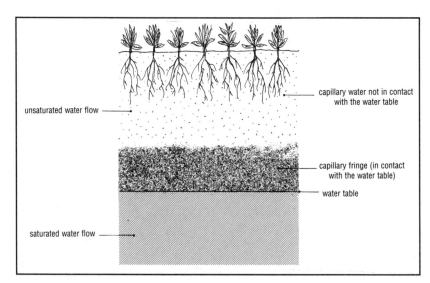

Fig. 2.11 Section through soil showing "perched" and true water tables

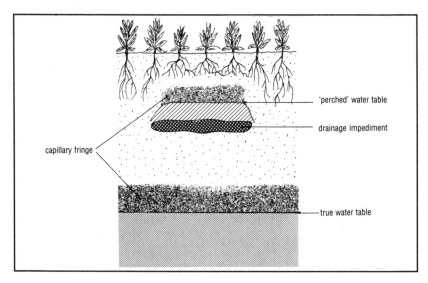

2. Saturated flow is important for the movement of water below the water table laterally to drains, streams or rivers. Saturated flow rates should be fast enough to dispose of all the

gravitational water arriving at the water table. Otherwise, the water table will slowly rise and the soil will eventually become saturated to the surface.

Downward flow of gravitational water under temporarily saturated conditions above the water table occurs during heavy rainfall. It is important in relation to nutrient leaching. Where flow rates are high, nutrient ions may be washed or leached out of the root zone leading to infertile soil conditions.

Saturated flow rates are highest in sandy and gravelly soils and in soils with very good structure development. They are lowest in silty soils and soils with poor structure.

2.3.5 Soil temperature

Soil temperature affects all physical, chemical and biological processes in soil. Chemical and biological reactions obey *Van't Hoff's Law* which states that the rate of all chemical reactions doubles for each 10 °C rise in temperature. In Ireland, soil temperatures are low and any practice which raises them usually gives a beneficial growth response.

In horticulture, glasshousing and mulches are commonly used to raise temperatures. In agricultural practice, the principal way in which soil temperature is raised is the use of artificial drainage in wet soils. The excess water removed by drainage is replaced by air which is more easily heated. Air has a specific heat value about four times smaller than that of water. As a result, crops growing on drained soils commence growth earlier in spring and produce higher yields over the growing season.

Exercises

Exercise 2. Estimation of soil texture by feel

Materials needed
1. Soils of contrasting textures (2 mm sieved)
2. Hand lens (magnification x10)
3. Water

Procedure
1. Using a sample of a *sand*, carry out steps (a) to (d).
   (a) Examine the dry soil under a lens and note the proportion of large and fine grains.
   (b) Handle the dry soil and note the feel of it, e.g. gritty or non-gritty.
   (c) Moisten the soil with some water and knead it with the fingers. Note cohesiveness and plasticity and its feel for grittiness. Knead the lump into a ball in the palm of the hand. Then see if it can be rolled into long threads (< 2 mm diameter). If it can, do the threads bend into rings?
   (d) Estimate the texture of the soil making use of the table on page 38 *(Table 2.5)*.
2. Using a *clay* soil, repeat steps (a) to (d).
3. Now attempt to classify soil samples of unknown texture.

Appearance under lens	Feel between fingers		Rolling between fingers	Texture
	Wet or dry	Wet		
Large grains absent or very few in amount	1. Smooth and non-gritty 2. Slightly gritty	Generally very sticky Plastic	Gives long threads which will bend into rings	1. Clay 2. Sandy clay
Many sand grains present	Slightly gritty	Moderately plastic	Gives threads with difficulty which will NOT easily bend into rings	Silty clay loam Clay loam Sandy clay loam
Sand grains present but silt and clay predominating	Smooth	Smooth	Forms threads with broken appearance	Silty loam
Comparable portions of sand, silt and clay	Gritty	Slightly plastic	Gives threads with great difficulty	Loam
Sand grains predominate	Gritty	Not plastic Only slight cohesion	Gives threads with very great difficulty	Sandy loam
Mostly sand	Very gritty	Forms flowing mass	Does not give threads	Loamy sand

Table 2.5 *Estimation of soil texture by appearance and feel*

Results

Record the results of your tests and estimations. Comment on the likely properties of each soil from the standpoint of management.

Precautions

Obtain estimates of soil texture from other pupils for each sample tested. Observe the variation and decide on a *class value* in each case.

Exercise 3. Determination of soil textural class

Materials Needed

1. Percentage sand, silt and clay values of soils
2. Soil texture triangle
3. Pencil
4. Ruler

Procedure

A procedure for using the textural triangle to determine the textural class of a soil containing 55% clay, 32% silt and 13% sand is as follows:

1. Take the soil's percentage clay (55%), find the value on the clay scale and draw a line parallel to the bottom of the triangle *(dotted line in Fig 2.12)*.

2. Take the soil's percentage silt (32%), find the value on the silt scale and draw a line parallel to left side of the triangle *(dotted line in Fig. 2.12)*.

3. The area in which intersection of the two lines occurs gives the textural class name of the soil. As a check, take the percentage sand (13%), find the value on the sand scale and draw a line parallel to the right side of the triangle. If all three lines intersect at the same place, the textural class has been determined correctly.

Use this procedure to determine the textural class of soils a, b , c and d.

Soil	Percentage			
	a	b	c	d
Sand	13	35	9	58
Silt	32	45	55	27
Clay	55	20	36	15

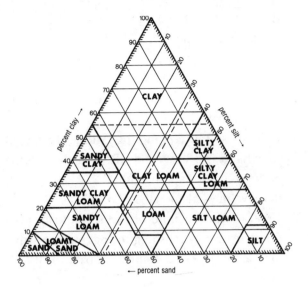

Fig 2.12 Soil textural triangle

Results

List results for soils a-d. Comment on the likely properties of each soil from the standpoint of management.

Exercise 4. Estimation of soil texture by sedimentation

Materials needed
1. Sample of soil (2 mm - sieved)
2. Graduated cylinder (100 ml)
3. Beaker (250 ml)
4. Water
5. Glass rod and rubber tubing.

Procedure
1. Take 20g of soil approximately (4 teaspoonfuls).
2. Place in a beaker and add 30 ml of hot water. Soak for 2-3 minutes.
3. Stir the soil/water suspension vigorously with a glass rod which has rubber tubing on one end. Break up the soil thoroughly by pressing it against the sides and bottom of the beaker with the rubber-covered end of the glass rod.
4. Pour the suspension into the graduated cylinder, washing out the beaker. Insert stopper and shake vigorously for one minute.
5. Add water to bring up to the 100ml mark.

Insert stopper, invert two or three times and place on the bench.
6. Allow sedimentation to occur. The coarse and fine sand will settle on the bottom of the graduated cylinder in a few minutes. Silt and clay will take much longer, perhaps up to 24 hours.
7. Measure the volumes of sand, silt and clay and express each as a percentage of the total of the three.

Note: Sand is characterised by its distinctly granular appearance. Silt appears granular also but the grains are so small that they are barely distinguishable as such. Clay appears to be amorphous. *(Fig. 2.13)*

8. Estimate the soil textural class using the procedure in *Exercise 3.*

Results

Record and comment on the result

Precautions

Ensure that the graduated cylinder is not disturbed during sedimentation or during measurement of the volumes of sand, silt and clay. Disturbance can cause the boundaries between the fractions to become indistinct and difficult to read accurately.

Fig 2.13 Estimating soil texture by sedimentation

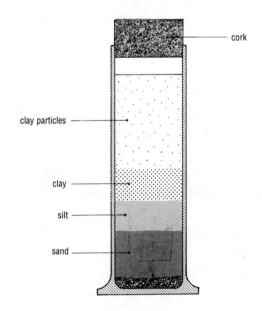

Exercise 5. Demonstration of flocculation of clay

Materials needed

1. Suspension of clay. This is prepared by adding 1 g of clay from a deep clay subsoil to 100 ml of de-ionised water and shaking thoroughly.
2. Reagents as follows: (a) 0.1 M hydrochloric acid, (b) 0.1 M sodium chloride, (c) 0.05 M calcium chloride, (d) 0.02 M aluminium chloride
3. Test-tubes, 4 (all of the same type)
4. Rubber stoppers to fit test-tubes, 4
5. Graduated cylinder, 10 ml
6. Test-tube rack (holder)
7. Watch or stopwatch

Procedure

1. Pour 10 ml of the suspension into each test-tube. Place the test-tubes in a test-tube rack. Label them (a) to (d).
2. Add 1.0 ml of reagents (a) – (d) to the four test-tubes. Mix thoroughly immediately (i.e., stopper and invert 3-4 times).
3. Note the time. Examine the tubes and record degree of flocculation after 5, 10, 20, 30 and 50 minutes.

Results

Make a table of the results. Comment on the results.

Precautions

1. It is important that the four test-tubes are of the same size. This makes recording of flocculation easier.
2. Use burettes or pipettes with pipette fillers for measuring the reagents.

Exercise 6. Demonstration of the effect of structure formation on total pore space

Materials needed

1. Sieved soil (2 mm sieve)
2. Two graduated cylinders (100 ml)
3. Two stirring rods
4. Water
5. Mortar and pestle

Procedure

1. Fill a 100 ml graduated cylinder to about the 55 ml mark with sieved soil.
2. Pack the soil by tapping the cylinder firmly on your hand for 30 seconds. Record the volume of the soil after tapping (A ml).
3. Remove the soil and label "Soil 1".
4. Take another sample of the soil and destroy the structure by crushing the aggregates with a mortar and pestle. Repeat steps 1 and 2 (B ml).
5. Remove the soil and label "Soil 2".
6. Fill a 100 ml cylinder to the 70 ml mark with tap water.
7. Slowly pour Soil 1 into the water in the cylinder.
8. Stir the mixture with a stirring rod and let stand for 5 minutes to allow the air to escape.
9. Repeat steps 6-8 with Soil 2 (structure destroyed).
10. Record the volume of each of the two soil/water suspensions (Soil 1: C ml, Soil 2: D ml).
11. Calculate the % total pore space for each soil sample as follows;

Sample Soil 1: % pore space

$$= \frac{\text{Pore space volume}}{\text{Soil volume}} \times 100$$

$$= \frac{(70 + A) - C}{A} \times 100$$

$$= \dots\dots\dots\dots \%$$

Sample Soil 2: % pore space

$$= \frac{\text{Pore space volume}}{\text{Soil volume}} \times 100$$

$$= \frac{(70 + B) - D}{B} \times 100$$

$$= \dots\dots\dots\dots \%$$

Results

Record the results for Soil 1 (structured) and Soil 2 (no structure). Explain the differences in pore space.

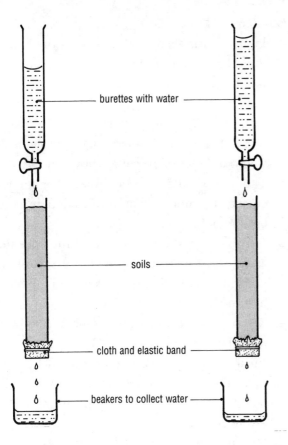

Fig. 2.14 Experimental set-up for determining infiltration rate and permeability

Exercise 7. Determination of infiltration rate and permeability in a sandy and a clay soil

Materials needed
1. Glass tubes, internal diameter 5-10 mm, 2
2. Sandy soil, clay soil; both dried and 2 mm sieved
3. Pieces of cloth, 2
4. Elastic bands, 2
5. Burettes, 2 [not essential]
6. Retort stand and clamps, 2
7. Metre stick or ruler
8. Beakers, 2
9. Graduated cylinder, 10 ml
10. Watch or stopwatch

Procedure
1. Attach cloth to the bottom of the glass tubes with elastic bands as shown in *Fig. 2.14*.
2. Fill each tube to the same height with soil. Put sandy soil in one tube, clay soil in the other.

Tap to compact.
3. Fill two burettes with water (these are not essential; a beaker of water is a suitable alternative).
4. Set up the burettes, glass tubes and beakers as shown in *Fig. 2.14*
5. Note the time. Begin adding water to the soil in each tube, either from the burettes or from a beaker.
6. Maintain 5 mm of water on top of the soil at all times. Measure and record the distance from the top of the soil to the wetting front every minute. The wetting front is the lowest level of water infiltration.
7. Keep measuring and recording the distance to the wetting front every minute until the wetting front reaches the bottom of the tubes.
8. Wait until the first drop of water comes through the cloth and falls into the beaker. Note the time again.
9. Wait 5 minutes, then remove the beaker and collected water.

Note: addition of water to the top of the soil should continue all the time up to this point.
10. Measure the volume of water collected in each beaker during the 5 minutes percolation and record (A ml, sandy soil; B ml, clay soil).
11. Measure the internal cross-sectional area of the glass tubes, i.e. of the soil columns ($C cm^2$).

Results
1. Plot distance to the wetting front (cm) against time (minutes) for each soil on a sheet of graph paper.
2. Compare the shapes of the curves and the total time (minutes) for complete infiltration.
3. Calculate mean infiltration rate for each soil as follows:

Mean infiltration rate

$$= \frac{\text{Length of soil column (cm)}}{\text{Time for complete infiltration (min)}}$$

$$= X\ cm\ min^{-1}$$

$$= \frac{X}{60}\ cms^{-1}$$

Comment on the results.

4. Calculate permeability for each soil as follows:
Permeability for sandy soil

$$= \frac{A \text{ ml}}{5 \text{ min}}$$

$$= \frac{A}{5} \text{ cm}^3 \text{ min}^{-1}$$

$$= \frac{A}{5C} \text{ cm min}^{-1}$$

$$= \frac{A}{300C} \text{ cms}^{-1}$$

Comment on the results.

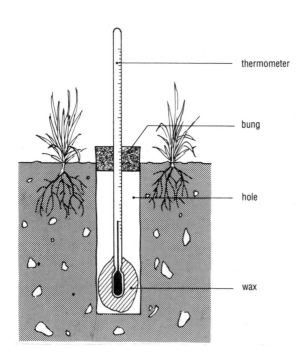

Fig. 2.15 Thermometer inserted in the soil

Exercise 8. Determination of threshold soil temperature for grass growth

Materials needed
1. Thermometer
2. Candle
3. Iron bar, 1 cm diameter approximately
4. Metre stick or ruler
5. Cork or rubber bung, bored to hold the thermometer

Procedure
1. Light the candle and drop wax on the bulb of the thermometer until the bulb is coated with wax to a thickness of 2-3 mm.
2. Select an area of grassland in an open situation (i.e. not sheltered by buildings or trees). Using the iron bar, make a hole in the soil to a depth of 10 cm as shown in *Fig. 2.15*. The hole should be wide enough for the wax coated thermometer bulb to fit snugly at the bottom of it.
3. Gently lower the thermometer into position and then fit the bung over the top of the thermometer so that it closes off the top of the hole as shown in the *Fig. 2.15*.
4. Remove and read the thermometer once daily from January 15 onwards. (The wax prevents sudden changes in the reading when the thermometer is removed from the soil.) Take readings at the same time each day and record carefully.
5. Measure the height of the grass daily from January 15 onwards. Record measurements.

Results
Observe records of grass height and soil temperature. Note the temperature at which grass growth commences.

3 – CHEMICAL AND BIOLOGICAL PROPERTIES OF SOIL

3.1 Chemical Properties

3.1.1 Cation exchange capacity

The soil colloids are the soil particles with the greatest level of chemical activity. This is related to their surface area. For example, within mineral particles the following is the case:

Particle	Surface area g^{-1}
Smallest fine sand particles	Up to $0.1 \, m^2$
Smallest silt particles	Up to $1.0 \, m^2$
Colloidal clay particles	Up to $1\,000.0 \, m^2$

In organic matter the comparisons are even greater than this.

The negative charges on the surfaces of the soil colloids arise in three ways:

1. Structural changes occurring within clay minerals during chemical weathering. If, for example, a magnesium ion, Mg^{++}, replaces an iron ion, Fe^{+++} in a mineral, one negative charge is left unsatisfied on the clay surface.

2. Unsatisfied negative charges at broken edges of clay particles.

3. Dissociation of protons from both (a) mineral and (b) organic surfaces.

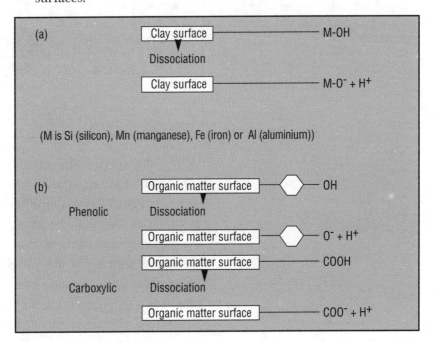

—43—

These reactions occur at millions of sites on the soil colloid surfaces. The result is the creation of a huge amount of negative charge which is satisfied by adsorbed cations. Cation exchange is a dynamic phenomenon with cations continually leaving the colloid surfaces either to replace ions withdrawn from the soil water or because they are being replaced by other cations which are temporarily more abundant in the soil.

3.1.2 Soil pH
Soil pH is defined as:

"the negative log of the hydrogen ion concentration in the soil solution".

The range of pH normally found in soil is shown in *Fig. 3.1*. Most agricultural land in Ireland has soil pH values in the 5.0 to 7.5 range with only mountain soils and peats being more acid than pH 5.0.

Fig. 3.1 Scale of soil pH values

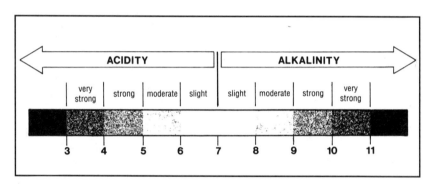

Fig. 3.2 Clay particle with its negative charges satisfied by cations. Note the ions in the soil solution – their concentration is greatest near the particle and decreases with distance from particle

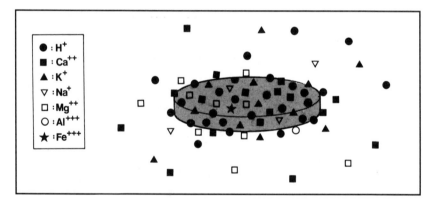

The amount of hydrogen ions in the soil solution is related to the amount of hydrogen and other acid-inducing ions on the soil colloids. *Fig. 3.2* is a simplified sketch of a clay particle with its adsorbed cations and the adjacent soil solution. It is the hydrogen ion concentration of the solution which is measured when soil pH is measured with a pH meter. This is the *active acidity* of the soil whereas the concentration of acid-inducing ions on the colloids is referred to as the *exchange acidity*. The exchange acidity is normally 30 000 to 60 000 times greater than the active acidity.

H^+ and Al^{+++} ions are the acid-inducing ions. If these dominate on the colloids, then the soil will be acid. This will occur (i) where felspars and micas (containing Al) are weathered from granite or sandstone or (ii) where carbonic acids and organic acids release H^+ ions for adsorbtion.

If basic cations, such as Ca^{++} and Mg^{++}, dominate on the colloids the soil will be alkaline or neutral. This might be the case when a soil is derived from weathered limestone or when a farmer spreads ground limestone on the land.

While H^+ ions directly influence pH in the soil solution, the action of Al^{+++} is indirect:

$$1. \quad Al^{+++} + H_2O \xrightarrow{\text{Hydrolysis}} Al(OH)^{++} + H^+$$

$$2. \quad Al(OH)^{++} + H_2O \xrightarrow{\text{Hydrolysis}} Al(OH)_2^+ + H^+$$

$$3. \quad Al(OH)_2^+ + H_2O \xrightarrow{\text{Hydrolysis}} Al(OH)_3 + H^+$$

Thus an Al^{+++} ion, once it leaves the colloid surface, has the ability to produce three H^+ ions in the soil solution and lower the pH accordingly.

Soil pH has a very important influence on all soil biological processes, including plant and crop growth. Measurement of pH and alteration by liming are commonly practiced in farming *(see page 69)*.

3.2 Biological properties

3.2.1 Soil organisms

Soil organisms can be grouped as shown in *Table 3.1*.

All of these organisms are involved in some way in the conversion of plant and animal debris to soil humus. In addition they physically churn the soil and help to create and stabilise soil structure. The great majority of soil organisms belong to plant life. Most organisms, both plant and animal, are *microscopic* in size.

High levels of biological activity are usually associated with favourable soil conditions and good potential for crop and animal production. The level of biological activity can be expressed in terms of *soil biomass*. This is the total amount of living matter in an area of soil (from the surface down to the depth at which biological activity ceases). The values in *Table 3.2* show the influence of vegetation on biological activity.

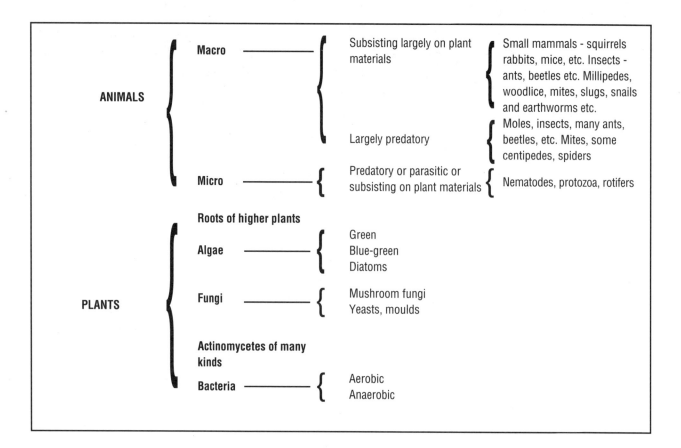

Table 3.1 Groups of organisms commonly found in soils

Table 3.2 Soil biomass values for three different vegetation types

Vegetation	Soil biomass (g m^{-2})
Grassland meadow	850
Oak forest	600
Spruce forest	355

The activity of *bacteria, fungi* and *actinomycetes* makes up 60 - 80 per cent of all soil biological activity and these three groups, together with *earthworms*, are of most practical importance. The important activities of these groups are summarised in *Table 3.3 (page 47)*.

All the activities listed in *Table 3.3* are beneficial to the soil except for Nos. 4 and 6. Degradation of soil organic matter *(Activity 1)* makes the plant nutrients contained in the organic matter more available and produces humus for structure formation and carbon dioxide to replenish atmospheric supplies. This activity is described in the next section of this chapter.

Activities 2, 3 and 4 are important in the nitrogen nutrition of plants and will be described later. Knowledge of mycorrhizal effects of fungi *(Activity 5)* is used in root innoculation of some trees and shrubs. The resultant fungal growth penetrates the tree roots and increases nutrient uptake. Species which benefit from mycorrhizal association include pines, spruces, oaks, maples, apples, laurels, azaleas and rhododendrons.

Group			Activity of Importance
Bacteria	1	(A)	Degradation of soil organic matter
	2		Conversion of atmospheric nitrogen from gaseous form to organic forms which can eventually be used by plants (nitrogen fixation)
	3		Oxidation of ammonium (from soil organic matter or inorganic fertilizers) to nitrate, a form in which it can be absorbed by roots (nitrification)
	4		Reduction of usable nitrate to unusable nitrogen gas (denitrification)
Fungi	1	(B)	Degradation of soil organic matter
	5		Combination with certain trees and other plants in a symbiotic relationship which makes plant nutrients more available to the plants (mycorrhizal effect)
	6		Parasitic attack on some crops
Actinomycetes	1	(C)	Degradation of soil organic matter
Earthworms	1	(D)	Degradation of soil organic matter
	7		Improvement of soil structure, aeration, and water movement
	8		Transportation of soil and organic matter (mixing of surface and lower soil)

Table 3.3 *Activities of the most important groups of soil organisms*

Parasitic attack by fungi *(Activity 6)* can have serious effects on crop growth, leading to complete crop failure in cases.

The benefits of the earthworm *(lumbricus terrestris) (Activities 7 and 8)* to soils and plant growth are numerous. Earthworms are very important in the first steps in the breakdown and incorporation into soil of plant debris. Leaf litter that has been passed through the earthworm's gut has the availability of its phosphorus (P) increased by over 100 per cent. The litter is also much more accessible to further degradation by micro-organism action.

Soil aeration and water movement are improved by the channels left by the earthworm's burrowing action. This is especially true in clay soils which have poor structural conditions in the absence of earthworms.

Fig 3.3 Influence of low (a) and high (b) levels of earthworm activity on soil structure and organic matter (OM) percentage

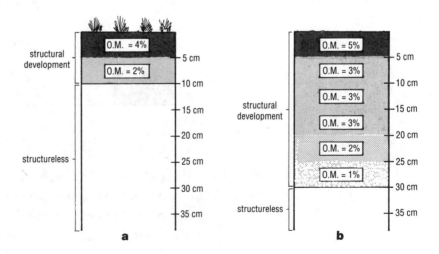

Earthworm activity is of special benefit in the renovation of barren, structureless materials such as *spoil* left behind after land drainage, building construction or any large-scale earth movements. In an experiment on one such material, the absence of earthworm activity caused the situation shown in *Fig. 3.3 (a)* to be found after a period of 5 years. Plant debris had been degraded and incorporated and soil structure had developed to a depth of 10 cm only.

In an adjacent location having a high earthworm population, the situation shown in *Fig. 3.3 (b)* was found. Here, soil organic matter was found at high levels down to a depth of 30 cm and good structure existed to that depth also. This is explained by *transportation* of organic matter to progressively deeper depths with time and the general mixing of the soil achieved by earthworm activity.

Earthworm numbers and activity are dependent on environmental factors. The optimum pH is 6 - 8 and earthworms require moist, warm (> 10° C) soil conditions with plenty of palatable organic matter. Populations of 30 - 300 m^{-2} are commonly found in arable soils while numbers in excess of 500 m^{-2} may be found in rich grassland. Even greater numbers occur in land recently spread with farmyard manure.

3.2.2 Organic matter degradation

Fresh plant debris is composed of water and solids; this and the elemental composition of the solids are shown in *Fig. 3.4*.

Fig. 3.4 Composition of fresh plant tissue. The organic materials contained are listed in order of ease of degradation (1, most easily degraded; 5, least easily degraded)

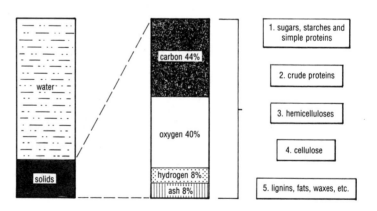

Degradation of most of the organic matter is essentially a "burning" or oxidation process. Aerobic bacteria, fungi and actinomycetes obtain energy for growth and metabolism by acting on the oxidisable fraction of the organic materials. This is the fraction composed mainly of carbon and hydrogen and the reaction is as follows:

$$-[C, 4H] + 2O_2 \xrightarrow[\text{oxidation}]{\text{Enzymic}} CO_2 + 2H_2O + \text{Energy}$$

Carbon- and hydrogen containing compounds   Oxygen   Carbon dioxide   Water

Organic materials containing other elements in addition to carbon and hydrogen are involved in more complex reactions. Protein substances, for example, contain nitrogen, phosphorus and sulphur. During degradation they produce *amides* and *amino acids* of various kinds in addition to carbon dioxide and water. These amides and amino acids are often constituents of microbial cells. When the cells die, they may be further degraded to yield nitrogen, phosphorus and sulphur compounds which may yield nutrient ions for uptake by plant roots.

At any one time, therefore, soil organic matter is composed of the following constituents: plant debris; microbial cells, living and dead; intermediate products; humus. *Humus* is a mixture of (1) partly modified lignins, fats and waxes and (2) complex compounds synthesized by the soil micro-organisms. It is resistant to further degradation, colloidal in nature, very reactive chemically and dark brown/black in colour.

Fig. 3.5 Changes occurring in soil organism numbers and volumes of fresh organic debris and humus during organic matter degradation

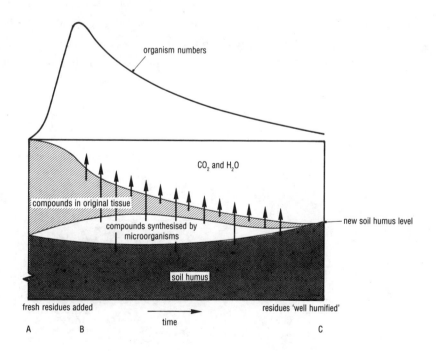

The events occurring during a period of organic matter degradation are shown in *Fig. 3.5*. When fresh material is added to the soil the soil micro-organisms first attack easily-degraded compounds. This leads to rapid build-up of microbial numbers accompanied by a reduction in the volume of fresh material as carbon dioxide and water are released from it *(period A —> B)*.

After the easily-degraded materials have been oxidised, organism numbers decline. So does the rate of loss of fresh material and the rate of carbon dioxide and water release *(period B —> C)*. This coincides with the degradation of the less-easily degraded materials.

The process described above is called *humification*. It refers to the degradation of organic debris with humus as the end-product. It occurs repeatedly and continuously in soil and, as is shown in *Fig. 3.5*, leads to a small increase in the level of soil humus. This small increase is usually balanced by leaching losses and humus levels tend to change little unless the vegetation is greatly altered.

Humification may be contrasted with *mineralisation*. In this process, easily-degraded organic materials, such as simple proteins, are fully degraded to their mineral constituents (e.g. nitrates, sulphates, phosphates). These may then be absorbed by plant roots. In the mineralisation process, very little humus is formed.

Humification and mineralisation apply equally to residues of both plant and animal origin. Both processes are dependent on soil conditions and they operate best in *moist, warm, aerated, high pH(> 6.0) soils.*

3.2.3 The carbon cycle

The activity of soil organisms in degrading soil organic matter is a component of the carbon cycle *(Fig. 3.6)*. As large amounts of carbon dioxide are taken from the atmosphere for photosynthesis, it is important that it is constantly replaced. This is achieved by means of the carbon cycle.

Fig. 3.6 The carbon cycle

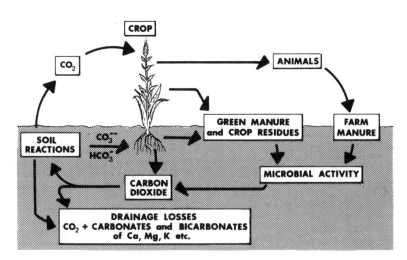

Exercises

Exercise 9. Demonstration of cation exchange

Materials needed
1. High-pH soil (pH 7.0 or greater); dried, sieved (2 mm)
2. Funnel
3. Filter paper (Whatman No. 50)
4. Test-tube
5. Retort stand and clamp
6. Test vials
7. Distilled water
8. Reagents as follows:
   (a) potassium chloride (1%) (b) ammonium oxalate (c) sodium cobaltinitrite
   (d) ethanol (e) hydrogen chloride (1%)

Procedure
1. Place 1 level teaspoonful of soil in a filter paper in the funnel.
2. Slowly (drop by drop) add reagent (a).
3. Test the leachate (first drops) for calcium. *Calcium test:* to 10 drops of leachate in a test vial add 1 drop of reagent (b). Shake and note the amount of white precipitate.
4. Continue the exchange process (slowly adding reagent (a)), testing occasionally for calcium. Continue until this test is negative. The colloids are now transformed from being calcium-dominant to potassium-dominant.
5. Wash potassium chloride from the soil pores and the filter paper by dropping distilled water onto the soil. This procedure may be speeded up by transferring the soil to a clean filter paper. Test for potassium from time to time until a negative test is obtained. *Potassium test:* to 10 drops of filtrate in a test vial add 1 drop reagent (c) and a few drops reagent (d).
6. To prove that the colloids in the soil are potassium-dominant, another ion is introduced to replace the potassium ions. Add reagent (e) slowly and test the filtrate for potassium.

Results
Record the activities carried out in sequence and the results obtained. Explain the significance of the results.

Exercise 10. Determination of soil pH

Materials needed
1. Soil of contrasting pHs; finely broken down or sieved (2 mm)
2. pH meter
3. Distilled water
4. Glass rods
5. Small beakers (50/100 ml)

Procedure
1. Place a small quantity (two teaspoonfuls) of each soil in a beaker.
2. Add approximately the same volume of distilled water. Stir with the glass rod and allow to stand for 10 minutes. (Keep one stirring rod per soil and do not interchange them).
3. Stir again and insert the electrode into the soil/water suspension. Turn the dial to "read" (or "pH") and read the soil pH. If the reading fluctuates, wait for 30 seconds before taking the value.
4. Clean the electrode with distilled water, using a wash bottle.
5. Measure the next pH value, repeating steps 1-3 or store the electrode in distilled water and turn the dial to "stand-by".

Results
Record and comment on the results.

Precautions
1. The pH meter should be turned on at least 1 hour before making any measurements.
2. The pH meter should be calibrated after every 10 readings. Use a buffer solution, buffered at pH 4.0 or pH 7.0. Use whichever buffer is closest to the pHs of the soils being measured.

Exercise 11. Field-measurement of earthworm populations

Materials needed
1. Washing-up liquid
2. Water
3. Scissors or shears
4. Notebook

Procedure
Note: This exercise should be carried out on two soils which would be expected to contain contrasting numbers of earthworms, e.g., (a) an acid and a neutral soil, (b) a tillage and an old grassland soil.
1. Select a $1m^2$ level area of soil and remove all vegetation using the scissors or shears.
2. Make up a solution of washing up liquid, using approximately 20 ml of liquid to 2 litres of water.
3. Apply the solution evenly over the area.
4. Count and record the number of earthworms which come to the surface.

Results
1. Compare and comment on the earthworm numbers recorded in the two soils.
2. Express the population in earthworms ha^{-1}

Precautions
1. Try to apply the solution without allowing bubbles to form. Otherwise it will be difficult to see and count the worms.
2. Some earthworms may not come fully out of the soil. These should be caught and gently pulled out. Otherwise some worms may be counted twice.

Exercise 12. Determination of organic matter content of soils

Materials needed
1. Soil 1: sandy; dried, sieved (2 mm)
   Soil 2: peaty; dried, sieved (2 mm)
2. Silica-dishes, 2
3. Pipe-clay triangles, 2
4. Bunsen burners, 2
5. Laboratory tongs

Procedure
1. Weigh out 10 g of the two soils and transfer to weighed silica dishes (dish for sandy soil = Ag; dish for peaty soil = Bg).
2. Place the dishes and contents on pipe-clay triangles on tripods. Label the tripods "sandy" and "peaty". (Labelling will burn off the dishes.)
3. Heat with bunsens until all the organic matter has been burnt. The samples will first smoke and then become red.
4. Cool the dishes and soils in a dessicator (memorise the placing, since the dishes are not labelled).
5. Weigh the dishes and contents (weight of dish + sandy soil = Cg; weight of dish + peaty soil = Dg).

Results
1. Calculate per cent organic matter as follows:
   Sandy soil:

   $$\% \text{ organic matter} = \frac{\text{wt of organic matter} \times 100}{\text{wt of soil}}$$

   $$= \frac{(10 + A - C)\ 100\ \%}{10}$$

   Peaty soil:

   $$\% \text{ organic matter} = \frac{\text{wt of organic matter} \times 100}{\text{wt of soil}}$$

   $$= \frac{(10 + B - D)\ 100\ \%}{10}$$

2. Comment on the results

Precautions
1. Wear protective glasses during the burning process.
2. Handle the silica dishes carefully with laboratory tongs after burning.

4 – SOIL TYPES

To manage land properly for farming or other purposes, it is important to know the soil type(s) with which one is dealing. Even small farms can, and usually do, contain more than one soil type. Each has different properties and should be managed differently.

There are three phases in the study of soil types. These are: (1) soil formation; (2) soil classification; (3) soil survey and mapping.

4.1 Soil Formation

4.1.1 Factors of soil formation

A number of factors influence soil formation and development. They are: (1) climate; (2) parent material; (3) living organisms; (4) topography; (5) time.

(1) Climate: climate is the most important factor influencing soil formation. This is so because, in addition to its direct influence on parent material weathering and soil development, it is largely responsible for variation in plant and animal life. Its influence overrides that of the other factors. *Rainfall* and *air temperature* are the most important climatic criteria. On the basis of these, the world can be divided into climatic regions or zones. Each climatic region contains a range of soils specific to it. Ireland's climate is dominated by low air temperature and evaporation rate. As a result, rainfall exceeds evaporation and most soils tend to be leached of bases. This makes them acid, requiring regular liming and fertilizer addition. Regional variation in rainfall and evaporation is reflected in soil type variation.

(2) Parent material: the nature of the parent material greatly influences the characteristics of the derived soils. This is particularly true in Ireland where our soils are young, having developed since glaciation. In very old soils, chemical weathering may alter rock minerals to such a degree that there is little or no relationship between soil and parent material.

The influence of rock texture and acidity on soil texture and acidity has already been mentioned. This relationship becomes more important in Ireland's humid climate with its natural tendency toward acidification. Sandy soils allow freer downward flow of water and acidity develops more quickly. This is especially true if the sand is derived from quartz and is therefore acid in nature itself.

Where *limestone* is present in the parent material, the development of acidity is delayed in two ways. Firstly, the abundance of Ca^{++} and Mg^{++} ions in the developing soil raises the pH directly. Secondly, the species of trees usually found on limestone (ash, birch, hazel) are relatively high in bases. The action of the trees in

—53—

continually bringing these bases to the surface as constituents of leaves and twigs *(Fig. 4.1)* causes a further, indirect, delay in acidification.

(3) Living organisms: living organisms are involved in a range of processes which affect the development of differing soil types. These include organic matter degradation, mixing of soil constituents, development of soil structure, addition of nitrogen to the soil system and prevention of erosion of soil constituents by vegetative cover.

The most striking examples of the influence of different organisms are seen in (a) differences between soils developed under grassland and forest and (b) soil differences under different forest species.

(a) Soils developed under forest vegetation have more soil layers *(horizons)*, a more highly leached surface layer and more plant debris at the surface than those developed under grassland. This is due to the fact that the organic matter in forest soils is added in the form of leaves and twigs *on* the surface. That added to grassland soils is in the form of fibrous roots *within* the soil. This leads to better humification and higher humus levels in grassland soils. This in turn gives them better water- and cation-holding capacity which makes them less prone to acidification and leaching.

(b) The soil differences under different forest species result from the acidifying effect of *coniferous* leaves and twigs compared with the less severe acidification induced by the leaves and twigs of some *deciduous* species *(Fig. 4.1)*. Acidification leads to leaching of bases and the development of light-coloured, infertile horizons near the surface. Acidifying species include pines, firs and spruces while the deciduous species which slow down acidification include ash, birch and hazel.

Fig. 4.1 Nutrient recycling. If residues from the vegetation are low in bases, acidification is favoured (A). If residues are high in bases, acidification is delayed (B)

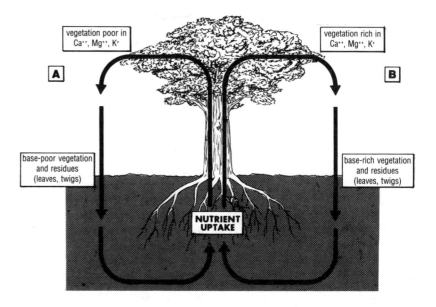

(4) Topography: the influence of topography is seen mostly at a local level, where differences in slope affect *water movement* and *erosion*. On steep hillsides, soils are shallower than on gently sloping hillsides. This is because on the steep slopes water moves along the soil surface *(runoff)* instead of percolating through the soil. The runoff causes surface erosion. The eroded soil material accumulates lower down on gentler slopes and gives deeper soils.

In valley bottoms, the leached bases and some eroded clay particles from the surrounding higher areas accumulate. This tends to give rise to deep, fertile soils high in organic matter. If the bottoms of the slopes are landlocked depressions, however, wet marshy conditions result which may give lakes and basin peats. The influence of topography on soil formation is shown in *Fig. 4.2.*

Fig. 4.2 Influence of topography on soil development. In location 1, a river removes water from the valley bottom; in location 2, a lake develops.

A: Shallow soils
B: Deeper soils
C1: Deep, fertile, humus-rich soils
C2: Wet soils, or basin peats

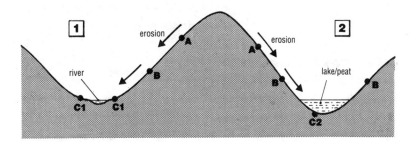

(5) Time: while soil formation can occur in as short a time as 200 years under ideal conditions, it is more common for it to take several thousand years. While conditions remain favourable, soil formation and ageing continue and some soils in unglaciated areas are very old. As has been pointed out already *(see page 53)*, Irish soils are young and therefore their properties are strongly related to their parent materials.

4.1.2 Weathering and soil profile development
A soil profile may be defined as:

> *"a vertical section of the soil through all its horizons (layers) and extending into the parent material".*

The process by which the upper part of the soil profile develops from the parent material is influenced by *physical and chemical weathering* and by *soil organisms and organic matter.*

The physical and chemical destruction of rock and synthesis of new minerals *(see Section 1.4)* begin the soil forming process. The weathered rock and synthesised clay minerals retain water and release nutrient ions. These nourish simple plant and animal life forms such as bacteria, fungi and lichens. Residues from these are returned to the weathering mass and are degraded to humus, whose water- and nutrient- holding powers are a further stimulus to plant and animal life.

As soon as plants begin to grow on the new soil, the soil profile begins to develop. Plant and animal remains are deposited on and in the soil material. They are degraded there giving the surface layer a slightly darker colour than the deeper layers.

The organic matter in this *new surface horizon* releases acids as it decomposes. These acids speed up the chemical weathering of the rock minerals causing more soluble nutrients to be released. These may stimulate further plant growth, increased rooting and deepening of the surface horizon *(Fig. 4.3a)*. If downward movement of water is large and conditions acidic however, these soluble nutrients may be washed down in the water. They are then, together with other soil constituents such as clay and humus particles, deposited at a lower depth *(Fig. 4.3b)*.

Fig. 4.3 Soil profiles developed under (a) low-rainfall, slightly acid conditions, and (b) high rainfall, more acid conditions

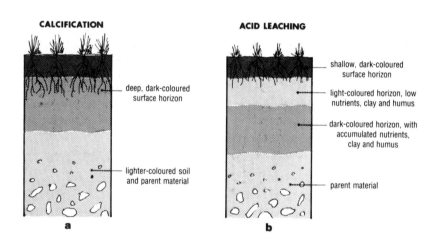

The processes just described constitute two of the three soil-forming processes of most importance in Ireland. The first process, known as *calcification*, occurs where rainfall is low (< 750 mm year^{-1}) and the parent material contains substantial amounts of calcium, i.e., where the pH is neutral or only slightly acid. When these soils support grassland or deciduous forest (which recycle bases), acidification is prevented. The result is deep, humus-rich soils with little horizonation, which are moderately base-rich and fertile.

The second process, known as *acid leaching*, occurs where rainfall is high and parent materials are acid. Under such conditions, soluble nutrients are carried downwards in acid percolating water. This process is accentuated when the vegetation is coniferous forest as was the case in many areas in the past in Ireland.

The soil becomes progressively more acid and the leached horizon becomes progressively lighter in colour and lower in bases.

Clay and humus are also leached. The light colour of the leached horizon is caused by the absence of iron and humus. All the leached materials accumulate deeper in the profile when their concentration reaches a high level. The results of this process are variable. Some soils are deep and only moderately leached. Others have very shallow, acid surface horizons overlying severely leached horizons, both being of very low fertility.

The third soil-forming process of importance is referred to as *gleisation* and is independent of rainfall amount and parent material. Gleisation is caused by water-logged conditions. These may arise either because of a high watertable or due to the impermeable nature of the soil itself. Leaching does not occur and anaerobic conditions lead to the chemical conversion of many soil constituents to the reduced form.

Reduction of iron causes gleyed soils to have grey or blue colours with some red mottling where the iron has been partly re-oxidised. Crop production on gleyed soils is usually limited by spring and autumn wetness. In many cases, artificial drainage can bring about some improvement.

4.1.3 The soil profile

The soil profile may be composed of a number of *soil horizons*. Soil horizons are roughly horizontal layers of soil which differ from adjacent horizons in properties such as colour, texture, structure, organic matter content or chemical characteristics.

The system of profile and horizon nomenclature is shown in *Fig. 4.4.*

Fig. 4.4 Soil layers, horizons and horizon characteristics

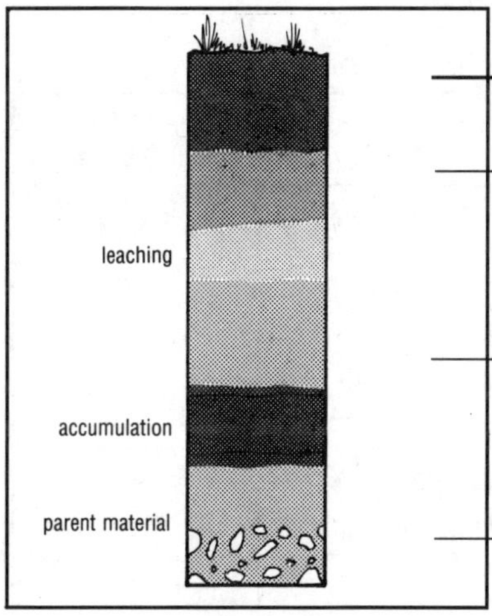

Soil layer	Soil horizon	Horizon characteristics
O	O1	Organic, not degraded
	O2	Organic, degraded
A	A1	Mineral & organic mixed, dark coloured
	A2	Horizon of maximum leaching of nutrients, clay, etc., light coloured
	A3	Transitional. More like A than B
B	B1	Transitional. More like B than A
	B2	Horizon of maximum accumulation of nutrients, clay, etc., dark coloured
	B3	Transitional. More like B than C
C	-	Parent material

The O layer is organic or peaty in nature. It is only sometimes present.

The A layer is mineral in nature. It may contain a leached horizon. It is dark coloured at the top and has good rooting and structure. It is often referred to by farmers as the *topsoil*.

The B layer is mineral in nature. It may contain a horizon of accumulation. It is light-coloured except for the B2 horizon and has poor rooting and structure. It is often referred to by farmers as the *subsoil.*

The C layer is mineral in nature. It is light coloured and has poor structure and no rooting.

4.2 Soil Classification

A number of international systems of soil classification were devised between 1900 and 1967. The system used by the *National Soil Survey of Ireland* is a modified version of the system proposed by the United States Department of Agriculture in 1938. It is based on a system of Orders, Suborders and Great Soil Groups and is summarised in *Table 4.1.* The descriptions of Orders and Suborders show the importance of climate, vegetation and topography in soil formation. The Great Soil Group is the basic classification unit. It can be seen that there are a total of 35 Great Soil Groups worldwide. Of these, 10 are found in Ireland.

These are:

1. Podzols
2. Brown podzolics
3. Brown earths
4. Grey brown podzolics
5. Gleys
6. Blanket peats
7. Basin peats
8. Rendzinas
9. Regosols
10. Lithosols

These are described below.

Table 4.1 *Classification of soils into Orders, Suborders and Great Soil Groups*

Order	Suborder	No. of Great Soil Groups
Zonal soils (Determined by climatic zone)	1. Soils of the cold zone 2. Light-coloured podzolised soils of timbered regions 3. Soils of forested warm-temperate and tropical regions 4. Soils of the forest- grassland transition 5. Dark-coloured soils of semi-humid and humid grasslands 6. Light-coloured soils of arid regions	1 5 1 3 5 4
Intrazonal soils (determined by local conditions)	1. Hydromorphic soils of marshes, swamps and seepage areas 2. Halomorphic (salt-affected) soils of imperfectly drained arid regions 3. Calcimorphic soils	8 3 2
Azonal soils (Soils without horizon development)	(No suborders)	3

1. *Podzols. (Fig 4.5)* These soils occupy 6.8% of the country. They exhibit the fullest effects of acid leaching seen in Ireland, referred to as *podzolization.* This occurs when the pH of the leaching water

Fig 4.5 Podzol soil profile

Fig 4.6 Brown podzolic soil profile

Fig 4.7 Brown earth soil profile

becomes sufficiently acid to leach iron and aluminium from the A horizon and deposit them in the B horizon. When the iron is deposited in a thin layer the soil is called an *iron pan podzol.* The word podzol is Russian and means "ash-like", referring to the colour and appearance of the leached A2 horizon.

Podzol profiles usually have a distinct sequence of horizons. At the surface, there is an O horizon caused by poor organic matter degradation due to the very low pH, which is often less than 4.5. Where an iron pan has formed lower down, water-logging above the impervious pan may cause the O horizon to become very deep and blanket peat is often found overlying podzols.

The O horizon is usually underlain by a thin A1 horizon and a thicker A2 which is bleached in colour. The B2 horizon may be thin and impervious (iron pan) or thick. It contains accumulated iron, aluminium, humus and clay, the iron giving it its characteristic red colour. The profile is underlain by the C horizon.

Podzols are poor soils with high lime and fertilizer requirements. They are usually found on acid parent materials in hill and mountain areas and are commonly devoted to forestry or very rough grazing.

2. *Brown podzolics.* (Fig 4.6) These soils occupy 8.5% of the country. They are rather similar to podzols, but have not been as severely leached. The A1 horizon has high levels of organic matter mixed with mineral matter and overlies a weakly developed A2 horizon. The B2 horizon is thick and reddish-brown and contains accumulated iron, aluminium and perhaps humus.

Brown podzolics are found in locations where the rainfall and parent material combination favours a lower level of leaching than that found with podzols. They have a wider use range than podzols, and, when limed and fertilized, can be suited to arable crops and intensive pasture production.

3. *Brown earths.* (Fig 4.7) These soils occupy 12.6% of the country. They are characterized by an apparent absence of horizons. Apart from having a dark layer at the surface due to higher levels of organic matter, they display a uniform brown colour down to the parent material. Chemical analysis of the profile for calcium and magnesium may reveal some leaching and accumulation, however.

Brown earths are found in low rainfall areas and/or on lime-rich parent materials. They have relatively low lime and fertilizer requirements and usually have texture, structure and drainage characteristics suited to arable cropping. They have a very wide use-range and are considered to be among the best agricultural soils in the country.

4. *Grey brown podzolics.* These soils occupy 18.3% of the country. Like brown earths, they are uniform in colour from the soil surface down to the parent material. Without laboratory analysis, it is difficult to distinguish them from brown earths. However, they are usually formed on limestone parent materials and this means that acid leaching does not occur. Clay particles are leached from the A2 horizon and accumulate in the B2 horizon, however. This can be confirmed by laboratory testing or by the "feel" method.

Grey brown podzolics have high pH values and low lime requirements. They have wide use-range and are considered to be excellent agricultural soils.

5. *Gleys.* *(Fig 4.8)* Gleys occupy 27.5% of the country. Where gleys are formed by water-logged conditions in topographical depressions, they are called *ground water gleys.* Those occurring over impervious layers are known as *surface water gleys.* Both soils have wet, badly-structured conditions and a short growing season.

Since there is no leaching they do not possess A2 or B2 horizons. Instead, they are said to have an A layer (topsoil with moderate structure development due to the influence of rooting and biological activity) and a B layer (subsoil with poorer structure and mottling of blue/grey and red colours) overlying the parent material. The soil shown in *Fig 4.8* is a surface water gley.

Gleys have limited use-range and are only suitable for low-intensity grassland farming. Where drainage can be successfully carried out, their potential may be improved considerably.

6. *Blanket peats.* *(Fig 4.9)* These soils occupy 12.2% of the country. They are so called because they cover large areas of land like a blanket. They are also called *climatic peats,* since their development is a result of adverse climatic conditions, principally high rainfall. The blanket peat profile consists of a single O horizon which varies from one to two metres in depth and is uniformly black/brown in appearance. Closer examination may show differences in degree of humification. The mechanism of formation of blanket peats has been described already *(see page 19).*

Blanket peats have poor drainage and moisture contents in excess of 90%. These features, together with their very low pH (3.8-4.1) and their wet, windy locations, make them soils of very limited use-range. They are mainly used for forestry. They can also be harvested for fuel.

7. *Basin peats.* Basin peats occupy 7.3% of the country. The profile, as with blanket peat, consists of a single O horizon uniform in colour and appearance. It is normally deeper than that of blanket peat, ranging from 3 to 10m. The degree of organic matter degradation increases with profile depth.

In contrast to blanket peats, which are found only in areas of high rainfall, basin peats are distributed throughout the country. They often occur in isolated depressions in areas of other soil types.

Fig 4.8 Surface water gley soil profile

Fig 4.9 Blanket peat soil profile

The mechanism of their formation has been described already *(see page 20)*.

In their natural state, they are of limited use-range being wet and acid. When drained, limed and fertilized, however, basin peats have a wide use-range in agriculture and can be used for a range of cultivated crops as well as grassland. They may also be harvested for fuel.

8. *Rendzinas.* These are rather limited in extent and importance, occupying only 2.0% of the country. They are derived from limestone rock and are shallow, often being less than 20 cm in depth. They have alkaline or neutral pHs and excellent soil structure. They are often found intermingled with limestone rock outcrops. This feature limits their use-range and they are usually confined to grassland production.

9. *Regosols.* These soils are also limited in extent and occupy 0.2% of the country. They are derived from river alluvium and are local in nature. Where they are not subject to river-flooding, they have a wide use-range.

10. *Lithosols.* These soils occupy 4.0% of the country. They are shallow stony soils usually closely intermingled with rock outcrops. They are often associated with podzols at high elevation. Their use range is usually limited to rough grazing.

4.3 Soil Survey and Mapping

The soils of Ireland have been surveyed and mapped by the National Soil Survey of Ireland which is a branch of Teagasc. A soil map of the country prepared at a scale of 1:575 000 was published in 1980. More detailed maps (at a scale of 1:126 720) of some counties are also available.

The *mapping unit* in the Soil Map of Ireland is the Great Soil Group. More detailed subdivisions of Great Soil Groups (soil *series* and *phases*) are used in county maps. These sub-divisions take into account such soil properties as depth, slope, stoniness, texture, organic matter content and degree of leaching, all of which are of practical importance at farm level.

A simplified version of the Soil Map of Ireland is presented in *Fig. 4.10*. It shows the location of the more important and extensive Great Soil Groups. It can immediately be seen that the better and more productive soils (categories 1 - 4) are in general located in the east, south and midlands while the poorer soils (categories 5 - 7) are located in the west and north.

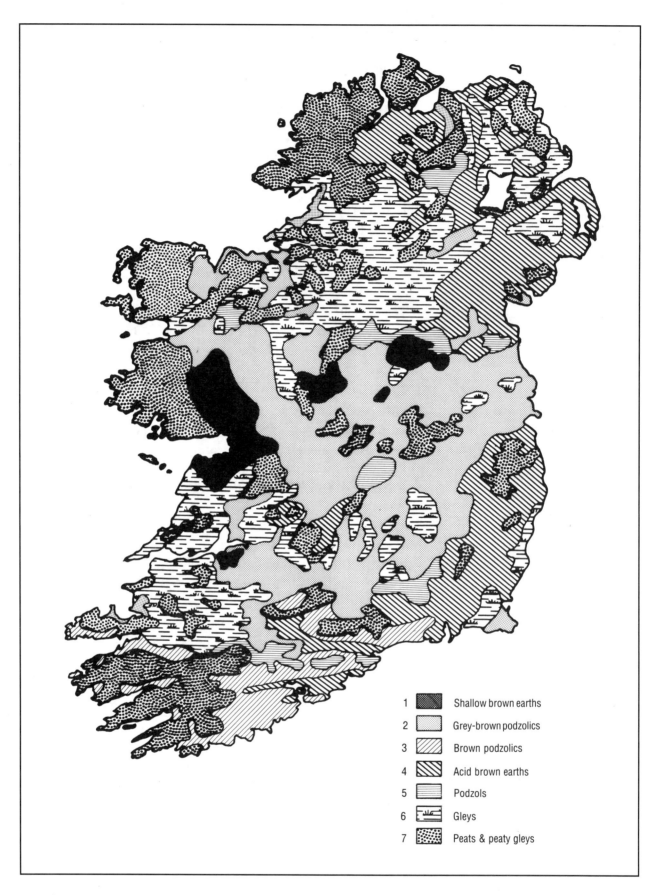

1		Shallow brown earths
2		Grey-brown podzolics
3		Brown podzolics
4		Acid brown earths
5		Podzols
6		Gleys
7		Peats & peaty gleys

Fig 4.10 A simplified soil map of Ireland

Exercises

Exercise 13. Examination of colour and texture in soil profiles using a sampling auger

Materials needed
1. Soil-auger
2. Penknife

Note: a soil-auger is a wood-auger, usually 2.5 cm in diameter, used for soil study.

Procedure
1. Screw the auger into the soil to the depth of the threads. Slowly pull the auger up out of the soil (be careful: see Precautions).
2. The soil retained in the threads of the auger represents the soil from the surface down to the depth of the threads (i.e. the depth sampled). Using a penknife, clean off the outer 1 mm of soil from the auger. This soil may have been smeared from the sides of the auger-hole during removal of the auger.
3. Remove the soil carefully from the auger and place on the ground (or on white paper) in the correct position i.e. surface soil at one end and deeper soil underneath.
4 . Drop the auger into the auger-hole until it comes to rest on the bottom. Screw the auger down the depth of the threads again. (The depth of the threads should be marked with paint or some other means repeatedly up the shaft of the auger.) Slowly pull the auger up again, clean off the outer 1 mm of soil as before. Remove the soil from the auger and place on the ground as before. Make sure that the soil is placed adjacent to the previous samples in the correct position.
5. Repeat step 4 as often as required to obtain a good indication of changes in the soil from the surface downwards. The samples laid out in the correct sequence accurately reflect the *soil profile.*
6. The colour and texture may be examined *in situ.* The soil can also be placed in carefully labelled plastic bags and brought back to the laboratory for further examination and testing.

Results
1. Record all your observations and textural test results on the soil.

2. Comment on any variation in properties observed in the profile.

Precautions
1. Be *very careful* each time in pulling the auger up out of the soil. It is very easy to injure your back in this operation. For removing the deepest samples, it is advisable to use *two people* pulling together.
2. No observations on soil structure can be made in this exercise. The structure is destroyed during the sampling treatment.

Exercise 14. Examination of excavated soil profiles

Materials needed
1. Spade
2. Hand trowel
3. Atomizer (watering spray gun)
4. Water
5. Hydrochloric acid (dilute)

Procedure
1. Find suitable locations for examining the soils chosen. Road cuttings, excavations near construction work, open drains are ideal. If none of these is available, a pit has to be dug using the spade.
2. Clean the face of the excavated soil profile using the spade and/or hand trowel. Clean down to the parent material.
3. If the soil is dry, spray it with the atomizer to moisten it. This enables the true soil colours to be seen.
4. Identify the soil horizons in each soil. Describe them under the following headings: (a) Thickness; (b) Colour; (c) Structure; ("open", "loose", "crumb", "compacted", etc.); (d) Extent of rooting; (e) pH .
5. Examine the parent materials for the presence of limestone or carbonates, using the hydrochloric acid. Frothing indicates presence of carbonates. Identify rock types.

Results
1. Record all observations.
2. Comment on the potential land use of the soils.

5 – Soil Fertility and Crop Growth

5.1 Source and Nature of Plant Nutrients

An essential element may be defined as:

"a chemical element required for the normal growth of plants".

There are 17 essential elements and they are listed in *Table 5.1*. Carbon, hydrogen and oxygen make up approximately 95% of fresh plant tissue. They are taken up by plants as carbon dioxide from the atmosphere and water from the soil pores. These three elements rarely limit crop growth through deficiency; the most usual exception is when root uptake of water is seriously reduced by drought, waterlogging or plant disease.

Table 5.1 Essential nutrient elements

Essential elements used in relatively large amounts		Essential elements used in relatively small amounts	
Mostly from air and water	From the soil solids	From the soil solids	
Carbon Hydrogen Oxygen	Nitrogen Phosphorus Potassium Calcium Magnesium Sulphur	Iron Manganese Boron Molybdenum	Copper Zinc Chlorine Cobalt

The essential elements obtained from the soil solids, on the other hand, are more likely to become deficient and restrict crop growth, especially where intensive farming is practised.

The six nutrient elements taken up in relatively large amounts from the soil solids are known as the *macro* or *major* elements. The eight used in smaller amounts are known as the *minor* or *trace* elements. Within the major elements, nitrogen, phosphorus and potassium are taken up by crops in greatest quantity (*Table 5.2*) and have the greatest tendency to become deficient. They are often called the *fertilizer elements* because they are regularly applied by farmers in fertilizer form.

Table 5.2 Major elements removed by normal yields of common crops

Element	Crop uptake (kg ha^{-1})		
	Wheat	Barley	Silage (single cut)
Nitrogen	168	122	86
Phosphorus	37	24	40
Potassium	70	65	73
Calcium	10	15	36
Magnesium	22	8	16
Sulphur	14	15	14

5.2 The Major Elements

The major elements occur in soils in two contrasting forms: (1) complex, relatively insoluble forms and (2) simpler, more soluble forms. These are listed in *Table 5.3*. The conversion from complex to simpler forms is of great importance, since the simpler forms are the direct source of the nutrient ions. The soil factors affecting the rate of conversion of each nutrient will be dealt with individually.

Table 5.3 *Principal forms in which the major elements occur in soil*

Major element	Complex, relatively insoluble form (A) inorganic; (B) organic	Simpler, more soluble form	
		Forms	Ions
Nitrogen (N)	(B) Organic materials (proteins, amino acids, etc)	Ammonium salts Nitrite salts Nitrate salts	NH_4^+ NO_2^- NO_3^-
Phosphorus (P)	(A) Primary (rock) minerals (e.g. apatite) Secondary calcium, iron and aluminium phosphates (B) Organic materials (phytin, nucleic acid, etc)	Phosphates of calcium, magnesium, potassium Soluble organic compounds	HPO_4^{--} $H_2PO_4^-$
Potassium (K)	(A) Primary (rock) minerals (felspars, micas) Secondary aluminium silicates, including clays	Potassium ions on soil colloids Potassium salts	K^+
Calcium (Ca)	(A) Primary (rock) minerals (felspars, hornblende, calcite, dolomite)	Calcium ions on soil colloids Calcium salts	Ca^{++}
Magnesium (Mg)	(A) Primary (rock) minerals (micas, hornblende, dolomite, serpentine) Secondary aluminium silicates, including clays	Magnesium ions on the the soil colloids Magnesium salts	Mg^{++}
Sulphur (S)	(A) Primary (rock) minerals (pyrite, gypsum) (B) Organic materials (proteins, amino acids, etc)	Sulphites and sulphates of calcium, magnesium, potassium, etc.	SO_3^{--} SO_4^{--}

5.2.1 Nitrogen and crop nutrition

Nitrogen is an important constituent of plant proteins, chlorophyll and nucleic acids. Thus, it is intimately involved in growth, photosynthesis and cell reproduction. Nitrogen is the most important and widely used fertilizer element. Deficiency causes sharp reductions in crop yield. When nitrogen is abundant in soil, plant growth is rapid, vegetation is dark green in colour and fruits and seeds have increased protein content. When nitrogen is deficient, growth is restricted and vegetation becomes yellow in colour. The ways in which nitrogen is supplied, used and re-used in soil constitute the *nitrogen cycle (Fig. 5.1)*.

The important parts of this cycle are:

1. *Fertilizer application.* Inorganic nitrogen fertilizers contain nitrogen in urea, ammonium and nitrate forms. Urea and ammonium are converted to nitrate in moist, warm soil conditions. Some of this

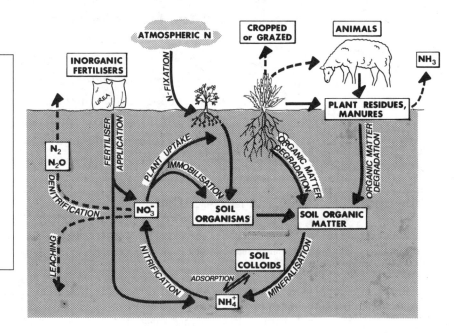

Fig. 5.1 The nitrogen cycle. Losses of nitrogen are indicated by dashed lines

Nitrogen inputs from:

Inorganic fertilizers
Plant residues
Organic manures
Nitrogen fixation

Nitrogen depletion due to:

Crop and animal removal
Gaseous loss (denitrification, volatilization of manure)
Leaching in drainage water

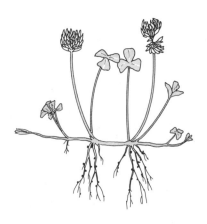

Fig. 5.2 Nodules on the roots of a white clover plant

nitrate is then absorbed immediately by crop roots. Some is converted to protein by soil micro–organisms *(immobilization)* and is not available until the micro-organisms die and decompose.

2. *Nitrogen fixation.* Nitrogen fixation has already been defined *(Table 3.3)*. The organisms of greatest importance in the process are *Rhizobium* bacteria which have a symbiotic relationship with leguminous plants. The bacteria form *nodules* on the roots of clover, peas, beans and other legumes *(Fig. 5.2)*.

   The nodules contain large numbers of bacteria which obtain energy in the form of starches from the root tissue. Some of the nitrogen fixed diffuses through the walls of the bacterial cells as simple compounds which are absorbed by the host plant. The remainder is released for use by the host plant and other plants on the death and decay of the nodule bacteria. Farmers make use of nitrogen fixation when they sow grass/clover mixtures in pasture land. The clover contributes the equivalent of 5 - 9 bags of nitrogen fertilizer per hectare each year for use by the grasses.

3. *Organic matter degradation and mineralization.* When plant residues and animal manures are added to soil, they are degraded in the manner already described *(see section 3.2.2)*. This is a key component in the nitrogen cycle as it begins the recycling of nitrogen, converting it from complex organic forms to the mineral form of ammonium ions.

4. *Nitrification.* The recycling of nitrogen begun by organic matter degradation and mineralization is carried a stage further by nitrification. Nitrification is achieved with the help of two species of aerobic bacteria, *Nitrosomonas* and *Nitrobacter.* The reactions involved are:

				Enzymic								
1.	$2NH_4^+$	$+$	$3O_2$	$\xrightarrow{\text{oxidation}}$	$2NO_2^-$	$+$	$2H_2O$	$+$	$4H^+$	$+$	Energy
	Ammonium ions		Oxygen	Nitrosomonas species	Nitrite ions		Water		Hydrogen ions		

				Enzymic				
2.	$2NO_2^-$	$+$	O_2	$\xrightarrow{\text{oxidation}}$	$2NO_3^-$	$+$	Energy
	Nitrite ions		Oxygen	Nitrobacter species	Nitrate ions		

Thus, ammonium ions, which cannot be absorbed by plant roots, are converted to nitrate ions which can be absorbed. Nitrification is necessary to make urea and ammonium fertilizers available for plant uptake also. The process is favoured by moist, well-aerated, warm, high-pH soil conditions.

5. *Plant uptake.* This completes the nitrogen cycle.
6. *Denitrification and leaching.* All the parts of the nitrogen cycle described so far are favoured by good soil aeration. In contrast, denitrification occurs in very *wet or waterlogged soil conditions.* It results in loss of nitrogen from the soil. The bacteria involved function very well in anaerobic conditions and the process is an enzymic reduction of nitrate to nitrous oxide (N_2O) and nitrogen (N_2) gases which are lost to the atmosphere.

Nitrates are *water-soluble* and thus subject to leaching in drainage water. Leaching losses of nitrates are both costly to the farmer and a major cause of water pollution. For this reason, spreading of nitrogen fertilizers should not be carried out in autumn or winter when large amounts of drainage occur.

5.2.2 Phosphorus and crop nutrition

Phosphorus is involved in cell division and plant growth processes. It is the second most critical plant nutrient. Deficiency of phosphorus results in stunted growth with discoloured (bluish) vegetation.

Phosphorus in soil exists in a range of complex inorganic and organic compounds *(Table 5.3).* Phosphate ions are released by chemical and biological weathering/degradation processes. If the soil pH is less than 5.5, these ions form insoluble iron, aluminium and manganese compounds and become almost unavailable for crop uptake. If the soil pH is greater than 7.5, a similar phenomenon occurs. In this case, calcium phosphate is the insoluble material formed. *(See Fig 5.3).* Phosphate ions released from added inorganic fertilizers suffer the same fate. This phenomenon is known as *phosphorus fixation (immobilization)*. To improve *phosphorus availability* to crops, therefore, the soil pH should be kept between 5.5 and 7.5 and for maximum availability it should be kept between 6.0 and 7.0.

5.2.3 Potassium and crop nutrition

Potassium performs a variety of functions in plant growth, including the translocation of carbohydrates and the promotion of disease resistance. Deficiency of potassium causes loss of yield and scorching or withering of the outer margins of older leaves.

Potassium availability for uptake is affected by clay mineral composition. Potassium ions are cations and are held on the soil colloids until root uptake. Some clay minerals have the ability to trap K^+ ions in *inner surfaces* during *swelling/shrinking* cycles. These ions then become unavailable to roots. This is known as *potassium fixation (immobilization)*.

The location of the soil types which have this problem is known from the laboratory analysis carried out during soil survey and mapping procedures. Farmers growing crops on these soils must apply extra amounts of potassium fertilizer to counteract this problem.

5.2.4 Calcium, magnesium, sulphur and crop nutrition

These three nutrients are considered together because, although they are major elements, they are generally not added to soil in fertilizer form. This is so for two reasons:
1. They are relatively abundant in soils.
2. They are not subject to serious immobilization (lack of availability) in the soil as are nitrogen, phosphorus and potassium.

The lime used by farmers to raise soil pH contains calcium and magnesium and the main nitrogen fertilizer used, calcium ammonium nitrate, contains calcium. Application of these two materials, therefore, helps to keep plants supplied with calcium and magnesium.

Recently, *sulphur deficiency* has begun to appear in some areas where sulphur amounts in soil are low. In the past, this scarcity was masked as the fertilizer materials used contained sulphur as an impurity. The replacement of these by newer materials has resulted in fertilizer manufacturers now having to add sulphur to nitrogen fertilizers for use in these areas.

5.3 Trace Elements

Whereas the major elements are used in building the structure of plants, trace elements are important in *enzyme systems* and contribute to the plant's function rather than to its structure.

Deficiency of the major elements (especially the fertilizer elements nitrogen, phosphorus and potassium) is rare nowadays because the use of inorganic fertilizers has become routine with most farmers. Deficiency of trace elements still does occur, especially on *recently reclaimed soils.*

Deficiencies occur for two reasons:

1. Absence of the element from the parent material. Peat soils and soils developed from very sandy materials have most problems in this respect.

2. Inadequate availability due to over-liming and high soil pH *(see Fig. 5.3).*

When deficiencies occur they may be rectified by soil applications (*prevention*) or foliar sprays (*cure*). The inclusion of small amounts of boron in fertilizers for sugar beet is now routine practice. If the problem is caused by overliming, then liming should be discontinued. If the soil has a high pH due to the parent material, the problem is less easily resolved.

Some diseases of crops and animals caused by trace element deficiencies are shown in *Table 5.4.* Individual examples are dealt with later.

Table 5.4 Diseases caused by trace element deficiency

Element	Disease	
	Crop	Animal
Iron (Fe)	Yield reduction in apples	Anaemia in pigs reared indoors
Manganese (Mn)	"Grey-speck" in oats	Infertility in cattle
Boron (B)	Heart-rot in sugar beet	—
Molybdenum (Mo)	"Whiptail" in cauliflower and broccoli	—
Copper (Cu)	Yield reduction in cereals	"Swayback" in sheep
Zinc (Zn)	Yield reduction in cereals and potatoes	Parakeratosis (dry skin) in pigs
Chlorine (Cl)	—	—
Cobalt (Co)	—	"Pining " (illthrift) in sheep and cattle

5.4 Soil pH and Liming

Soil pH influences the availability to crops of both major and trace elements in soil *(Fig. 5.3).* When elements are *available,* they are present in soluble form and so their ions can be taken up from the soil solution. When elements are *unavailable,* they are in insoluble form because they have been immobilised chemically, biologically or by clay minerals.

It is very noticeable in *Fig. 5.3* that all the nutrient elements except for the Fe/Mn/Cu/Zn/Co group are at maximum availability *between pHs 6 and 7.* The availability of the Fe/Mn/Cu/Zn/Co group

Fig. 5.3 Relationship between soil pH and availability of essential elements

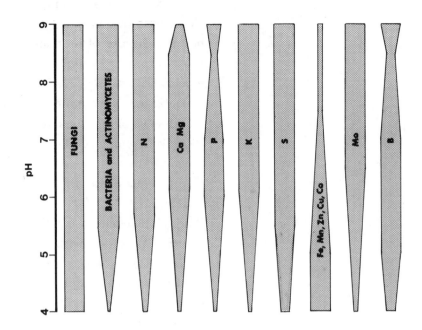

is sufficient to meet crop needs in this range also (these elements may, in fact, become *toxic* at lower pH values). This is the pH range, therefore, that should be the objective in liming and soil management.

Liming is an essential farming operation in Ireland because of acid leaching. It has to be carried out every five to ten years, depending on *soil texture* and *rainfall/evaporation* amounts. Application amounts are decided on as a result of a lime requirement test *(see p. 74)*.

Lime raises soil pH by causing Ca^{++} ions (and some Mg^{++} ions) to replace H^+ and Al^{+++} ions in the soil colloids. This leads to a reduction in the H^+ ion concentration in the soil solution. It takes one and a half to two years for liming to have its full effect on soil pH. This is an important consideration when planning to grow pH-sensitive crops such as barley or sugar beet.

The principal liming material used in Ireland is *ground limestone*, which is simply finely crushed limestone. Ground limestone must meet the following requirements:

1. The product must have a total neutralising value (TNV) of not less than 90%. TNV is a measure of its effectiveness in raising soil pH.
2. All of the product must pass through a 3.35 mm sieve.
3. Not less than 35% of the product must pass through a 0.15 mm sieve.
4. The moisture content must not exceed 3.0%.

Other materials used in limited amounts for liming purposes are *shell-sand* (sea-sand composed of shells with variable amounts of

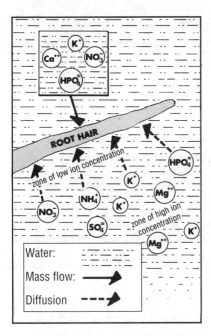

Fig. 5.4 Mass flow (movement of ions in water being taken in by plant roots), and diffusion of nutrient ions from zone of high concentration (soil solution) to zone of low concentration (immediate vicinity of root hair). The low concentration near the root hair is caused by ion uptake

lime) and *sugar-factory waste lime*. This is a waste material from sugar manufacture and is used in the vicinity of the sugar factories. It is a wet material and 2.5 tonnes of it correspond to one tonne of ground limestone.

5.5 Mechanism of Nutrient Uptake by Plants

Nutrients are absorbed by plant roots in ionic form *(Table 5.3, right-hand column)*. The sources of these ions are:
1. Adsorbed ions on the soil colloids (cations).
2. Compounds which dissolve to supply ions to the soil solution (cations and anions).

The uptake of these ions involves two distinct phases. *Firstly,* ions move through the soil solution to the root surface. *Secondly,* ions enter the root through the cell wall. The movement of ions to the roots occurs by mass flow, diffusion and root interception. The first two processes are explained in *Fig.5.4*. Root interception is essentially the opposite of mass flow; i.e. roots move towards the soil solution. This is accomplished by root hairs growing through and exploring new areas in soil and intercepting ions in these areas. A good system of soil pores facilitates this process.

Ion entry through the root cell wall is complicated because ions have to work against a concentration gradient. The process involves energised *nutrient carriers* which are organic compounds found in the cell wall. The process is shown and explained in *Fig. 5.5.*

A balance exists between the nutrient ions in the soil solution and those on the soil colloids and in the nutrient-containing compounds. As the soil solution becomes *depleted* of ions due to root uptake, ions are released from the colloids and compounds in an attempt to maintain the concentration of the soil solution. When

Fig. 5.5 Simplified mechanism of nutrient ion entry through root cell wall. Energised nutrient carrier transports ion across the cell wall against a concentration gradient. It loses its energy in doing this but is then re-energised to allow it to transport another ion. This process occurs repeatedly

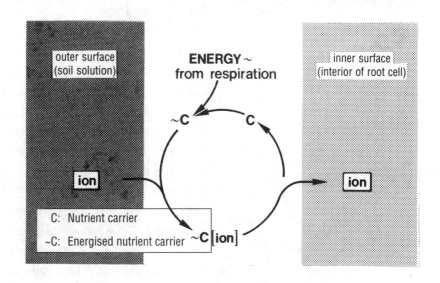

the soil pH is between 6 and 7, this release of ions proceeds satisfactorily: the further the pH varies from these values, the less satisfactory is the release process.

5.6 Soil Sampling and Analysis

Soil is analysed to determine its level of fertility and its fertilizer requirements. The full procedure involves the following steps:

1. Soil sampling
2. Soil analysis
3. Interpretation of soil analysis data

Step 3 leads to making *recommendations* on fertilizer requirements. These recommendations should then be implemented.

5.6.1 Soil sampling

Before beginning to sample, the area should be examined for any obvious differences within it. In a tilled field, differences in colour might be seen. Differences in slope, texture and natural vegetation may also be observed.

The past history of the area should be considered. For example, two fields may have been joined into one; some of the area may have been limed, some may not. Where differences are seen to exist, each sub-area should be sampled separately.

A minimum of 25 samples should be taken from the root-zone of each area sampled. These are then mixed to give a *composite* sample for the area. It is very important that the sample obtained is representative of the area. To ensure this, a "W" sampling design can be used *(Fig. 5.6)*. Small parts of the area which might be non-representative should be excluded. These would include gateways, headlands and wet areas.

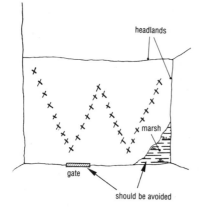

Fig. 5.6 Design for sampling an area for soil analysis

5.6.2 Soil analysis

Soil analysis usually consists of determining lime requirement, available phosphorus and available potassium. There is no reliable test for available nitrogen so other methods have to be used to decide on the nitrogen requirements of the crop being sown.

Most of the routine soil testing for farmers is carried out in the Soil Testing Laboratory of Teagasc, located at Johnstown Castle, Co. Wexford. The soil samples are first dried and sieved. A subsample is treated with *Morgan's extracting solution* and the extract tested for available phosphorus and potassium. Lime requirement is determined on a separate subsample of the sieved soil.

Morgan's extracting solution is a chemical designed to remove amounts of phosphorus and potassium equivalent to those removed by a growing crop. The results of these tests are expressed as parts per million (ppm) available phosphorus, ppm available potassium and tonnes per hectare of ground limestone.

5.6.3 Interpretation of soil analysis data

The data obtained from soil analysis for available phosphorus and potassium are of little or no value in themselves. It has been stated by a US scientist, R.L. Donohue, that:

"... a soil test is only as successful and usable for a region as the degree to which it is correlated and calibrated for the soils and crops of the area".

Thus, when the test data are interpreted, reference is made to an extensive series of trials carried out by Teagasc using a range of soils, crops and fertilizer treatments.

In these trials, the relationship between crop yield and fertilizer application on soils of different fertility status was determined. An example of the results of one trial is shown in *Fig. 5.7*. The curve shows that on a loam soil with 6 ppm available phosphorus, optimum yield of barley will be obtained if 60 kg ha^{-1} of phosphorus are applied. If a range of curves is available, then a set of guidelines can be prepared for easy interpretation of soil test data. The analysis data for lime requirement are expressed in tonnes ha^{-1} of ground limestone *required to raise the soil pH to 6.8*. They do not require any further interpretation.

Fig. 5.7 Relationship between yield of spring barley and application of phosphorus on a loam soil with available phosphorus of 6 ppm

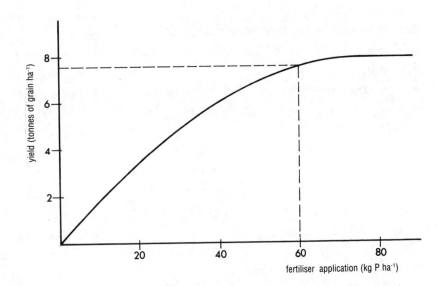

Exercises

Exercise 15. Examination of soils for the presence of NPK

Materials needed

1. Soils (a) Low pH (< 5), dried, sieved (2mm)
(b) Neutral pH (near 7.0), dried, sieved (2mm)
2. Conical flasks (100-200 ml), 2
3. Bungs to fit flasks, 2
4. Funnels, 2
5. Filter paper (Whatman No. 50)
6. Beakers (100 ml), 2

7. Test tubes, 8
8. Reagents as follows:
    (a) Diphenylamine, 0.5%
    (b) Ammonium molybdate solution
    (c) Barium chloride solution
    (d) Silver nitrate solution

Test for	Add to the filtrate	Positive result
1. Nitrates (NO_3^-)	A few drops of diphenylamine reagent	Blue colour
2. Phosphates (HPO_4^{--})	A few drops of ammonium molybdate reagent	Yellow precipitate
3. Sulphates (SO_4^{--})	A few drops of barium chloride solution	White cloudiness
4. Chlorides (Cl^-)	A few drops of silver nitrate solution	White precipitate

Procedure

Note: Testing soils for available nutrients is a procedure requiring sophisticated chemicals and measuring techniques. This exercise is simpler and demonstrates the existence of some water soluble nutrients and the influence of pH on their abundance.

1. Place 1 teaspoonful of each soil in a conical flask and label.
2. Add approximately 50 ml of distilled water.
3. Stopper the flasks and shake vigorously for 3-4 minutes.
4. Filter the contents of each flask into a beaker.
5. Place 8 test-tubes in a rack and label four "(a)" and four "(b)".
6. Pour equal quantities of the acid soil filtrate into test-tubes (a). Do the same with the neutral soil filtrate and test-tubes (b).
7. Perform the tests shown in the table on each set of filtrates.

Results

1. Record the results carefully.
2. Answer the question: does soil pH affect the content of water soluble nutrients?

Exercise 16. Determination of lime requirement of soils

Materials needed

1. Acid soil; dried, sieved (2 mm)
2. Small screw-cap bottles (50-100 ml) with necks wide enough to admit the pH-meter electrode, 6
3. Calcium hydroxide ($Ca(OH)_2$)
4. Water
5. Chloroform
6. pH-meter
7. Distilled water

Procedure

1. Weigh 10 g of soil into each bottle.
2. Add 0, 0.01, 0.02, 0.04, 0.08 and 0.16 g of calcium hydroxide into the bottles. Label each bottle according to the amount of calcium hydroxide added.
3. Add 25 ml of water and 2 drops of chloroform to each bottle.
4. Screw on the caps, shake vigorously for 5 minutes and allow to stand for *one week.*
5. Remove the caps and measure the pH of the soil suspension in each bottle. Wash the electrode with distilled water between measurements.

Results

1. Plot the graph of pH (vertical ordinate) against amount of calcium hydroxide added.
2. Read the *lime requirement* ("X"g) necessary to raise the pH to 6.5 from the graph.
3. Convert the lime requirement figure to tonnes ha^{-1} of ground limestone using the following calculation:

$$\text{Tonnes ha}^{-1} \text{ ground limestone} = \frac{\text{"X" x } 100 \text{ x } 227}{74}$$

Note: 100 = molecular weight of $CaCO_3$
74 = molecular weight of $Ca(OH)_2$
227 = conversion factor (to convert $g(10g)^{-1}$ to tonnes ha^{-1}).

Section 2
Fertilizers and Manures

6 – Fertilizers and Manures

Fertilizers and manures are materials which contain one or more of the *essential elements* and which are added to land to encourage crop growth. The amounts to be added are decided on after soil sampling and analysis have been carried out and the results interpreted.

Fertilizers are *manufactured materials*, mainly inorganic in nature, whereas manures are *animal and plant wastes* and are organic in nature.

6.1 Fertilizers

Most of the fertilizers sold in Ireland contain *nitrogen* (N), *phosphorus* (P) and *potassium* (K), either singly or in combination. Fertilizers are manufactured from the following raw materials:

atmospheric nitrogen, converted to ammonia or nitric acid;

mineral rock phosphates. Those used in Ireland are calcium phosphate rock deposits imported from north Africa;

natural potassium ("potash") salts. Most of those used in Ireland are mined in central and eastern Europe and imported from there.

Fertilizers containing one nutrient element only are described as *straight* (or simple) fertilizers. Those with two or more nutrients are known as *compound* fertilizers.

6.1.1 Straight fertilizers

Information on the straight fertilizers used in Ireland is shown in *Table 6.1.*

Table 6.1 Names, formulae, percentages of nutrients and sales of straight fertilizers sold in Ireland

* Citrate insoluble

Fertilizer	Formula	% Nutrient	Sales, tonnes, 1990
Calcium ammonium nitrate (CAN)	$NH_4NO_3 + CaCO_3$	27.5 N	489 500
Urea	$CO(NH_2)_2$	46.0 N	133 000
Sulphate of ammonia	$(NH_4)_2SO_4$	21.0 N	10 000
Superphosphate	$Ca(H_2PO_4)_2 + CaSO_4$	7.0 P	< 5 000
Triple superphosphate	$Ca(H_2PO_4)_2$	16.0 P	< 5 000
Ground rock phosphate	$CaPO_4$ (apatite)	*14.5 P	8 500
Muriate of potash	KCl	50.0 K	< 5 000
Sulphate of potash	K_2SO_4	42.0 K	< 5 000

Only calcium ammonium nitrate, urea and ground rock phosphate are important as straight fertilizers. The remainder are almost exclusively used in the manufacture of compound fertilizers.

Calcium ammonium nitrate (CAN) is the largest-selling fertilizer in the country. Half of its nitrogen, 13.75%, is in the ammonium form.

The other half is in the nitrate form. The ammonium ions have an acidifying effect in soil as follows:

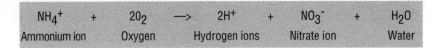

$$NH_4^+ + 2O_2 \longrightarrow 2H^+ + NO_3^- + H_2O$$

Ammonium ion   Oxygen   Hydrogen ions   Nitrate ion   Water

The calcium acts as a buffer against this acidifying action. CAN has replaced sulphate of ammonia in recent times as the principal nitrogen fertilizer sold in Ireland, mainly because of its lesser acidifying action. As a result of this change in usage, sulphur has now become deficient in some parts of the country.

These areas of *sulphur deficiency* occur where the soils are high in sand and low in organic matter. Such soils give low levels of sulphur release into the soil. To deal with this problem, fertilizer manufacturers now add sulphur in small amounts to the nitrogen fertilizers sold in these areas.

As CAN is hygroscopic, both the straight fertilizer and compounds containing it must be carefully stored and spread as soon as they are exposed to the air. Otherwise, caking and wastage will result.

Urea is a fertilizer which is increasing in popularity. It is highly concentrated (46% N) and so is less wasteful of labour and fuel during spreading. It gives a slightly slower crop response than CAN. This is because the N must be converted from the ureic form, firstly to the ammonium form and then to the nitrate form.

Urea also has some problems due to volatilization of ammonium during this process. The gas can diffuse into the atmosphere in warm dry weather and can cause toxicity to germinating seeds of tillage crops. Consequently, it is recommended that urea be used as a *top-dressing* (i.e. applied on the surface) on established crops and only when there is a strong likelihood of rain and moist soil conditions. Teagasc suggests that urea can be safely spread before May 1 and after August 15. Between these dates it should only be spread when rain is forecast.

Urea production is still being developed and refined and, if the problems with usage described above can be overcome, it is likely to increase greatly in importance in the future.

The use of *ground rock phosphate* as a straight fertilizer in Ireland is confined almost entirely to forest-tree fertilization. Most of our forests are located on acid soils. The P in finely ground rock phosphate dissolves slowly in such soils and becomes available for uptake over a long period. The rate of release of P in the less acid soil conditions favoured by other crops is too slow for ground rock phosphate to be of much value.

6.1.2 Compound fertilizers

Compound fertilizers are prepared either by *mixing* straight fertilizers, or by *chemical synthesis* from the raw materials already mentioned. During chemical synthesis, the P in the mineral rock phosphates is made more soluble and, thus, capable of being more quickly released for crop use. Sulphate of potash is manufactured from muriate of potash (using sulphuric acid). This makes it more expensive than muriate. Despite this, it is used in the preparation of compound fertilizers for potatoes as it gives drier, more floury tubers.

Compound fertilizers are named by listing their percentage content of N, P and K in order. Thus, in *Table 6.2*, the first fertilizer, 18:6:12, contains 18% N, 6% P and 12% K. The remaining 64% is made up of chemicals and impurities of various kinds. Some of these have nutrient value but most do not. For example, in compounds for potato-growing, the sulphate of potash is a source of the major essential element sulphur.

Table 6.2 Names and sales of the compound fertilizers most widely used in Ireland

Fertilizer	Sales, tonnes, 1990
18 : 6 : 12	254 000
27 : 2.5 : 5	240 000
0 : 7 : 30	123 500
0 : 10 : 20	77 000
10 : 10 : 20	130 500
24 : 2.5 : 10	154 000
	979 000

Each of the compound fertilizers listed in *Table 6.2* has been prepared for a specific use and the nutrient balance reflects the likely uptake by the particular crop in mind. Thus, 18:6:12 is designed for use on silage and hay crops, 27:2.5:5 for heavily-stocked grassland, 0:7:30 for autumn spreading on land planned for silage, and so on. The farmer must choose whichever compound best meets the nutrient requirements of his particular crop.

6.1.3 Fertilizer application

Fertilizers may be applied in three ways:
(a) They can be *placed* in the soil in a band near a line of sown seeds. This is achieved using specially-designed planters or drills, such as potato planters and combine corn drills *(see page 161)*.
(b) They can be *broadcast* onto the soil surface and mixed through the seedbed using cultivation implements.
(c) They can be broadcast onto the growing crop. This is referred to as *top-dressing*.

A fertilizer spreader for broadcasting fertilizer is shown in *Fig. 6.1*. It consists of a storage hopper which feeds a regulated supply of fertilizer into a spreading device. This can be a *reciprocating arm* as in *Fig. 6.1* or a *rotating disc*.

Straight and compound fertilizers are both sold in granulated form. This facilitates spreading in two ways. Firstly, it reduces their hygroscopicity, since the surface area of granules exposed to moisture in the air is much lower than that of a powder. This means that the fertilizers do not cake and block the spreader so easily. Secondly, more uniform and accurate spreading is possible. This is because all granules are of approximately the same size and thus travel the same distance through the air in the spreading procedure.

Fig. 6.1 Fertilizer spreader (reciprocating arm type)

6.2 Organic Manures

6.2.1 Farmyard manure

Farmyard manure is a by-product of the winter housing of animals. It is a mixture of faeces, urine and bedding which has rotted during storage. The main feature of farmyard manure which distinguishes it from inorganic fertilizers is its organic matter content. This organic matter contributes to the maintenance and improvement of soil structure as well as supplying plant nutrients. Where land is repeatedly cropped over long periods, as in horticulture, farmyard manure is of great value in preventing structure deterioration.

There is a low concentration of nutrients in farmyard manure, making it a bulky material as a fertilizer. The average composition is:

0.50 % N   0.15 % P   0.60 % K

Not all the nutrients are immediately available since they are mostly present in organic form. They are released slowly as the organic compounds become degraded. Old, well-rotted manure releases nutrients and humus more quickly than fresh manure.

On average, an application of 25 t ha^{-1} of manure will release, in the first growing season, 40 kg of N, 20 kg of P and 80 kg of K. When planning to use both manures and fertilizers, these figures can be used to adjust the amounts of fertilizer applied.

Usage of farmyard manure has declined in Ireland in recent years. This is due mainly to changes in animal housing from open sheds to cubicle and slatted houses where no bedding is used. The manure is used on the farms on which it originates, except for the amounts used in horticulture. If *organic farming* increases in extent in the future, the use of farmyard manure will become more widespread.

Farmyard manure can be spread on both tillage and grazing land. Losses of nitrogen due to volatilization of ammonia are minimised by *ploughing in* the manure immediately after spreading. When spread on grazing land, large losses of N result. In addition, there is a risk of spreading animal diseases and pests (e.g. stomach worms) if the land is grazed before rain has washed the herbage clean. For this reason, use of farmyard manure on grassland is usually confined to fields planned for silage or hay.

6.2.2 Animal slurry

The decline in usage of farmyard manure has been accompanied by an increase in animal slurry usage. Slurry is a mixture mainly of dung and urine. Where it accumulates under the floors of slatted houses, it is more concentrated and less variable in composition than when it comes from cubicle houses. This is because of the dilution by water which occurs when *cubicle houses* and adjacent yards are washed. In addition, as storage pits for slurry from cubicle houses are often located in the open, dilution by rainwater results. The average composition of cattle slurry is:

$$0.45 \% \text{ N} \qquad 0.10 \% \text{ P} \qquad 0.50 \% \text{ K}$$

It is, therefore, similar in concentration of nutrients to farmyard manure. It contains less organic matter, about 10 % on average compared to 25 % in farmyard manure. This makes slurry of less benefit to soil structure than farmyard manure but it is better than manufactured fertilizers which have no organic content.

Slurry, like farmyard manure, is almost always used on the farms on which it originates. It is an important source of nutrients on dairy farms, where it is used extensively on silage fields. It is less subject to losses of N than farmyard manure because it seeps quickly into the soil. It has the same *disease and pest hazards*, however, which is why its use is mostly confined to grass being grown for silage. It may also be spread on tilled land.

6.2.3 Other organic manures

The only other organic manures of any importance are straw, seaweed and sewage sludge.

Straw, when ploughed back into the soil after a cereal crop, decomposes and releases amounts of organic matter and plant nutrients which are only slightly less than those in farmyard manure. These constituents are more slowly released, however, because no decomposition has taken place prior to ploughing-in. It is a mistake to expect a big response from straw in the first year after ploughing-in.

Seaweed is used as a manure to a limited extent in coastal areas. The organic matter it supplies to sandy soils in such areas improves their structure and water-holding capacity. It is fairly similar to farmyard manure in chemical composition.

Sewage sludge is the solid material remaining after sewage (domestic waste in cities and towns) has been treated to make the liquid safe for disposal into waterways. It is available to farmers in the vicinity of sewage treatment plants. Its composition is fairly similar to that of farmyard manure in respect of nutrients and organic matter. In highly industrialized areas, however, it may contain toxic levels of heavy metals (lead, zinc, copper, chromium and nickel). All sewage sludges made available for agricultural use should, therefore, be analysed for heavy metal content.

6.2.4 Application of organic manures

Farmyard manure is spread using a muck spreader *(Fig. 6.2)*. The spreader is filled using a tractor and front-loader. The manure is

Fig. 6.2 Muck spreader

then torn up and thrown out sideways by a series of chains with flails attached which revolve at high speed.

Slurry spreaders *(Fig. 6.3)* suck the slurry into the tank, the suction being developed by a tractor-driven pump. When full, the tank is driven to the spreading area. The suction pump is then converted to a *pressure pump* which forces the slurry out through the rear outlet. A *deflector plate* spreads the slurry in a band about 6 m wide.

Fig. 6.3 Slurry spreader

Exercises

Exercise 17. Examination of fertilizers

Materials needed
Samples of fertilizers

    Straight: CAN, CAN + S,
                  Urea, Urea + S
                  Superphosphate
                  Ground rock phosphate
                  Muriate of potash
                  Sulphate of potash
    Compound: 0 : 10 : 20
                  0 : 7 : 30
                  10 : 10 : 20
                  18 : 6 : 12
Ground limestone

Procedure

1. Examine each of the "straight" fertilizers. Answer the following questions: (a) which samples are crystalline? (b) which samples are granulated? (c) why do ground rock phosphate and superphosphate appear so different?

2. Examine each of the compound fertilizers. Answer the following questions:
   (a) which fertilizer(s) are *chemically combined?*
   (b) which fertilizers are *mixtures* of straight fertilizers.

3. Examine ground limestone (note: this is not a fertilizer, strictly speaking).

4. Answer the question: which two materials have the finest particle-size and why?

Results

Record your descriptions of the materials examined. Record the answers of the questions asked at 1, 2 and 4 above.

Precautions

Keep all materials away from mouth and eyes.

Exercise 18. Study of spreading pattern of a fertilizer spreader

Materials needed
1. Tractor
2. Fertilizer spreader
3. Flat trays or boxes (as large as possible), 10
4. Old newspapers

Procedure
1. Attach the fertilizer spreader to the tractor.
2. Fill the spreader with fertilizer.
3. Bring the tractor and spreader to a large, flat, accessible area (a yard or field is suitable).
4. Operate the spreader for a short time (10-20 seconds) with the tractor stationary.
5. Stop the tractor and spreader. Turn off the tractor engine.
6. Measure the *spreading-width* (i.e. the width behind the tractor over which fertilizer particles are found).
7. Distribute the 10 trays or boxes *evenly* across the spreading-width and at a distance from the tractor at which fertilizer was found on the ground in 6. Label them 1-10. Measure and record their positions (*see Fig. 6.4*).
8. If the trays/boxes are *shallow*, cover their bases with slightly-crumpled newspaper. This will minimise the risk of fertilizer particles bouncing off the bases and out again.
9. Start the tractor and operate the spreader for *1 minute.*
10. Stop the tractor and spreader and turn off the tractor engine.
11. Collect the fertilizer from each tray/box carefully and place in 10 *labelled* plastic bags.

12. Bring the bags of fertilizer back to the laboratory and weigh the contents of each bag. *Record the weights.*

Results
1. Draw out the positions of the trays/boxes on graph paper and write in the weight of fertilizer found in each position.
2. Draw a graph of the spreading-pattern. Plot weight of fertilizer against distance from the centre of the tractor ("a" in figure).
3. Calculate the amount of "overlap" required to ensure that spreading is uniform.

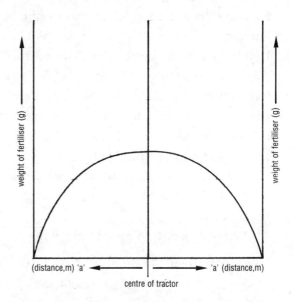

Fig. 6.4 Spreading-pattern (amount of fertilizer vs distance from the centre of a fertilizer spreader)

Precautions
1. This exercise should be carried out under the supervision of an experienced machinery operator.
2. Keep *well clear* of the tractor and spreader at all times while they are in operation.
3. Be especially careful of the tractor *power take-off (PTO)* and the *PTO shaft.*

Exercise 19. Examination of farmyard manure and slurry

Materials needed
1. Sample of farmyard manure (fresh)
2. Sample of farmyard manure (well-rotted)
3. Sample of cattle slurry

Procedure
1. Examine samples of fresh and well-rotted farmyard manure (FYM). Compare the following: (a) smell (b) colour (c) evidence of organic remains (straw etc.) (d) feel (dryness, wetness).
2. Examine the cattle slurry. Note its degree of liquidity.
3. Determine the moisture content of each of the three samples. For each, do the following:
   (a) Place a small amount in a weighed evaporating dish (wt of dish, Ag)
   (b) Weigh sample + dish (Bg)
   (c) Dry in an oven to constant weight (max temp, 100°C), cool in a dessicator and reweigh (Cg).
   (d) Calculate moisture content as follows:

$$\text{Moisture content} = \frac{\text{wt of moisture} \times 100}{\text{wt of fresh material}}$$

$$= \frac{(B-C) \times 100}{B-A}$$

$$= \dots\dots\dots\%$$

Results
1. Record observations made at 1 and 2 above. The well-rotted FYM should have a weaker smell and be darker in colour than the fresh FYM. It should show less evidence of organic remains and feel drier.
2. Record the moisture content results.
3. Comment on all results.

Section 3
Plant
Science

7 – Cells and the Chemicals of Life

7.1 Cells

Cells are the basic unit of all plants and animals. Groups of cells which perform specialized functions are called tissues. Originally, most of what is known about cells was discovered using light microscopes. Microscopes used in classrooms are *light microscopes.* Today additional information comes from studies using electron microscopes. *Electron microscopes* allow much higher magnifications but they are large, expensive and are confined to research.

7.2 The Compound Microscope

Microscopes are precision instruments and must be used with care. After use, clean the stage and put away, carefully covered with a dust jacket. Use the diagram in *Fig. 7.1* to identify the main parts of the microscope. Sometimes, an in-built light source is available, otherwise use natural daylight (near a window) directed through the condenser with the flat side of the mirror. If a condenser is not being used, use the convex side of the mirror.

Practise viewing with both eyes open. Often, too much light gets through and a better view can be got by changing the diaphragm lever. Put an object on the stage. Use the low power objective. Carefully use the *coarse focus* adjuster to bring the object nearly into focus. Now use the fine focus adjuster.

Material has to be prepared for viewing. *Temporary mounts* are often used to examine living material. Generally, a small amount of the material is placed on the centre of a microscopic slide, a drop of water is added and a cover slip is put on. Sometimes, stains are used to colour parts otherwise difficult to see. *Methylene blue* is an example of a stain. Permanent mounts are often commercially produced. Instead of mounting in water, the material is dehydrated (water fully removed) and mounted in a resin material (e.g. Canada balsam).

7.3 Structure of Cells

The basic structure of a cell is shown in *Fig. 7.2*. The living part of each cell is called the *protoplasm* and it is surrounded by a cell membrane. In addition to this membrane, *plant cells have a rigid cell wall* which is composed mainly of *cellulose.* (Important biological chemicals will be covered later in this chapter.) Another important characteristic of plant cells is that they have chloroplasts (see below) which make photosynthesis possible.

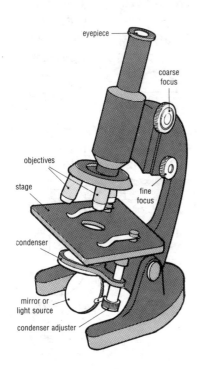

eyepiece

coarse focus

objectives

stage

fine focus

condenser

mirror or light source

condenser adjuster

Magnification =
eyepiece magnification
x
objective magnification

Fig 7.1 A typical compound microscope

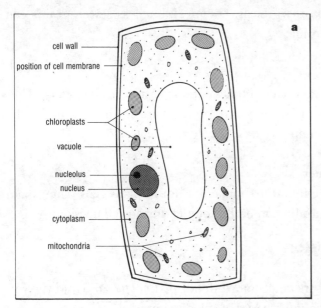
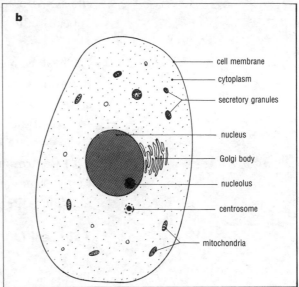

Fig 7.2 Diagrams of cells: (a) plant (b) animal

The vast majority of cells contain a nucleus. The nucleus contains granular areas called chromatin and denser areas called nucleoli (singular, nucleolus). The nucleus is covered by a nuclear membrane. During cell division, the chromatin appears as the *chromosomes*. Cell division is discussed later in this chapter.

The protoplasm outside the cell nucleus is called the *cytoplasm*. It contains many other sub-cellular components called *organelles*. Organelles carry out specialized functions. Important organelles include mitochondria, chloroplasts, ribosomes and centrosomes.

7.3.1 Mitochondria

Mitochondria are small, elongated bodies in the cytoplasm. Those from mammalian liver cells are about 1.5 μm long and 0.5 μm wide. They are most common in cells which are very active and use a lot of energy. For example, mitochondria are very common in muscle cells. Electronmicrographs have shown us that their outer wall is smooth but that internally they have folds on their inner walls, called cristae. The main function of mitochondria is the production of the chemical ATP from ADP during *respiration*. This will be covered in greater detail in *Chapter 8*. ATP is the main energy storing compound in the cell.

7.3.2 Chloroplasts

Chloroplasts occur in all plants which photosynthesize. They are relatively large: up to 10 μm in diameter and 3 μm thick. Their internal structure (based on an electronmicrograph) is shown in *Fig. 7.3*. The photosynthetic pigment, *chlorophyll*, is located in sheet-like structures called *lamellae*. In places, the lamellae are thickened to form *grana*. These are suspended in an aqueous matrix called the

Fig 7.3 Chloroplast structure

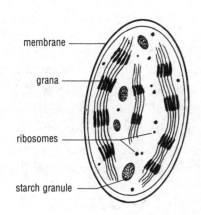

stroma. After photosynthesis, chemicals such as starch grains can appear in the stroma.

7.3.3 Ribosomes

Ribosomes are very small bodies (about 15 nm in diameter). They are very important as sites where proteins are synthesized under the control of the genetic code *(see 7.5.4 and Chapter 27)*.

7.3.4 Centrosomes

Centrosomes are found in animal but not in plant cells. Their main function is the production of the spindle during cell division.

7.4 Cell Division

This is covered in much more detail in *Chapter 26*. However you need to understand the basics of cell division now.

Nuclei of plant and animal cells have chromosomes. Normal plant and animal cells have a pair of every chromosome; each member of the chromosome pair is identical or almost so. For example, humans have 23 pairs of chromosomes. This is referred to as the *diploid* number *(2n)* of chromosomes. There are two kinds of cell division. *Mitosis* occurs when a cell divides to form two daughter cells with the same number of chromosomes as its parent cell. However the formation of *gametes* (sex cells) involves a special kind of division called *meiosis*. Gametes have only half the number of chromosomes as normal cells. This is called the *haploid* number *(n)*. When fertilization occurs, two gametes *(n)* fuse and the diploid number *(2n)* is restored.

7.5 Chemicals of Life

The main chemicals found in living organisms are carbohydrates, proteins, amino acids and lipids. We will also examine two other very important groups of chemicals, vitamins and minerals. You will also learn to carry out food tests.

7.5.1 Carbohydrates

Carbohydrates are chemicals which contain the elements carbon, hydrogen and water. They have the general molecular formula of $(CH_2O)_n$ where n can range from 1 to a large number. They tend to be simple sugars (glucose is an example of a monosaccharide), or sugars composed of two simple sugar units (called a disaccharide; sucrose or household sugar is a common example), or long chains of sugar units (called a polysaccharide; starch is an example). *(See Fig. 7.4.)*

Sugars are soluble in water. Plants and animals have difficulty in storing large quantities of simple sugars. Instead, they convert sugars to long chains of the basic sugar units – *polysaccharides* for storage. The storage polysaccharide of plants is called starch. In animals the storage polysaccharide is called *glycogen*. Another polysaccharide, *cellulose,* is the main component of the cell-wall of plants and a vital foodstuff for grazing animals.

Try to remember the following examples of carbohydrates:

monosaccharides: glucose and fructose

disaccharides: sucrose, maltose and lactose

polysaccharides: starch, glycogen and cellulose

Sugars can be monosaccharides or disaccharides. The molecular formula for glucose is $C_6H_{12}O_6$ and is given in *Fig. 7.4*. In reality, these molecules exist in a molecular ring structure. Study the example of glucose. When two monosaccharide sugar molecules join together they form a disaccharide such as sucrose which is the common sugar obtained from sugar beet. Sucrose is formed from one molecule of glucose and one molecule of fructose. Because of the way the sucrose molecule is formed, this sugar does not react with alkaline solutions of copper (Cu^{++}) ions — this is the usual test for "reducing sugars", and is used in the investigations on food tests which you will carry out. Hence, we call sucrose a non-reducing sugar.

Fig 7.4 *The structure of carbohydrates*

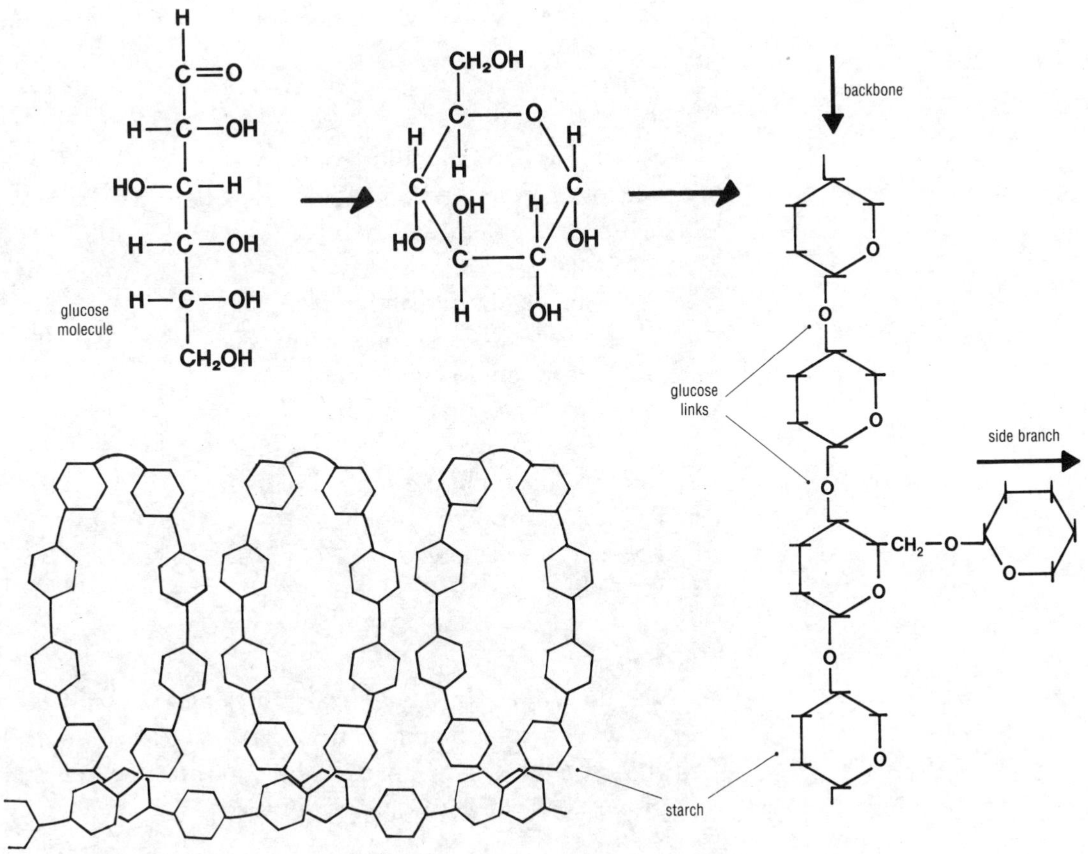

Starch is the main storage carbohydrate of plants. It is formed by the linking together of many glucose molecules. The advantages for the plant are that the sugars formed by photosynthesis are effectively stored. If they were not converted to starch, the plant would have to cope with the osmotic problem of all that extra sugar. *(See Section 7.6.1)*

In animals, the main storage carbohydrate is *glycogen*. It is found in the muscles and liver. Its molecular structure is very similar to starch.

Cellulose is the most abundant organic chemical in the world. At least 50% of all the carbon in vegetation is in cellulose. However, not all animals can digest cellulose. For example, it passes undigested through the digestive system of humans. Even so, it is important as "roughage". As we shall see, some animals exploit other organisms to digest cellulose for them. This makes this huge food resource available to them.

When polysaccharides are broken down, they first yield short chains of sugar units, and eventually the monosaccharide of which they were formed. Then the monosaccharide itself is broken down by the process of respiration to release the energy which was trapped in the sugar unit when the sugar was formed during photosynthesis.

Food Tests

Food testing and using a refractometer to measure sucrose concentration

Materials needed
1. Starch powder and iodine solution
2. Glucose powder and Benedict's reagent
3. White of egg, dilute sodium hydroxide and 1% copper sulphate
4. Some fat, e.g. butter, and brown paper
5. Vitamin C tablets (ascorbic acid) and DCPIP tablets (dichlorophenol - indophenol)
6. Variety of foodstuffs of unknown composition
7. Test-tubes on a rack
8. Bunsen burner and test-tube holder
9. Pipettes or dropping pipettes
10. Pocket refractometer
11. Household sugar (sucrose)

Procedure
1. Test for *starch*. Put some starch powder in a test-tube and shake with some water. Boil to make a clear solution. When cooled, add 3 or 4 drops iodine solution. When starch is present, a dark blue-black colour forms.

contd. –

2. Test for *sugar*. This is a test for reducing sugars. Put a pinch of glucose in the bottom of a test-tube and add about 1 cm depth of water. Shake. Add a similar quantity of Benedict's reagent. Boil carefully. When a reducing sugar is present, the solution turns greenish to reddish. If allowed to stand, a rusty coloured precipitate forms. Sucrose gives a negative result to this test. However, if the sucrose molecule is split, e.g. using an enzyme, the resulting solution may give a positive result. (Can you explain why?)

3. Test for *protein*. Dilute egg white (the protein albumen) with water in the ratio of 1 to 20. Place about 1 cm depth of the dilute albumen in a test tube. Add 5 cm^3 of dilute sodium hydroxide and then slowly pour 5 cm^3 of 1% copper sulphate solution down the wall of the tube. A purple colour indicates protein.

4. Test for *fats*. Rub some fat or oil on brown paper or filter paper. Observe the grease test on the paper.

5. Test for *vitamins*. Use a 0.1% solution of DCPIP (dichlorophenol-indophenol). This is a blue dye which goes colourless with vitamin C. Use freshly prepared 0.1% vitamin C (or use citrus fruit juices such as orange squash). Put 2 cm^3 of vitamin C solution into a test-tube and add DCPIP, counting the number of drops necessary to change the colour. Different vitamin C solutions require different amounts of DCPIP according to their concentration.

6. Estimate sucrose concentration using a pocket refractometer. Look through the refractometer and satisfy yourself that nothing is visible. Depending on the concentration of sugar present, a scale is revealed and you can read off the sugar concentration. Make up a few different solutions of household sugar (you only need a drop of each). Now place a drop of sugar solution on the stage of the refractometer and close it. Examine it by looking through the eyepiece and read off the percent sucrose at the top of the part of the scale now visible.

Precaution

When boiling material in test-tubes, the mouth of the tube MUST be pointed away from others in the classroom. Practise keeping small quantities "just on the boil" by flicking them in and out of the flame. Otherwise the material tends to "bump" - i.e. spurt out of the tube.

7.5.2 Fats or lipids

Chemists call fats lipids. The term lipids also includes oils — the main difference is that fats are normally solid at normal temperature whereas oils are liquid.

Lipids are biological chemicals which can be dissolved in the so-called "fat solvents" such as ether or chloroform. They are not soluble in water. Lipids consist of long chains of *fatty acids*. Sometimes, tiny fragments of lipids can be *permanently suspended in an aqueous mixture*. This is called *an emulsion* and milk is an example. Enzymes *(see 7.5.3)* which act to break down lipids are collectively called *lipases*.

7.5.3 Proteins and amino acids

Proteins are extremely important chemicals. All *enzymes* are proteins. Other proteins are found in cell-walls. Hair, wool and collagen (important in connective tissue) are all proteins. Muscular contraction involves proteins. Some hormones are proteins. Antibodies, so important in the body's defence system, are proteins. Thus, we can say that proteins are involved in nearly all physiological functions. Proteins can constitute up to three-quarters of the dry matter of animal tissue.

Proteins are very large molecules. They consist of chains of basic units called *amino acids*. Twenty amino acids occur commonly in proteins. Look at the chemical structure of one amino acid called alanine. You do not need to memorize the structure. Note one important detail: all amino acids have an *amino group*. This is the $-NH_2$ part. We will come across this again in excretion. When proteins are broken down, they yield the amino acids which formed them. When the amino acids are broken down, this amino group forms ammonia which is poisonous. Excretion deals with this problem. Some of the amino acids are *essential* in an animal's diet — this means that they cannot be manufactured by the animal itself.

All enzymes are proteins. *Enzymes* are biological *catalysts*. Catalysts do not themselves take part in a reaction but they enable a reaction to take place. Nowadays, enzymes are named by adding "-ase" to the name of the chemical they act upon. Examples are lip*ases* (acting on lipids), protein*ases* (acting on proteins) and amyl*ases* (acting on starch - amylin is a form of starch). A few well-known enzymes are still known by their old names. Examples are *pepsin* and *trypsin* which are two proteinases important in the digestive system.

The white of an egg is a protein called albumen. When boiled, it goes solid and white. The albumen has been denatured. Heating a protein, in general above the body temperature of mammals (about 40°C), denatures a protein. Protein can also be denatured by mixing it with acid. Since enzymes are proteins they can also be denatured in this way. When you perform the investigation on the enzyme catalase, can you explain why you heated one of the tubes?

7.5.4 DNA

DNA is the main chemical found in the chromosomes. The letters *DNA* stand for *deoxyribonucleic acid*. This chemical is the basis for the

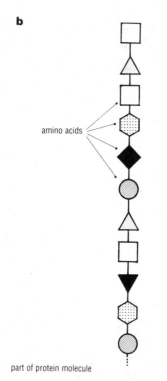

Fig 7.5 (a) An example of an amino acid and (b) different amino acids linked together in a protein molecule

genetic code. Additional information on DNA is included in the genetics chapter *(Chapter 27)*.

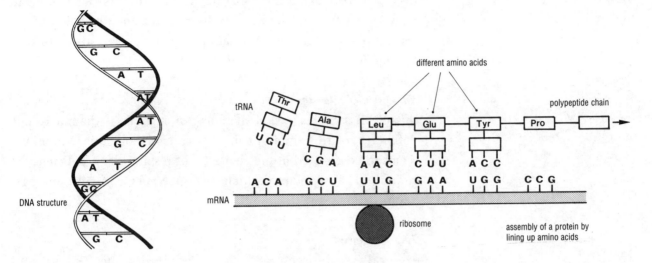

Fig 7.6 DNA structure and the assembly of a protein by lining up amino acids

The structure of DNA was discovered by Watson and Crick in 1952. The DNA molecule consists of two long chains of the sugar deoxyribose and phosphates. Each chain is coiled into what is called a *"double helix"* structure. Between each chain are bases called adenine, cytosine, guanine and thymine. *Adenine* always bonds with *thymine*, and *cytosine* with *guanine*. The genetic code is based on the fact that three of these bases (triplets) code for an individual amino acid. There are 20 common amino acids and 64 different combinations of base triplets. A diagram of DNA structure is in *Fig. 7.6.*

In the nucleus, DNA forms messenger *RNA (ribonucleic acid)* which leaves the nucleus and transfers to the ribosomes. Thus, the function of the DNA is to form RNA which lines up the various amino acids in the correct order for them to form the protein which the genetic code has directed. Since many proteins are enzymes or very important structural proteins it is easy to see how the genetic code is eventually implemented. It will be useful to return to this section when studying genetics *(Chapter 27)*.

7.5.5 Vitamins

For normal healthy living, the diet of an animal must include chemicals other than carbohydrates, lipids and proteins. Vitamins are an example. Vitamins are organic chemicals which cannot be made by the animal itself and must be included in its diet. One of the best known example is vitamin C. Since the middle of the 18th century, it has been known that fresh fruit (especially citrus fruit) and vegetables in the diet prevent scurvy. Broadly speaking, vitamins can be divided into two groups: *fat soluble* and *water soluble.*

> **There is an old name for a sailor with a vitamin connection.**
> **Find out what it is.**

Fat soluble vitamins

Vitamin A is chemically related to the carotene in carrots. It is necessary for making the visual pigments and a deficiency leads to night blindness. Vitamin D is involved in calcium absorption and is very important for bone formation. A deficiency leads to rickets. Vitamin K is necessary for blood-clotting.

Water soluble vitamins

Vitamin B includes several vitamins. An example is vitamin B_{12}. A deficiency of this vitamin causes pernicious anaemia. Vitamin C seems to be involved in the chemistry of respiration. A deficiency of vitamin C causes scurvy which was once very common amongst sailors on long voyages.

7.5.6 Minerals

Minerals are inorganic nutrients required by both plants and animals for a variety of functions. They will be referred to throughout the book. An investigation on the importance of minerals for plant nutrition is in Exercise 33.

7.6 Cell Physiology

Materials can enter and leave cells by *diffusion* and *osmosis* and *active transport.*

Molecules in gases and liquids are free to move. Because of this random movement, molecules of gases and liquids tend to distribute themselves throughout the space which confines them. This is called diffusion. In single-celled animals (Protozoa), diffusion might be enough to account for the entry of gases such as oxygen and the removal of waste material.

7.6.1 Osmosis

Osmosis is a special kind of diffusion which occurs in nature. Membranes occurring in cells are said to be *semi-permeable membranes.* This means that they have pores which allow the passage of small molecules such as water but do not allow larger molecules such as sugars, proteins or starch to pass through. Thus, when a semi-permeable membrane separates two solutions of different concentration, only the water molecules can pass through. Osmosis is the movement of water across a semi-permeable membrane from a region of lower concentration to a region of stronger concentration. When two solutions of different concentration are separated by a semi-permeable membrane, the more concentrated solution is said to be *hypertonic* to the other. The less concentrated solution is said to be *hypotonic* in comparison to the more concentrated solution.

Osmosis is of great importance in living cells and many examples will be mentioned in the following chapters. When plant cells are placed in a hypertonic salt solution, their protoplasm shrinks away from the rigid cell-wall. This is called *plasmolysis*. If the solution is replaced by water, the protoplasm swells again. When water enters the protoplasm of a cell by osmosis, it exerts turgor pressure on the cell-walls. A cell is then said to be *turgid*.

7.6.2 Active transport

Active transport is in effect the opposite of osmosis. It is the transfer of a substance from a region of low to a region of high concentration. Active transport involves the *use of energy* by cells. This is a common function of cells: one example is the *"sodium pump"* in the kidney *(Chapter 33)*.

Exercises

Exercise 20. Examination of cells using a microscope

Materials needed
1. Microscope, microscope slides and coverslips
2. Dissecting pin (or straight pin) to manipulate material
3. Green algal filaments from a pond
4. Cells from the lining of the mouth
5. Methylene blue
6. Onion cells
7. Cork from a bottle
8. A soft plant stem
9. Razor blade

Procedure
Prepare temporary mounts as described in the text. Observe the cells and produce labelled drawings of what you see. The cheek cells are obtained by scraping the inside of your mouth with your (cleaned!) fingernail. Place the material on a slide and add a drop of methylene blue stain. Carefully apply a coverslip. Put on the stage of the microscope and focus. The cell nuclei stain darker. A thin strip of onion cells can be got as follows: take a scale from an onion and bend it backwards until it breaks. Now quickly pull the two pieces apart and use the thinnest piece of tissue. Mount with water and a coverslip. Cut thin sections of cork from a bottle and of a soft plant stem. Mount with water and a coverslip, as before.

Exercise 21. Demonstration of an enzyme: liver catalase

Principle:
Hydrogen peroxide is a poison in the body. Catalase breaks this down to harmless water and oxygen.

$H_2O_2 \longrightarrow H_2O + O_2$ (greatly speeded up by the presence of catalase)

Materials needed:
1. Dilute hydrogen peroxide
2. Fresh liver
3. Mortar, pestle, washed sand
4. Test tubes on rack

Procedure
1. Put a lump of liver in the bottom of a test tube. Add a 2 cm depth of dilute hydrogen peroxide. Note the extent of any bubbles given off.

2. Grind the same sized lump of liver using the mortar, pestle and sand. Now put the ground liver in the tube and repeat stage 1, above.

3. Grind another piece of liver, again the same size. Put in test tube. Put tube down into almost boiling water for about a minute. Now add the hydrogen peroxide and note any reaction.

Do you know why each stage of the procedure was carried out? Explain your results.

Exercise 22. Investigations on diffusion and osmosis

Materials needed
1. Wide glass tube (diameter 20 mm, length about 30 cm)
2. Piece of wire longer than tube and a forceps
3. Pieces of litmus paper 1 cm square
4. Bung for tube with a hole bored in it
5. Cotton wool
6. Dilute ammonia solution
7. Dropping (teat) pipette
8. Dialysis (visking) tubing - or use "Glad" freezer polythene bags
9. Beaker three quarters full of 1% starch solution
10. Dilute iodine solution
11. Burette or small funnel
12. Piece of twine
13. Microscope, microscope slide and coverslip
14. Piece of fresh rhubarb stalk
15. Pinch of salt
16. Blotting (or filter) paper

Procedure
1. Demonstration of diffusion of a gas. Mark the tube every 2 cm. Close one end of the tube with an ordinary bung. Using forceps, dip a square of litmus paper in water, shake it and place it inside the tube. Use the wire to move it to the first mark. Continue until you have a piece of litmus paper at each mark (*Fig. 7.7a overleaf*). Stuff cotton wool into the bore of the bung. Now use a dropping pipette to add 20 drops of the ammonia solution to the cotton wool. Place this bung on the tube and note the time as each litmus square turns from red to blue (why?). Explain your observations.

2. Demonstration of osmosis across a semi-permeable membrane. Cut the dialysis tubing into 15 cm lengths and soak in water before use. Knot one end of the tubing. Fill the tubing with the starch solution (*Fig. 7.7b*). Be careful not to spill starch along the outside: try filling the tubing using a burette or small funnel. Tie and suspend in a beaker of dilute iodine. Keep another beaker of dilute iodine to compare the exact colour when the investigation is finished. Examine the following day. Note any colour changes. Compare the colour of the iodine remaining in the beaker with the beaker set aside on day 1. Has iodine travelled across the membrane? Has starch travelled across the membrane? What evidence have you for your answers?

3. Demonstration of osmosis in living tissue. Prepare three hollowed-out half-potatoes as in the diagram (*Fig. 7.7c*). Place one in boiling water for a few minutes. This kills it. Now set up all three in Petri dishes of equal quantities of water. Place a teaspoon of salt in the dead potato and in one of the others. About 2-3 hours later, note and explain if any liquid is within the potato cavities.

4. Demonstration of plasmolysis in red rhubarb cells. Make a temporary mount of red rhubarb epidermal cells using the method used for onion cells in Exercise 20. Examine them and draw them. Place a pinch of salt crystals at one side of the coverslip. Touch a piece of blotting paper at the far side of the coverslip. This draws a strong salt solution over the rhubarb cells. Observe and make drawings showing plasmolysis - notice that the protoplasm shrinks away from the cell. Plasmolysis can be reversed by drawing water over the cells in the opposite direction, again using blotting paper.

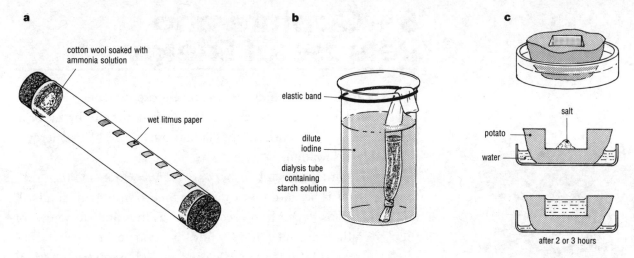

a

cotton wool soaked with ammonia solution

wet litmus paper

b

elastic band

dilute iodine

dialysis tube containing starch solution

c

salt

potato

water

after 2 or 3 hours

Fig 7.7 Investigating diffusion and osmosis (Exercise 22)

8 – Capture and Release of Energy

In this chapter, we will study how organisms capture energy and how it is released. Green plants capture energy from the sun by a special process called photosynthesis (or "light-production"). This energy is released by respiration.

Green plants are said to be *autotrophic*, which means "self-feeding". This is because they can make their own organic food. All other organisms depend on green plants as the ultimate source of their organic material ("food") and are said to be *heterotrophic*. Energy captured by green plants passes through a food chain when plants are eaten by animals who eat plants ("herbivores") and when herbivores are themselves eaten by other animals ("carnivores"). Another group of organisms, such as many fungi and bacteria, feed on decaying organic matter and recycle the energy in it. To summarize: all energy comes to the Earth from the sun; green plants capture this energy and make it available for themselves and other living organisms. A diagram showing the role of green plants is given in *Fig. 8.1*.

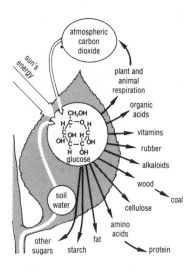

Fig. 8.1 Green plants link solar energy to life on earth

8.1 Photosynthesis

The reactions of photosynthesis are summarized in *Fig. 8.2*. Light energy is absorbed by the chlorophyll in the chloroplast. Its effect on the chlorophyll results in the splitting of a water molecule into H^+ and OH^- ions. The hydrogen ions are held temporarily by a "hydrogen carrier". The OH^- ions are further split. This results in the release of oxygen and, most importantly, the release of energy. This energy is captured by a special compound in the cell called *ADP* (adenosine diphosphate). In the presence of energy and phosphate ions, ADP is converted to *ATP* (adenosine triphosphate). ATP releases its energy when it is converted back to ADP. Thus ATP is the universal energy currency in the cell and is used for many reactions which require energy to drive them. This is the main function of light:

solar energy is used to produce a high energy compound for later use.

So far in photosynthesis, oxygen has been released. The sun's energy has been converted to ATP and hydrogen ions are being held by a hydrogen carrier. Carbon dioxide is now combined with the hydrogen ions to yield sugar. This reaction requires the energy trapped in ATP. The overall reaction is: *(overleaf)*

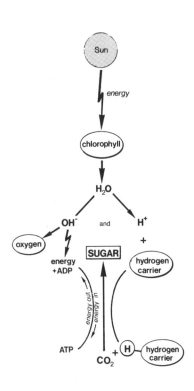

Fig. 8.2 The main events in photosynthesis

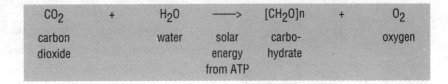

CO_2	+	H_2O	$\longrightarrow$	$[CH_2O]n$	+	O_2
carbon dioxide		water	solar energy from ATP	carbo-hydrate		oxygen

Thus, in photosynthesis, the sun's energy is used to split a water molecule. This releases energy. This energy is used to form carbohydrates. *Oxygen is released.*

8.2 Respiration

Fig 8.3 Summary of events during respiration

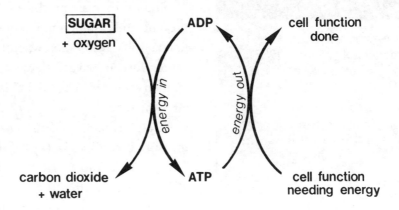

Respiration is the process used by organisms to *release energy.* Whereas photosynthesis was confined to green plants, respiration occurs in all living organisms. The basic reaction is the opposite to that of photosynthesis. A sugar molecule is broken down to carbon dioxide and water. *Oxygen is used in the reaction.* Energy is released and stored for future use in ATP. This ATP is then available as an energy source for other cell functions. These reactions are summarized in *Fig. 8.3.* The overall reaction is:

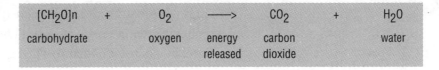

$[CH_2O]n$	+	O_2	$\longrightarrow$	CO_2	+	H_2O
carbohydrate		oxygen	energy released	carbon dioxide		water

The kind of respiration described so far which uses free oxygen is the most common form of respiration. It is *aerobic* respiration. Aerobic respiration consists of a series of reactions whereby a molecule of glucose is oxidized to carbon dioxide and water. Some organisms do not use oxygen for respiration. Instead they convert glucose to either lactic acid or alcohol. This is called *anaerobic* respiration.

Basically, all kinds of respiration follow a common first pathway. This is called *glycolysis* (gluco = sugar; lysis = to split). Oxygen is not required for this stage. Anaerobic respiration results in either lactic

Hans Krebs, b. 1900
Shared Nobel Prize in 1953 for the
discovery of the citric acid cycle.

1 Calorie = 1 000 calories
           = 4.2 kJ

acid or alcohol. Aerobic respiration involves passing the products of glycolysis through a further series of reactions called the *TCA (tricarboxylic acid)* or Krebs' Cycle. Oxygen is required at this stage. The TCA cycle yields much more energy than glycolysis. For each molecule of glucose, glycolysis yields 8 ATP molecules. A further 30 ATP molecules are produced by the TCA cycle. These reactions take place in the mitochondria. Mitochondria are abundant in tissues such as muscles which respire a lot.

Even though anaerobic respiration does not yield as much energy, it is sufficient for some organisms. Anaerobic respiration by bacteria produces lactic acid which sours milk. Anaerobic respiration by yeast produces alcohol and is very important for the brewing and distilling industries. Mammalian muscle cells can resort to anaerobic respiration when there is not enough oxygen: sprinters can endure an oxygen debt and a temporary build up of lactic acid in their muscles. The "debt" is repaid during the recovery period after the race.

Energy is measured in *joules* (J). Foodstuffs usually have values measured in *kilojoules* (kJ). Energy values used to be measured in calories. One kilocalorie was often written as a Calorie (4.2 kJ = 1 Cal). Remember that the term calorie is no longer valid. However, calories are often given on food packages and the term "calorific value" is still used to mean energy value. Energy values are obtained by burning a sample of the food in a *bomb calorimeter*. The temperature rise is carefully measured and converted to the energy value. Exercise 24 includes a demonstration of a calorimeter.

8.3 Energy Compensation Points

The production of organic energy by photosynthesis needs light. The release of energy by respiration can take place in the dark. Light intensity varies between different habitats. For example, compare the intensity of light falling on a field with that at ground level in a dense woodland. The light intensity which allows a plant to exactly balance energy synthesis and energy consumption is called the *compensation point*. Different species of plants are adapted to survive in different conditions and have different compensation points. Species, such as mosses, which survive low light intensity have low compensation points and are described as shade plants. As a general rule, plant species used as houseplants tend to be shade plants since light levels within houses, even on sunny windowsills, are relatively low.

Exercises

Exercise 23. Investigations on photosynthesis

Materials needed
1. Test-tubes, glass funnel and beaker
2. Industrial methylated spirits (called "alcohol" here)
3. Supply of Canadian pondweed *Elodea*
4. Strong light source - sunny window or light projector
5. Variegated geranium *(Pelargonium)* plant
6. Iodine solution
7. Beaker of boiling water
8. Forceps

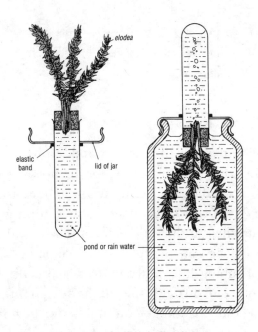

*Fig 8.4 Using **Elodea** to study photosynthesis*

Procedure
1. The presence of chlorophyll. Chlorophyll is readily soluble in alcohol. Cut up some leaves, place them in alcohol and notice the colour of the solution.
2. Observations on the production of oxygen. To monitor the production of oxygen, the water plant called Canadian pondweed *(Elodea)* is used. Set up cut stems of this plant as shown in the diagram *(Fig. 8.4)*. A problem with this investigation in school laboratories

is that good sunlight is needed. You can replace this by using a bright light source such as a slide projector. Set up the apparatus and use the bright light. Check that you can see the small bubbles of gas appearing. Switch off the light source. Continue observing and time how long it takes for the bubbles to stop.

3. Identify the gas produced in photosynthesis. To do this you will require a reasonable quantity of gas. This takes some days. Place the apparatus on a sunny windowsill. Once a few cm^3 of gas have formed, test for the presence of oxygen. (Does it relight a smoldering splinter?)

4. Investigate the importance of light for photosynthesis. Place just a few stems of *Elodea* in the apparatus and use a bright light source. Count the number of gas bubbles released in 30 seconds. Move back the light source and wait about a minute before you count the gas bubbles again. Repeat this until you have counted the number of gas bubbles produced in 30 seconds with the light at five distances from the *Elodea*. Graph the number of bubbles released in 30 seconds against the distance of the light source from the *Elodea*. Explain your results.

5. Investigate the effect of light of different wavelengths. You can use a similar set up as used in Investigation 4. This time, keep the distance of light source to apparatus constant but put coloured filters in the projector. (If you do not have proper filters, try red and yellow cellophane sweet wrappers but be careful as parts of a slide projector are very hot.)

6. Investigate the effect of adding sodium bicarbonate. Add some sodium bicarbonate (10%) to the beaker containing the *Elodea*. This has the same effect as adding carbon dioxide. Carbon dioxide gas is sometimes used in protected crops to increase yield. Can you explain why?

7. Is chlorophyll necessary for photosynthesis?

Get a variegated geranium plant. Place it in a sunny position for at least a few hours on the day you carry out this practical. Otherwise, shine an electric light (60 W bulb) onto the leaves from a distance of 15 to 20 cm overnight. Now test a leaf for the presence of starch, as follows:

Read the precautions before proceeding.

Remove a leaf from the plant and draw the pattern of variegation. Immerse a leaf in boiling water for a few seconds to kill it. Use a forceps to handle it. Place the leaf in a test tube of alcohol. Place the test tube in the beaker of boiling water for a few minutes. This removes the chlorophyll. Test the leaf for starch using iodine (chapter 7). Draw the leaf again showing where starch was present. Explain your results. Explain the reason for each stage in the investigation.

Precautions

Alcohol is highly inflammable. This is the reason for the beaker of boiling water. Ensure that all naked flames (e.g. Bunsen burners) are switched off before opening the bottle of alcohol. Industrial methylated spirits is poisonous.

Exercise 24. Investigations on respiration and energy value of food

We can monitor respiration by looking for two of its products: carbon dioxide and energy (heat).

Materials needed

1. Test- tubes
2. Lengths of glass tube
3. Rubber tubing
4. Limewater
5. Two screw top jars - same size
6. Germinating peas
7. Cotton wool
8. Stump of candle (or a night light)
9. Two vacuum (e.g., "thermos") flasks
10. Wheat or pea seeds, soaked overnight
11. 1% formalin
12. Two glass rods, 20 cm
13. Thermometer
14. Two crucibles
15. 1 g each cooking oil and sugar
16. Metal can
17. Retort stand
18. Tripod stand and triangle fitting
19. 100 cm^3 graduated cylinder
20. Bunsen burner

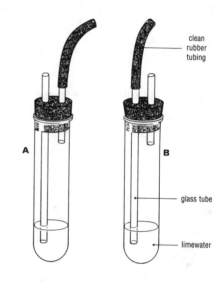

Fig 8.5 Comparing inspired and expired air

1. Comparison of inspired and expired air. Limewater is used to test for the presence of carbon dioxide. Set up two test-tubes as in *Fig. 8.5*. Note that the rubber tubing is attached to the short tube in tube A and to the long tube in tube B. Why? Put both ends of tubing into your mouth and breathe in and out through the tubing for about 30 seconds. Compare the limewater in both tubes and explain your results.

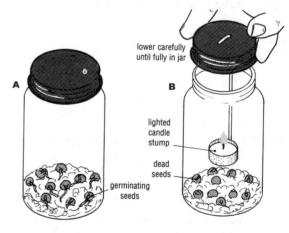

Fig 8.6 Which gas is used during germination?

2. Which gas is used up when seeds respire during germination? Get two screw-top jars of the same size and a supply of germinating seeds (e.g. peas). Kill half of the peas (boil them and let them cool). Put some moist cotton wool in the bottom of each jar. Place an exact number of germinating peas into jar A and the same number of dead peas into jar B. Leave for 24 hours or more. For the next stage, you will need a short candle on a special holder *(see Fig. 8.6, page 102)*. Unscrew but do not remove the lids from jars A and B. Now carefully remove the lid of jar A and lower the lighted candle into it. Time how long it continues to burn. Repeat for jar B. Explain your results.

3. Is energy released by germinating seeds? Obtain two small vacuum flasks and enough seeds (peas or wheat) to fill them. Soak the seeds overnight. Divide the seeds into two equal sized batches, A and B. Boil the seeds of batch B for 5 minutes to kill them and allow them to cool. Soak both batches of seeds in a solution of 1% formalin for about 5 minutes. This kills fungi and bacteria that might grow on them. Pour off the formalin from both batches and wash the seeds in two changes of water. Now set up the vacuum flasks as in *Fig. 8.7*. Put the seeds loosely into the flasks, filling them almost to the top. Plug each flask with cotton wool which has a glass rod through it extending down into the

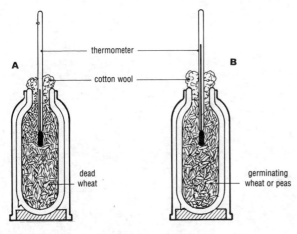

Fig 8.7 Is energy released during germination?

seeds. Put the flasks where they will not be subject to heat from radiators or sunshine. Leave for two to four days. Then carefully remove the glass rod from each flask and replace with a thermometer. Note the temperature and explain your observations.

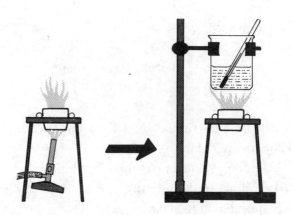

Fig 8.8 1. Practice movements before lighting Bunsen 2. Light material in crucible 3. Slide burning crucible under can

4. Demonstration of simple calorimeter. It is important that you read and understand all the instructions for this investigation before you proceed. Set up the apparatus as in *Fig. 8.8*. Place the crucible with the oil on a triangle on the tripod stand. Clamp the metal can at a height so that when the tripod stand is moved under it the distance will be about 5 cm. Check this in advance. Now use the graduated cylinder to measure 100 cm^3 water into the can. Note the temperature. Light the Bunsen burner under the crucible. From time to time bring the flame of the Bunsen to the mouth of the crucible until the oil just starts to burn. Now carefully slide the tripod across under the can. If the oil quenches move the tripod back to the Bunsen - do not bring the Bunsen across under the can. When the oil is fully burned note the final temperature. Repeat for 1 g sugar.

Calculations

Subtract the first temperature from the final temperature to give the rise in temperature

(T°C). Remember that 1 calorie raises the temperature of 1 g water by 1°C. If 1 g oil raised the temperature of 100 cm^3 by T°C, then 1 g oil produced:

$$100 \times T \text{ calories} = \ldots\ldots\ldots \text{ calories}$$

or 1 g oil gave

$$\frac{\ldots\ldots\ldots \text{ kilocalories per gram}}{1000}$$

Multiply this figure by 4.2 to convert it to kilojoules per gram.

  5. Energy values of common foodstuffs.

 (i). Collect and study the energy value tables printed on food packages.

 (ii). Study the values in *Table 8.1*. Calculate the energy value of each food (in kJ per g) by summing the contribution of the protein, fat and carbohydrate. Use the following conversion figures: fat 39 kJ g^{-1}; protein 23 kJ g^{-1} and carbohydrate 17 kJ g^{-1} (these are average figures since different kinds of proteins, for example, give slightly different energy values).

Table 8.1 *Typical composition and energy values of various foods. The values are per 100g sample. Read through this table and get an overall view of food composition. You do not need to memorize the values*

Food	Protein (g)	Lipid (g)	Carbohy-drate (g)	Energy (kJ)
Milk (whole)	3	4	5	272
Yoghurt (natural)	4	3	5	239
Cheddar cheese	25	35	0	1726
Butter	0.5	83	0	3122
Beef (average)	15	28	0	1311
Chicken (roast)	30	7	0	771
Cod (fried in batter)	20	10	8	834
Eggs	12	12	0	662
Honey	0.4	0	76	1270
Cauliflower	3	0	3	101
Potatoes (boiled)	1	0	20	331
Apple	0.3	0	12	193
Oatmeal	12	9	73	1676

9 – Living Organisms Part 1

In this chapter, we will consider the general structure and life cycles of micro-organisms, such as viruses and bacteria and fungi, and of green plants such as the fern, the pine tree and the flowering plants. We will study the life cycles of animals in *Chapters 28 and 29.*

9.1 Scientific Names

This topic is covered in more detail in *Chapter 28.* The basic unit of classification is the *species.* A species is *a group of closely related organisms which interbreed and produce fertile offspring.* Species are named by a system first proposed by *Linnaeus* from Sweden in about 1750. Each species is given two names. The first is the *genus* name. Each genus contains a number of related species. For example, buttercups belong to the genus *Ranunculus.* The creeping buttercup belongs to the species *Ranunculus repens.* The second word is the specific name. However, there are many other species of buttercup, also in the genus *Ranunculus* but with different species' names. Scientific names of plants are properly written with capital letters for the genus name and small letters for the specific name.

9.2 Viruses

Viruses are very small ranging from 20 to 400 nm in size. Electron microscopes are needed to see them. Individual viruses are called *virions.* All viruses are obligate parasites which means that they must live within the living cells of a host. It is the damage they cause which makes viruses so imporant. Some viruses attack bacteria: they are called *bacteriophages.*

The basic structure of a virion is a genome of either DNA or RNA sometimes enclosed in a coating or capsule *(Fig. 9.1).* Once a virus invades a host, it can reproduce itself repeatedly, thus causing the disease. Frequently viruses are transmitted by sucking insects. Greenfly or aphids transmit yellows virus in sugar beet. The rabbit flea transmits the myxoma virus which causes myxomatosis. Other examples of viruses in humans include poliomyelitis, influenza and rabies.

9.3 Bacteria

Bacteria (singular bacterium) are larger than viruses. They range from 0.5 to 5 μm in size. Under the microscope they have a variety of shapes. As an example, a rod-shaped bacterial cell is called a

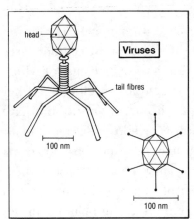
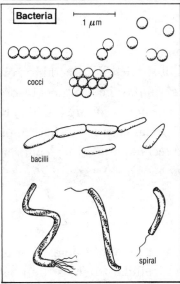

Fig. 9.1 Viruses and bacteria. Note the different scales

Louis Pasteur, 1822 – 1895
French microbiologist who has given his name to pasteurization

Pasteurisation, named after Louis Pasteur, kills disease causing bacteria, e.g. TB. Milk is pasteurizes by heating it to 72°C for 15 seconds and then cooling it rapidly. UHT milk is *sterilized* by blowing superheated steam (135 – 160°C) through it for a few seconds. This kills spoiling organisms and lengthens the shelf-life of the product.

bacillus and a spherical bacterium is called a coccus, see *Fig. 9.1*.

Most bacteria live on decaying organic matter or as parasites. A few can make their own simple sugars using a process similar to green plants. Many bacteria can respire in the absence of oxygen - anaerobic respiration.

In mammals, bacteria cause diseases such as pneumonia, botulism, dysentery and tuberculosis *(TB, see page 330)*. Their modes of transmission can be by air, food, water or by blood-sucking parasites (bubonic plague is transmitted from rats to humans by fleas). Bacterial diseases of plants include swollen tissues called galls, wilts (which block the water-conducting cells, or xylem, in plants) and cankers which cause tissue decay.

Gut bacteria are of major importance to mammals. Herbivores such as the cow have a rumen for the digestion of cellulose (see *Chapter 30*). Within the rumen are micro-organisms, of which bacteria are very important for the digestion of cellulose. Other herbivores without a rumen, such as the horse and rabbit, have bacteria within their large intestines for cellulose digestion. Many mammals, including humans, obtain vitamins B and K from bacteria in their guts. Bacteria are very important for soil chemistry where their function includes the fixation of atmospheric nitrogen to nitrates. Bacterial starter cultures are used in the manufacture of cheese and yoghurt.

9.3.1 Growing bacteria in the laboratory

Normally, bacteria occur as mixtures of species. For scientific work in the laboratory pure cultures are required, i.e. cultures of one species only. When other species are present the culture is said to be *contaminated*. Bacteria are grown in special cultures which supply them with nutrients for survival. The technique used for culturing bacteria is referred to as *sterile* or *aseptic technique*. *See exercise 26*.

9.4 Fungi

Fungi range in size from microscopic to large mushrooms, bracket fungi and puff balls. They can be unicellular, such as the yeast *Saccharomyces*. Usually fungi consist of a mycelium which consists of a network of threadlike hyphae. Examples of fungi include moulds *(Mucor)*, blight *(Phytophthora)*, mildews, yeasts *(Saccharomyces)*, blue moulds *(Penicillium)*, rusts such as the wheat rust *(Puccinia)* and the field mushroom *(Agaricus)*.

An important characteristic of fungi is that they *lack chlorophyll*. This means they are heterotrophic, i.e. they depend on other organisms for their food source. Some feed on decaying organic matter; others are parasites on both plants and animals.

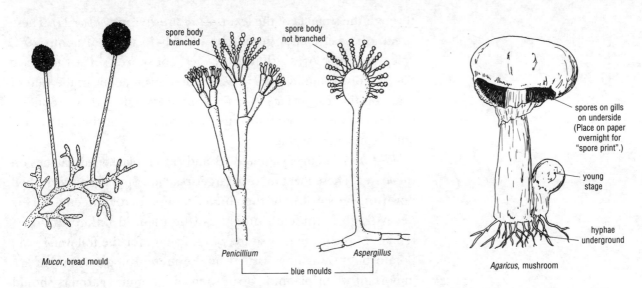

Fig 9.2 Variety of fungi

Fungi reproduce by means of spores. The spores may be produced either by sexual or asexual reproduction. A variety of fungi are shown in *Fig. 9.2.* Try to examine some of the spore-producing structures under a lens or microscope.

9.4.1 Parasitic fungi: potato blight

Some fungi are *pathogens* - i.e. they cause diseases in animals and plants. An animal pathogen is the ringworm fungus. Related to this is the athlete's foot fungus in humans. Plant pathogenic fungi include *rusts* of grain crops, *damping off* disease in seedlings - very important in horticulture - and *blight.*

Potato blight is an example of a very important plant pathogen. The fungus concerned is *Phytophthora infestans.* It was the major cause of the Irish potato famine. It continues to be of major economic importance to Irish agriculture.

Phytophthora is an obligate parasite. This means it can only live as a parasite. *Hyphae* grow between the cells of the potato leaf. Fine branches called *haustoria* penetrate the cells and absorb food from them. Later, spore-producing bodies called *sporangiophores* protrude

Fig 9.3 Diagram of a potato leaf invaded by blight (transverse section)

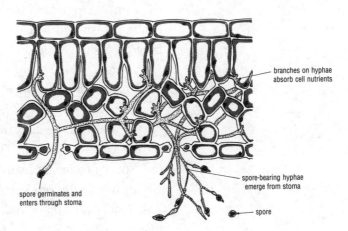

through the stomata of the leaf *(see leaf structure in Chapter 11)*. These break off easily. They germinate quickly in water at about 20°C releasing zoospores - they are called zoospores since they have flagella for swimming *(see Fig. 9.3)*. These swim about in the film of water on the leaf surface for a few hours. Eventually they produce a germ tube which penetrates the epidermal cell of the potato leaf and forms a new hypha.

Phytophthora quickly establishes and causes blackened patches on the leaves. These meet to form larger patches. Sporangia are washed down to the soil where they infect tubers. Badly infected tubers decay. Lightly infected tubers can be planted unknowingly or remain in the ground as sources of infection for the following year. Potato blight warnings issued by the meteorological service are important when planning a spraying programme. Farmers should also be aware that the fungus develops strains resistant to the fungicide sprays used to control it. The use of different sprays in different years is recommended to try to stay ahead of the natural resistance developed by the fungus.

Blight also infects tomato plants. This is interesting since the tomato and the potato belong to the same genus, *Solanum*.

9.4.2 Useful fungi

Fungi which live on decaying organic matter release the nutrients. This is important for nutrient-cycling. Some species of mushroom such as *Agaricus* are cultivated as a food crop. Yeasts are important in the brewing, distilling and baking industries. Many *antibiotics* made by fungi have been isolated. Antibiotics can be used to control bacterial infections. One example of an antibiotic is *penicillin* isolated from the mould *Penicillium*.

9.5 Green Plants

We will now consider the life cycles of three groups of green plants, the fern, the pine and the flowering plant. Before studying these in detail, you should be clear about the definitions of mitosis, meiosis, haploid *(n)* and diploid *(2n)* - *see Chapter 7*.

9.5.1 Life cycle of the fern

The life cycle of the fern *Dryopteris* is shown in *Fig. 9.4*. The obvious part of a fern is the leafy frond. This has spore-producing sporangia on the back of the leaf. The frond is called the *sporophyte*, literally the "spore-producing plant". At the back of the frond are sporangia. Under dry conditions the sporangia burst open and release spores. The spores germinate under suitable damp conditions and develop into a *prothallus*. This is a few millimetres in size. This develops sex

Alexander Fleming, 1881 – 1955 Shared Nobel Prize in 1945 for the discovery of penicillin.

Fig 9.4 The life cycle of the fern

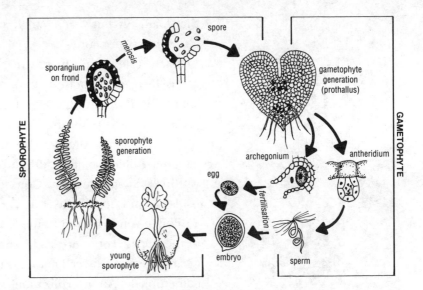

organs which produce the male and female gametes by meiosis. The prothallus is called the *gametophyte* (or "gamete-producing plant"). The male gametes enter the female organs and fertilization occurs. The new plant that grows up from the prothallus is a young fern frond or *sporophyte*.

9.5.2 Seed-bearing plants

At this stage you need to be very clear as to the difference between a sporophyte and a gametophyte. The seed-bearing plants are often considered as the "higher plants" in the Plant Kingdom. The plants we see, be they trees, shrubs, cabbages or tulips, are all sporophytes. The *gametophyte* stage is *greatly reduced* and is represented only by a passing microscopic stage during the formation of seeds. Seed-bearing plants used to be divided into two groups according to whether the seeds they produced were not covered (*"gymnosperms"* produce "naked" seeds) or covered by various coverings or coats (*"angiosperms"*). Often these coverings are what we call fruits. Although the terms gymnosperms and angiosperms are not formally recognized now, the terms are still useful for the concepts they describe.

Gymnosperms are all woody and are generally trees or at least shrubs. The Scot's pine, *Pinus*, will serve as an example. Angiosperms also include woody trees and shrubs, such as oak and hawthorn, but herbaceous species, which are green and soft in texture, outnumber the woody species. Grasses and daisies are examples of herbaceous angiosperms.

9.5.3 Life cycle of *Pinus*

Examine a branch of a pine tree during April. Use the diagram in *Fig. 9.5* to identify the following parts: the larger cones from last year,

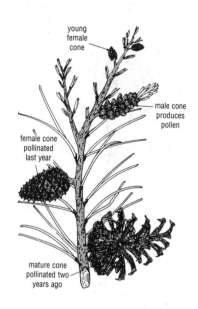

young
female
cone

male cone
produces
pollen

female cone
pollinated
last year

mature cone
pollinated two
years ago

Fig 9.5 A branch of **Pinus**

the small, current year's female cones and the male cones. You may also find mature cones.

Each scale in the current year's cones are called sporangia. They are of two types, male and female. In the male cone, two male sporangia develop on each scale and produce large quantities of *pollen*. This occurs during late April. Two female sporangia develop on each scale in the developing female cones. A single female gamete, called an *ovule*, develops by reduction division or meiois within each sporangium. Consequently, the ovule is haploid. The ovule remains inside the cone and it is the female gametophyte.

Pollen is transferred to the female cones by *wind pollination*. Parts of the female cones are sticky and pollen sticks to them. The pollen germinates and the cell contents undergo meiosis. It is now the male gametophyte. After fertilization occurs, it develops into a seed which remains within the scales of the cone until it matures. The seed is an *embryo sporophyte*. Each scale in a mature cone bears two seeds. This is easy to see if you examine a mature cone before it sheds its seeds.

9.5.4 Life cycle of flowering plants

The life cycle of flowering plants, or *angiosperms*, is actually very similar to that of *Pinus*. The flower consists of both the male and female sporangia. Many parts of the flower have evolved to attract pollinators. In Ireland, these are mainly insects. Other flowers are mainly pollinated by the wind. Flowers pollinated by insects often have marks to guide the insects. *Nectar* and *scents* may be produced also.

The female parts of the flower are called the *carpels*. The ovule develops within an enlarged area at the base of the carpel called the *ovary*. The other parts of the carpel are a sticky, receptive stigma and a "stem" portion called the style. Pollen is produced in the *stamens*. It is shed and transferred to the female stigma during pollination. (Do not confuse pollination and fertilization.)

As in the case of *Pinus*, development of the female ovule involves reduction division. It is now the female gametophyte. After pollination, pollen germinates to form a pollen tube which grows down the style. When meiosis takes place within this tube it becomes the male gametophyte. Fertilization takes place and the diploid "zygote" develops into a seed. As was the case with *Pinus*, the newly formed seed is an embryo sporophyte. The main difference between the seeds of *Pinus* and of flowering plants is that the *Pinus* seed is naked whereas the seed of flowering plants is covered. This means that it is formed within fruits or capsules which develop from the female parts of the flower. The structure of the angiosperm seed and examples of fruits are covered in the next chapter.

Exercises

Exercise 25. Preparation of microbiological media

Materials needed
1. Filter funnel and filter paper
2. 5 g each of Oxo cube and glucose powder
3. 1.5 g agar per 100 cm^3 (see below)
4. Graduated cylinder
5. Flask (suitable for use in pressure cooker)
6. Cotton wool
7. Cooking foil
8. Pressure cooker
9. Oven gloves
10. Disposable sterilized Petri dishes
11. Bunsen burners or hot plate

Suggestion
Get a lesson in using a pressure cooker first.

Procedure
Dissolve the Oxo cube and glucose in about 30 cm^3 water. Filter. Make up to 1 litre. Divide into containers for sterilization. Solid medium is prepared by adding 1.5 g agar to each measured 100 cm^3 at this stage. Only half fill bottles. Plug with a bung of cotton wool and add a cover of cooking foil. Put about 1 cm water in pressure cooker. Place flasks in cooker - never more than 2/3 of the volume of the cooker. Use the lid to close but do not put on weights yet. Use a few Bunsen burners or a hot plate to bring to pressure - steam hissing from the vent indicates this. Now put on the weights. When steam hisses from the weighted vent again the correct internal pressure has been reached. One Bunsen should be enough now. Sterilization is complete after 15 minutes. Do not attempt to open the pressure cooker until sufficiently cooled to reduce pressure - gently touch the weights to see if there is any further hissing. Media will be very hot and you should use insulating gloves. Allow flasks to cool to 60°C before pouring into Petri dishes.

Exercise 26. Growing a pure bacterial culture and making yoghurt

Materials needed
1. Mixed source of bacteria, e.g. shake up soil in water
2. Agar plates produced in Exercise 25 (or purchased)
3. Vacuum flask
4. Enough milk to fill the vacuum flask
5. Thermometer
6. Saucepan and hot plate
7. Natural yoghurt

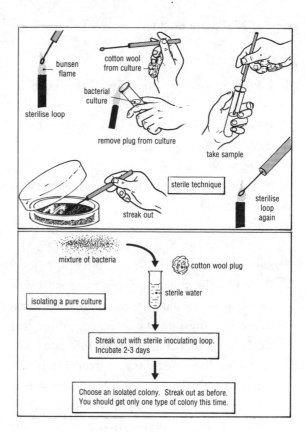

Fig. 9.6 Sterile technique

Procedure
1. Growing a pure bacterial culture. Follow the sterile technique outlined in *Fig. 9.6*.
2. Making yoghurt. Bring the milk to almost boiling point. Allow to cool to about 40°C. Scald the vacuum flask with boiling water. Pour milk into the flask and add a

dessertspoonful of natural yoghurt. Cover flask and leave for up to 24 hours. Open and taste (see precautions). Provide a microbiological explanation for what has happened. Why use a vacuum flask? What was the function of the yoghurt?

Precautions

Do not use laboratory utensils and try to use a site other than a science laboratory (e.g. Domestic Science room) for this practical if the product is intended for consumption. Alternatively, you could do this exercise at home.

Exercise 27. Potato blight

Materials needed

1. Leaves with potato blight – fresh or preserved
2. Preserve in formal-acetic acid – optional
3. Tubers with potato blight
4. Straight pin
5. Microscope, microscope slides and coverslips
6. Cooking foil
7. Alcohol

Procedure

1. Potato blight in leaves. Fresh material is best. Using a strong hand-lens, it may be possible to see sporangia on the underside of the leaf. Remember that the fungus is only alive and active at the boundary of green leaf and blight patch. In the middle of a patch of blight, the leaf and fungus are dead. Tease some of this material with a needle and mount on a microscope slide with water. Examine. It may be possible to see some hyphae.
2. Potato blight in tubers. Tubers with potato blight tend to be blackened below the surface. However, blight is not the only cause of blackening. Carefully scrub some potatoes which are thought to be blighted. Dip in alcohol, if possible. This is to reduce the possibility of bacterial infection. Now cut into

halves and wrap each half loosely with cooking foil. Keep at 25°C for a few days. Examine. Most potatoes set up this way rot – this is soft rot caused by bacteria. If you are lucky, some may develop a furry growth of fungal hyphae. This is potato blight.

Exercise 28. Examination of fern fronds, Pinus and flowering plants

Materials needed

1. Branch of *Pinus* during April-May
2. Buttercup flowers
3. Hand lens

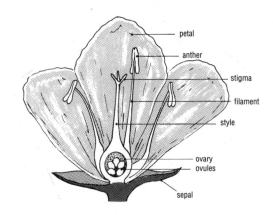

Fig 9.7 A typical flower

Procedure

1. Examine the material. Identify and draw the structures observed. Can you clearly point out sporophyte and gametophyte parts? This is described in the text for the fern and the pine.
2. Flower structure. Obtain specimens of flowers buttercups or lesser celandines. Use the diagram in *Fig. 9.7* to identify the following parts: the green sepals, the yellow petals, the stamens and the carpels (each including a stigma, style and ovary). Draw a sketch of the flower.

10 – Seeds, Germination and Growth

In this chapter we will study seed structure, various fruits and the ways used by plants to disperse seeds, germination and the beginnings of life as an independent plant.

10.1 Seed Structure

The seeds of flowering plants contain an *embryo* which develops into a seedling and a supply of *food* reserves. The food reserves account for the importance of seeds, especially cereals, in human history. In many seeds, the food reserves are contained within the embryo itself. In this case, the embryo makes up the bulk of each seed. In some seeds, however, the food is contained within a special tissue called the *endosperm*. In fact all seeds have an endosperm: in some the food is absorbed by the embryo early in the formation of the seed. These are called *non-endospermic* seeds. The remainder retain the endosperm as a food source: these are called *endospermic* seeds.

The outside of the seed is called the *testa*. At the base of the broad bean seed is a scar called the *hilum* which was the site of attachment to the pod when the seed was formed. At one end of the hilum is a small hole called the *micropyle*. (To find the micropyle, dry the hilum of a soaked seed. Now squeeze and you will see some water pressed out.)

The embryo consists of a *radicle*, which forms the root, a *plumule* which forms the shoot, and one or two seed leaves. The seed leaves are called *cotyledons*, they are rounded and do not look like the normal leaves of the plant. The cotyledons are fleshy in non-endospermic seeds since they contain the seed's food reserves. Plants whose seeds have one cotyledon are called monocotyledons and those with two are called dicotyledons (often shortened to *monocot* and *dicot*).

The grass family, which includes the cereals, are an important group with monocot seeds. Most of the other common families of flowering plants have dicot seeds. The broad bean is an example of a dicot seed which is non-endospermic. The maize seed is an example of a monocot which is endospermic. (The presence or absence of an endosperm does not mean a plant is a monocot or dicot – it just happens to be so in these examples.)

10.2 Fruits

Once seed development takes place in angiosperms (flowering

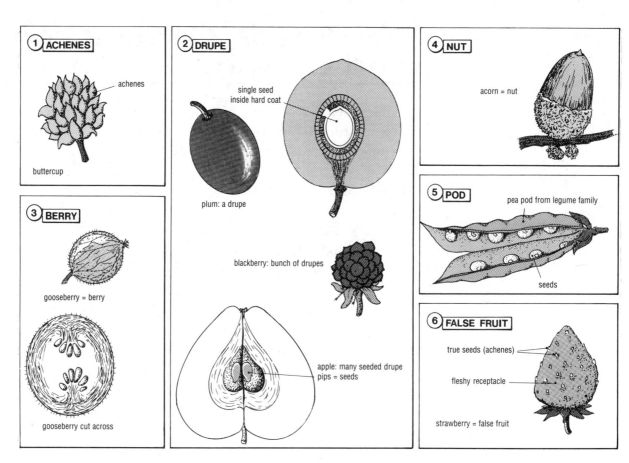

Fig 10.1 Various fruits

plants), hormones cause the ovary wall to develop into a fruit. This is sometimes exploited in agriculture to produce seedless fruit, e.g. oranges and grapes. Instead of pollination, the flowers are sprayed with the plant hormones normally associated with the development of fruits.

It is convenient to divide fruits into a few sorts: *succulent* fruits provide tissue which attracts animals to eat it and so disperse it whereas *dry* fruits provide only the nourishment contained in the seed. Fruits can also be described as *dehiscent* which open to release their seed and *indehiscent* which do not. Some examples of fruit are: the *pod,* found in the legumes family Leguminosae (we will study the plant families in chapter 13); the *berry* is an indehiscent fruit with a fleshy outside and usually many seeds inside: gooseberry, blackcurrant, tomato and orange are examples; *drupes* have a fleshy outside and the real seed is borne within a hard covering inside. A plum is a good example. Apples can be thought of as drupes with multiple pips inside. Blackberries consist of numerous individual small drupes. NB The biologist's definition and the normal English definition of berries are not the same. *Nuts* are any one-seeded indehiscent fruit with a woody outside. Strawberries are an example of a *false fruit*: the fleshy part is the receptacle of the flower, the fruits (called *achenes*) are borne on the surface of the false fruit. *(See Fig. 10.1.)*

10.3 Dispersal of Seeds

Mechanical dispersal of seeds is often by *explosion* of the fruit. Pods explode when they dry out. Stand near a gorse (furze or whin) bush on a warm summer's day to hear this happening. Dispersal by wind includes the *parachute* fruits of dandelions and the *winged* fruits of ash and sycamore. Dispersal by animals is either by *hooks* such as in the bedstraw *Galium,* or by providing a fleshy covering attractive to fruit-eating animals. Many fruits depend on *partial digestion* before they germinate.

10.4 Germination

Germination is divided into two kinds according to whether or not the cotyledons come above the ground and photosynthesize. Where the cotyledons do emerge, the type of germination is called *epigeal* (literally, above ground), whereas when they remain below ground it is called *hypogeal* (or below ground) germination. Various conditions such as moisture and temperature affect germination. You should investigate these by carrying out *Exercise 30.*

10.5 Sensitivity of Plants – Tropisms

Nearly everyone has observed how plants growing on a window generally face outwards. When turned around, the leaves grow to face outwards again in a few days. You should try this to convince yourself. Seedlings provide an excellent means of investigating this phenomenon. A *tropism* is a plant's response to a stimulus such as light *(phototropism)* and gravity *(geotropism).*

A *clinostat* is a useful apparatus for investigating tropisms: it provides a continually rotating stage. When potted plants or young seedlings are placed on a clinostat, they are continually, but very slowly, turned. The growth of these plants can be compared with that of plants not on the clinostat but otherwise similarly treated.

10.6 Mineral Nutrition of Plants

Minerals have already been defined as *inorganic substances* required by both plants and animals for their existence. Minerals can be divided broadly into *macronutrients* and *trace* elements. Macronutrients include sodium, potassium, calcium and phosphate ions. As you study different chapters in this book note examples where these macronutrients are involved.

Trace elements tend to be needed only in very small amounts. In larger quantities they can be poisonous. Magnesium is part of the chlorophyll molecule. Deficiency in sulphur inhibits grass growth and boron deficiency can be a problem in sugar beet crops. Refer to the relevant chapters for further details of these.

You will investigate the effect of different mineral deficiencies on young seedlings in *Exercise 32*. For convenience, the investigation will be set up using commercially available water culture chemicals which have been developed to provide all the mineral nutrients needed except the one stated on the pack. In this way, it is possible to grow young cereal seedlings in nutrient-solutions deficient in one of the following: sulphur, magnesium, phosphorus, potassium, iron, calcium and nitrogen, and to compare growth in the deficient medium with growth in "normal" medium with the complete range of minerals *(see Fig. 10.5)*.

10.7 Photoperiod

Many organisms react to day length. Depending on how they react, species are divided into *short day* and *long day* types. Photoperiod is very important in some plants and needs to be considered if they are being grown as crops. The basic concept is that certain parts of the life cycle are triggered by a change in *day length*. Onions, for example, form their bulbs when the day length begins to shorten (after mid-summer's day). To grow large onion bulbs, it is necessary to plant them as early in the year as possible. Curd formation in cauliflower also depends on the photoperiod. Different varieties have been bred to crop at different times of the year. Many gardeners grow a variety called 'All Year Round' to avoid this problem. A good seed-catalogue will provide more details.

10.8 Plant Hormones

A chemical related to 2-4-D called Agent Orange causes leaves to fall from trees. It was used as a form of chemical warfare during the Vietnam War.

Plant hormones are chemicals which influence the growth of plants. The best known is a chemical called *IAA* (indole acetic acid). Other substances called *plant growth substances* do not occur naturally but have similar effects. Only minute quantities (parts per million) of these hormones or substances are needed to produce major effects in plants. Many are now in everyday use in farming and horticulture: *2-4-D* kills broadleaved plants but has no effect on grasses. It is used as a selective weedkiller in lawns and cereal crops. *Cycocel* is a dwarfing agent used in the potplant industry ("potmums" are dwarfed chrysanthemums; geraniums) and in field crops (to shorten straw length in barley to prevent lodging). Fruit setting agents cause unfertilized flowers to produce seedless fruits (grapes, bananas, tomatoes). *Rooting hormones* are used to speed rooting of cuttings. *Sprout inhibitor* is used for storing potatoes (see page 175); obviously "seed" potatoes should not be treated!

Exercises

Exercise 29. Examination of seeds and fruits

Materials needed
1. Broad bean and maize seeds. Soak these in water overnight.
2. Variety of fruits: pea pod (or vetch), gooseberry, tomato, plum, apple, blackberry or raspberry, a nut such as hazelnut, strawberry
3. Hand lens
4. Straight pin
5. Iodine

Procedure
Carry out this procedure on both the broad bean (dicot seed) and maize (monocot) seed.
1. Examine and draw external structure. Find all the parts in *Fig. 10.2*. Draw.
2. Use the pin to remove the testa. Carefully prise open the cotyledons and use the lens to examine the embryo structure. Use the diagrams in *Fig. 10.2* to guide you. Draw and label what you see.
3. Test the different parts of the seed for the presence of starch and note your

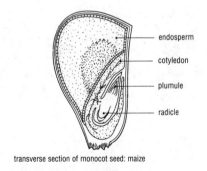

transverse section of monocot seed: maize

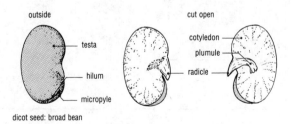

dicot seed: broad bean

Fig 10.2 Monocot and dicot seeds

observations *(method on page 90)*.
4. Examine a range of fruits and classify them as described in the text.

Exercise 30. Observations on germinating seeds

Materials needed
1. Large seeds such as broad bean and sunflower
2. Small seeds such as cress
3. Cereal seeds such as wheat or barley
4. Some containers or flower pots
5. Compost or damp sawdust
6. Petri dishes
7. Some thread and cotton wool
8. 2 conical flasks, 2 pins bent to form a hook
9. Sodium hydroxide
10. Pyrogallic acid
11. Mortar, pestle and some washed sand

Procedure
1. Investigate hypogeal and epigeal germination by sowing broad bean and sunflower seeds. Broad bean have hypogeal and sunflowers have epigeal germination. Examine, observe and draw every few days. If you use damp sawdust it is easy to shake from the roots. Another suitable technique is to trap the seeds between damp paper and inside the walls of a glass jar. If you use this technique, cover the glass to exclude light when observations are not being made. Keep the compost moist.
2. Investigate the conditions necessary for germination. To do this, place a test module under various conditions. Each test module consists of a Petri dish with a piece of damp filter paper and some cress seeds. To test if moisture is necessary, set up two test modules, one with damp filter paper and the other with dry filter paper. To test if light is necessary, place one test module in a dark place and another on a windowsill. To test for the importance of heat, put one module near a radiator and another in a domestic fridge (not a freezer!).

3. Is carbon dioxide or oxygen necessary for germination? Sodium hydroxide absorbs carbon dioxide from the air. Sodium hydroxide plus pyrogallic acid (called "alkaline pyrogallol") absorb both oxygen and carbon dioxide from the air. Set up two conical flasks, labelled A or B, as in *Fig. 10.3*. Roll a piece of cotton wool, dampen it, tie a piece of thread to it, dip into cress seeds and hang carefully on the hook. After about one week observe and explain your results.

4. The use of food reserves in germination. Soak about 20 wheat seeds overnight. Place in a mortar and add some washed sand. Grind with pestle. Perform an iodine and a Benedict's test on this material *(see page 90)*. Repeat this procedure on seeds which have been germinating for three to five days. Explain your results.

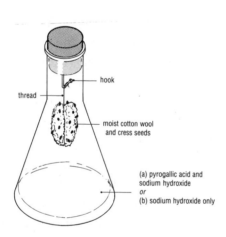

Fig 10.3 The set-up for Exercise 30

Precautions

1. It is important to keep germinating seeds moist, not waterlogged.
2. The sodium hydroxide and pyrogallic acid must be mixed just before use. The concentrations are given in the Reagents' Appendix. Note that care must be used when using sodium hydroxide and wash off any spills immediately.

Exercise 31. Phototropism and geotropism

Materials needed

1. Two small actively growing potplants
2. A supply of recently germinated broad bean seeds with straight radicles (see *Fig.10.4* for

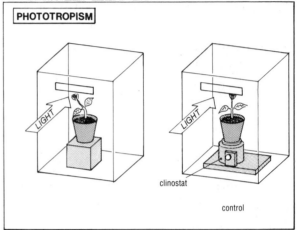

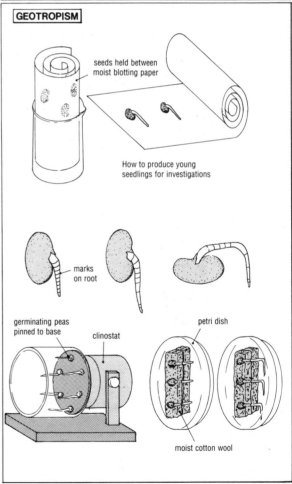

Fig 10.4 The set-up for Exercise 31

technique)

3. Petri dishes

4. Cotton wool

5. Fine marker (permanent, not water soluble, e.g. those used for overhead transparencies)

Procedure

1. Investigation on phototropism. Set up the potted plants as in *Fig. 10.4*. Observe and interpret your results.

2. Geotropism in roots. Set up young broad bean plants as in *Fig. 10.4*. Observe over the next few days, draw labelled diagrams of what you observe. Interpret.

3. Another investigation on geotropism is to put evenly spaced marks on broad bean radicles using a fine marker. Place the seeds at different orientations (horizontally, vertically, upside down). Observe how the radicles react by noting the regions of growth where the marks stretch apart, and any changes in direction.

Exercise 32. The importance of certain elements for normal plant growth

Materials needed

1. Sach's water culture solutions (the different solutions are mentioned in the text); distilled water

2. Polystyrene (aerobord) cut to the size of the sandwich boxes

3. One sandwich box for each nutrient solution

4. Simple air pump

5. Rubber tubing and Y-junctions to reach each sandwich box (from pet shops)

6. Large nail and pliers with well-insulated handle

7. Bunsen burner

8. Place some wheat (or barley) seeds on damp paper a few days in advance. They should be just germinating.

Procedure (See Fig. 10.5)

1. Arrange the rubber tubing so that air is delivered to each sandwich box. Cut a piece

Fig 10.5 The set-up for Exercise 32

of polystyrene to fit each box and place it on a piece of timber to protect the bench. Now hold the nail with the pliers and heat it in the Bunsen. Then quickly make holes in the polystyrene using the hot nail. Repeat for each piece of polystyrene.

2. Make up the nutrient solutions by following the directions with the kit. Place the same volume in each sandwich box and carefully label. Put the polystyrene on top and drop a germinating seed into each hole. Switch on the air – you may have to use clamps to get air distributed to each sandwich box.

3. Observe the subsequent growth of the seedlings and compare the effects of the different nutrient deficiencies. Try to explain why the observed effects occurred. Can you provide a biological basis for your answer.

11– Plant Structure and Function

In this chapter, we will study the structure and function of the various parts of the plant. This will include the structure of the root, stem and leaf, and the uptake and transport of materials through them. Many parts of the plant are modified for special purposes such as food storage. We will also study these now.

11.1 Plant Tissues

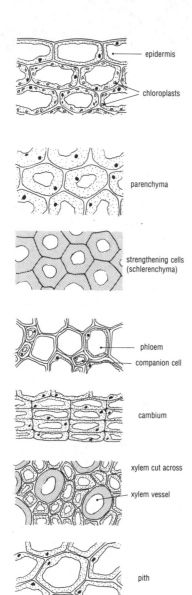

Here we are concerned with how the basic plant cells described in *Chapter 7* are modified into various specialized plant tissues. You could practise drawing each type of cell as they will be encountered when carrying out the exercises which follow. The types of tissues include the outer epidermal layer, tissues where photosynthesis takes place, tissues used for transporting materials, strengthening tissues, meristem tissues (areas where cell division takes place) and storage tissues. *Fig. 11.1* shows various kinds of plant cells.

The outer layer of cells is called the *epidermis*. It covers the complete outer surface of plants. The cells are flattened. They fit closely together and there are no spaces between them. Epidermal cells of the aerial parts of plants have a *waxy cuticle* on their outer layer *(Fig. 11.1)*. Also included in the epidermal cells is a special type of cell which allows communication in and out of the plant. The openings are called stomata and each stoma consists of two guard cells lying close together. The guard cells are able to change their shape (more on this later) and in this way, can open and close the pores. Stomata are most abundant on the underside of leaves. Chloroplasts are absent from all epidermal cells except the guard cells.

Inside the epidermis are the cells where photosynthesis takes place. This mainly takes place in leaves. The photosynthetic cells are mainly a type of cells called *parenchyma*. These are relatively large cells which are of fairly uniform shape. There are many air spaces between them. Immediately under the upper epidermis of leaves are a few layers of specialized photosynthetic cells called the *pallisade layer*. Below this are cells with more air spaces called the *mesophyll*. The important thing to note about all these cells is the presence of *chloroplasts*.

Cells used for transporting materials are called *vascular* tissues. These are of two types, *xylem* and *phloem*. These cells are the *plumbing system* of the plant. Xylem is responsible for the upward transport of water. Xylem cells are actually dead cells which have thick cell-walls

Fig 11.1 Various plant cells

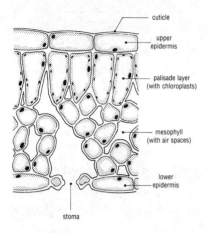

Fig 11.2 Structure of a leaf (transverse section)

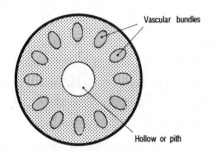

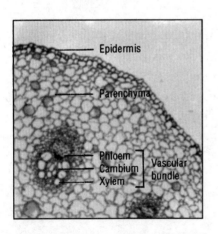

Fig 11.3 Structure of a stem. Diagram (above) and photomicrograph of one vascular bundle (below)

supported by rings of lignin. In contrast, phloem cells are living. They are elongated cells. However, their end walls are perforated and this region of the phloem cell is called the sieve plate. Each phloem cell has a small cell called a *companion cell* associated with it.

A *meristem* is a region in a plant where there is active cell division. The principal meristems occur in the tips of the roots and shoots. Another meristem is the region in the stem and root which forms the xylem and phloem. This actively dividing layer of cells is called the *cambium* layer.

Support tissues include *collenchyma* and *schlerenchyma*. Collenchyma tissue is composed of living cells whose original cell wall is thickened to provide strength. Schlerenchyma cells are often dead cells and have developed a second cell wall which is strengthened with lignin fibres.

Storage cells occur, for example, in potato tubers and in seeds. Because they are fleshy, it is difficult to cut them thinly enough to see under a microscope. However, the diagram in *Fig. 11.1* will show you what to expect if you succeed.

11.2 Cross Section of a Leaf

Observe the overall structure of a leaf. Notice the *netted venation* in the leaf – this is easily seen in partly decayed leaves found in autumn. We will study a part of a leaf which does not include a vein. The diagram in *Fig. 11.2* shows the usual structure: the upper epidermis with a waxy cuticle. Beneath this is the palisade layer and then the spongy mesophyll cells. Both of these contain many chloroplasts. The lower epidermis has *stomata* in it which allow gaseous exchange.

11.3 Cross Section of a Stem

When you examine a cross section of a *dicot* stem (e.g. sunflower) under the low power of a microscope, the overall picture seen is given in *Fig. 11.3*. This shows that the transport tissues are arranged in a circle of distinct *vascular bundles*. Under higher magnification *(Fig 11.3)*, it is possible to see the arrangement of the different tissues: an outer layer of epidermis. Inside this is a strengthening region of collenchyma and then a layer of general packing cells called parenchyma. The vascular bundle has a region of strengthening schlerenchyma fibres. Now notice the position of the cambium tissue. *Phloem cells*, with their companion cells, are located outside the cambium, while *xylem* vessels are inside the cambium region.

Monocot stems have a different structure. Here, the vascular bundles are *scattered* around the stem and not distributed in a circle as in a dicot stem.

The structure just described is the general type of structure found in a stem which lives for just one season. Stems of plants which live longer (e.g. trees) develop what is called *secondary thickening.* Here is a brief account of how this occurs: the cambium region of the different vascular bundles joins up to form a complete *circle of cambium.* It produces new phloem tissue to its outside and new xylem vessels to its inside. In temperate climates, such as the Irish climate, there are distinct growing seasons, spring and summer, followed by periods of slow growth, late summer and autumn, and of no growth, winter. The xylem produced in spring and early summer has larger vessels than that produced at the end of the season. Then after a period of no growth, large vessels are produced again the following spring. This means that distinct rings are produced, one for each season of growth and that is why we can tell the age of a tree by counting the *rings* in the xylem. Although phloem is also continually produced, it is a softer tissue located just inside the bark of trees, and rings are not obvious in it. Mature trees also develop a specialized protective layer called the *bark. Cork* from the cork oak is an extreme example of bark.

11.4 Root Structure

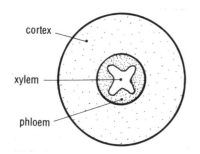

The structure of the transverse section of a dicot root is shown in *Fig.11.4.* The outside layer is the root epidermis. Inside this is parenchyma tissue. This is called the *cortex* of the root. The vascular tissues are in the centre surrounded by a special layer, the endodermis. The xylem cells are in a cross in the very centre with the phloem cells in the axes of the cross.

11.5 Transport in Plants

Before studying this topic, you should have covered the material on photosynthesis in *Chapter 8* and the basic functions of cells, especially osmosis, in *Chapter 7.* Here, we are concerned with how materials are absorbed from the soil and how the products of photosynthesis are moved around the plant. Two types of transport are involved, *transpiration* and *translocation.*

11.5.1 Transpiration

Transpiration is the loss of water vapour by the plant to the atmosphere around it. Most of the water vapour is lost through the pores or stomata. You should now carry out *Exercise 34* to investigate transpiration and the factors which influence it. Part of *Exercise 34* also demonstrates *root pressure.* We must distinguish between root

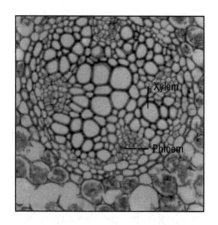

Fig. 11.4 Transverse section of a dicot root. Diagram (above) and photomicrograph (below)

pressure which is an upward pressure from the roots and *transpiration* which is a pulling pressure originating at the leaves. Root pressure sometimes causes the production of drops of sap at the tips of leaves by a process called *guttation* (and sometimes mistaken for dew on, e.g. grass). Root pressure starts off the rising sap in trees in spring.

About 5 mm back from the tip of a root is the root-hair region. The root hairs are important for absorption of water and mineral ions from the soil. It is generally thought that water is absorbed into the root hairs and then from one cell to the next along an osmotic gradient. Eventually, water enters the xylem vessels.

How is water transported to the top of the highest trees? The American redwood trees *(Sequoia)* grow to over 100m. Normal atmospheric pressure at sea level (101.3 kilopascals) can raise a column of water to a height of about 10m. Root pressure accounts for, at most, an additional 200 kPa or 2m of water column. The *cohesion theory*, proposed by the Trinity College, Dublin biologists *Dixon* and *Joly* in 1894, is the generally accepted explanation for this phenomenon. This theory suggests that the water columns in the xylem vessels are continuous from the roots to the leaves through the stem. As the leaves transpire, the water columns come under tension. Bonding between individual water molecules prevents the columns of water from breaking. Tension pressures of up to 3000 kPa have been demonstrated in leaves. This pressure could pull columns of water to a height of 300m – much higher than the redwood trees. Minerals absorbed by the roots are transported along with the water. It is therefore important to cut the stem of the plant under water when you are setting up the potometer investigation in *Exercise 34.*

It has been mentioned that the guard cells can open and close the stomata in the leaf epidermis. The guard cells are long and ovalshaped. They are thickened along the side near the opening of the stomata. It was also mentioned that they are the only cells in the epidermis with chloroplasts. This means that photosynthesis takes place in guard cells. When photosynthetic products (sugars) are produced, the turgor pressure in the guard cells rises. This causes the guard cells to open. You can demonstrate the effect for yourself using a long balloon. Put some air in it. Now thicken one wall with a strip of sellotape. When you blow in more air, the balloon will curve. This is similar to the effect of increased turgor pressure in the two guard cells.

11.5.2 Translocation

Translocation is the term used for the transport of organic materials in the *phloem* tissue. This is not as well understood as the transpiration stream just described. It involves the *movement of sugars* produced by photosynthesis either to storage sites (e.g. bulbs or tubers) or to areas of rapid growth (shoot tips). This means that translocation can occur both upwards and downwards and the way the phloem manages to do this is not known. (Distinguish between transpiration and translocation.)

Exercises

Exercise 33. Structure of stems, roots and leaves

Materials needed
1. Suitable material or prepared sections. If possible you should try to cut your own sections. The following material is suitable for cutting: leaves: privet; dicot stems: sunflower; monocot stems: maize. Roots tend to be difficult to cut but buttercup-roots can be tried.
2. Elder pith or carrot
3. Razor blade (use one-sided safety blades)
4. Microscopes and microscope slides
5. Small dish of water

Procedure
1. Place the material to be cut between pieces of elder pith or pieces of carrot. Rigid stems, such as maize, are easy to cut without this.
2. Carefully cut the thinnest possible sections using the blade.
3. Do not let your sections dry out. Drop them temporarily into water.
4. Mount on the microscope slides, examine under the microscope and draw.

Exercise 34. Transport of water in plants

Materials needed
1. Supply of actively growing plants – geraniums are very suitable
2. Narcissus flower, celery stems
3. Flower pot, compost and cress or mustard seeds
4. Coloured water: use the red colouring used for icing
5. Razor blade
6. Polythene bags
7. Vaseline

Procedure
1. Demonstration of water movement in a stem. Place a white Narcissus (daffodil) flower in coloured water. Observe. Place a fresh celery stem in coloured water. The following day, carefully cut thin cross sections and see which cells have been stained.
2. Simple demonstration of root pressure. Grow some cress or mustard seeds to the stage when they are ready to eat (about two weeks). Cut as if to eat. Observe the cut stumps an hour later.
3. Demonstration of root pressure. Use an actively growing plant. Cut it off a few cm above the soil surface (you can use the cut portion in the next investigation). Use a piece of rubber tubing to attach a glass tube to the cut stem. Add some coloured water to the tube and mark the level. Keep the root watered. Note the water level over the next few days. Any rises are due to root pressure.
4. Demonstration of transpiration using a potometer. Set up the potometer as in *Fig. 11.5*. Use a leafy stem from an actively growing plant. Immediately after cutting it, place it under water and cut a few cm from the base of the stem if there has been any delay in setting up the potometer. Take care

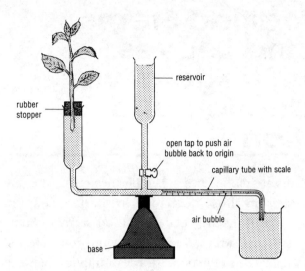

Fig. 11.5 Potometer

not to include any air bubbles. Seal all joints with vaseline. Note the rate of transpiration by following the progress of an air bubble in the water column in the capillary tube. You can investigate the effect of factors such as wind-transpiration, use a hair drier, heat and cold, on the rate once the potometer is set up successfully.

5. Demonstration of the production of water vapour during transpiration. Enclose an actively growing plant in a polythene bag and tie the bag around the base of the stem. Place for a few hours in direct sunlight and observe.

6. Which is more important for transpiration – upper or lower leaf surface? Devise an investigation for this by either modifying 3 or 4 above. You could block the stomata on the leaf surfaces using vaseline.

12 – Modified Stems, Roots and Leaves: Storage, Vegetative Reproduction and Protection

Various parts of plants are modified. This simply means that they are somehow different from those described in the last chapter. Sometimes the modifications are related to food storage. Some modifications are associated with a form of reproduction, referred to as vegetative or asexual reproduction. Clearly distinguish between asexual and sexual reproduction: the result of asexual reproduction is genetically identical to the plant which formed it whereas sexual reproduction involves the fusion of genes from two parents *(see Chapter 25)*. Yet other modifications of plants are associated with protection, for example from extremes of drought and from plant-eating animals *(herbivores)*.

Often the storage modifications are associated with the type of life span of the plant. We can distinguish between *annuals*, which grow and flower in one season, *biennials*, which grow in one season and flower the following season and the third sort, *perennials*, which live for many years. Food storage organs are often associated with biennials or perennials. As an example, consider the carrot which has a *tap root (more on this below)*. The tap root acts as a *food source*. When grown as an agricultural crop, carrots grow in a single season. However, carrots do not complete their cycle until the second season when they flower and produce seeds. The same is true of many of the examples in this chapter.

12.1 Storage modifications

Carry out *Exercise 35*. Corms, bulbs, tubers and rhizomes are common modifications of plants (*see Fig. 12.1*). *Corms* arise where plants store food at the base of the stem. The following year the food stored in the corm is used to start the growth of the shoot and flower. Later food is stored, not in the old corm, but at the base of the stem just above the old corm. Special roots, called adventitious roots, shrink and thus hold the new corm at the same depth as the old corm. New corms are formed at the bases of shoots arising from lateral buds. The *Crocus* is an example of a plant with a corm. *Montbretia*, a plant with an orange-coloured flower common in the hedges in the west of Ireland, often has a series of former seasons' corms at the base.

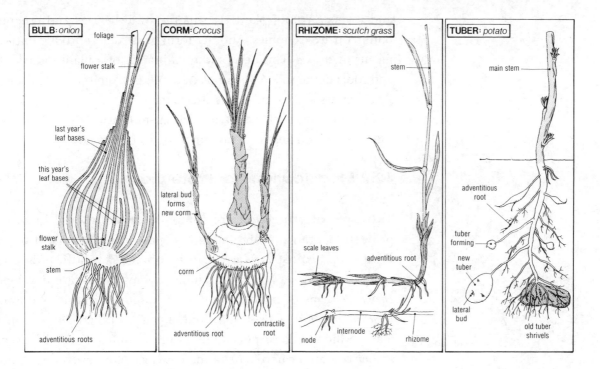

Fig. 12.1 Modifications of plant structures

12.1.1 Modified leaves

Bulbs are modified leaves used for storage of food. The stem is greatly condensed at the base of the bulb. As in the case of the corm, food stored during the previous season is used to form the new leaves and flower. Later in the season, these form new food reserves at the bases of the current leaves. These form the bulbs for the following season. New bulbs form from lateral buds which arise at the base. The onion is an example of a bulb.

12.1.2 Tubers

Tubers are a different form of *underground stems.* The potato is an example. When potato tubers are planted, the old tuber sends up shoots and forms leaves. Underground lateral buds spread out. As food is formed, it is transported to the underground shoots for storage. These form the new tubers. The old tuber shrivels and is usually rotted by the time the potatoes are dug out at the end of the season. The "eyes" of the potato are the young lateral buds which will sprout the next season.

12.1.3 Rhizomes

Rhizomes are another form of underground stem. This time however the swellings are more even. *Scutch grass* is an example and its rhizome makes it a persistent weed in some crops (sugar beet).

12.1.4 Other modifications

Some plants produce *runners.* This is a form of vegetative reproduction where a young shoot grows away from a parent plant and forms a young plantlet at its tip. Strawberries and creeping buttercup are examples. Another form of asexual reproduction is by means of *stolons*. This occurs when a branch of a plant loops down and roots in the soil. A young plant develops from the rooted stolon. Blackberries and loganberries are examples.

Some plants, such as carrot and parsnip, produce swollen roots called *tap roots*. These roots are their food storage sites.

12.2 Modifications for Protection

Two types of protection are commonly encountered in plants: protection against being eaten and protection against drought. Protection against *herbivores* can be obtained in a few ways: the evolution of *thorns* are one example. Some plants have developed *chemical* forms of protection. One common example is ragwort (*Senecio jacobaea*). This has evolved chemicals called *alkaloids* in its leaves which make it poisonous to most animals – the black and amber coloured caterpillars of the cinnabar moth are an exception. Stinging glands found on nettles *(Urtica)* also provide protection. The development of hairs on the leaves provides protection from the attacks of aphids (greenfly).

We have seen how leaves are the main site for water loss by transpiration. Plants which live in a *desert environment* have reduced their leaves to non-transpiring thorns. In addition to water conservation, they provide protection. A cactus is an example. *Marram grass* growing on Irish coastal sand dunes has special hinge cells which allow the leaf to roll up under dry conditions and so reduce water loss from the stomata on the inside *(Fig. 12.2)*.

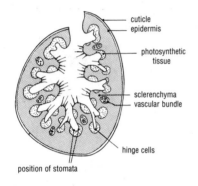

Fig 12.2 A transverse section of marram grass

12.3 Vegetative Reproduction and Agriculture

The various forms of storage organs and *vegetative reproduction* just described are often exploited in horticulture to form new plants. Vegetative reproduction is another term for asexual reproduction or a form of reproduction which does not involve fertilization of two gametes. Corms, tubers, bulbs and rhizomes are lifted and divided to form new plants. The farming practice associated with potatoes should give some idea of the possibilities here.

Artificial techniques have also been developed to exploit the asexual reproduction of plants. *Cuttings* and the various forms of *grafting* are examples of this. The recently developed technique of micropropagation is a major development in this area.

12.3.1 Cuttings

There are different types of cuttings. *Softwood cuttings* are taken when the plants are growing strongly; they are short pieces of stem about 5 cm in length with about three pairs of leaves. They are trimmed below a bud, dipped in rooting hormone and placed in compost. Sometimes they are protected with polythene and given bottom heat. *Hardwood cuttings*, usually taken at the end of the season, are about 20 cm long. Some cuttings are difficult to root. One technique which may succeed is called *layering*: a low branch near the ground is selected, it is carefully slit about half-way across near a bud and pegged into the ground so that the slit is kept open. This means that it is partially connected with the mother plant until it roots. Then it is separated and transplanted.

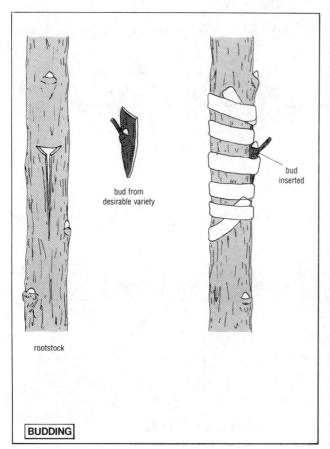

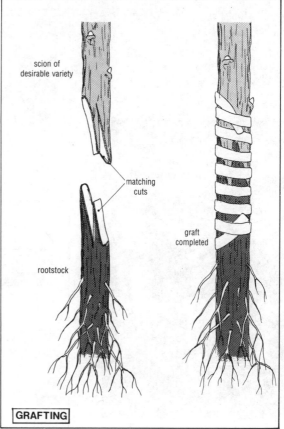

Fig 12.3 Grafting and budding

12.3.2 Grafting and budding

Grafting and *budding* are kinds of artificial vegetative reproduction. The principle involved here is that tissue from a desirable variety of plant, called the *scion*, is grafted or budded onto a *rootstock*. The rootstocks are produced in bulk either from seed or by cuttings. This means that a much greater number of the desirable variety can be produced. Another advantage is that rootstocks (e.g. of apples) have been bred to enable the eventual size and vigour of the variety grafted onto them to be controlled.

12.3.3 Micropropagation

Micropropagation is an exciting development in vegetative reproduction. The technique involves *micro-cuttings* such as a shoot tip 10-20 mm in length. This is grown on a culture medium (macronutrients, micronutrients, vitamins, sugar and growth hormones) and kept at 20-25°C under good light conditions. Since this culture medium and conditions are also ideal for bacterial growth, completely sterile conditions must be maintained. In roses 8-12 shoots are produced every six weeks for each shoot cultured. Some of these are put in a different medium to stimulate root production for eventual sale, the rest are cultured again to produce more shoots. A summary is given in *Fig. 12.4.*

Fig 12.4 A summary of micro-propagation

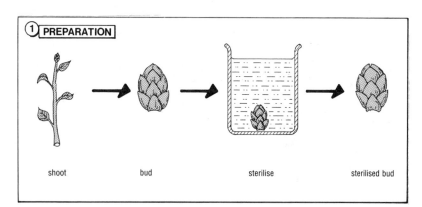

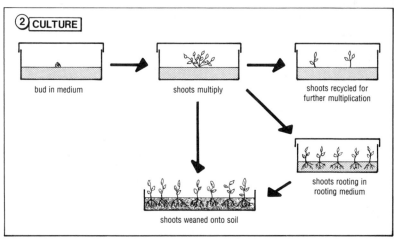

Fig 12.5 A micropropagated plant

Micropropagation is now routine for some horticultural crops such as African violets *(Saintpaulia)*, dwarf roses and rhododendrons. Another application is to quickly multiply a new variety once it has been bred by sexual reproduction *(see Chapter 27)* e.g. strawberries and potatoes. The technique has also been used to produce virus-free stock of potatoes when the original stock became infected. New applications are constantly being discovered.

Exercises

Exercise 35. Examination of various stem, root and leaf modifications

Materials required
1. Corms, e.g. *Crocus* or montbretia
2. Bulbs, e.g. onion
3. Tubers, e.g. potato
4. Rhizome, e.g. scutch grass
5. Tap root, e.g. carrot

Procedure
Examine the material. Compare to the drawings in the text. Now draw your own material and make notes.

Exercise 36. Vegetative reproduction techniques

Procedure:
1. Propagate some material from cuttings. Geraniums are an easy example for soft cuttings. Take a cutting of three pairs of leaves. Remove the bottom leaves and trim cleanly just below the node. Dip in rooting hormone and place in a 5 cm pot. Alternatively, you could put about five cuttings in a 10 cm pot. Do not cover geraniums in polythene. Busy Lizzie *(Impatiens)* cuttings are even easier: just place in water and wait about two weeks for rooting to take place. Blackcurrants are very easy to propagate from hardwood cuttings almost any time during the dormant season. Cut a blackcurrant branch into 20 cm lengths of stem and trim the base below a bud and the top above a bud. (To produce "proper" blackcurrant bushes you should remove all the buds which would end up underground.)
2. Examine examples of apple trees and rose bushes. At the base of the stem you should see a swelling which represents the joining between scion and stock. "Suckers", if you observe them, are shoots from the rootstock and they have to be removed.

13 – Plant Families and Field Study

In this chapter we will study the structure of the flower in different plant families. This information is then used for a field study.

13.1 Families of Flowering Plants

Flowering plants are classified mainly by their flower structure. Flower structure was introduced in *Chapter 9*. You may need to revise the terms introduced there. This basic structure differs between different families of plants. Some of these families are very important in agriculture. By knowing which species are related, we can often predict a lot about their biology since related species often share the same diseases, pests and problems. In the long term, this is easier than learning the information separately for each species. If we recognize which family a plant belongs to, identifying it to species' level becomes much easier. It will be easier when studying this chapter if you carry out *Exercise 37* as you proceed.

Fig. 13.1 Cruciferae: floral diagram (upper) and half-diagram (lower)

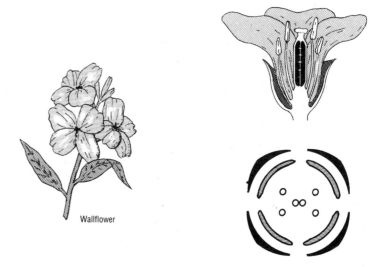

Wallflower

13.1.1 Cruciferae

This family includes wall-flowers and many vegetables such as cabbages, Brussels sprouts, broccoli, cauliflower (collectively called brassicas since they belong to the genus *Brassica*), turnips, radish and mustard. Note that they have floral parts mainly in fours: i.e. four sepals, petals and stamens. The flower is in the form of a cross, hence the name of the family. Diagrams of the flower and the floral diagram are included in *Fig. 13.1*.

Learn either "half-diagrams" or "floral diagrams". Floral diagrams summarise the main parts of a flower (sepals, petals, stamens and carpels) in transverse section.

Fig. 13.2 Rosaceae, rose family

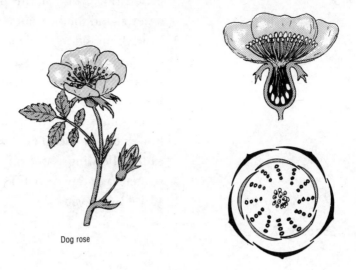

Dog rose

13.1.2 Rosaceae

This family includes the dog rose, fruit trees such as apple, plum, pear, cherry, and fruits such as raspberry, blackberry and strawberry. Since the flowers are all large, they can be easily studied. Use the diagrams in *Fig. 13.2* to help identify the parts. The dog rose has five each of sepals and petals and numerous stamens and carpels.

13.1.3 Leguminosae

Fig. 13.3 Leguminosae, pea family

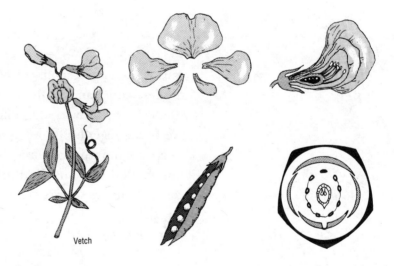

Vetch

This is the pea family. Members range from tiny herbs to large trees and include peas, beans and many fodder crops such as clovers (Ireland) and lucerne (abroad). If possible, get a specimen of a large flower for study (e.g. a sweet pea). If not, any member of the family will do. The diagram in *Fig. 13.3* will help in identifying the parts. The flower structure in this family enables pollination by large pollinating insects such as bumblebees. The flower provides a stage, called the keel, for the pollinator. If heavy enough the keel is lowered and the bee can insert its tongue to obtain a nectar reward. Note the position of the stamens and stigma relative to the position of a large bee. The design is ingenious: pollen is transferred to the thorax (middle segment) of a bee and then transferred to the next flower the bee flies to.

Legumes have five petals: two enclose the central part of the flower called the keel; two are on each side of the keel and are called the wings, and one large petal. There are five sepals, ten stamens and one carpel. The fruit is called a pod.

13.1.4 Compositae

Fig. 13.4 Compositae

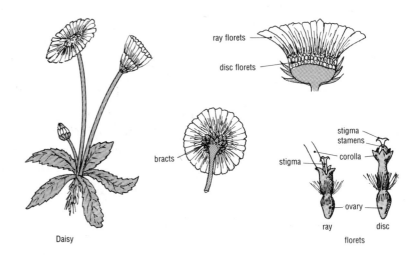

This is the largest family of plants. It includes daisies, dandelions, thistles, lettuce and sunflowers. The family is so called because each "flower" is actually a composite or collection of many florets which are borne together on a flat receptacle. Examine a daisy "flower". There are two types of floret: the white ray florets and the yellow disc florets. Pull some of the florets free for examination. Each is a complete flower with petals and carpels. The *ray florets* lack stamens but these are present in the *disc florets*. These are shown in the diagram in *Fig. 13.4.*

13.1.5 Umbelliferae

Members of this family have a typical *inflorescence* (collection of flowers) borne on spokes somewhat like an umbrella *(Fig. 13.5)*. Each individual flower is very small but complete with sepals, five petals, five stamens and two carpels. Members of the family include parsley, dill and vegetables such as celery, carrots and parsnips.

Fig. 13.5 Umbelliferae

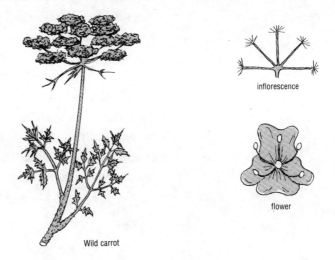

inflorescence

flower

Wild carrot

13.1.6 Gramineae

This is the grass family. In addition to the grass species used as fodder crops, the family also includes cereals such as wheat, oats, barley, maize and rice. Grass flowers are specialized for *wind pollination*. Most of their floral structures can be understood if this point is remembered: those floral parts used for attracting insects in other plants, such as petals, are greatly reduced. Wind pollinated plants produce large amounts of pollen, which is not sticky, in order to maximize their chances of pollination. The large quantity of pollen is often the cause of an allergy called hay fever.

Grass flowers have both male and female parts *("hermaphrodite")*

Fig. 13.6 Gramineae, grass family

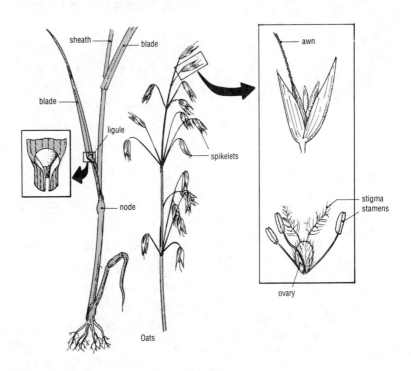

sheath · blade · awn · blade · ligule · spikelets · node · stigma stamens · ovary · Oats

and are borne on an inflorescence. Obtain a grass in full flower. The diagram in *Fig. 13.6* should help you to identify the various parts. Note especially the very prominent stamens. Individual flowers are borne within protective bracts. Sometimes these bracts have bristles which are called *awns*.

13.1.7 Liliaceae

This family is another monocot family whose members include onions, garlic and hyacinths. The sepals and petals are fused into a single structure. Their floral parts are in multiples of three: six sepals/petals, six stamens and three carpels *(Fig. 13.7)*.

Fig. 13.7 Liliaceae

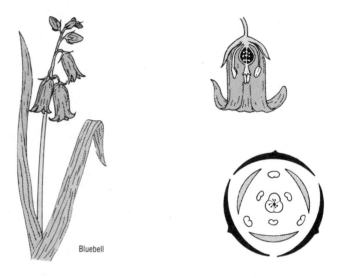

Bluebell

13.2 Identifying Plants

Plants are identified using *identification guides.* Sometimes these are collections of diagrams or photographs of each species. A better approach is to study the structure of the specimens and use this with an identification *"key"*. *Exercise 38* includes a very simplified key to illustrate the point. It may be used to identify some common farm grasses. This exercise must be carried out when grasses are in flower around the end of May, or on dried specimens.

13.3 Description of Grassland

Once you can identify some common grasses and some other common plants, you can undertake a description of grassland. Two techniques are often used for this purpose: using *transects* and using a *quadrat.*

A *transect* is a length of rope marked at regular intervals. The length and the intervals depend on the site being studied. A 10 m length marked at 10 cm intervals is often suitable. Transects are often used to study change in vegetation e.g. across a trampled area where cattle walk, or when studying the change in vegetation going from a wet to a dry part of a site. To use a transect, peg out both ends and identify the plants at each marked interval.

A common type of *quadrat* is a wooden square 0.5 m by 0.5 m. Quadrats are placed randomly e.g. by throwing and studying the vegetation where they land. It is usual to estimate the area occupied ("percent cover") of the important species. It is useful to have a smaller square (e.g. 5% of the area of the quadrat) as a guide for correct estimation. Quadrats are suitable for comparing two or more sites: at each site record the values for about 10 quadrats and average the results.

You will apply these techniques in *Exercise 39*. When discussing your conclusions you should take additional information on grassland *(Chapter 19)* into account.

Exercises

Exercise 37. Families of flowering plants

Materials needed
1. Flowers representing the families mentioned in the text: buttercup, wallflower, dog rose, sweet pea, ox-eye daisy, wild carrot, a grass flower (different species can be used), hyacinth
2. Hand lens
3. Straight pin

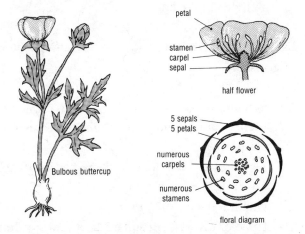

petal
stamen
carpel
sepal
half flower

5 sepals
5 petals
numerous carpels
numerous stamens
floral diagram

Bulbous buttercup

Fig. 13.8 Ranunculaceae, buttercup family

Procedure
1. Start with a buttercup flower. Buttercups belong to the family Ranunculaceae.

Examine the flower and identify the petals, sepals, stamens and carpels. Remove each item as you find it and count them. Write down this number. If there are more than 10 of any item, record them as "numerous". The number of petals varies between different species of buttercups - this is especially true if you are examining a lesser celandine flower. Draw what you see. The petals can be free or fused. Collectively the petals are referred to as the corolla. Note also the "floral diagram" in *Fig 13.8*. This is another way of representing the floral structure. Basically, it represents a diagram of a cross section through the flower.
2. Repeat this exercise for the other families.

Exercise 38. Identifying common farm grasses

Materials needed
1. Read the procedure first. Now collect grass specimens in the field.
2. Hand lens

Procedure:
1. When collecting specimens, ensure that you have the various parts of the grass plant,

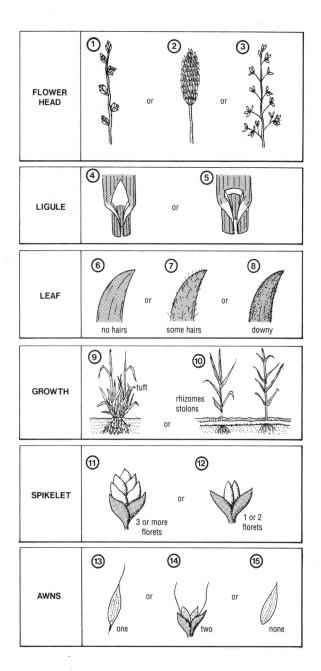

Fig. 13.9 Grass characters for grass key

especially the flowering head. Also note whether the plant is growing in tussocks or has underground stolons or rhizomes. Refer to the drawings in *Fig.13.9* and note the number of the type of each character as it occurs in the specimen you are identifying (characteristics 1 to 10 are easy and may be sufficient). Take each specimen in turn and note:

Flower head: *1.* Unbranched, flower spikelets attached alternatively at different sides

2. Like a cat's tail

3. Branched loosely

Ligule: *4.* Ligule longer than half its width, often pointed

5. Ligule shorter than half its width

Leaf blades *6.* Completely hairless to naked eye

7. Some hairs

8. Soft and downy

Growth form *9.* Tussocks

10. With underground stolons or rhizomes

Spikelets *11.* Three or more flowers which extend beyond the bracts

12. One or two flowers smaller than the bracts

Flowers *13.* Awns (bristles) on outer bracts

14. Two awns coming from inside the flower

15. No awns

2. Consult the key to common grasses in *Fig.13.10 (page 139)* for the final identification. Note that only common meadow grasses are included in the key.

Exercise 39. Investigating the species' composition of grassland

Materials needed

1. Identification guides to common grasses and plants

2. Light rope, 10 m long and marked at 10 cm intervals

3. Quadrat 0.5 m x 0.5 m

4. Piece of card 11 cm square (= 5% of quadrat area)

5. Compass

6. Clinometer (weighted string on a protractor will suffice)

7. Ordnance Survey map which includes site

character number	1	2	3	4	5	6	7	8	9	10	11	12	13	14	15	species
	◆	◇	◇	◇	◆	◆	◇	◇	◆	◇	◆	◇	◇	◇	◆	perennial ryegrass
	◆	◇	◇	◇	◆	◇	◆	◇	◇	◆	◆	◇	◇	◇	◆	scutch grass
	◇	◆	◇	◆	◇	◆	◆	◇	◆	◇	◇	◆	◇	◇	◇	sweet vernal
	◇	◆	◇	◇	◆	◆	◇	◇	◆	◇	◇	◆	◇	◆	◇	meadow foxtail
	◇	◆	◇	◆	◇	◆	◇	◇	◆	◇	◇	◆	◆	◇	◇	timothy
	◇	◆	◇	◇	◆	◆	◇	◇	◇	◇	◇	◇	◆	◇	◆	crested dogstail
	◇	◇	◆	◆	◇	◇	◇	◇	◇	◆	◇	◇	◆	◇	◇	Yorkshire fog
	◇	◇	◆	◆	◇	◆	◇	◇	◆	◇	◇	◇	◆	◇	◇	cocksfoot
	◇	◇	◆	◇	◆	◆	◇	◇	◆	◇	◆	◇	◇	◇	◆	meadow fescue
	◇	◇	◆	◇	◆	◆	◇	◇	◇	◆	◆	◇	◇	◇	◆	smooth meadowgrass
	◇	◇	◆	◆	◇	◆	◇	◇	◆	◆	◆	◇	◇	◇	◆	rough meadowgrass
	◇	◇	◆	◇	◆	◆	◇	◇	◆	◇	◇	◆	◇	◇	◆	common bent

character is:

◆ present
◇ absent

Fig. 13.10 Key to common grasses found in Irish meadows

Procedure

1. Produce a simple map of site giving dimensions, aspect (use compass), gradient (clinometer), altitude (from Ordnance Survey map), local geology and soil characteristics *(see Section 1, Soils)*. Note type of management, especially grazing.

2. Use transect as described in the text to investigate effect of trampling. You could relate vegetation to soil characteristics such as soil moisture and other characteristics *(Section 1)*.

3. Use quadrats to describe the grassland composition in two contrasting sites e.g. different management practices, or at different altitudes or between a wet and dry site. Relate to soil characteristics *(Section 1)* if possible.

Section 4

Cultivation of Tillage Crops

14 – Cultivation Machinery

The creation of a suitable soil environment is essential for successful tillage crop production. The soil provides *mechanical support, air, water and nutrients* for crops. In addition, the condition of the soil influences the amount of *heat* available to the crop's root system. Tillage operations (subsoiling, ploughing and cultivation) are one of the two keys to optimizing the soil environment, the other being fertilizer application.

14.1 Subsoilers

On heavy or poorly-structured soils it is sometimes necessary to loosen the soil to a greater depth than that reached by normal cultivations. This is done in order to improve drainage and root penetration. The problem may be due to a *plough pan*, which is a compact layer resulting from repeated ploughing to the same depth. The compaction is caused by the pressure of the plough and the tractor wheels on the soil. *General compaction* in and below the root zone, caused by the heavy machinery used to harvest sugar beet in late autumn/winter, is another problem which may be alleviated by soil-loosening.

Fig. 14.1 (a) Two-tine subsoiler; (b) section through the soil showing the loosening which has occurred. Note the raised soil surface resulting from the loosening action

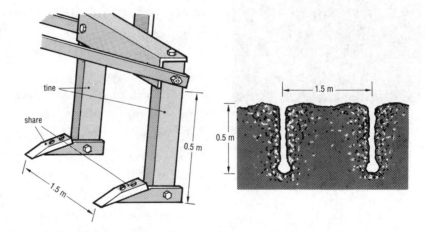

Subsoilers are commonly used to deal with soil compaction. They are comprised of one or more heavy vertical *tines (Fig. 14.1)*, each with a replaceable foot or share. Single-tine subsoilers may be operated by medium-powered tractors. Those with two or more tines require much larger tractors and perhaps tracked vehicles. For greatest effect, subsoiling should be carried out in dry soil conditions at 40-50 cm depth and 1-2 m spacing *(Fig 14.1)*. This usually leads to very effective loosening and shattering of the soil. It is desirable that the soil regions loosened by the tines meet.

14.2 Ploughs and Ploughing

The plough is an implement designed to turn over a layer of soil in preparation for further cultivations and sowing the crop. Ploughs may turn over one, two or more *furrow-slices* or *furrows*. Large ploughs, which plough six or eight furrows, are capable of very fast work-rates but require very powerful tractors to operate them.

Fig 14.2 Three-furrow plough, showing the parts of one plough unit.: A, frame; B, rear wheel; C, leg; D, disc coulter: E, share; F, mouldboard: G, landside: H, skim coulter

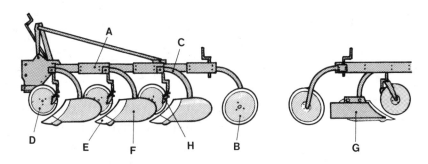

Fig. 14.3 Ploughing on grassland

The layout and parts of a three-furrow plough are shown in *Fig 14.2*. The purposes of the parts are as follows:

(A) The *beam* or *frame* is a single horizontal bar to which the *plough units* are attached.

(B) The *rear wheel* is a wheel attached to the beam at the rear of the plough. It can be adjusted vertically and controls the *depth* of ploughing.

(C) The *leg* is the link between the beam and an individual plough unit.

(D) The *disc coulter* makes a vertical incision in the soil, cutting the *side* of the furrow about to be turned.

(E) The *share* makes a horizontal incision, cutting the *bottom* of the furrow about to be turned.

(F) The *mouldboard* lifts and turns the furrow.

(G) The *landside* presses against the side of the unploughed ground (the *furrow wall*) and helps to keep the plough aligned properly.

(H) The *skim coulter* cuts a small slice off the corner of the furrow being turned and throws it into the previous *furrow bottom*. This reduces the risk of vegetation from the previous crop growing up between the furrows. High quality ploughing on grassland is shown in *Fig 14.3*.

14.2.1 Ploughing in "lands"

The plough shown in *Fig. 14.2* turns over the soil by throwing furrows *to the right*. When ploughing a large field, this results in a lot of travel with the plough raised and not in operation *(Fig. 14.4a)*.

This is referred to as *idle time* and is wasteful of fuel and labour. The traditional method of keeping idle time to a minimum is known as ploughing in lands. It involves dividing the field into sections or lands and ploughing these separately as shown in *Fig 14.4b*.

Fig 14.4 Ploughing a field, (a) as one unit and (b) in lands

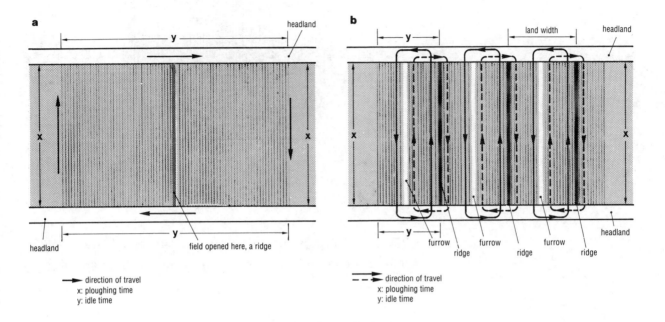

14.2.2 Reversible ploughs
The plough shown in *Fig 14.2* is known as a conventional plough whereas that shown in *Fig. 14.5* is a reversible plough.

Fig. 14.5 Reversible two-furrow plough

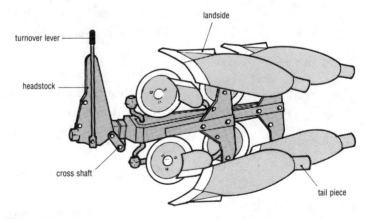

A reversible plough consists of *two sets* of plough units, one of which is idle while the other ploughs. One set of units throws the furrows to the right while the other throws them *to the left*. This allows a field to be ploughed with a minimum of idle time *(Fig. 14.6)*.

It also leaves the field level after ploughing, since there are no ridges or furrows. This makes later cultivations easier. Another advantage is the time saved in not having to mark out the field into lands.

Fig. 14.6 Ploughing with a reversible plough ("one-way" ploughing)

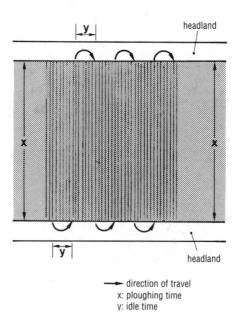

direction of travel
x: ploughing time
y: idle time

Reversible ploughs are expensive and are usually used only by agricultural contractors, with whom savings in time are of great importance.

14.2.3 Autumn vs spring ploughing

When land is ploughed in autumn, the turned-up surface is exposed to the effects of wetting/drying and freezing/thawing cycles over the winter. These weather effects have been described already. *(See page 32.)* As a result, the surface soil of autumn-ploughed land is more broken-up and easier to cultivate the following spring than that of spring-ploughed land. Seed beds are more easily and quickly achieved. This leads to earlier sowing dates and better soil conditions generally.

Autumn ploughing has become an almost essential part of growing deep-rooting crops like sugar beet and potatoes, especially on clay and silty clay loam soils.

14.3 Cultivators and Harrows

Fig. 14.7 Soil conditions suitable for germination and development of fine-seeded crops

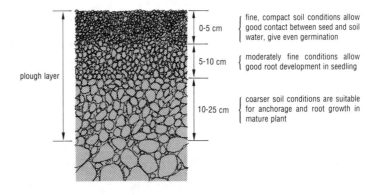

plough layer

0-5 cm { fine, compact soil conditions allow good contact between seed and soil water, give even germination

5-10 cm { moderately fine conditions allow good root development in seedling

10-25 cm { coarser soil conditions are suitable for anchorage and root growth in mature plant

The cultivation operations used between ploughing and sowing are designed to provide (a) a suitable seedbed for seed germination and plant establishment and (b) a suitable soil environment for subsequent crop growth.

The conditions required for small-seeded crops such as cereals, sugar-beet and most horticultural field crops are shown in *Fig. 14.7*. Thus, cultivation operations become *lighter* and *shallower* as one approaches final seedbed preparation. Very fine soil conditions caused by *over-cultivation* below the seedbed (0-10 cm) depth can lead to poor aeration and restricted root development.

Cultivation machinery may be divided into (a) *heavy-duty* machinery for operations immediately after ploughing, (b) *harrows* for lighter work leading to seedbed formation and (c) *"one-run" harrows*, designed to bring the soil from ploughed to "ready for sowing" state in one operation.

14.3.1 Heavy duty cultivators

These implements consist of a frame with a number of tines which break and stir the soil *(Fig. 14.8)*. They vary in weight, width and number of tines, depending on the type of work to be done. The heaviest and strongest of these are called *chisel ploughs* and can be used instead of mouldboard ploughs in situations where there is little surface vegetation to bury.

Three types of tine are found on heavy duty cultivators *(Fig. 14.9)*. *Rigid tines* are used for heavier work. The tines are staggered across the frame to reduce soil blockages.

Spring-loaded tines are non-flexible tines held in position by heavy springs. The tines lift on hitting a large clod or stone and spring back into position after it has been passed. This action helps to shatter the soil. *Spring tines* are flexible and spring up on hitting large clods or stones. They vibrate in the soil, thus increasing their shattering effect.

All of these tines have *replaceable shares*. Some shares are reversible so that they can be reversed and then replaced as they wear.

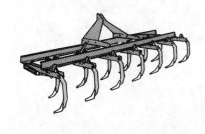

Fig. 14.8 Heavy-duty cultivator

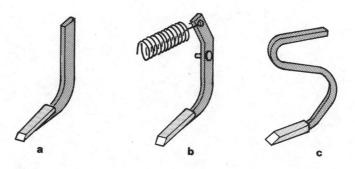

Fig. 14.9 Cultivator tines and shares.: (a) rigid; (b) spring-loaded; (c) spring

14.3.2 Harrows

Most of these implements are broadly similar in design to heavy-duty cultivators. They are, however, much lighter and are used for seedbed preparation. They have rigid or spring tines and replaceable shares. They have working widths of up to 10 m.

Two additional types of harrow are *disc harrows* and *chain harrows*. Disc harrows *(Fig. 14.10)* contain two or more sets of saucer-shaped discs fixed to a frame. They are heavy harrows which cut and consolidate the soil. They are used mainly for preparing a seedbed after ploughing in grass, where a tined implement would pull the grass sod to the surface.

Fig. 14.10 Disc harrow

Chain harrows are used for very light seedbed work and for covering seeds after sowing. They consist of a large number of small spikes carried on flexible frames *(Fig. 14.11)*. In addition to their use in tillage work, they are often used on grassland to break up matted swards or to spread dung patches after grazing.

Fig. 14.11 Chain harrow

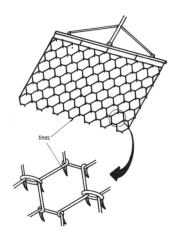

tines

14.3.3 "One-run" harrows

These can be used on sandy and loam soils to create a seedbed in one operation after ploughing. There are many different designs but most of them contain three basic components *(Fig. 14.12)*.

Fig. 14.12 "One-run" harrow

Firstly, there is a *levelling bar*, which breaks some clods and makes the surface roughly level. This is followed by a series of rows of *spring tines* designed to create progressively finer soil conditions. The rows of tines are separately adjustable for this purpose. Finally, there is a *soil crumbler*, also adjustable, which creates the final seedbed and compacts it ready for sowing.

14.4 Power-driven Implements

All the cultivation machinery described so far is *pulled* through the soil. The amount of shattering and soil disturbance caused is largely dependent on the forward speed of the implement.

Power-driven implements are basically different. They consist of a set or sets of tines or blades which are *driven at high speed* by the power transmission of the tractor. These implements therefore, in addition to being mounted on the tractor, are connected to the tractor's transmission by a detachable *power shaft*. The tractor's power is then adjusted, through a series of gears, to operate the cultivating tines or blades.

14.4.1 Rotary cultivators

The principal operating part of a rotary cultivator or *rotavator*, is a rotating horizontal bar *(rotor)* carrying a number of L-shaped blades *(Fig. 14.13)*.

The blades bite into the soil and throw it backwards against a hinged metal hood at the rear of the machine; this helps to shatter clods. The rotor and blades run at speeds of 90 to 240 rpm, having

Fig. 14.13 Rotary cultivator

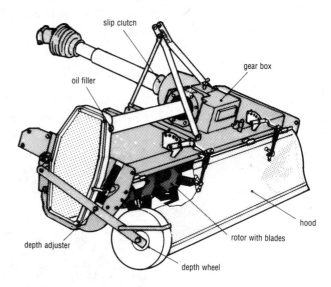

been geared down from the power shaft speed of 540 rpm. Low speeds give coarse soil conditions, high speeds fine conditions.

The rotary cultivator is a very powerful implement. It can easily produce a seedbed in one run, even on heavy soils. If used at high rotor speeds in dry soil, there is a risk of damaging soil structure, so its use must be carefully controlled. It is a very expensive implement with high maintenance costs and a small (1-2 m) working width.

It is used mostly for seedbed work for potatoes and sugar beet, but is also useful for cutting up and incorporating crop residues into the soil. It is used extensively in horticulture, where high levels of organic manuring offset the risk of soil structural damage.

An alternative version, with *spikes* instead of blades, can be used for seedbed preparation and this implement is less destructive of soil structure.

14.4.2 Power harrows

These implements consist of two *reciprocating* tine-bars *(Fig. 14.14)* which cut and crush soil clods. A crumbler, similar to that used in one-run harrows, is usually fitted behind the tine-bars.

Fig. 14.14 Power harrow

14.5 Rollers

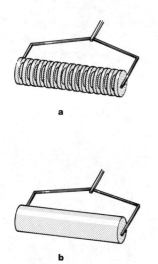

Fig. 14.15 (a) Cambridge (ribbed) roller, (b) smooth roller

Rollers are used for two purposes, breaking large clods and smoothing and firming the surface soil. In addition to their use in preparing the soil for sowing, they are often used *after* sowing cereals and other fine-seeded crops to compact the soil around the seed and thus improve water intake and germination.

Rollers are of two kinds, Cambridge or ribbed rollers and smooth rollers *(Fig. 14.15)*. The Cambridge roller is made up of a number of cast-iron rings on an axle. It has a better compacting effect and leaves a corrugated surface. Smooth rollers may be made up of separate metal rings or may be hollow drums which can be filled with water to increase their weight.

Rollers are usually used in groups of three, giving a working width of up to 8 m. The compacting effect of rollers may be improved by driving slowly, since this will increase the length of time the roller's weight is in contact with the soil.

Exercises

Exercise 40. Examination of plough, plough parts and ploughing operations

Materials needed
1. Plough
2. Tractor
3. Area of land

Procedure
1. With the plough mounted on the tractor and resting on ground (preferably a yard or roadway), make a rough sketch of the plough and its attachment to the tractor.
2. Identify and carefully examine each of the following plough parts: (a) beam, (b) rear wheel, (c) disc coulter, (d) share, (e) mouldboard, (f) landside and (g) skim coulter.
3. Observe ploughing in progress. Examine the action of each of the seven plough parts identified above. Observe the effects of (a) ploughing too deeply (b) ploughing too shallow (c) ploughing without skim coulters (d) ploughing slowly (e) ploughing at high speed.

Results
Record and comment on the effects of 3(a) to 3(e) above.

Precautions
1. Stand well back from the plough when it is being raised or lowered.
2. Keep a safe distance from the tractor wheels at all times.

Exercise 41. Comparing the action of a harrow and a rotavator

Materials needed
1. Tractor
2. Harrow (any kind)
3. Rotavator
4. Recently-ploughed land

Procedure

1. Attach harrow to tractor and use it for one run, going 12 cm deep, in the ploughed ground.
2. Disconnect harrow. Attach the rotavator and rotavate a strip, again going 12 cm deep, adjacent to the harrowed strip. Use high rotor speed and low forward tractor speed.
3. Compare soil conditions in the two strips of land. How do they compare as potential seedbeds?

Results

1. Record results
2. List the advantages and disadvantages of each of the two methods.

Precautions

1. This exercise should be carried out under the supervision of an experienced machinery operator.
2. Keep well clear of the tractor and implements at all times while they are in operation.
3. Be especially careful of the *power take-off (PTO)* and the *PTO shaft*.

15 – Tillage Crops: General Principles

Before dealing with individual crops, three features/practices common to them will be discussed. These are (A) location of tillage crops; (B) crop rotation; and (C) weed, disease and pest control.

15.1 Location of Tillage Crops

The geographical location of tillage crops in the country was shown in *Fig. 2* in the *Introduction*. The main factors influencing this location are (a) climate/weather patterns in the country and (b) soil type distribution. *Fig. 15.1* shows this relationship.

Fig. 15.1 Relationship between "rain-days" per year, predominant soil type and location of tillage crops

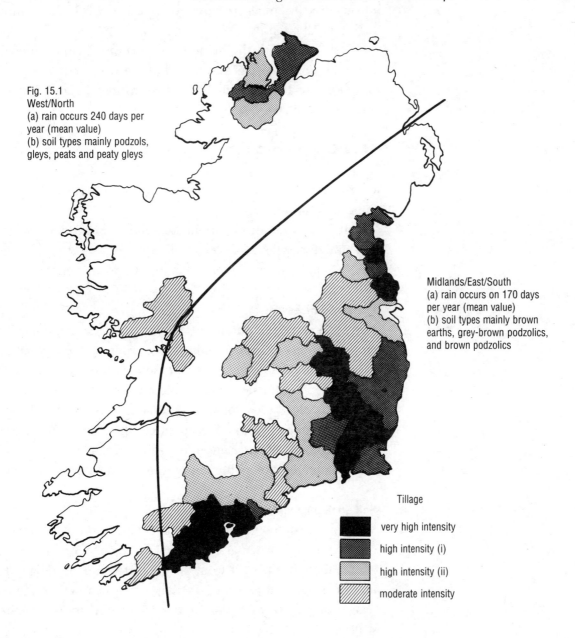

Fig. 15.1
West/North
(a) rain occurs 240 days per year (mean value)
(b) soil types mainly podzols, gleys, peats and peaty gleys

Midlands/East/South
(a) rain occurs on 170 days per year (mean value)
(b) soil types mainly brown earths, grey-brown podzolics, and brown podzolics

Tillage

very high intensity

high intensity (i)

high intensity (ii)

moderate intensity

The number of "rain-days" per year (a rain-day is a day on which at least 0.2 mm of rain falls) is very important in relation to the growing of tillage crops. Where the number is high, as in the west/north, the soil is unlikely to be dry enough for spring cultivations. There will also be difficulty in obtaining fine weather conditions for harvesting cereal crops. The number of rain-days in the midlands/east/south is substantially lower than in the west/north.

The soil types predominant in the midlands/east/south are free-draining. This makes them more suitable for spring cultivations and less likely to be damaged by harvesting machinery. They are also fertile and less in need of frequent lime and fertilizer applications.

The isolated areas of tillage crops found in east Donegal and east Galway are explained by the occurrence in those areas of good quality, free-draining brown earths (see *Fig. 4.10*) which offset the high rainfall intensity.

The county with the greatest proportion of land under tillage crops is Carlow with 25-30%. The county with the smallest proportion is Leitrim with 1.3%. In Northern Ireland, Fermanagh has 0.8% of tillage crops.

15.2 Crop Rotation

Crop rotation, or the growing of crops in a definite sequence, is important for two reasons:
1. It helps to control certain soil- and crop residue-borne pests and diseases.
2. It helps to maintain soil structure and organic matter.

Pests and diseases
Many soil- and crop residue-borne pests and diseases are specific to a crop or group of crops. Growing these crops *too frequently* allows the pests and diseases to build up in the soil to serious infestation levels. If this happens, further crops of the same type will grow very badly or fail completely. The organisms responsible must then be starved out by growing crops not susceptible to them. Since the organisms may be capable of surviving in the soil for many years, it is safer to adopt a sound rotation, thereby preventing them from building up.

Soil structure and organic matter
Soil structure and organic matter content are improved and increased under grassland. When grassland is ploughed under and tillage crops grown, the crops benefit from the good structure and high organic matter. Repeated growing of tillage crops, however, leads to a progressive loss of organic matter and deterioration of the soil structure.

On many *silty* and *clayey* soils, this quickly leads to serious *soil compaction*, with resultant poor crop growth. On these soils it is recommended that a *tillage/grassland* rotation is adopted. One such rotation is four years tillage/two years grassland and this helps to maintain soil structure.

15.3 Weed, Disease and Pest Control

Weeds, diseases and pests of tillage crops may be controlled by *indirect, biological* or *direct* means.

15.3.1 Indirect control
There are a number of means of indirect control:

Crop rotation is a major means of controlling the numbers of weed seeds and pest and disease organisms in soil.

The influence of rotation on pests and diseases has just been described. In the case of weeds, practising a rotation means that the different conditions occurring from year to year (different cultivations; different sowing dates; crop competition and shading) discourage the build-up of weed seeds associated with any individual crop.

Growth encouragement leads to healthy vigorous crops which resist weed invasion and pest and disease attack. Factors leading to growth encouragement include good seedbed preparation, early sowing, and use of sufficient fertilizers and lime.

Sowing resistant crop varieties, where such varieties exist, gives protection against some pests and diseases.

Harvesting without delay is important because over-ripe crops are highly susceptible to pest and disease damage.

Stubble cleaning is a term applied to a technique for controlling weeds in the period between growing two tillage crops. The soil is harrowed to encourage weed germination. When germination has occurred, the soil is again harrowed to kill the seedlings.

This procedure is repeated as often as time and weather permit. The result is clean, weed-free seedbeds.

15.3.2 Biological control
This mainly concerns crop pests and involves introducing a *predator*, a *parasite* or an *infectious agent* of the pest causing damage. The main application in Ireland is in horticulture, where some glasshouse crop pests are routinely biologically controlled (e.g., red spider mite and whitefly in tomatoes).

15.3.3 Direct (chemical) control
Materials used in chemical control include herbicides, fungicides and pesticides.

(A) Herbicides

Herbicide treatments may be total (non- selective) or selective. *Total herbicides* kill all vegetation. They are used either before planting the crop or in non-crop situations, e.g. paths, waste ground.

Selective herbicides, if properly used, check or kill weeds without damaging the crop. Their action is related to the extent of their absorbtion by plant tissue and they are often used to control broad-leaved weeds in cereals (the weeds, with greater leaf area, absorb more herbicide). If the application rate is too high, selective herbicides become total herbicides.

The mode of action of herbicides may be contact, translocated or soil-acting (residual). *Contact herbicides* kill only plant tissues with which they come into contact. They "scorch" or dessicate tissues. If the shoot is extensively affected by the herbicide spray, annual weeds are killed while perennial weeds recover due to regrowth from their unaffected root systems.

Translocated herbicides are absorbed by plant tissues and translocated within the plant to all parts. This means that extensive covering of the vegetation is not necessary and low-volume sprays may be used. Translocated herbicides kill by affecting the plant's growth processes and sprayed plants become distorted in shape and finally die. Translocated herbicides affect the root system and thus kill perennial weeds as well as annuals.

Soil-acting (residual) herbicides are applied to the soil and remain active there for some time, killing all germinating seeds. Soil-acting herbicides are taken up by roots of young seedlings and move to the actively-growing parts, slowly killing them. They are not absorbed by leaves, so they can be used after crop emergence. They are active only in the upper 3-5 cm of soil, so deeply sown or well- established crop plants are not killed.

(B) Fungicides

Fungicides are compounds which kill or inhibit the growth of fungi. They are normally applied as sprays. Fungicide action may be eradicant, protective or systemic (translocated).

Eradicant fungicides kill fungal infections at the site of application. It is necessary to achieve good coverage of the crop vegetation when spraying.

Protective fungicides work by protecting the plant from fungal attack at the site of application. They should be applied in dry weather so that they are not washed from the vegetation. Good coverage is needed.

Systemic fungicides are a very important group. These compounds are absorbed by plant tissue and moved to different parts of the plant, including the roots. Systemic fungicides can kill existing infection within the plant and also protect the plant from fungal attack. Complete coverage of the vegetation is not essential.

(C) Pesticides

Pesticides are available for controlling a wide range of crop pests. While insecticides are best known and most widely used, chemicals for killing slugs and snails, mites and vertebrate pests also exist.

Most pesticides are applied by *spraying* a solution or colloidal suspension of the chemical onto the crop. The pests are then killed either by contact with the chemical or by eating sprayed foliage (*contact/ingestion* effect). Some sprays are absorbed and moved around the crop plants in a similar way to the action of translocated herbicides and systemic fungicides and pests feeding on the foliage are killed by the chemical (*systemic* effect).

Some pesticides are applied as *baits* which are mixtures of food attractive to the pest and of poisonous chemicals. Finally, some pesticides are applied as *fumigants*. This has to be done in a confined space (e.g., glasshouse, sealed rabbit burrow) and poisonous gases are used.

Great care must be taken when using pesticides, especially some insecticides, because of their *toxicity* and *persistence*. If vegetable or fruit crops, for example, are sprayed with insecticide too close to harvest time, persons consuming these crops may be poisoned. Persons applying insecticides without the correct protective clothing run the risk of toxic effects. The *persistence* of some insecticides refers to the fact that their rate of degradation is extremely slow. The presence of these materials in the soil and on vegetation affects wildlife and pollutes the environment.

Because of these two potentially dangerous aspects of pesticides, there are strictly-controlled schemes and legal requirements governing their purchase and use.

16 – Cereals

The cereals commonly grown in Ireland are barley, wheat and oats. These are all members of the *Order Gramineae*, which is by far the most important order of plants from an agricultural standpoint. Grasses, which cover more than two-thirds of the world's agricultural land, belong to this order as do the tillage crops listed in *Table 16.1.*

Table 16.1 *Area of cereal crops, 1990*

Crop	Area under crop worldwide (ha)
Wheat	242 million
Rice	148 million
Maize	124 million
Barley	98 million
Millet	53 million
Sorghum	51 million
Oats	25 million
Rye	16 million

16.1 Recent Trends in Cereal Production

The changing land area under the main cereals is shown in *Fig. 16.1.* Barley has increased steadily in popularity over the last 30 years, mainly because it grows well under Irish climatic conditions. The area under wheat has fluctuated greatly and is at present increasing. The steady decline in the area under oats is mostly explained by the disappearance of the working horse, its main consumer.

Fig.16.1 Recent trends in cereal crop areas

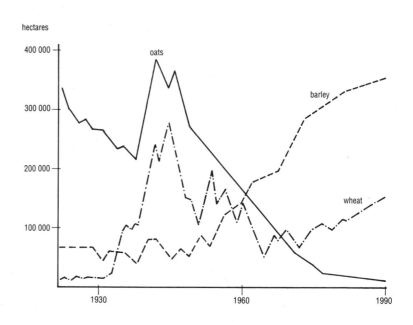

16.2 Identification of Cereals

The seed-heads of mature plants of barley, wheat and oats as well as individual grains are shown in *Fig. 16.2*. Barley may be distinguished from wheat by presence of *awns* or *beards* on the grain. The seed-head of oats has a different form from the others, being a loose, spreading *panicle*.

In the younger, vegetative stage, the cereals may be identified by the appearance of the leaf, especially the auricles *(Fig.16.3)*.

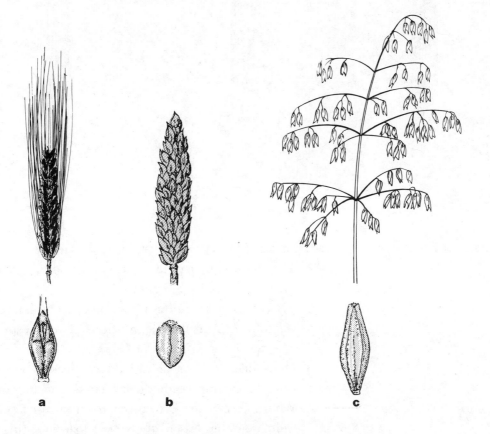

a   b   c

Fig. 16.2 Seed-heads and grains of (a) barley, (b) wheat, (c) oats

16.3 Winter and Spring Varieties

Cereals may be sown in winter or spring. *Winter varieties* are sown from mid-September to early November and have the ability to survive winter frosts. They reach the *grass corn* stage (8-10 cm tall) before growth stops in winter. They resume growth in early spring. This gives them a longer growing season and greater yield capacity than spring varieties. They are harvested from mid-July onwards.

Spring varieties are not fully frost-resistant and must be sown in spring. Consequently, they have a shorter growing season and lower yield capacity than winter varieties. They are harvested from early August onwards.

Cereal farmers usually sow as much of their land as possible with winter varieties and the remainder with spring varieties. The

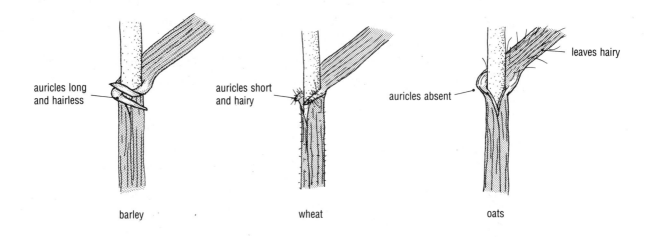

auricles long and hairless

auricles short and hairy

auricles absent

leaves hairy

barley

wheat

oats

Fig. 16.3 Leaves and auricles of the cereals

advantages of sowing winter varieties are as follows:

1. They have higher yield capacity than spring varieties, yielding on average 20 % more grain.
2. Their earlier ripening allows them to be harvested in good weather and firm soil conditions. This is especially true of wheat.
3. Over-reliance on spring varieties can lead to serious yield losses when bad spring weather delays cultivation and sowing.
4. Where cereals are grown in mixed farming systems, sowing winter varieties lessens the labour load in spring when calving and lambing activities are at a maximum.

16.4 Seed Certification

Almost all cereal seed sown in Ireland is Government-certified seed. This is seed produced by the Department of Agriculture and Food under strictly-controlled conditions. The properties of certified seed are listed in *Table 16.2*.

Table 16.2 *Guaranteed characteristics of Department of Agriculture and Food Certified Seed*

1.	Minimum germination rate of 85 per cent.
2.	Minimum analytical purity of 98 per cent.
3.	Completely free from wild oat *(Avena fatua)* seed.
4.	Seed is treated with fungicide/insecticide.

16.5 Cultivation of Barley

16.5.1 National importance

Two types of barley are grown in Ireland. *Feeding barley* is used for animal feed, being suitable for all livestock. About 30% of the crop is retained by farmers for feeding cattle, sheep and pigs on the farm. The remainder is sold to animal-feed compounders for the manufacture of animal rations. Barley straw can be fed to cattle. Because of its low feeding value, however, this is usually done only in bad winters when feed supplies are scarce.

Malting barley is used in the brewing and distilling industries. It is grown only on very good soils and the quality of the grain harvested is very important. Much of the crop is grown under contract to brewing and distilling companies. There is an export trade in malting barley.

16.5.2 Features of cultivation

1. *Soils and climate:* Feeding barley grows best on deep, sandy loam soils, brown earths and grey brown podzolics being most suitable. It will, however, grow satisfactorily on a wide range of soil types. Good drainage and a soil pH of greater than 6.0 are essential; a pH of 6.5 is ideal.

   Soil type is of greater importance for malting barley, only the best soils being suitable. Grey brown podzolics, whose clay-rich B horizons retain moisture in dry summers and ensure proper ripening, are considered best. Soil pH should be kept at 6.5.

   Barley requires a steady supply of moisture over the growing season. *Drought in mid-season* lowers the yield and quality of grain. This is specially true for malting barley. Dry soil conditions during ripening and at harvest time are of benefit, however. They lead to improved grain quality and drier grain at harvest.

2. *Place in rotation:* Barley is not seriously affected by soil-borne pests and diseases; therefore rotation is not of great importance. If barley is grown very intensively, occasional grass breaks (1-3 years) will help to maintain soil structure.

3. *Varieties:* A "Recommended List of Cereal Varieties" is published every year by the Department of Agriculture and Food. Varieties on this list have been extensively tested over a three-year period for characteristics such as yielding capacity, shortness of straw, strength of straw, earliness of ripening and resistance to disease. New barley varieties with improved characteristics are continually being introduced and the varieties most extensively sown by farmers change from year to year.

4. *Cultivations:* For spring barley, a seedbed similar to that shown

in *Fig. 14.7 (page 144)* should be prepared. This should be done without "forcing", i.e. with a small number of well-timed cultivations. Rigid-tined, spring-tined, one-run and disc harrows are commonly used. Autumn ploughing is a valuable aid in minimising forcing. Rolling after sowing is also important.

For winter barley, the seedbed should not be so fine as the soil is usually moist after sowing. Rolling is not necessary and should not be done. It can lead to soil "capping" (breakdown of structure in the top few mm) if prolonged heavy rainfail follows sowing.

5. *Sowing:* The optimum date for sowing winter barley is October 1st. If the seed is sown too long before this date the crop grows past the grass corn stage before winter. It will then be too tall and advanced when growth begins the following spring and may lead to *lodging* (falling over) of the crop later in the year. If the seed is sown too long after October 1st., it will not reach the grass corn before winter. The yield will suffer as a result.

When sowing winter barley the aim should be to have 250-300 plants per m^2 established by early spring. These plants will produce 900-1 000 ears at harvest, due to *tillering*. Barley, like all graminaceous plants, tillers. This means that the main shoot produces a number of side shoots or tillers, each of which develops its own root system and grows into a mature plant, although still attached to the main plant.

If the grain weight and the percentage establishment are known, the weight of seed to be sown in order to obtain 250-300 plants per m^2 can be calculated *(see Exercise 44)*.

Spring barley should be sown as early as weather conditions permit a seedbed to be properly prepared. Late sowing causes reduced yields. Sowing rates may be calculated using similar

Fig. 16.4 Cross section through a combine drill, showing one seed and one fertilizer chute. There are 20-40 of each

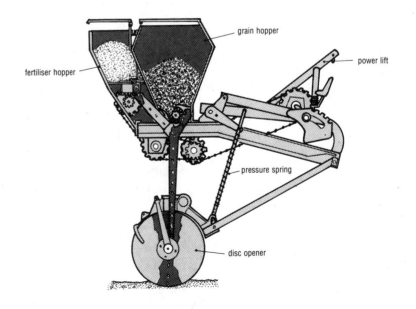

grain hopper

power lift

fertiliser hopper

pressure spring

disc opener

information to that used for winter barley. Because spring barley tillers very vigorously and has a higher percentage establishment than winter barley, sowing rates are usually lower. Barley is usually sown with a *combine drill (Fig. 16.4)*. This drills in seed and fertilizer adjacent to each other in lines 18 cm apart.

6. *Fertilizers:* P and K fertilizers are applied *at sowing* for both winter and spring barley. They are usually applied using the combine drill but they can also be *broadcast* and harrowed into the soil. The amount applied is decided after soil-testing has been carried out.

   N is always applied in the spring and summer. Some farmers apply all the N in one spring application. This is broadcast on winter barley and applied at sowing on spring barley. Others apply it in *split dressings*, some at sowing and the remainder in one or two further applications.

   Split dressings tend to give higher yields but should not be practised on malting barley as they give rise to high grain-N levels which make the grain unacceptable for malting. The amounts of N applied depend on a number of factors such as soil organic matter content and recent cropping history.

7. *Weed control:* Weeds must be controlled in order to maximise crop yields and ensure that harvested grain is clean and free of weed seeds. Growing barley in a *rotation* is one way of controlling weeds *(see page 153)*. Stubble cleaning *(see page 153)* is another.

   Weeds found in the growing crop must be controlled by the use of *herbicides*. The usual procedure is to identify the weeds present and their abundance and then choose suitable selective herbicides to control them. Since herbicides vary in their effectiveness in controlling different weed species, a mixture often has to be used. Correct application rate and time of application of selective herbicides are very important in ensuring effective weed control.

8. *Disease and pest control:* Barley, throughout its life, is subject to attack by a wide range of diseases and pests. Some are *seed-* or *soil-borne* such as *loose smut* (a seed-borne fungal disease which attacks the ears), and *wireworms,* insect larvae which attack seeds and underground stems. These are protected against by *seed treatment* which consists of covering the seed with a thin coating of a mixture of a systemic fungicide and a contact insecticide. All Government-certified seed is treated in this way.

   The most important of the *air-borne* diseases and pests is *powdery mildew* which affects leaves and is seen as a grey-white fungal growth *(Fig. 16.5)*. Once it is observed, the crop should be

Fig. 16.5 Powdery mildew on barley

immediately sprayed with a suitable systemic fungicide. Seed treatment with a systemic fungicide is also practised as a control measure.

Many more diseases and pests affect barley during growth. Some of the more important are listed in *Table 16.3*. In all cases, the procedure for their control is similar to that employed in weed control, namely:

1. identify the pest or disease causing the crop damage,

2. apply a suitable fungicide or pesticide promptly.

Table 16.3 *Some diseases and pests of barley and their symptoms and treatment*

Disease/pest	Causal organism	Symptoms	Form of treatment
Diseases			
Powdery mildew	*Erysiphe graminis*	Grey-white fungal growth on leaves	Seed treatment / foliar spray
Leaf blotch	*Rynchosporium secalis*	Pale grey-green blotches on leaves	Foliar spray
Brown rust	*Puccinia hordei*	Orange-brown raised specks on leaves	Foliar spray
Loose smut	*Ustilago nuda*	Grains in seed-head destroyed and replaced by black fungal spores	Seed treatment
Pests			
Barley yellow dwarf virus	Virus transmitted by aphids *Rhopalosiphum padi*, *Sitobion avenae*	Leaves turn bright canary yellow	Foliar spray
Wireworms	*Agriotes spp*	Plants turn yellow and die due to damage to under- ground stem	Seed treatment
Leatherjackets	*Tipula spp*	Plants die due to damage at and below ground level	Poison baits

9. *Harvesting* When barley is fully ripe, the straw becomes dry and bleached in colour. The grain becomes very dry and hard and the ear bends over and finally lies parallel to the stem *(Fig. 16.6)*. At this stage, the crop is ready for harvesting.

Barley is harvested using a combine harvester. This is a complex machine *(Fig. 16.7)* which cuts the crop, threshes it (separates the grain from the rest of the plant), and delivers clean grain to a storage bin. From there it is transferred by a conveyor chute to tractor-trailers for transporting to the farmyard or grain merchant. It is important to have all parts of the combine harvester set and working properly so that grain damage and loss are kept to a minimum. This is of greatest importance with malting barley because damaged grain will not be accepted by maltsters.

The average yield of barley in Ireland at present is about 5 tonnes per ha , this figure having been reached by means of a steady increase over the last 100 years *(Fig. 16.8)*. This increase

withered flag leaf at harvest

Fig. 16.6 Barley plant fully ripe

Fig. 16.7 Combine harvester

Fig. 16.8 Average barley yields in Ireland, 1890 – 1990

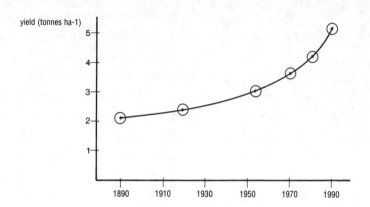

was brought about by improved varieties, better weed, disease and pest control, and by increased fertilizer usage. Winter barley outyields spring barley by about 25%. Good management, especially in the area of disease control and fertilizer use, can give higher yields and the best cereal growers have achieved yields of up to 10 tonnes per ha .

10. *Storage:* The main sources of damage in stored barley are germination or *sprouting,* bacterial and fungal attack and attack by insects and other pests.

High grain moisture-content encourages the processes listed above and *grain drying* is the most widely used technique for prolonging the storage life of barley and other cereals. For long-term storage, grain merchants have to dry barley to 14% moisture. The higher the moisture content of the harvested grain, the more expense is incurred in drying it. For this reason, grain merchants usually pay for all cereals on a sliding scale using 20% moisture content as their baseline.

When very dry barley is rolled for animal feed, the product may be dusty and may cause respiratory irritation to the animals being fed. Barley retained on the farm for rolling, therefore, is often stored at high moisture contents by using *acid-treatment.* In this procedure, propionic or sulphuric acid is sprayed onto the grain at rates of 3 – 5 l per tonne. This kills the embryo, preventing sprouting, and also protects the grain against bacterial, fungal, insect and other pest attack.

16.6 Cultivation of Wheat

16.6.1 National importance

Wheat is grown in Ireland for human and animal consumption. The *endosperm (Fig. 16.9)* may be separated from the embryo and outer layers and ground to make flour for bread-making. The flour is not of high quality, however. This is because our climate does not contain sufficient late summer sunshine to allow the grain to mature and ripen correctly. As a result, less than 50%, on average, of home-grown wheat is accepted for milling. The flour manufactured from it must be mixed with flour from high-quality imported wheat to produce acceptable bread.

The rest of the wheat produced is used for animal feed. This gives the farmer a lower financial return than if the wheat were of milling-quality. Yet, winter wheat's yield potential, which is the highest of all cereals, makes it worth growing on some of the better soils.

Wheat is lower in fibre than barley or oats. It must be mixed with fibre-rich feeds when compounding animal rations to prevent animal digestive disorders.

Wheaten straw is of low feeding value and is used for animal bedding only.

16.6.2 Features of cultivation

The cultivation of wheat is generally similar to that of barley. Important differences are:

Soil pH is less restrictive than in the case of barley . Wheat will grow well at pHs of 5.5 upwards. The *weather* required for satisfactory growth and ripening of the crop needs to be warmer and sunnier than that required for barley.

Harvest dates are later than for barley. Winter wheats are usually ripe in mid-August, spring wheats in late August/September.

Diseases and pests are, in many cases, different from those affecting barley. The general principles governing their control are similar, however.

16.7 Cultivation of Oats

16.7.1 National importance

Oats have declined greatly in national importance in recent times. In 1950, oats occupied 55% of land under cereals but this had

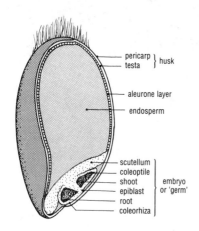

Fig. 16.9 Longitudinal section of a wheat grain

fallen to 6% in 1990 *(Fig. 16.1)*. The main reason for this was the replacement of oats by barley as animal feed. Barley has higher potential yields and is a more concentrated feed, containing a smaller amount of indigestible husk. Other reasons have been the decline in numbers of working horses and farmyard poultry for which oats were an important foodstuff.

Although oats are now of minor importance nationally, they are important in the small farms of the west and northwest because of their ability to grow on acid soils and in rainy conditions. As these farms are not highly mechanised, wet soil conditions at harvest time do not present problems with heavy machinery.

Oaten straw, if cut before the crop is fully ripe, has a feeding value similar to that of moderate quality hay. This makes oats a useful crop on the small western and northwestern farms where winter feed for livestock is often scarce. On these farms, oats may be cut early, allowed to dry out in the field and threshed later with both the grain and straw being kept for winter feed.

16.7.2 Cultivation

Oats are cultivated in the same way as barley and wheat, the main differences being:

Oats grow satisfactorily on soils with *pH values* of 5.5 or greater.

Climatic requirements are not as demanding as those for barley and wheat. Oats grow well in cool, rainy conditions provided soil drainage is adequate.

Crop yields are lower than those for the other cereals; the figures are:

Oats ("good" yield) : 4-5 tonnes per ha
Barley ("good" yield) : 7-8 tonnes per ha
Wheat ("good" yield) : 8-9 tonnes per ha

Exercises

Exercise 42. Examination of wheat, barley and oat plants

Materials needed
Complete, mature (ready for harvest) plants (including root systems) of wheat, barley and oats.

Procedure
Note: The plants for this exercise should be collected at harvest time and stored carefully until used.

1. Examine general structure of the plants. Identify roots, stems, seed-heads (ears), grains, awns. Compare the seed-heads with the sketches shown in *Fig. 16.2*.
2. Count the number of stems bearing seed-heads in each plant. One of these is the main stem, the others are tillers. Calculate the class mean number of tillers for each of the three cereals.
3. Concentrate on the barley plants. Each pupil determine for his/her plant:
   (a) Number of tillers (n1).

(b) Average number of seeds per seed-head (n2).

Collect individual pupils' results for n1 and n2. Plot n1 against n2. Is there a definite relationship between them?

4. Break up and thresh the seed-heads by hand. Compare the grains with the sketches in *Fig. 16.2*. Try to separate the outer fibrous coat from the grain (caryopsis) in barley and oats.

Results

There should be an inverse relationship between n1 and n2. This is explained by the plant's ability to *compensate* for small numbers of tillers by producing more grains per seedhead. (It also tends to produce larger, heavier grains.)

Comment on the differences in the amount of fibre in the three different grains.

Exercise 43. Determination of germination percentage of certified seed and home-produced seed of barley

Materials needed

1. Sample of certified spring barley seed.
2. Sample of home-produced seed.
   Note: The home-produced seed should have been dried naturally. If heated air was used, the temperature should not have exceeded 50°C. The grain should not have been treated with acid. High temperatures and acid kill the embryo.

Procedure

1. Count out 100 grains of each type of seed.
2. Soak the grains in water for 24 hours in *labelled* beakers.
3. Place each sample on moist filter paper in *labelled* petri dishes (or any small flat containers).
4. Allow the seeds to germinate. This can take up to 6 days. Keep the filter paper moist at all times.
5. When the grain has germinated, and the shoots are 1 cm long on average, count the number of germinated grains in each container. The number of grains *is* the germination percentage.

Results

Obtain class mean values for (a) certified seed, (b) home-produced seed. Compare the values. The value for certified seed should be higher than that for home-produced seeds.

Exercise 44 Calculating seeding rate for winter barley

Materials needed

Information on seed weight, germination percentage and establishment percentage of winter barley

Procedure

1. Assume the following information:
   (a) The 1 000 grain weight is 50 g
   (b) The germination percentage is 96 %
   (c) The establishment percentage of germinated grain is 85%.

2. The aim is to have 250-300 established plants per m^2. Take a figure of 275 plants.
   (a) 275 established plants require:
   $$\frac{275 \times 100}{85} \text{ germinated seeds}$$
   $$= 323.53 \text{ germinated seeds}$$
   (b) 323.53 germinated seeds require:
   $$\frac{323.53 \times 100}{96} \text{ seeds sown}$$
   $$= 337.01 \text{ seeds sown}$$
   (c) These weigh:
   $$\frac{50 \times 337.01}{1\,000} \text{ g}$$
   $$= 16.85 \text{ g}$$

3. This amount of seed is needed for 1 m^2. There are 10 000 m^2 in 1 ha. The amount of seed to be sown per ha is:
   $$16.85\text{g} \times 10\,000 = \frac{16.85 \times 10\,000}{1\,000} \text{ kg}$$
   $$= 168.5 \text{ kg}$$

Exercise 45. Identification and collection of weeds of cereals

Materials needed
Access to a field of cereals in springtime (April/May).
Note: Many of the weeds of importance in cereals are found in any cultivated area or even in recently disturbed ground, such as is found in building sites, roadworks etc. These areas may be used instead of cereal fields.

Procedure
1. Using a guide to common weeds of tilled ground, identify the following: Fat hen (Lamb's quarter), Redshank, Chickweed, Speedwell, Fumitory, Mayweed, Creeping buttercup, Charlock, Wild turnip, Groundsel, Dock, Knotgrass, Black bindweed.
2. Collect a sample of each weed and label carefully.

Results
1. Press the weed samples collected.
2. Mount them in a notebook and label.

17 – Roots

17.1 Recent Trends in Root Crop Production

The root crops of most importance in Ireland are potatoes and sugar beet. The changing land area under these crops is shown in *Fig. 17.1.* The steady decline in the area under potatoes is explained by two factors. Firstly, there has been a decrease both in the number of human consumers of potatoes (due to a population decline) and in their *per capita* potato consumption.

Fig. 17.1 Recent trends in root crop areas

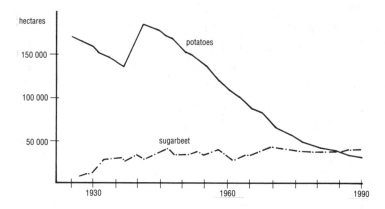

Secondly, consumption of potatoes by livestock has diminished greatly as the popularity of feeding-barley has grown. The sharp increase in the area under potatoes in 1939-41 was caused by a government compulsory tillage programme designed to deal with food shortages during the second world war.

The area under sugar beet increased from zero in 1925 to 25 000 ha in 1935 as the Irish Sugar Company became established. It has fluctuated between 25 000 and 35 000 ha since then, meeting domestic demand for sugar.

17.2 Seed Certification

The quality of seed is closely controlled, for potatoes by the Department of Agriculture and Food and for sugar beet by the Irish Sugar Company.

The seed potato industry is located principally in county Donegal, where *cool windy conditions* keep aphid populations low. Aphids transmit the viruses which cause a number of serious diseases in potatoes. One of the main objectives of the *Seed Potato Certification Scheme* is to keep viral infestation of seed to a minimum.

Production of seed under the Scheme consists of the following procedures:

1. *Selection:* Potatoes to be used as the source of seed are selected from Department of Agriculture and Food farms in Donegal. These potatoes must come from fields free of *Potato root nematode (see page 253)* infestation and must themselves be completely free of this pest. They are also rigorously tested for *virus Y, leaf roll* and *leaf mosaic* diseases, the three principal viral diseases of potatoes.

2. *Initial propagation:* The selected potatoes are propagated under strictly-controlled growing conditions in *high-elevation, windy* "nucleus plots" in Donegal. These plots are isolated from other potato crops and the growing vegetation is tested frequently for viral infection. Alternatively, these potatoes are propagated by *micro-propagation* techniques. This involves growing virus-free plants from meristem tip cuttings under controlled laboratory conditions.

3. *Further propagation:* When sufficient seed is available, it is distributed to selected growers nationwide and propagated further, again in isolated and strictly supervised situations. The crops are tested regularly for viral and other diseases. The potatoes from this propagation are sown again on selected farms the following year. Potatoes from this final propagation are sold as *certified seed* to commercial growers and farmers.

Seed used in sugar beet production is produced to standards similar to those applying to seed potatoes. Thus, seed must be pure, healthy, and free from pest damage and disease organisms.

17.3 Cultivation of Potatoes

17.3.1 National importance

The potato *(Solanum tuberosum)* is a member of the Order Solanaceae which also includes tobacco and tomatoes. Although commonly called a root crop, potatoes are in fact *tubers* or swollen underground stems and it is these which are consumed or used as "seed".

Potatoes are used mostly for human consumption and Ireland is generally self-sufficient in potato production. Potatoes may be classified into three categories, depending on their date of harvest and degree of maturity at harvest. These are:

First earlies: potatoes which are harvested immature in early summer. The yield loss incurred by early harvesting is compensated for by high prices.

Second earlies: potatoes harvested immature later in the summer. The prices obtained are high but not as high as those obtained for first earlies.

Maincrop: these are potatoes harvested in the autumn at full maturity. They are used to supply the market over the winter and until the earlies are harvested the next year.

Increasing amounts of potatoes are processed into dried, mashed potatoes, chips (including frozen and oven-ready chips), crisps and canned potatoes. Further progress in diversifying potatoe products is likely in the future. Seed potatoes amount to 9-10% of total production and some of these are exported to Britain and other European countries.

17.3.2 Features of cultivation

1. *Soils and climate:* Potatoes grow well on a wide range of soils. Highest yields, however, are obtained on deep, well-drained loams and sandy loams. They are very tolerant of low pH and satisfactory growth can be obtained at pH 5.0.

   Potatoes are not frost resistant, so they must be sown at a time which ensures that the young plants will not be killed off by frost. First and second earlies can be grown successfully only in frost-free coastal areas such as parts of Wicklow, Wexford, Waterford and Cork. Light sandy soils and south-facing slopes are important for first earlies as they lead to warm soil conditions in spring.

   The mild showery weather common throughout Ireland is ideal for growth. Drought during the period of *tuber development* (July and August) seriously reduces yield. Research has shown that irrigation during this period may be economically feasible. Dry soil conditions at harvest make harvesting easier and protect soil structure. These conditions are more likely to be found on sandy and sandy loam soils.

2. *Place in rotation:* When potatoes are grown too frequently in the same field, they become affected by potato cyst nematode. This is a soil-borne nematode (or *eelworm*), microscopic in size, which affects the crop's root system. Although some potato varieties are resistant to eelworm attack and *nematicides* are available for soil use, the most effective control is obtained by practising a rotation.

   Potatoes should not be sown in the same area more than one year in four. In seed potato production, EC regulations stipulate that potatoes may only be sold for seed from fields which are eelworm-free on sampling. For this reason, seed potato growers in Ireland must limit sowings to one year in five.

   Potatoes grow satisfactorily at any point in a rotation of crops. Where farmyard manure is available, it is often applied to potatoes and they and the other crops benefit from the increased organic matter levels.

3. *Varieties:* Potato varieties used do not change as quickly as do cereal varieties and many of those widely used at present have been popular for many years. There are 40-50 varieties in the "National Catalogue of Agricultural Plant Varieties", published annually by the Department of Agriculture and Food. Some of these are listed in *Table 17.1*.

Table 17.1 Potato varieties grown in Ireland

Category	Variety	Comment
First early	* Home Guard	—
	Epicure	—
Second early	* British Queen	—
Maincrop	* Kerr's Pink	Good eating quality, high yielder
	* Record	Good eating quality, high yielder
	Clada, Pentland dell, Maris piper	—
	Golden Wonder	Excellent eating quality, low yielder
	Cara	Poor eating quality, very high yielder
	* Most widely sown	

4. *Cultivations:* Deep cultivations are required for potatoes. The land should be autumn-ploughed to a depth of at least 22 cm and then cultivated in spring to give a deep fine seedbed. Rotavators or power-harrows are often used to give a deep seedbed quickly without compaction.

   Stone removal is practised on some commercial potato farms to avoid the problems of bruising and contamination encountered when the crop is mechanically harvested. Cultivations are carried out almost to the seedbed stage. Then a machine similar to a potato harvester *(Fig. 17.3, page 175)* is used to lift the soil, separate the stones and deposit them in a band at the side of the machine.

   The stones are then pressed into the ground by the wheel of the tractor carrying out the *ridging* operation. Spacing of ridges is arranged so that the buried stones are located in the furrow between two ridges. The land is ploughed for the next crop at right angles to the ridges to spread the stones again. Stone removal is then practised each year potatoes are grown.

   Potatoes are usually grown on ridges and ridging is either the final cultivation operation before sowing or is performed during sowing.

5. *Sowing:* Potatoes are sown or *planted* about 10 cm below the surface of ridges 76 cm apart. The *spacing* of seed in the ridges is governed by the size of the seed. As seed-size increases, the number of "eyes" per tuber increases. These eyes are in fact axillary buds. Shoots develop from them and grow into individual potato plants, each with its own root system.

Large seed, therefore, produces more plants and tubers than small seed but average tuber size is smaller. This effect is modified by using wider spacing for large seed. In this way, a greater volume of soil is available to large seed to allow the tubers to grow to normal size.

The recommended procedure is to grade seed (which is 35-55 mm in size) into two sizes, 35-45 mm and 45-55 mm before planting. The seed is then planted at the spacings shown in *Table 17.2.*

Planting may be performed by hand in small units. On commercial farms semi-automatic potato planters (which require one or more persons working on the machine) or automatic planters are used. These machines make ridges and plant the seed in the same operation.

Table 17.2 Spacing of graded seed potatoes

Seed size (mm)	Spacing (cm)	No. of seeds ha^{-1}
35-45	20-25	60,000
45-55	30-35	40,000

Potato seed may be *sprouted* prior to planting. This is done by placing the seed in shallow sprouting boxes and placing them in greenhouses or well-lit buildings at temperatures of $5.5^{\circ}C$ or greater. The size and number of sprouts can be controlled by varying light and temperature conditions (*see Exercise 46*). Sprouting *speeds up growth* and plant emergence and *increases yield*. It is considered an essential part of the production of first earlies.

Certified seed, on account of the time and costs involved in its production, is rather expensive. Many growers buy certified seed every two or three years only and use it to produce *home-grown seed*. This is done by planting the certified seed in an isolated area of the farm and spraying with pesticides if necessary to control aphids.

The vegetation is then killed off early. This ensures the maximum number of potatoes in the seed size range. Research has shown that seed produced in this way gives satisfactory crops with reduced costs for up to two generations removed from the certified seed.

6. *Fertilizers:* It is important to apply fertilizer nutrients in balanced amounts to potatoes. Excessive applications of nitrogen, for example, give higher yield but lowered eating quality, the watery potatoes sometimes being unsaleable. Excessive potassium also depresses dry matter content and eating quality.

Application rates should be decided on after soil test results and previous cropping have been considered. Rates are usually in the following range:

Nitrogen : 125-150 kg per ha
Phosphorus : 125-150 kg per ha
Potassium : 250-300 kg per ha

Sulphate of potash gives rise to higher dry matter content than muriate of potash. It is most frequently used in manufacturing fertilizers designed for use on potatoes.

Fertilizers are normally broadcast on the soil surface prior to planting and incorporated into the seedbed during ridging/planting.

7. *Weed control:* The objective in weed control is to suppress the growth of weeds until the potato *haulms* (leaves and stalks) meet across the drills. After this happens, weeds are controlled by shading.

The usual procedure is to spray the crop, when 15-20% of the potato plants have appeared over the soil, with a mixture of a *total contact* herbicide and a *residual* herbicide of medium persistence. The contact herbicide kills all vegetation, including the young tips of the potato plants. The plants recover and continue to emerge, however. The residual herbicide controls emerging weed seedlings for long enough to allow shading to take over weed control.

8. *Earthing up:* This is an operation carried out when the crop is 20-25 cm high. A ridger is used to deepen the furrows and widen the ridges as shown in *Fig. 17.2.*

The objective in this operation is to ensure that developing tubers are not exposed to light. Light causes "greening" of tubers, leading to the formation of poisonous *alkaloids* in the skins. It is against the law to sell greened tubers, so they must be graded out and discarded.

9. *Disease and pest control:* The most important disease of potatoes is *potato blight,* caused by the fungus *Phytophthora infestans (see page 107).* This disease causes premature death of the haulms with resultant yield losses. In the case of bad infections, blight spores may be washed by rainfall from the haulms onto the soil and onto the tubers. This leads to tuber infection and rotting during storage.

The spread of potato blight is favoured by warm, humid weather conditions. Once infection occurs, it is almost impossible to control so preventative measures must be taken. When weather suitable to blight spread is expected, *potato blight warnings* are issued on radio and television by the meteorological service. This usually happens from mid- June onwards.

When warnings are issued, growers should spray crops

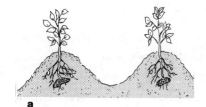

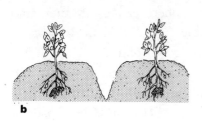

Fig. 17.2 Potato ridges (a) before and (b) after earthing up

immediately (i.e. before infection) with a suitable protective fungicide. Spraying should be repeated every 10 days thereafter until September 1. This will ensure satisfactory foliage growth, tuber formation and development and crop yields.

Potatoes are subject to several other diseases and some of the more important are listed in *Table 17.3*.

Table 17.3 *Some important diseases of potatoes*

Disease	Cause	Symptoms	Control
Leaf roll	Virus transmitted by aphids	Rolled leaves, stunted growth	Use certified seed. Use aphicides when required.
Leaf mosaics	Viruses transmitted by aphids	Mottled leaves, stunted growth	Use certified seed.
Blackleg	Bacterium (*Erwinia carotovora*)	Blackening of lower parts of stems. Blackening of stored tubers.	Use certified seed. Avoid poorly drained fields. Avoid putting wet tubers in stores.
Gangrene	Soil-borne fungus (*Phoma exigua*)	Dark coloured depressions on stored tubers. Secondary infection by bacteria.	Use certified seed. Avoid damage at harvest. Apply chemicals if necessary.
Common scab	Soil-borne bacterium (*Streptomyces scabies*)	Dark superficial scabs on tubers (which affect selling quality).	Use certified seed. Avoid high-pH soils. Do not lime potato crop or previous crop.

The principal pests of potatoes are potato root nematode, which is controlled by crop rotation, wireworms, slugs and aphids.

Wireworms are mainly a problem when potatoes are planted after pasture. The pest is the same species which attacks barley *(see Table 16.3)* and it attacks the tubers, eating into them and lowering tuber quality. A suitable contact insecticide, worked into the soil before planting, gives good control.

Slugs also feed on the tubers, making them unsightly and leaving them exposed to bacterial infection during storage. Where populations are high, slug pellets should be broadcast in July to control numbers.

Aphids are carriers of viral diseases already mentioned. Whenever populations are high (more than three per plant) the crop should be sprayed with a systemic aphicide.

10. *Harvesting:* Early potatoes are harvested from early June onwards depending on variety and part of the country. The earliest crops of "new" potatoes have low yield but obtain high prices.

Maincrop potatoes are harvested in late-September or October when the tubers are fully grown and mature. The haulms are killed off using a contact herbicide three weeks before harvesting. This is done to make harvesting easier and to prevent blight spores from being washed onto the soil and tubers. The three weeks wait allows the skins of the tubers to harden; this makes them less prone to bruising and scratching during harvesting .

The most commonly used potato harvester is the *elevator digger* (*Fig. 17.3*).

Fig. 17.3 Elevator digger potato harvester

This machine has a wide flat share which runs through the ridge just under the potatoes. The soil and potatoes are moved onto an elevator, composed of parallel bars, which carries them back towards the rear of the machine and agitates them at the same time. The soil and small stones fall through the spaces in the elevator. The potatoes remain on it until they fall back onto the soil behind the harvester. They are then picked by hand.

Complete potato harvesters are used by some large-scale producers. These lift and clean the potatoes in the same way as the elevator digger but the potatoes are then carried further by a conveyor and deposited in a storage bin.

Average yields of maincrop potatoes are about 30-40 tonnes per ha, varying considerably from year to year. Earlies yield less than this, with first earlies sometimes being harvested with yields as low as 7-10 tonnes per ha to avail of very high prices available early in the season.

11. *Storage:* Buildings used for storing potatoes should meet the following requirements:

(a) They should be *leak-proof* and *frost-proof.* Wetting and frost damage encourage rotting which can spread quickly and cause big losses. Potato stacks are commonly covered with a layer of loose straw to protect them from frost.

(b) They should be *well-ventilated*. This speeds up the drying of the potatoes and lessens the risk of sprouting, heating and rotting. Where potato stacks do not exceed 1.8 m in height, natural ventilation may be adequate. Where they exceed this height, a *forced-draught ventilation* system with fans and air-ducts is needed.

(c) They should be large enough for *easy access to tractors and trailers*. They should have *strong, reinforced walls* as potato stacks can cause walls to collapse.

Sprouted potatoes become dehydrated, shrivelled and unsaleable. Potatoes sprout rapidly in stores in springtime when temperatures rise. While those intended for sale before February 1 should keep satisfactorily, potatoes kept until later in spring should be treated with a *sprout inhibitor* or kept in a *refrigerated store.*

17.4 Cultivation of Sugar Beet

17.4.1 National importance.

Sugar beet (*Beta vulgaris*) is a member of the Order Chenopodeaceae. It has been developed by genetic selection from the commonly-found wild plant sea beet, strains of the species with large root size and high sugar content being developed over time.

Sugar beet is grown *on contract* to the Irish Sugar Company. The company supplies farmers with seed and fertilizers, and provides advice and technical help during the growing of crops. Harvested crops are accepted by the company at guaranteed prices and the sugar is extracted at one of its factories in Carlow and Mallow.

There are a number of important *by-products* of sugar beet production.

Beet tops (Fig. 17.4) are left in the field after sugar beet harvesting. They can be fed to cattle or sheep, having a food value equivalent to that of grass of moderate quality.

Fig. 17.4 By-products of sugar beet

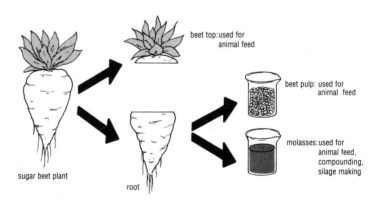

Beet pulp is dried, shredded root-material from which the sugar has been extracted. It is fed to cattle and sheep, having a food value similar to that of barley.

Molasses is a thick black liquid left after crystallisation of sugar from the water extract. It is very sweet and improves the palatability of animal feeds and its stickiness is used in *pelleting* animal feeds. It is also used as a silage additive. It has food value similar to that of barley.

17.4.2 Features of cultivation

1. *Soils and climate:* Deep, well-drained soils are required for sugar beet. On shallow soils or on soils with compacted layers, root forking may occur. This leads to a high level of tare (crop waste) at the factory. Sugar beet is very intolerant of bad drainage, plants dying at the seedling stage. It is also intolerant of acid soil conditions and pH should be in the 6.5-7.0 range.

   The sugar content of sugar beet is strongly influenced by the level of sunshine during the growing season. The average sugar content in Ireland is 16% but higher levels than this are found in areas with more sunshine such as eastern England. Low rainfall makes seedbed preparation and crop harvesting easier.

2, *Place in rotation:* To avoid serious build-up of *beet cyst nematode* a rotation is practised. Sugar beet and other host crops for this pest must not be grown on the same soil more frequently than one year in three. Host crops include fodder beet, mangels, beet roots and spinach beet as well as all brassica crops (turnips, swedes, rape, kale).

3. *Varieties:* A limited number of varieties is available and the Sugar Company advises farmers on which variety to sow, taking into account the soil type and location of their farm.

4. *Cultivations:* Sugar beet requires a fine seedbed for uniform seed germination and plant establishment. This is best achieved by autumn ploughing, followed by cultivation to a depth of 20 cm with a spike rotavator in spring.

5. *Sowing:* Sugar beet is sown early in spring to obtain a long growing season and high yields. The crop is sown using a *precision seeder*, which sows the seed at whatever spacing the grower chooses. The usual seed spacing is 18 cm in drills 56 cm apart. This gives approximately 100 000 seedlings per ha. Not all of these seedlings become established and 75-80 000 mature plants per ha is the usual population.

   Sugar beet seed is irregular in shape and to make it usable in a precision seeder it is *pelleted*. This involves coating the seeds with inert clay materials and moulding them into roughly spherical shapes. These pellets then fit easily into the circular holes in the seed belt of the precision seeder. The coating material dissolves in the soil.

6. *Fertilizers:* Specialized fertilizers are available from the Sugar Company. In addition to balanced amounts of N, P and K, sodium and boron are found in these fertilizers. *Sodium* is an essential nutrient for sugar beet because of the crop's development from salt-loving sea beet. *Boron* is routinely added to prevent the occurrence of *heart rot*, a disorder of sugar beet roots caused by boron deficiency.

   Fertilizers are spread on the ploughed ground and cultivated into the seedbed.

7. *Weed Control:* Weeds in sugar beet crops are controlled using an approach similar to that used in potatoes. This involves spraying with contact and residual herbicides twice between sowing and full leaf cover.

8. *Disease and pest control: Virus yellows* is the most important disease of sugar beet. It is caused by a virus transmitted by peach potato or green aphid, the same species involved in potato viral diseases. The foliage of infected plants becomes chlorotic and yield losses result.

   Sites where aphids can overwinter should be dealt with to keep down aphid populations; crop residues should be ploughed in quickly and headlands and loading areas cleaned off after use. During the growing season, crops should be sprayed with a systemic aphicide if aphid populations reach 1.5 per plant.

   The main pest of sugar beet is beet cyst nematode, which is controlled by rotation as already described.

9. *Harvesting:* Harvesting is carried out using special sugar beet harvesters. These machines *(Fig. 17.5)* lift the plants from the ground, remove the tops, and clean and convey the roots to a storage hopper or directly to a trailer being driven alongside.

   Sugar beet yields on average 40 tonnes of roots and 25-30 tonnes of tops per ha.

Fig. 17.5 Sugar beet harvester

10. *Storage and utilization:* Sugar beet is harvested from mid-September onwards. The sugar factories require a regular supply of beet over the processing period (October - January) but have limited storage facilities. If a farmer's crop is not required until late in the period, then he should harvest while soil conditions are dry and store the roots until they are collected.

Roots should be stored on concrete yards or on very dry, firm ground. Road sidings and lay-bys are often used. Clamps should be long and narrow and not higher then 2.5 m to minimise heating. They should be protected by covering with straw in frosty weather, since frost reduces sugar content and makes the roots unsuitable for processing.

If the crop has been harvested in wet soil conditions, leaving a lot of soil adhering to the roots, further cleaning may be carried out during the storage period. This minimises transport of soil to the factories.

Factories pay farmers on the basis of (a) weight of washed roots and (b) sugar content. The price per tonne is based on a sugar content of 16%. Bonuses and reductions are made for sugar contents above or below this value.

Sugar beet tops are normally left in the field after the harvesting operation. They can be fed to cattle or sheep *in situ* (using an electric fence to strip-graze them). They can also be transported to yards and sheds for feeding. They must be wilted for a few days, however, as, when fresh, they contain oxalic acid which causes diarrhoea (or scouring). Beet tops may be *ensiled* and fed later in the winter.

17.5 Cultivation of Other Root Crops

17.5.1 Fodder beet and mangels

These are root crops, similar to sugar beet, which are grown in mixed farming areas, mainly in the south-east, Cork and Galway. They give heavy yields of highly digestible nutrients and are fed to cattle and sheep on mixed farms where a cereal/root rotation is practised.

They are bulky, labour-intensive and have to be protected from frost during winter storage. For these reasons, grass silage is preferred by most farmers as winter fodder and the area under mangels and fodder beet has declined to only 5 500 ha in 1990. Recently, techniques have been developed for harvesting and shredding fodder beet and mangels and making silage from them in a single streamlined operation. This may increase their popularity in the future.

The cultivation practices used in growing fodder beet and mangels are similar to those used in growing sugar beet.

17.5.2 Turnips

Turnips are a brassica root crop grown for winter fodder for sheep on mixed farms. For many years, turnips were grown for feeding to cattle also and were harvested and stored over the winter on the same way as fodder beet and mangels. Having the same labour and storage problems, they were largely replaced by grass silage.

When grown for feeding sheep, however, they are less labour-intensive, as they are grazed *in situ* (*Fig. 17.6*). They are best grown in free-draining soils so that the sheep do not poach the soil too much during grazing.

The cultivation practices used are again similar to those used in growing sugar beet. A rotation must be practised to prevent the occurrence of clubroot ("finger and toe"), a soil-borne fungus disease.

Fig. 17.6 Sheep grazing turnips

Exercises

Exercise 46. Sprouting of seed potatoes: control of sprout number and size

Materials needed
1. Seed potatoes (need not be certified seed), 30
2. Refrigerator

Procedure
Note: If seed potatoes are sprouted at 15-16°C in early autumn, a single sprout develops which suppresses growth of all other sprouts. *Single-sprouted seed* produces a small number of large potatoes and is used for first early production. If the seed is sprouted late in the year (December/January) or if the single sprout is removed, a large number of sprouts is produced. *Multi-sprouted seed* produces a large number of small potatoes and is used for production of seed potatoes or potatoes for canning.

1. Sprout all the potatoes at 15-16°C in September. When the single sprouts have developed and grown to 15-20 mm length, place 10 of the potatoes in a regrigerator at 4°C (Group 1).

2. Remove the single sprout from each of 10 of the remaining potatoes and allow multiple

sprouts to develop (Group 2): When these reach 15-20 mm length, refrigerate them as before.

3. Allow the remaining 10 potatoes to continue to sprout at 15-16°C (Group 3).

Results

1. Compare sprout number and size in each of the three groups of potatoes when the multi-sprouted potatoes have been refrigerated for 3-4 weeks.

2. Comment on the results. It is expected that Group 1 will have single short sprouts. Group 2 should have many short sprouts. Group 3 should have long sprouts which will be easily broken at planting.

Exercise 47. Estimation of potato yield: total and ware

Note: Unprocessed potatoes offered for sale in 25 kg bags are referred to as *ware* potatoes. They must be graded into the 40-80 mm size range.

Materials needed

1. Drill of potatoes ready for harvest
2. Shovels or forks (for digging the potatoes)
3. Piece of strong wire, shaped into a 40 mm x 40 mm square
4. Piece of strong wire, shaped into an 80 mm x 80 mm square
5. Bathroom weighing scales
6. Metre stick or ruler

Procedure

1. Measure average width of the potato drill ("X" m).
2. Harvest 10 m of the drill.
3. Clean off the soil and bring the potatoes back to the laboratory.
4. Grade the potatoes into small (< 40 mm), ware (40-80 mm) and large (> 80 mm).
5. Weigh the amount of each type (kg).

Results

1. Calculate the yield of each grade of potatoes per ha as follows:
Yield (tonnes ha^{-1})
$$= \frac{\text{(yield recorded in 10 m) x 10 000}}{10 \text{ "X"}}$$

2. Comment on the use to be made of the three categories measured.

Exercise 48. Determination of eating quality of ware potatoes

Materials needed

1. Golden Wonder potatoes, 5
2. Record potatoes, 5.
3. Kind Edward potatoes, 5.
4. Beakers (600 ml), 9.
5. Oven

Procedure

Note: The main characteristic influencing eating quality in ware potatoes is dry matter (DM) content. Teagasc has assessed the three varieties being tested as follows:

	DM content (Max., 9)	Eating quality (Max., 9)
Golden Wonder	9	9
Record	7	8
King Edward	5	6

1. Wash all the potatoes and dry with tissue.
2. Weigh three beakers, record the weights and label them Golden Wonder A, B, C.
3. Repeat step 2 with three beakers for Record and three for King Edward.
4. Cut the Golden Wonder potatoes into cubes and fill the three beakers. Discard excess potato cubes. Weigh the beakers and contents and record the weights.
5. Repeat step 4 with Record and King Edward potatoes.
6. Place all beakers in the oven at 100°C and dry to constant weight.
7. Cool *in the oven* and weigh again as soon as

the beakers are cool enough to handle easily.

Results

1. Calculate the DM% for each sample as follows:

$$DM\% = \frac{\text{Wt of bkr + dry p'toes} - \text{Wt of bkr}}{\text{Wt of bkr + fresh p'toes} - \text{Wt of bkr}} \times 100$$

2. Calculate the *mean* DM values for Golden Wonder, Record and King Edward.
3. Rank the varieties in order of DM content.
4. Compare the rank order obtained with that of Teagasc.
5. Comment on the results.

Exercise 49. Relating sugar content of sugar beet to weather conditions during growth

Materials needed

1. Sugar beet roots
2. Refractometer
3. Meteorological data

Procedure

1. Cut a sugar-beet root across and obtain a drop of sap.
2. Measure the sugar content with the refractometer *(see the method in Exercise 21)*.
3. Obtain meteorological data on total sunshine amounts (March – September, inclusive). This should be obtained from the meteorological station closest to where the sugar beet was grown.

Results

1. Add the sugar content and total sunshine amount data to the data already available. These data can be collected by the school over a number of years from one area. Alternatively, data from other areas may be obtained from other schools or from other sources.
2. Observe whether there is a relationship between the two parameters. It is expected that there is a positive correlation (i.e. more sunshine - more sugar) between them.

18 – Horticultural and other crops

18. 1 Horticultural Production

18.1.1 National importance

Although horticultural crops occupy only 2.0% of tillage land, they account for more than 20% of the value of tillage crop output. This is because horticulture is both land and labour-intensive, and a high level of efficiency has been achieved. Crops produced are high-value crops for human use.

There is considerable scope for expansion in horticulture, especially in the area of fresh vegetables and protected crops. At present, large quantities of these commodities are being imported because of problems with domestic production. These problems have been in the area of quality and marketing of produce, mainly. Poor development of co-operation among growers has also meant that the industry has had difficulties competing with outside interests.

18.1.2 Horticultural crops

Horticulture is a complex area within agriculture and a wide range of crops is grown. These crops can be roughly grouped into four categories: field vegetables, fruit, ornamentals and protected crops.

1. *Field vegetables:* These account for about 75% of the total area of horticultural crops. The major area of importance is north county Dublin where the *fresh vegetables* for both Dublin and much of the rest of the country are produced. The factors influencing this location are (a) ease of access to the Dublin city market, (b) availability of light sandy soils very suitable for tillage and (c) low incidence of frost due to the area's proximity to the sea. There are also areas of fresh vegetables in the vicinity of the other main centres of population.

   Large areas of vegetables, mainly *peas* and *beans,* are cultivated for *processing* (freezing and canning) near vegetable processing factories mainly in Dublin and Carlow. These are grown on contract to the factories in the same way that sugar beet is grown, and their cultivation is a specialised operation.

2. *Fruit:* Fruit is mostly produced in the Suir valley and around Dungarvan (apples) and in Wexford and Dublin (soft fruits). Most of the apples grown are cooking apples; many of these are processed for cider at a factory in Clonmel. Some dessert (eating) apples are also grown.

Soft fruits *(strawberries, blackcurrants, gooseberries and raspberries)* are produced in county Dublin for both fresh consumption and processing (jam-making, canning). Elsewhere, principally in Wexford, they are grown mainly for processing.

3. *Ornamentals:* Ornamentals include *horticultural bulbs, cut flowers, potted plants* and *trees and shrubs.* The large production units are found in the midlands and around Dublin mainly. Smaller units are located near all the large centres of population. Their operations are highly specialized and labour intensive.

4. *Protected crops:* Protected crops are those grown in buildings and they represent the most intensive type of cultivation found in Ireland. Although the land area under protected crops is very small (650 ha), output from it accounts for about half of the total value of horticultural output. Capital and labour inputs are very large but products are mostly of high value *(Fig 18.1).*

The buildings used are glasshouses, plastic tunnels and sheds. They may be heated or unheated. Crops grown in glasshouses and plastic tunnels include *tomatoes, lettuce, cucumbers, flowers and potted plants. Mushrooms* are grown in specially designed sheds but may also be grown in heated, darkened glasshouses or plastic tunnels or in converted farm buildings.

Cultivation of protected crops is very highly specialized. Features include *soil sterilization, irrigation, hydroponics, light and temperature control, biological pest control and growing of a succession of crops throughout the year.*

Fig 18.1 Production of ornamental plants in a plastic tunnel

18.2 Production of Other Agricultural Crops

These crops occupy only 2.5% of tillage land, so they are of minor importance nationally at present.

18.2.1. Rape and kale

These are brassica crops grown for winter fodder for dairy cows. They are grazed *in situ* and can be the cause of severe soil damage unless grown on very free-draining soils.

Where rape or kale are sown in late summer for grazing in the December-February period they are referred to as *catch crops,* i.e. crops grown between two main crops. Two examples of catch cropping are:

	Year	Crop
(a)	1	(i) Early potatoes
		(ii) Rape for winter grazing
	2	(iii) Cereal
(b)	1	(i) Winter barley
		(ii) Rape for winter grazing
	2	(iii) Spring cereal, potatoes, sugar beet, etc.

18.2.2. Oilseed rape

This is a brassica crop grown for its seed, which is processed to yield an oil used for a variety of purposes. These include the manufacture of margarine, cooking oils, lubricating oils and detergents.

Oilseed rape is popular with intensive cereal growers for a number of reasons. *Firstly*, it is grown using the same cultivation and harvesting machinery as cereals. It demands husbandry skills which the cereal grower has. *Secondly*, it is a useful break crop from cereals, since it does not harbour their pests and diseases. *Thirdly*, it is a valuable crop giving a good return for the labour and other investments made.

Oilseed rape is highly susceptible to clubroot *(see page 180)*, so it must not be grown on land which has grown brassica crops in the previous five years.

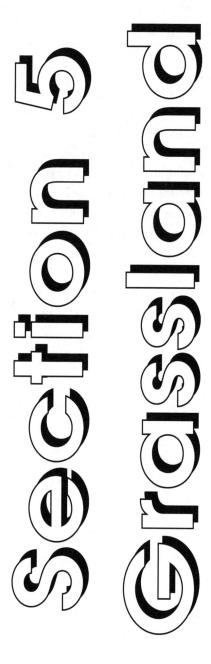

Section 5
Grassland

19 – Extent and Importance of Grassland

Grassland occupies about 70% of the world's agricultural land, making it the most important crop. In Ireland, 91% of our agricultural land is grassland and this provides 70-80% of the feed requirements of our cattle and more than 90% of those of our sheep. Grassland is, therefore, a major resource in our agricultural industry.

19.1 Categories of Grassland

There are three main categories of grassland; *rough mountain and hill grazing, permanent grassland* and *leys.*

19.1.1 Rough mountain and hill grazing
This land is more appropriately called grazing than grassland since it often contains more heather, gorse, bracken and *scrub* than grasses. It is characterized by the following properties:
1. Extreme variability in botanical composition
2. Low stocking rates
3. Low levels of production.

Such land is usually acidic and can be peaty or stony with *rock outcrops*, making it difficult or impossible to cultivate. Where cultivation and/or liming and reseeding are possible, very large increases in production can be achieved.

19.1.2 Permanent grassland
This is grassland which is *never ploughed.* It differs from the previous category in that,
(a) it is dominated by perennial grasses and
(b) scrub and trees are scarce or absent.

It displays great variability in botanical composition, however, ranging from communities of three or four productive grasses and clover to weedy unproductive grassland not much better than rough mountain and hill grazing.

In general, permanent grassland has higher levels of production and management and is more heavily fertilized and stocked than rough mountain and hill grazing.

19.1.3 Leys
These are areas of grassland *sown by farmers* and are characterized by:

1. Little variability in botanical composition, the sown species being dominant
2. High stocking rates
3. High levels of production

Leys are normally associated with good farming practices and high levels of management. They are resown or reseeded regularly.

19.2 Grassland Distribution

Grass is the predominant crop in all counties of Ireland. Its distribution is complementary to that of tillage crops shown in *Fig. 15.1 (see page 151)*. Thus, the percentage of agricultural land occupied by grassland varies from well in excess of 90% in most of the southwest, west, north and north midlands to 70-85% in the remainder of the country (the tillage crop areas).

The relative amounts of the three grassland types described above are shown in *Table 19.1*. Rough mountain and hill grazing and

Table 19.1 Distribution of grassland types, 1990

Category of grassland	Area (ha, millions)	% of total agricultural land
1. Rough mountain and hill grazing	1.04	18.2
2. Permanent grassland	2.93	51.3
3. Ley	1.24	21.7

permanent grasslands are found throughout the country. Leys are most commonly found in the tillage crop areas and on intensive dairy farms.

19.3 Grassland Ecology

The natural vegetation for most of Ireland is *deciduous forest*. In the absence of grazing, therefore, grass would be merely the first phase of vegetation in the natural progression from bare soil to forest. The phases of this progression are:
1. Bare soil
2. Grasses
3. Shrubs, such as bramble, hawthorn, hazel and blackthorn
4. Forest species such as oak, ash, birch and others which form the final natural vegetation, eliminating shrubs by their shading effect

Intensive grazing prevents this progression from going further than the grassland stage. This is so because grasses are able to regenerate themselves from growing points *close to the ground* and *below grazing height (Fig. 19.1)*. Thus they are able to compete favourably with shrubs which do not have this property and so they

Fig 19.1 Structure of grass plant: (a) general structure: note main shoot and tillers, (b) position of stem apex and tiller bud

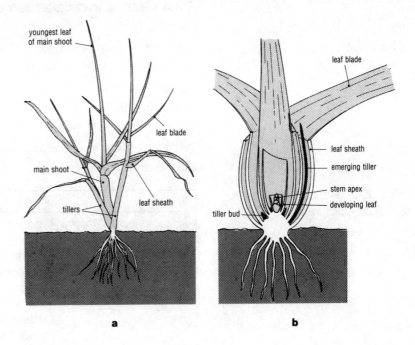

remain dominant. Grassland is, therefore, a *semi-natural association of plants* which, if grazing is reduced, tends to revert to scrub or forest.

In the same way that taller species (trees) become dominant in the natural change from bare soil to forest, in grassland ecosystems *taller species* tend to dominate whenever grazing intensity is light. The *shorter, leafier* species are, however, more nutritious and are thus of more agricultural value. Growth of these species (the "agricultural" species) is encouraged by *intensive grazing* and *high levels of soil fertility.*

This principle applies to all categories of grassland.

(A) In *rough mountain and hill grazing,* increased stocking and lime and fertilizer use encourage bent grasses, sheep's fescue and creeping red fescue at the expense of heathers, purple moor grass and mat grass *(see Table 19.2).*

(B) In *permanent grassland,* perennial ryegrass, white clover and other agricultural species increase in amount at the expense of a range of less valuable weed grasses such as sweet vernal grass, Yorkshire fog and meadow foxtail.

(C) In *leys,* perennial ryegrass and clovers are the principal sown species and their dominance in the sward (or short grazed pasture) continues only as long as it is heavily stocked and soil fertility maintained at a high level.

The farmer, therefore, can *manage* his grassland in such a way as to maintain or improve its botanical composition and production capacity.

19.4 Grassland Species of Agricultural Importance

About 200 grasses and other grassland species are indigenous to Ireland but only a small number of these are of practical agricultural importance. These are listed in *Table 19.2*. Species which are palatable to stock and productive are denoted by an asterisk. Perennial ryegrass, short duration ryegrasses and white and red clover are given extra asterisks on account of their great importance.

Table 19.2 *Grassland species of agricultural importance*

Species	Common name	Scientific name
A. Species found in *rough mountain and hill grazing*	Mat grass Heathers Purple moor grass *Bent grasses *Sheep's fescue *Creeping red fescue *Meadow foxtail *Meadow grasses	*Nardus stricta* *Calluna* spp. *Molinia caerulea* **Agrostis* spp **Festuca ovina* **Festuca rubra* **Alopecurus pratensis* **Poa* spp.
B. Species found in *permanent grassland*	Bent grasses Sheep's fescue Creeping red fescue Meadow foxtail Meadow grasses Crested dogstail *Cocksfoot *Meadow fescue *Timothy ***Perennial ryegrass **White clover	*Agrostis* spp. *Festuca ovina* *Festuca rubra* *Alopecurus pratensis* *Poa* spp. *Cynosurus cristatus* **Dactylis glomerata* **Festuca pratensis* **Phleum pratense* **** Lolium perenne* ***Trifolium repens*
C. Species found in *leys*	Cocksfoot Timothy ***Perennial ryegrass ***Short duration ryegrasses **White clover **Red clover	*Dactylis glomerata* *Phleum pratense* ****Lolium perenne* ****Lolium* spp. ***Trifolium repens* ***Trifolium pratense*
* Palatable, productive species - valuable in sward		
, * Most palatable, productive species - very valuable in sward		

It can be seen that there is some overlapping of species in *Table 19.2*. Species considered valuable in the acid soil conditions of rough mountain and hill grazing are present in permanent grassland also. They are, however, of less value there because of the better soil and climatic conditions which are capable of supporting other, more productive species.

Farmers aiming for top productivity from permanent grassland would lime, fertilize and graze heavily to promote the growth of perennial ryegrass, white clover, cocksfoot, meadow fescue and timothy.

There is further overlap between the species in permanent grassland and leys. However, only perennial ryegrass and white and red clover are considered fully desirable in leys because of the high level of productivity expected.

19.4.1 Characteristics determining agricultural importance

Grassland in Ireland is utilized solely for feeding farm animals and the characteristics which determine the merit of individual species are related to its usage. They are: productivity, palatability and digestibility.

1. *Productivity:* Grassland species vary in their productivity, i.e. in their ability to produce large quantities of herbage. The potential to respond to fertilizer use is the first essential of any species considered for sowing or encouraging its growth in grassland. Productivity values for some of the species already listed in *Table 19.2* illustrate this point *(Table 19.3)*.

Table 19.3 Productivity of four grass species

Species	Productivity
(a) Mat grass	Very low
(b) Crested dogstail	Low
(c) Bent grasses	Medium
(d) Perennial ryegrass	Very high

Species (a) and (b) are suitable only for sheep grazing in areas not easily improved by reclamation and fertilization. Species (c) is somewhat better but only species (d) is considered suitable for sowing.

2. *Palatability:* If species are not palatable, then they are undesirable in grassland. This is because cattle and sheep are *selective* grazers and tend to ignore the unpalatable species and concentrate on palatable ones. This leads to the pasture becoming patchy. The ungrazed areas develop into strong tufts which increase in size over time and lower the overall productivity of the sward. *Table 19.4* shows the extent to which palatability varies between species.

Table 19.4 Palatability rating (maximum 100) of five grass species

Species	Palatability rating (max: 100)
(a) Mat grass	25
(b) Bent grasses	40
(c) Sheep's fescue	70
(d) Cocksfoot	85
(e) Perennial ryegrass	100

3. *Digestibility:* Digestibility refers to the degree to which a food material is retained and assimilated by the body. Food material which passes through the animal body unaltered and is voided in faeces or urine is wasteful as it does not contribute to the production of milk, meat or wool.

Table 19.5 Digestibility of some constituents of grass

Constituent	Digestibility (%)
Soluble carbohydrates	100
Protein	80
Cellulose	70
Fibre	35

Fig. 19.2 Changes with time in the dry matter digestibility (DMD) of grass; (a) and (b) are explained in the text

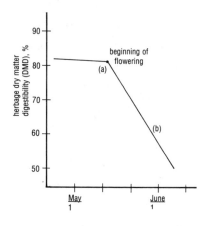

The constituents of grass vary greatly in digestibility *(Table 19.5)*. When growth is vegetative, there is a large concentration of soluble carbohydrates (starches and sugars) in the plant. When grass begins to produce flowering stems, however, these need strength to support the seed heads. This is provided by an increase in fibre at the expense of soluble carbohydrates and protein. This causes a reduction in the overall digestibility of the grass, from values of 80% or greater before flowering to 50-60 % one month later *(Fig. 19.2)*.

There are differences between grass species and varieties in date of flowering ("a" in *Fig. 19.2*) and rate of decrease of digestibility after flowering ("b" in *Fig. 19.2*). These lead to differences in the amounts of digestible dry matter produced (dry matter is vegetation from which the water has been removed). *Table 19.6* shows these differences and the superiority of perennial ryegrass is clearly seen.

Table 19.6 Amounts of digestible dry matter produced by four grasses

Species/strain	Digestible (i.e. > 65% DMD) dry matter produced in early summer growth, tonnes ha^{-1}
(a) Cocksfoot	5.5
(b) Timothy	6.5
(c) Perennial ryegrass, strain 24	7.8
(d) Perennial ryegrass, strain 23	8.4

19.4.2 Species sown by farmers

The principal species sown by farmers and the amounts sown are shown in *Table 19.7*.

(a) *Perennial ryegrass:* This is a grass whose superiority to all others in productivity, palatability and digestibility has already been shown. It is by far the most important agricultural grass in Ireland. Apart from the amount sown in leys by farmers *(Table 19.7)*, it makes up a large part of much well-managed permanent grassland.

Table 19.7 Grassland species used in agricultural seeds mixtures in Ireland 1990

Species	% of weight of seed sold
Perennial ryegrass	84.70
Italian ryegrass	5.60
White clover	4.10
Red clover	0.01
Other grasses	5.59

Perennial ryegrass, in its vegetative stage of growth, is characterised by a dark green colour and shiny leaves which give the sward a glistening sheen *(Fig. 19.3)*. Its inflorescence is shown in *Fig. 19.4*.

Fig. 19.3 Sward dominated by perennial ryegrass

It has a longer growing season than most other grasses. Its early spring and late autumn growth are of special value to farmers as they mean a saving on winter feed costs.

Perennial ryegrass *tillers more vigorously* and has a more *prostrate growth habit* than other grasses. This means that it is an "aggressive" grass. When properly managed (i.e. regularly grazed and well-fertilized), it tends to become the dominant species in the sward. It also has a high level of *persistence* and thus is very suitable for sowing in long-term leys.

To grow satisfactorily, however, perennial ryegrass needs good soil conditions, namely *free drainage, high soil pH (> 6.0)* and a *moderate/high level of soil fertility*. It is, consequently, a grass usually associated with good soils and high levels of farm management.

(b) *Short-duration ryegrasses:* The principal grass in this category is *Italian ryegrass (Lolium multiflorum)*, a biennial which may persist into a third year. It is similar in general appearance to perennial ryegrass but has awned seeds *(Fig. 19.5)*, a more

spikelet

Fig. 19.4 Inflorescence of perennial ryegrass

Fig. 19.5 Inflorescence of Italian ryegrass

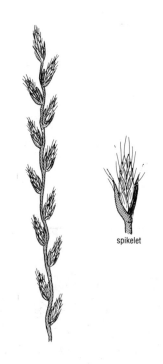

spikelet

Fig. 19.6 White clover plant

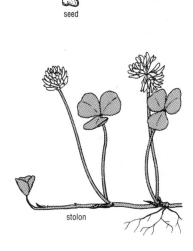

seed

stolon

erect growth habit and less vigorous tillering capacity.

Italian ryegrass has a longer growing season and produces 15-20 % more herbage than perennial. It can thus provide "early bite" for dairy cows but its main use in farming is as a grass sown to give heavy yields of *high quality silage*. It can be cut 4 or 5 times per season for this purpose. The best-known variety is RVP. Italian ryegrass, like perennial, requires good soil conditions and liberal fertilizer use.

Hybrid ryegrasses are crosses between Italian and perennial ryegrasses. The objective in making such crosses is to combine the high yields and long growing season of Italian with the persistence of perennial ryegrass.

(c) *Clovers (white and red):* These are legumes, having the ability to fix atmospheric N *(see page 65)* both for their own use and that of accompanying grasses. *White clover* is the more important and is an integral part of most long-term leys. It contributes protein-rich herbage as well as improving the N status of the soil. White clover is a glabrous perennial plant with white flowers. Its prostrate growth habit makes it very suited to grazing situations, with leaves growing upwards directly from the stolons *(Fig. 19.6)*.

The stolons root easily at the nodes on being trodden into the soil and the resulting dense ground cover gives good weed control in pastures.

When white clover makes up 30% of the herbage of a sward, it is capable of fixing 200-250 kg N ha^{-1} y^{-1}. Up to 130 kg ha^{-1} y^{-1} is transferred to the grass. However, the application of fertilizer N to a sward causes the clover content to decrease. As a rule of thumb, every 2 kg ha^{-1} of fertilizer N applied leads to a decrease of 1 kg ha^{-1} of clover N. Therefore, where heavy N fertilization is practised (i.e. more than 200 kg ha^{-1} y^{-1}), the N contribution of clover to the sward is negligible. In most farming situations in Ireland, however, this is not the case and white clover makes an important contribution to pasture growth.

Red clover is of less agricultural significance than white clover. It is used only to a limited extent in very short-term leys sown for silage crops. It has a more upright growth habit than white clover with hairy leaves and stems and red flowers. Its capacity to fix atmospheric N and its reaction to artificial N fertilizers are similar to those of white clover.

19.4.3 Other species

While the species dealt with above (perennial ryegrass, short-duration ryegrasses and clovers) have superseded all others in seeds mixtures, many other valuable species exist and are found in abundance in Irish pastures. Some of these have already been listed in *Table 19.2*. Some, such as *timothy, meadow fescue, cocksfoot* and the *meadow grasses* were widely sown by farmers in the past. They were gradually replaced in seeds mixtures, however, by strains of perennial and short duration ryegrass which were found to produce larger quantities of palatable digestible herbage. Nevertheless, these grasses are of great importance in permanent pastures and farmers should be able to recognise them and encourage their presence by proper management. The inflorescences of the most important of these grasses are shown in *Fig. 19.7*.

Fig. 19.7 Inflorescences of (a) timothy, (b) meadow fescue, (c) cocksfoot, (d) meadow grass

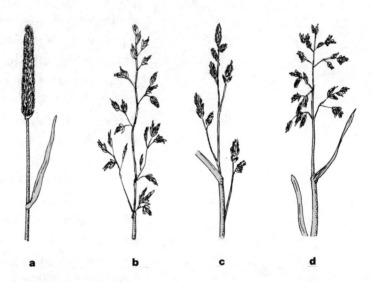

16.4.4 Seeds mixtures

(a) *For grazing:* In the past, seeds mixtures used in sowing leys for grazing were complex, with up to eight or more different grasses and clovers included. This was the case because perennial ryegrass, the main ingredient, tended to have a growth pattern with spring and autumn production peaks and a mid-season trough *(Fig. 19.8, a)*.

Fig. 19.8 Growth pattern of (a) earlier and (b) present-day strains of perennial ryegrass

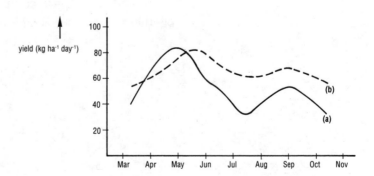

Clovers and some non-ryegrass species (e.g. timothy, cocksfoot, meadow fescue) which all have *mid-season growth peaks* were sown to ensure uniform production over the whole growing season. However, it was found in practice that sowing seeds mixtures such as these influenced the botanical composition of the pasture for only a year or two. After this, perennial ryegrass and white clover became the dominant species.

In recent years there has been a swing towards the sowing of ryegrasses and clovers only and this is reflected in figures shown earlier in *Table 19.7*. This swing has been further influenced by the successful breeding of new *strains* of perennial ryegrass which have mid- and late-season growth peaks. Thus, seeds mixtures now contain a number of varietal strains of perennial ryegrass with a range of heading dates, together with white clover.

This gives the following advantages:

1. It encourages a uniform growth pattern over the grazing season *(Fig. 19.8, b)*.

2. It increases the feeding value of the grass. Sowing a mixture of strains ensures that a proportion of the sward is always in the young, leafy, highly-digestible stage of growth.

3. It makes grazing management easier. The timing of grazings is less critical than with single-strain pastures, since the whole sward cannot go stemmy at the same time if grazing is neglected.

(b) *For cutting (silage):* In contrast to the grazing situation, mixtures for silage are either made up of strains of ryegrass with similar heading dates or contain a single strain only. This is because the crops are cut for conservation on a small number of occasions per season. The farmer is more interested in obtaining large amounts of digestible dry matter than in a steady supply of feed for grazing animals.

In addition to the differences attributable to grazing/cutting requirements, further differences in composition are found between seeds mixtures designed for short-, medium- and long-term leys. *Table 19.8* shows typical compositions for the full range of ley types, together with two seeds mixtures commercially available.

(a)	Short-term (2-3 yrs)	Medium-term (3-5 yrs)	Long-term (> 5yrs)
Cutting (silage)	20 of IRG 15 of PRG	10 of IRG 10 of PRG (early) 10 of PRG (intermediate)	
Grazing	20 of IRG 15 of PRG	12 of PRG (early) 6 of PRG (intermediate) 4 of PRG (late) 2 of white clover	10 of PRG (early) 10 of PRG (intermediate) 6 of PRG (late) 2 of white clover
General purpose (cutting and grazing)		8 of PRG (early) 8 of PRG (intermediate) 8 of PRG (late) 2 of white clover	8 of PRG (early) 8 of PRG (intermediate) 8 of PRG (late) 2 of white clover, 2 of red clover

(b) Silage mixture	General purpose mixture
10.0 Citadel tetraploid PRG 4.5 Everest tetraploid PRG 7.5 Magella PRG 7.5 Parcour PRG 1.2 New Zealand white clover	3.5 *Lemtal* RVP (IRG) 3.5 *Green Isle* (tetraploid) PRG 3.5 *Frances* PRG 4.0 *Talbot* PRG 2.0 *Sisu* PRG 6.5 *Meltra* (Tetraploid) PRG 5.5 *Vigor* PRG 2.0 *Grasslands Huia* white clover

Notes:

1. PRG = perennial ryegrass; IRG = Italian ryegrass

2. All rates in kg ha^{-1}

3. Tetraploid strains give increased yield, frost resistance, palatability and digestibility

4. "Early", "intermediate" and "late" refer to times of growth-peaks for different strains of PRG

Table 19.8 (a) *Seeds mixtures for short-, medium- and long-term use, (b) two commercially available mixtures*

Fig 19.9 Cage made of netting wire and stakes. Note: the netting wire should be attached to the stakes in such a way that it can be easily removed to allow botanical analysis

Exercises

Exercise 50. Examining the effects of grazing on the botanical composition of grassland

Materials needed
1. Stakes (wooden or metal, 0.7 m long), 12
2. Netting wire, 6 m

Procedure
1. Select an area of well-managed permanent grassland, i.e. one dominated by ryegrasses.
2. Install three cages in the area, using the stakes and netting wire (see *Fig. 19.9*).
3. Encourage the continuation of good management in the grassland outside the cages. Ensure that fertilizer-use and grazing intensity are high.

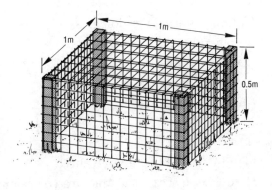

4. Do not fertilize the area under or around the cages. A strip 1m wide around each cage should not be fertilized.
5. Do not graze or cut the grass in the cages.
6. Compare the botanical composition of general *vs* caged grassland initially and twice per year thereafter. In addition to detailed botanical analysis, analysis under the following headings will be useful:
    (a) Agricultural grasses and clovers
    (b) Weed grasses
    (c) Broad leaved weeds
    (d) Woody-stemmed plants etc.

Note: The exercise should be carried out on an on-going basis over a number of years.

Results

1. Record results regularly. Add your results to those already collected so that a picture of the gradual change in botanical composition can emerge.
2. Relate the results to your knowledge of grassland ecology.

Exercise 51. Identification of grass inflorescences

Materials needed

1. Preserved (dried) inflorescences of:
    (a) Perennial ryegrass
    (b) Italian ryegrass
    (c) Cocksfoot
    (d) Timothy
    (e) Meadow fescue
    (f) Rough-stalked meadow grass
    (g) Smooth-stalked meadow grass
    (h) Meadow foxtail
    (i) Crested dogstail
    (j) Sweet vernal grass

Procedure

1. Identify each of the inflorescences.
2. Make a sketch of each and write an accompanying note on the importance or otherwise of the grass.
3. Collect samples of the inflorescences and press and mount them to make a collection.

20 – Sowing and Establishing Grasses

20.1 Methods of Sowing

Leys may be sown in four different ways: *direct sowing, undersowing, direct drilling* and *"stitching-in"*. The essentials of these methods are as follows:

20.1.1 Direct sowing

This is the most reliable way to obtain a good ley. In this method, the seeds mixture is sown directly into a seedbed prepared specifically for it by ploughing and harrowing the ground. The seedbed should be finer than that for cereals on account of the smaller seed size.

In *spring-sown leys*, fertilizer is broadcast onto the soil and worked in during the final seedbed preparations. The seeds are then drilled into the soil using a drill similar in design to a corn-drill (combine drill). However, it sows the seed in closer lines (10 cm) and at a shallower depth (2 cm). They can alternatively be broadcast onto the soil and covered using a chain harrow.

In either case, the seedbed should be fine and firm and the land should be rolled after sowing to give good soil/seed contact and germination. Spring-sown leys should not be sown after May 1 due to the risk of *drought*.

In *autumn-sown leys*, the seedbed is prepared and the seeds sown in the same way as for spring-sown leys. Most of the N fertilizer is not spread until the following spring, however. The seedbed is only lightly rolled unless the weather is very dry. These leys should not be sown later than mid-September; otherwise *cold conditions* may kill the young seedlings.

20.1.2 Undersowing

This method is most commonly practised by farmers who employ tillage/grass rotations. The grass seeds are sown with a tillage crop, usually a spring cereal. The two crops grow together over the summer *(Fig. 20.1)*. Then, after the cereal has been harvested, establishment and utilization of the grassland begins.

Fig. 20.1 Grass seeds undersown to barley

barley ('nurse' crop)

undersown grasses

The land should be ploughed in the autumn and then the seed-bed prepared and the cereal sown in the usual way the following spring. The grass seeds are sown immediately after the cereal, preferably using a drill, and the land is finally rolled.

There is always some degree of competition between the "nurse" crop and the undersown grass. Because of this, spring barley is the most suitable cereal for undersowing, having short straw and an early harvest. To lessen the risk of lodging of the cereal, which would damage the grass, N application should be reduced by 30%. The use of herbicides on the cereal crop has to be restricted if clover is included in the undersown seeds mixture. Because of these constraints, specialised cereal farmers, who aim for very high yields, have abandoned the practice of undersowing.

Undersowing grass to an arable silage crop (e.g. oats/vetch, oats/beans) is good farming practice. The silage is cut early and the grass crop has a very good chance of becoming well-established.

20.1.3 Direct drilling

This is a recently developed technique in which grass seeds are drilled into unploughed ground. The drilling machine *(Fig. 20.2)* cultivates a narrow strip of soil and sows the seeds in it. If grass seeds are direct drilled into stubble, the operation is straight-forward and usually successful.

Fig. 20.2 (a) Section through a direct drill, showing one cultivating and seeding unit, (b) section through the ground surface after drilling

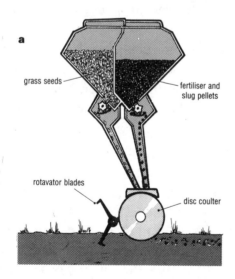

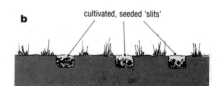

Direct drilling into grassland presents more problems. Firstly, the old sward should be grazed bare or mown and then killed with a herbicide (usually paraquat, applied at 5 l ha^{-1}). Then fertilizer and slug pellets are drilled with the grass seeds to give them the best chance of growing well and establishing a thick, dense sward.

Direct drilling is of most value on (a) *shallow soils* which cannot be easily ploughed and on (b) *heavy soils subject to poaching* by animals, the root-mat of the old sward giving extra strength to the soil.

20.1.4 "Stitching-in"

This method is also known as *slit-seeding* and uses machinery very similar to that used in direct drilling. Stitching-in is always used on grassland and differs from direct drilling in that the old grassland is not killed. Thus, if the "stitched-in" seeds do not grow successfully, the old grassland continues to grow and quickly colonises the cultivated slits. If, on the other hand, the sown seeds grow well, then the aggressiveness of the ryegrasses causes them to become dominant in a year or two giving a dense, highly productive sward.

Successful germination and establishment of the stitched-in seeds may be encouraged by a number of measures, including:

(a) checking the growth of the old grassland by severe grazing and cutting back on N use. A small amount (0.75 l ha^{-1}) of paraquat herbicide may also be used,

(b) drilling fertilizer into the cultivated slit with the grass seeds,

(c) drilling slug pellets into the cultivated slit with the grass seeds.

As with direct drilling, stitching-in is of most value on shallow soils and soils subject to poaching.

20.2 Grassland Establishment

This refers to the progression from newly emerged grass seedlings to thick, closely knit grassland. Good establishment is of most importance in *pasture*, since a close sward with a well-developed root-mat is required to support grazing animals and prevent poaching. The most important factor in grassland establishment is the extent to which *tillering* occurs.

Tillering is encouraged by defoliation and/or damage to the main shoots of the grass plants. This is best achieved by grazing newly sown pastures with light stock such as calves or sheep. Heavy animals such as cows should not be used for most or all of the first year as they tend to poach the land due to soft soil conditions.

Spring-sown pastures (except for undersown ones) are most easily established in this way. This is so because they can be grazed repeatedly with light stock over the summer, when the soil is relatively dry and resistant to poaching. This ensures that the pastures achieve good ground cover quickly without allowing the entry of weeds. With autumn-sown pastures, wet soil conditions often limit the farmer to one grazing with very light stock.

Annual weeds in newly sown pastures are easily controlled. Repeated grazing and/or *topping* (mowing at a height of 8-10 cm) encourages tillering of the grasses and prevents the weeds from seeding themselves. They will then disappear at the end of the first year. *Perennial weeds* such as dock, may present more of a problem. Grazing and topping help to control them, but if they persist, the pasture may have to be sprayed with a selective herbicide.

Soil fertility must be kept at a high level during the period of establishment. This encourages the sown grasses to tiller well and become quickly dominant and is achieved by adequate use of fertilizers *(see page 204).*

Exercises

Exercise 52. Comparison of establishment and botanical composition of direct-sown and undersown grassland

Materials needed
1. Area of direct-sown grassland
2. Area of undersown grassland
3. Sampling quadrat (1 m x 1 m)

Procedure
Note: Ideally, this exercise should be carried out 1-2 years after the grasses have sown. Otherwise, a false impression of the merit of the two methods of establishment may be obtained.
1. Place the sampling quadrat randomly in the direct-sown area. Decide on the percentage of area occupied by:
   (a) Perennial ryegrass
   (b) Clover
   (c) Other grasses
   (d) Broad-leaved weeds
   (e) Bare soil
   Carefully record your findings.
2. Repeat step 1 for undersown grassland.
3. Repeat steps 1 and 2 in two or three further randomly selected locations.

Results
1. Obtain mean values of (a) - (e) above for the two methods of establishment.
2. Answer the question: on the basis of the results, which method do you consider the better?

21 – Grassland Management

Good grassland management involves:
1. deciding on the amount of output of herbage required,
2. applying enough fertilizers to achieve this output, and
3. managing utilization (grazing and conservation) in such a way as to maximise the intake of digestible dry matter.

The *level of herbage output required* is decided by every farmer individually. It is governed by the type and number of grazing animals on the farm. When these are expressed in the form of *livestock units*, the total amount of herbage required to feed the stock can be calculated, using the rule that 1 livestock unit consumes 12 tonnes of herbage dry matter per annum.

21.1 Fertilizer Use

21.1.1 Grazing land

Since *new pastures* are not grazed as intensively as established pastures, the amounts of fertilizers applied are not as great. When sowing is done in spring, fertilizers are usually worked into the seedbed. The amounts applied depend on soil test results. At average levels of soil fertility, the recommended amounts of fertilizers would be:

$$N: 48 \text{ kg ha}^{-1}$$
$$P: 20 \text{ kg ha}^{-1}$$
$$K: 38 \text{ kg ha}^{-1}$$

On autumn-sown pastures, about the same amount of P and K is applied. N is reduced to 30 kg ha^{-1} or less, since the pasture will probably either not be grazed at all before winter or grazed very lightly once. If the grass grows too tall and cannot be grazed, it may fall over and rot at the base, leaving bare patches the following spring.

The amounts of N applied for the remainder of the first year depend on the rate at which the pasture establishes itself and becomes capable of supporting high grazing intensities. The farmer's priority should be the satisfactory development of the sward rather than productivity.

Fertilization programmes for *established pastures* depend very much on the level of farm management and grazing intensity. Recommendations made by Teagasc take these considerations into account and are as shown in *Table 21.1*.

Grazing intensity over the growing season	Soil fertility	Fertilizer application (kg ha^{-1})		
		Phosphorus	Potassium	Nitrogen
Medium (2.5 LU ha^{-1})	High	18.75 in spring	37.5 in spring	56.0 in spring
	Low	37.5 in spring	75.0 in spring	100.0 in *two* applications
High (3.7 LU ha^{-1})	High	do.	do.	250.0 in *six* applications
	Low	do.	do.	350.0 in *six* applications
Very high (4.5 LU ha^{-1})	High	do.	do.	375.0 in *nine* applications
	Low	do.	do.	475.0 in *nine* applications

Table 21.1 Teagasc recommendations for fertilizer application on established pastures

Table 21.2 Teagasc recommendations for fertilizer application for silage and hay

21.1.2 Land for Silage and Hay

Grassland may be cut repeatedly for silage over the grazing season, whereas a crop of hay is taken only once. Fertilizers must be applied in advance of each harvest. Teagasc recommendations are given in *Table 21.2*.

Crop	Fertilizer application (kg ha^{-1})								
Silage:	1st. Cut			2nd. Cut			3rd Cut		
	N	P	K	N	P	K	N	P	K
1 cut	100	35	150	–	–	–	–	–	–
2 cuts	125	35	150	88	9	38	–	–	–
3 cuts	150	44	188	100	18	75	81	–	–
Hay:	75	26	112	–	–	–	–	–	–

21.2 Grazing Management

Short, leafy grass, in the vegetative stage of growth, is palatable to grazing animals and highly digestible. The key to good grazing management is to ensure that grass of this type is available to animals at all times. The best way to ensure this is to adopt a system of *rotational grazing*.

Rotational grazing involves rotating stock around a series of grazing areas in such a manner that they always graze short leafy grass. These areas may be *fields*, *paddocks* or *strips* of pasture and the system contrasts with set-stocking as shown in *Fig.21.1*.

21.2.1 Paddock-grazing

In this, the most efficient form of rotational grazing, 20-25 paddocks are created, using electric fencing *(Fig. 21.2)*. The paddocks are tailored to the herd size, using the rule of thumb that *120 cows will graze down 1 ha of young leafy grassland in one day*. Thus, the correct paddock size for a 60-cow herd is 0.5 ha, for a 180-cow herd 1.5 ha, and so on.

The herd grazes one paddock per day in a rotational manner. Each paddock is spread with N fertilizer as soon as the animals are

Fig. 21.1 Set-stocking vs rotational grazing (not all paddocks or strips are shown)

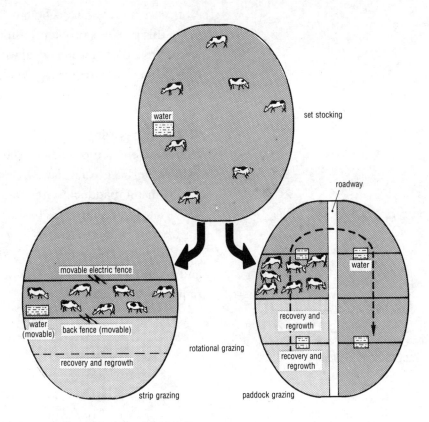

Fig.21.2 Paddock grazing system

removed. By the time the herd grazes the last paddock, the first paddock has again reached the correct growth stage for grazing and the cycle begins again.

Fencing, the creation of permanent roadways giving access to the paddocks, and the need to supply water to all paddocks are features which make this a very expensive system. The high incomes from dairy farming justify the costs involved, however, and paddock-grazing is widely used on dairy farms.

If excess grass has to be cut for silage in the May/June growth peak, this presents problems using cumbersome machinery in small areas. Most dairy farmers deal with this by grazing such excess grass with other stock (e.g. calves, replacement heifers) and keeping the silage fields independent of the paddock system.

21.2.2 Strip-grazing

In this system, a movable electric fence is used to give stock a fresh strip of herbage each day. Grazed strips are fertilized in the same way as in the paddock system and stock return to grazed strips 3-4 weeks later when the grass has regrown to the correct stage. For best utilization of the pasture, a *back fence* should be used, with or without a movable water supply *(Fig. 21.3)*. This prevents regrazing and treading of regrowth. Use of a back fence increases the labour requirements greatly, however,

Fig. 21.3 Strip-grazing (a) with a movable water supply, (b) without a movable water supply

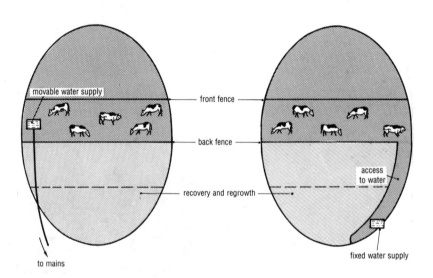

Strip-grazing is not as costly to set up as paddock-grazing. However, the high labour content, together with the problems of containing stock with temporary electric fencing, means that it is not commonly used on its own for rotational grazing purposes. It is, however, widely used in conjunction with block-grazing (*see below*).

21.2.3 Set-stocking

This is the simplest, least expensive to operate, but worst system of grazing management. Stock are allowed free access to all the grazing land over the grazing season. Pastures tend to be undergrazed during the May/June growth peak, giving rise to poor quality stemmy material later in the year. Set-stocked pastures also tend to become patchy and develop tussocks of unproductive grasses due to selective grazing.

Set-stocking is usually associated with poor farm management, low stocking rates and little or no use of fertilizers.

21.2.4 Block-grazing

This is also known as *field-by-field* grazing and is the system most commonly employed in Ireland.

In block-grazing, the grazing area is divided into blocks which provide grazing for periods of up to 7 or 8 days. The size of individual blocks is usually determined by the size and shape of existing fields, with only large fields being subdivided. This generally reduces fencing costs.

Stock graze the blocks in a rotational manner returning to each block 3-4 weeks after its previous grazing. Pasture management can be improved by using an electric fence to *strip-graze* blocks. Larger blocks can be set aside once or twice a year for silage production.

Block-grazing is not as efficient as paddock- or strip-grazing, because the grass in most blocks cannot *all* be grazed at the optimum growth stage. It is, however, a cheaper and easier system to set up and is used widely with all types of livestock - cows, beef animals and sheep.

22 – Conserving Grass as Silage or Hay

22.1 Principles of Conservation

The pattern of grassland production and use is shown in *Fig.22.1*. It shows that grass, in one form or another, provides almost all of the animals' feed requirements over the year.

Fig. 22.1 Pattern of grass production and use

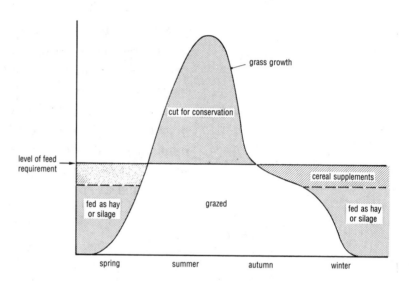

Conservation of grass for winter feed involves restricting the activity of bacteria and other micro-organisms which would otherwise cause spoilage or rotting. This involves using one of two contrasting approaches:

1. *Controlled fermentation* to reduce the pH of the grass to a level at which all microbial activity ceases. This approach is used in silage-making.

2. *Dehydration* of the grass to a level of dryness at which all microbial activity ceases. This approach is used in haymaking.

Silage-making is much more independent of the weather than haymaking. This makes it the better system of conservation for Irish farmers, given the showery nature of our summer weather. Grass can be cut for silage in May at the leafy, digestible stage, ensuring a high-quality winter feed. It is not feasible to cut grass for haymaking at this stage of growth, because sufficiently-long periods of warm dry weather cannot be expected.

Grass for hay, therefore, is allowed to grow to a more mature stage and is cut in June when it is not so lush and when the weather is warmer and drier. This means that hay has a lower feeding value than silage.

Silage-making is the more costly way of conserving grass, since it involves the use of expensive machinery and farm buildings. The high quality product is an essential part of winter feeding in well-managed dairy, beef and sheep farming, however. For this reason, silage at present accounts for 65% of grassland conserved. This compares with 45% twenty years ago.

22.2 Silage-making

22.2.1 Biochemical processes involved

When freshly cut green vegetation is made into a heap, it continues to respire until all the oxygen available is used up. Respiration involves oxidation of carbohydrates to carbon dioxide which means a loss of food value in the vegetation. Thus, as much of the air as possible should be squeezed out of the vegetation. In farming practice this is done by rolling the silage pit with a tractor.

When the oxygen is used up and the environment *anaerobic*, bacteria present on the vegetation begin to cause fermentation - conversion of carbohydrate to organic acids. This continues until the pH falls to a level at which all bacterial activity is inhibited and the material is "pickled" or preserved.

When the concentration of carbohydrates in the vegetation is *high*, the bacteria which control the fermentation process are *Lactobacillus* and *Streptococcus* spp. The acid produced is lactic acid. *Lactic acid* silage is palatable to stock, highly nutritious and can be kept safely for years provided air is excluded from it.

If, on the other hand, the concentration of carbohydrates is *low*, fermentation is controlled by *Clostridium* which leads to the formation of *butyric acid*. Butyric acid silage is unpalatable to stock, less nutritious than lactic acid silage and far less stable, lasting only a few months. Fuller details of the different silage types are shown in the table in *Exercise 55 (see page 217)*.

A farmer can encourage high levels of carbohydrates in the grass being ensiled by the following means:
1. Ensuring that the crop is not cut during or immediately after rain. Water on the grass reduces carbohydrate concentration.
2. Allowing the crop to wilt for some time (1-2 days) after cutting. This increases carbohydrate concentration.
3. Using double-chop or precision-chop harvesting equipment. These cut the grass into shorter lengths (5.5 cm and 1.0 cm, respectively) than the more common single-chop machines. While this practice does not alter the concentration of carbohydrates, it makes them more accessible to bacterial action.

4. Using a carbohydrate-rich *additive* (e.g. mollasses) on grass cut early in the year when it is likely to be lush and "sappy".

22.2.2 Practical procedures

Most silage is cut from fields of permanent grassland. Two cuts are normally taken, the first in mid-May and the second around July 1. On leys sown specially for silage, on the other hand, 3-5 cuts may be taken.

The grass should be cut at the correct *stage of growth*, i.e. when digestibility is high. In perennial ryegrass-dominant grassland, the dry matter digestibility (DMD) is 75-78% at the "heading-out" stage (this is defined as the stage when *half* the ryegrass plants have their seed-heads showing). The grass should be cut at this point, because DMD falls by 0.5% per day thereafter *(see Fig. 19.2, page 192)*. This loss in DMD more than offsets any increase in herbage yield obtained by delaying harvesting beyond the heading-out stage.

Fig.22.2 Forage harvester in operation

The sequence of events in the successful manufacture of silage is as follows:

1. The grass is harvested with a forage harvester which cuts, macerates and blows the grass into a silage-trailer *(Fig. 22.2)*.
2. The harvested grass is transported to the silage pit and heaped there.
3. An additive *(see below)* is used either at the pit or during harvesting, if it is considered necessary.
4. Matted lumps of grass, if present, are shaken loose and the surface levelled to lessen the risk of air pockets.
5. The grass in the pit is *rolled* repeatedly with tractors during the filling process to compact it and get rid of entrapped air.

6. When all the grass is in the pit and rolling completed, the pit is *sealed* with at least two layers of heavy-gauge polythene sheeting. This should then be further covered with ground limestone, farmyard manure, soil, old tyres, etc. This ensures that the upper layers of silage remain compact and reduces the risk of entry of air through the plastic, which is slightly porous.

7. The edges of the polythene sheeting are pulled tight and weighted down securely to complete the sealing of the pit. This is repeated once or twice more as the silage subsides over the following 2-3 weeks. A well-covered pit of silage is shown in *Fig. 22.3*.

Fig.22.3 A pit of silage, properly covered and sealed

22.2.3 Use of additives

Additives are used when the concentration of carbohydrates in the grass being ensiled is known or expected to be low. For safety, some farmers always use additives. Additives are of two types, stimulants and inhibitors.

*Stimulant*s are sources of carbohydrates and their presence ensures that lactic acid silage is formed. The stimulant most commonly used is *molasses* which contains 53% sucrose, and is applied at a rate of 10 l per tonne of cut grass. Molasses is applied onto the grass in the pit, an application being made to each layer of grass before it is rolled.

Inhibitors are acids which may initially encourage lactobacillus activity. Their main purpose, however, is to rapidly lower the pH to a level at which the grass is preserved and *all* bacterial activity inhibited. The acids commonly used are sulphuric and propionic. They are applied at rates of 3-5 l per tonne of cut grass during the cutting operation.

This results in very thorough mixing of the acid and the grass, and excellent conservation. The acids are highly corrosive to machinery, however, and it is recommended that acid should not be added to the last load of grass cut each day in order to clean out the harvesting machinery. Acids should also be handled carefully to avoid skin burns.

In practice, molasses is used more by farmers making small amounts of silage with their own machinery. Silage contractors and farmers making large quantities of silage rely almost exclusively on acids.

22.2.4 Silage storage

Silage is most commonly stored in pits or clamps. These may be either *wedge clamps* or *run-over clamps (Fig. 22.4)*. They should always be located on concrete so that effluent can be safely collected. Clamps made without the use of side walls involve lower capital costs but the sides of the clamp cannot be as easily rolled and there is a risk of tractor accidents.

The only other system of storage of silage of importance in Ireland is *round-bale silage*. In this system, the grass is cut with a mowing machine, wilted for 1 - 2 days, and then collected and made into round bales which are covered with plastic to make them airtight. The plastic can be either a large bag (which can be reused) or a self-sealing "bandage" wrapped mechanically around the bale.

wedge clamp

run-over clamp

Fig. 22.4 Types of silage clamps

Fig. 22.5 Round bales

The resulting product *(Fig. 22.5)* consists of heavy (500 kg approximately) separate units of silage which may be stored in the open and fed as required over the winter. Round-bale silage is more expensive than clamp silage but its manufacture is of value to the farmer in the following situations:

1. Silage can be made in this manner on soft, wet land which would not support conventional silage-making equipment.
2. Round bales can be made on land on which the cost of

constructing concrete silage-storage facilities is not justified. Examples of such land are small fields far from the farmyard and rented land.

3. Where the farmer intends to sell the silage, round bales are an easily handled, saleable product.

22.2.5 Silage effluent

This is a by-product of the fermentation process. It is an acidic material rich in nutrients which seeps from silage for 2-3 weeks after it has been sealed. Effluent has a high Biological Oxygen Demand value *(see p. 385)*. If it is allowed to make its way to rivers or streams, it will kill many organisms there, including fish.

For this reason, effluent should be collected and stored carefully before being safely disposed of. Effluent is usually stored in underground pits and then diluted with water before being spread on land, where it has a small fertilizer value. Care should be taken to spread it only when there is no risk of surface run-off.

Table 22.1 Effect of moisture content at ensiling on amount of effluent produced

% Moisture at ensiling	Amount of effluent produced per tonne of silage, l
85-90	400
80-84	150
75-79	60
<75	0

The quantity of effluent produced is related to the moisture content of the grass being ensiled as shown in *Table 22.1*. The highest moisture content values are the result of cutting after rainfall while the lowest are brought about by wilting. Wilting, therefore, has the double advantage of (a) minimising effluent storage and disposal problems and (b) ensuring high carbohydrate concentration in the grass with consequent good conservation.

22.2.6 Silage quality

Table 22.2 Parameters of silage quality and how they are influenced

The main criteria of silage quality and the management practices influencing them are shown in *Table 22.2*.

Parameter	Correct value	Factors affecting
pH	4	(a) Procedures used in ensiling (use of additives, compaction etc.)
DM (%)	20	(a) Stage of growth at cutting, (b) wetness at cutting
DMD (%)	70-75	(a) Stage of growth at cutting, (b) grass variety, (c) procedures used in ensiling
Protein (%)	14-16	(a) Stage of growth at cutting
*ME (MJ kg^{-1})	10-11	(a) Stage of growth at cutting, (b) procedures used in ensiling
*See page 302		

Silage quality can be accurately assessed by laboratory analysis. Many farmers arrange for this to be done so that they can make fullest use of it as a foodstuff. A simpler means of estimating silage quality is described in *Exercise 55*.

22.3 Haymaking

Baled hay is a clean, conveniently handled winter feed with very little waste. It is particularly useful for farmers out-wintering stock on land far removed from the farmyard. There are problems associated with the use of hay, however, the main one being its generally low feeding value. This can be the result of cutting the crop too late in the year, or encountering bad weather during the hay-making process, or both.

The chances of successfully making good quality hay are greatly improved if attention is paid to the principles outlined below. Since 35% of grass for winter fodder is still conserved as hay, it is desirable that farmers become more aware of these principles and put them into practice.

1. *Cut at the correct growth stage.* Grass for hay should be cut as close to June 1 as the weather allows. While grass cut earlier has a higher level of DMD, it is difficult to save it (dry it) unless a prolonged spell of hot dry weather occurs. Thus, it is safer to wait until early June. To ensure a heavy crop of hay, the field should be closed to grazing animals and fertilized in mid-April. A typical fertilizer application is 75 kg ha^{-1} N, 26 kg ha^{-1} P and 112 kg ha^{-1} K.

2. *Cut when dry weather is expected.* The objective in haymaking is to dry the crop from its moisture content at the time of cutting, 80%, to a moisture content safe for storage, 20% or less. This is most easily achieved in warm dry weather, preferably with some wind. Farmers should wait for the first expected period of such weather after June 1 before cutting their crop.

   While the general weather forecasts broadcast on radio and television are useful for predicting dry spells, regional forecasts are more useful and reliable. These are available from the Meteorological Service throughout the year and special emphasis is placed on likely drying conditions during the hay-making season. These regional forecasts are available on an automatic phone-in recording basis. They are available for all regions of the country and are updated several times daily.

3. *Use the correct machinery.* Unrestricted access to three items of machinery is essential. These are:

   (a) Rotary mower: this machine can cut at a rate of 1.2 - 1.5 ha hr^{-1} and can be operated easily and without breakdowns in

heavy or lodged crops. This is important if short periods of good haymaking weather are to be fully utilized.

(b) Power-driven rotary tedder: this machine has the abiltiy to work at high speed and to shake out and separate the grass stems thoroughly. This leaves a "fluffed-up" swath of grass which dries quickly *(Fig. 22.6).*

Fig.22.6 Power-driven rotary tedder in action

(c) Baler: when the crop has been dried to the safe moisture content, it is essential to protect it from rainfall immediately. This is best achieved by using a *baler* (which has the capacity to bale 8-10 ha day^{-1}) and then moving the bales into covered storage as quickly as possible.

4. *Cut the crop in manageable amounts.* Where large quantities of hay are being made, it is important to cut only as much hay in a day as can be conveniently (a) tedded *twice* in a day and (b) baled in a day. If this rule is not observed, then the crop cannot be saved in the fastest possible time, and the risk of weather-damage is greatly increased. Baling is the slowest operation in haymaking. Therefore, if the baler being used has a maximum capacity of 10 ha day^{-1}, the crop should be cut in 10 ha lots.

5. *Ted frequently to ensure fast drying.* Fast drying is important for two reasons; firstly it lessens the risk of weather damage. Secondly, since grass continues to respire after cutting, fast drying minimises respiration and consequent losses of carbohydrate from the crop.

The power-driven rotary tedder *(see above)* gives the best swath conditions for fast drying. Tedding should commence as soon as possible after cutting. Unless hay is cut late in the evening, it should be tedded the same day. Thereafter, hay should be tedded whenever the top of the crop is *noticeably drier* than the bottom. In good drying conditions, this means tedding two or even three times in a day. Special attention should be given to frequent tedding in unsettled weather as it may enable the baling of the crop one or two days earlier and possibly before the weather breaks.

The rotary hay tedder can be *adjusted* to ted with varying degrees of roughness. The crop can and should be tedded roughly immediately after cutting. It is still soft and pliable and is not easily damaged. It also needs to be well shaken out so that it covers the ground fully. As drying proceeds, however, tedding should be gentler as there is a greater risk of mechanical damage. If damage occurs, it is the most nutritious leaf material which is lost *(Fig. 22.7)*.

Fig.22.7 Mechanical damage caused by tedding: (a) properly tedded stem, (b) stem which was tedded too roughly

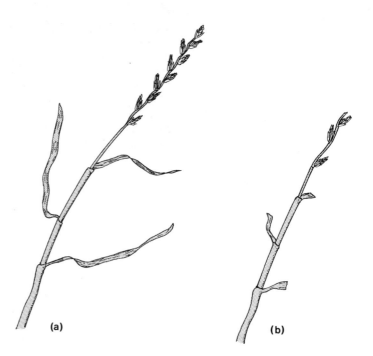

(a)   (b)

6. *Bale and remove to storage without delay.* The last operation before baling is to use the tedder to gather the crop into rows which are picked up by the baler. In good weather this may be done before the crop is fully dry, the final drying being allowed to take place in these rows. Usually, however, baling begins as soon as rowing is completed.

Baling should not be delayed once the crop is fully dry as further drying reduces the food value of hay by oxidising starch and denaturing proteins. Likewise, when fully dry hay is baled, it should be removed to storage immediately. Every day it is left in the field represents a gamble. This is because, while bales can withstand small showers, they take in water during prolonged rainfall and may rot and be lost completely.

Exercises

Exercise 53. Determination of dry matter content of grass, hay and silage

Materials needed
1. Samples of fresh grass, hay and silage
2. Beakers (600 ml), 6
3. Oven

Procedure
Measure the DM content, in duplicate, of the samples in the manner already described for potatoes *(see Exercise 48, page 181)*.

Results
1. Record results.
2. Comment on them.
3. Using the results for fresh grass and silage, calculate the quantity of effluent which might be expected when making silage. Assume that the quantity made was 200 tonnes.

Exercise 54. Estimation of sugars in grass for silage

Materials needed
1. Sample of fresh grass at the young leafy stage
2. Plastic bag
3. Freezer
4. Refractometer

Procedure
1. Ensure that the sample of grass is dry, i.e. no moisture on the leaves. A wet sample leads to dilution of the sugars and incorrect results.
2. Place the sample in a plastic bag and roll up the bag so that the air is removed.
3. Place in a freezer and leave there until frozen.
4. Remove from the freezer. The cells in the leaves have burst during freezing. Squeeze out a drop of cell sap onto the refractometer and obtain a reading *(see Exercise 21)*.

5. Obtain readings with two further drops of sap.

Results
1. Calculate the mean refractometer reading.
2. Estimate the percentage soluble carbohydrates using *Table 22.3*.
3. Estimate the amount of additive (acid) to add to the grass during silage-making.

Refractometer reading	0-4	5-6	7-8	9-10	>10
% water-soluble carbohydrates in grass	<1.5	1.5-2	2-3	3-4	>4
Required addition of acid (l tonne $^{-1}$)	4.5	3.5	2.5	1.5-Nil	Nil

Table 22.3 *Percentage soluble carbohydrates in grass and required addition of acid for silage-making at five refractometer readings*

Exercise 55. Determination of silage quality in situ

Materials needed
1. Access to silage pit
2. Portable pH-meter, if available

Procedure
1. Go to a freshly cut face of the silage pit. Remove samples and examine for:
   (a) colour, (b) smell, (c) texture, (d) DM content, (e) pH
2. Make a visual assessment of the colour.
3. Hold a sample close to the nose and note its smell.
4. Feel the sample. Rub individual leaves and stems between finger and thumb.
5. Squeeze a sample using one hand. Wring the sample using two hands.
6. Touch the tip of your tongue to a sample and note the taste *or* squeeze out sufficient liquid to permit the pH to be measured using the pH-meter.

Results

1. Compare your observations and results with the criteria in column 2 of *Table 22.4*.
2. Assess the type of silage - 1, 2 or 3?
3. Assess the feeding value.
4. If the quality is poor, suggest ways in which the farmer made errors in making the silage.

Table 22.4 *Silage types and quality*

Type	Sample characteristics	Feeding value	Reasons	Prevention
1. Overheated	*Colour:* brown/black *Smell:* sweet, like burnt sugar *Texture:* Dryish	Poor	Too much air in the vegetation at making	Use younger, leafier grass Roll more carefully
2. Butyric acid	*Colour:* Dark green *Smell:* Unpleasant, rancid *Texture:* Slimy. Soft tissues easily rubbed from fibres *pH:* (1) Not sharp to the tongue (2) ≥ 5.0	Poor to moderate	(1) Vegetation may have been too wet or lush (2) Not enough additive added	Ensile dry, preferably wilted, vegetation Use an additive
3. Lactic acid	*Colour:* Light yellowish green *Smell:* Little smell, sharp and vinegary *Texture:* Firm. Soft tissues not easily rubbed from fibres *pH:* (1) sharply acid to the tongue (2) < 5.0	Good	Lactic acid bacteria have dominated the ensiling process or Correct amounts of acid additive were used	
DM Content:	(1) Liquid can be squeezed out using one hand: < 20%, indicates poor quality (2) Liquid can be wrung out using two hands: 20 – 25%, indicates good quality (3) Liquid cannot be removed by hand: > 25%, indicates very good quality			

Section 6
Forestry

23 – Forestry in Ireland and the EC

Forests are of two kinds, natural and those planted by man. *Natural forests* are the result of areas of land reaching their vegetative ecological forest climax and being allowed to remain in that condition. If trees are selectively removed in limited quantities from natural forests by man, the forest maintains itself by natural regeneration (young trees growing from seed and replacing dead or removed trees).

Some countries, such as the United States (23% of the land area), Germany (18%) and France (14%) have substantial amounts of natural forest. In Ireland, on the other hand, the amount is very small, 0.4% of the land area.

Forests planted by man, *or commercial forests*, are planted, managed at all stages of growth and harvested by man. Only commercial forests are of significance in Ireland as regards timber production and use.

23.1 History of Forestry in Ireland

The vegetative ecological climax of Ireland is deciduous forest. As recently as 1600, more than 60% of the country was forest. From that time onwards, however, massive forest clearance without replanting occurred. By 1900, the area under forest had fallen to less than 2%.

In 1910, the Irish Forestry Commission was established. Its initial aim was to plant 120 ha yr^{-1}. By 1923, when the Commission was replaced by the Forest and Wildlife Service, plantings had reached a level of 400 ha yr^{-1}. Planting targets and achievements were steadily increased until by 1980, 10 000 ha yr^{-1} were being planted.

Since 1980, there has been an increase in private planting of commercial forests. This, together with further increases in Government planting, has brought total plantings of commercial forestry at present to 25 000 ha yr^{-1}.

25.2 Ireland vs other EC Countries

Despite the dramatic increase in plantings in Ireland since 1900, the present Irish level of forestry is the lowest in the EC *(Table 23.1)*. This is partly due to the large scale forest clearance referred to earlier. There is another reason, however. The ratio of lowland (suitable for intensive agriculture) to mountain land is higher in Ireland than in all of the other countries with the exception of the Netherlands,

Country	% area
Greece	43.2
Portugal	32.4
Luxembourg	31.7
Germany	29.6
France	26.9
Spain	24.8
Belgium	23.1
Italy	22.0
Denmark	12.1
Netherlands	10.0
UK	9.5
Ireland	5.8
Overall	*24.2*

Table 23.1 Percentage of land area under forests, EC countries, 1990

County	Area, ha
Cork	51 300
Galway	42 000
Mayo	39 800
Donegal	37 300
Wicklow	35 400
Tipperary	32 900
Clare	22 700
Kerry	18 800
Waterford	18 500
Laois	12 900
Leitrim	12 000
Sligo	8 900
Roscommon	8 500
Limerick	7 600
Wexford	7 400
Kilkenny	7 000
Offaly	5 100
Kildare	4 400
Cavan	4 000
Carlow	3 600
Westmeath	3 600
Monaghan	3 200
Dublin	2 000
Longford	1 900
Louth	1 700
Meath	1 600

Table 23.2 *Importance of forestry in the counties of Ireland 1990*

Table 23.3 *Growth rates of sitka spruce achieved in Sweden, Great Britain and Ireland*

Country	Growth rate (m^3 timber ha^{-1}y^{-1})
Sweden	4
Great Britain	11-14
Ireland	20-24

Belgium and Luxembourg.

Thus it is to be expected that we would have less forestry than countries like Norway, Sweden and Italy which are largely dominated by high mountain ranges. However, the Netherlands, which is *all lowland* has more forestry than Ireland. This shows that we have much less forestry than would be consistent with our lowland/mountain land ratio. It has been estimated that the level of forestry for proper utilisation of our land resources is 11-12% of our land area.

23.3 Geographical Distribution of Forestry

Some forestry is found in every county in Ireland. The greatest amounts, however, tend to be found in counties containing mountain land or other poor quality land. Hence there are large expanses of forestry in counties Galway, Mayo, Donegal and Wicklow.

Other counties, such as Cork and Tipperary, have large amounts simply because of their large size. The area under forest for each county is shown in *Table 23.2*.

23.4 Potential for Forestry in Ireland

The Irish climate is ideally suited to the growth of coniferous trees. The soils being planted at present, while poor by local standards, are very good when compared with some of the mountain soils being planted in other countries. The effect of these factors on the growth rates of sitka spruce is shown in *Table 23.3*

Most of the increase in planting since 1980 has been carried out by private individuals (mostly farmers), banks, investment companies, and a variety of other large companies. This has come about for three reasons:

1. The long-term returns from forestry have been shown to compare favourably with low-management-level agricultural production on poor land.
2. The EC predicts a strong demand for timber well into the next century and has, as a result, introduced attractive subsidies for planting.
3. Large companies see investment in forestry as a "hedge against inflation" (that is, a way of maintaining the real value of their money assets).

In view of the above and the restrictions recently imposed on the production of traditional agricultural products in the EC, it seems likely that the land area under forestry will increase further in the future.

24 – Silvicultural Practice

Silviculture means the cultivation of trees and silvicultural practice covers all aspects of commercial forestry production.

24.1 Soil Type/Tree Species Relationship

The land which becomes available for forestry use in Ireland is usually either *exposed acid mountain soils* (peats, podzols and brown podzolics) or *lowland peats*. Such land is well suited to *conifers (softwoods)*. These trees grow most rapidly, produce the highest volume of timber, reach maturity in the shortest time and achieve the greatest profitability.

The other major group of trees is *broadleaves (hardwoods)*. These require better soils than conifers, grow more slowly, produce less timber and are less profitable to plant. As a result, commercial forestry is dominated by conifers.

When planting commenced in 1910, many different tree species were planted to test their suitability to Irish soil and climatic conditions. It quickly became evident that the species listed in *Table 24.1* showed the greatest potential and it has been planting policy to concentrate on these species since then. The two species of most importance, sitka spruce and lodgepole pine are shown in *Fig 24.1*.

Table 24.1 *Species found in Irish forests and their uses*

Species		% planted	Uses
Common name	Scientific name		
Sitka spruce	*Picea sitchensis*	70	Chipboard, fibreboard, pallet-wood, construction timber
Lodgepole pine	*Pinus contorta*	20	Chipboard, fibreboard, pallet-wood
Japanese larch	*Larix leptolepsis*	3	Boat-building, transmission poles
Other conifers	–	2	–
Broadleaves	–	5	Furniture, hurley-making

Fig. 24.1 Eight year-old specimen of (a) sitka spruce, (b) lodgepole pine

There are differences in soil and climatic requirements within the conifers, sitka spruce requiring higher levels of soil fertility and soil water than lodgepole pine. Japanese larch requires moderately high levels of fertility and good drainage conditions.

When land is being planted, the soil distribution is first studied. Then the species are planted in accordance with the criteria in *Table 24.2.*

Table 24.2 Planting locations and vegetation indicators for the main species planted

Species	Planting locations	Natural vegetation indicator
Broadleaves	Well-drained, fertile areas. Often planted near roadsides where the best soil conditions are found.	Agricultural grasses
Sitka spruce	Hollows on higher ground. These have high watertables and contain nutrients washed down adjacent sideslopes.	Grass/rush associations; *Calluna* heather
Lodgepole pine	Hill-crests and hummocks on higher ground. These have lost nutrients to the hollows.	*Erica* (bell) heather
Japanese larch	Well-drained areas - less fertile than those used for broadleaves.	Agricultural grasses

24.2 Source of Seeds and Plants

The sitka spruce and lodgepole pine found so abundantly in Irish forests originated in Western North America, mainly in Oregon and British Columbia. These areas have climates rather similar to ours. The strains developed there, when imported and tested in the 1920s, were found to grow exceptionally well in Ireland.

Seed: For some time, all seed used in sitka spruce and lodgepole pine plantings was imported. Since plantations reached the seed-production stage, some collection of home-produced seed has been practised. Considerable quantities of seed are still imported, however.

Plants: Nurseries for plant production, both Government owned and private, are found throughout the country. Here, seed is planted, either under cover or in the open, in sandy, acid soils. When the seedlings are one year old they are transplanted into lines in the open.

Further transplanting may occur at two years old if root development is being restricted. The objective is to have healthy plants with extensive, vigorous root systems available for *forest planting* at three years old. Fertilizers, herbicides and pesticides may be used to achieve this objective.

Seed and plants for the other species planted are propagated in the same way. Again, some of the seed is imported and some home-produced.

24.3 The Silvicultural Sequence

The silvicultural sequence refers to all practices from initial land acquisition to final harvest of timber. The length of the sequence varies from 30-35 years (sitka spruce on good locations) to 150 years (oak on moderately suitable locations). The principal stages of the silvicultural sequence are described below.

24.3.1 Land acquisition and drainage

Where forest establishment is being planned by anyone other than a farmer or landowner, acquisition of suitable land is the first step to be taken. The economic returns from forestry are low. Therefore only *low land purchase prices* can be justified and this limits buyers to poorer soils and land areas.

Trees will not grow satisfactorily in waterlogged soil conditions. If land for planting contains areas with such conditions, then they must be artificially drained. Open-ditch drainage, the least expensive type of land drainage, is almost always employed.

24.3.2 Planting

Trees are planted 2 m apart in rows which are also 2 m apart. On *drained* land, the material removed from the open drains is deposited between the drains in lines of mounds 2 m apart. The trees are planted on the mounds *(Fig. 24.2)*.

Fig. 24.2 Planting arrangement on drained land

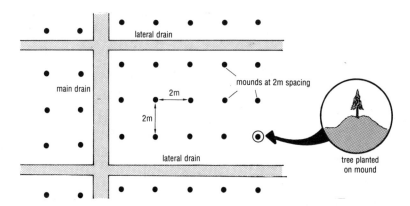

On *undrained* land, the trees are planted directly into undisturbed ground, again in the 2 m x 2 m spacing arrangement shown in *Fig. 24.2.*

The 2 m x 2 m spacing employed gives each tree 4 m^2 of ground. This means that 2 500 trees are planted per ha.

24.3.3 Fertilizer application

Forest trees use small quantities of soil nutrients. Most of the soils used for planting have sufficient N and K for tree needs. The N is present in the soil organic matter and is released during its natural degradation sufficiently quickly for satisfactory growth. The same is true for the release of K from the parent materials and soil minerals.

Due to the acid nature of most forest soils, P tends to be in limited supply *(see page 67)*. Thus, it is common practice to apply P in the form of ground rock phosphate at a rate of 250 kg ha^{-1} or 100 g per tree.

Only in the event of nutrient deficiencies showing up later on in the growth are any other nutrients applied.

24.3.4 Fencing, pest and weed control

As soon as, or before planting is completed, the planted area must be securely fenced. This is done in order to keep out cattle, sheep and other animals which might trample or otherwise damage the young trees. The normal procedure uses three strands of barbed wire with fence posts 4 m apart.

The principal *pests* of young trees are rabbits and hares, which can nibble the bark or bite off the tops of the stems. Where these pests are a serious problem, they should be driven out of the forest, and the fencing then reinforced with wire netting to prevent their reentry. Insect and other pests which attack forestry are generally not treated. They cause temporary set-backs in growth. Long-term predictions of forest growth and timber production usually assume a certain amount of such pest damage.

Weed control is essential for the first few years of a forest's growth. If weeds are allowed to grow unchecked, they greatly limit tree growth. If they collapse onto the trees in the first winter they can smother and kill large numbers (up to 100%) of trees.

Weeds must be controlled until the trees have grown above weed height. This usually does not occur until *two years* after planting where trees are planted on mounds and until *three years* where they are planted on the flat. The weeds commonly found are grasses and heathers. Weeds with tall growth habit such as gorse and rhododendron need to be controlled for a longer period.

In large areas, weeds are normally controlled *chemically* with sprays or pellets. In small areas, chemical control is also widely practised. However, *physical* control (trampling or cutting a small area around each tree) may also be practised.

24.3.5 Thinning

All the practices described so far take place in the first 2-3 years of forest establishment. When the trees are safely above the weeds, they are generally allowed to grow with only the occasional inspection for about fifteen years. After 8-10 years, the lower branches meet and *canopy closure* is achieved. Weeds now die away completely due to lack of light.

At 18-20 years, the first thinning is performed, one-third of the trees being removed. Thinning is *selective* with the poorest trees being removed and the better trees left standing. The thinnings are used for pulpwood (manufacture of chipboard, fibreboard). The remaining trees now grow at an increased rate because of the reduced competition for water and nutrients.

Further thinning operations occur at regular intervals and the thinnings become progressively larger in size and of more commercial value. The population of standing trees falls as shown in *Table 24.3*.

Table 24.3 *Timetable of growth, thinning and harvest of sitka spruce on *mineral soils*

Year	Tree population, ha^{-1}	Use of harvested trees
1	2 500	—
18	1 650	Chip-board, fibreboard, fence posts
23	1 300	Fence posts, pallet-wood, chipboard
28	950	Pallet-wood, fence posts, chipboard
33	600	Pallet-wood, saw-log (construction) timber
40	250	Saw-log timber
* On organic soils, growth is slower. Final harvest does not occur until 60-70 years.		

24.3.6 Final harvest (clear felling)

This is the last operation in the *first forest rotation* (the rotation is the number of years from planting to clear felling). Clear felling means the total clearance of trees from the area. This leaves the area ready for work preparatory to commencing the *second rotation*.

The timber removed at clear felling is the most valuable and is used for building construction.

24.3.7 Stump clearance and preparation for replanting

This is actually the beginning of another silvicultural sequence. The stumps of the trees which have just been clear felled are chemically treated to make them decay quickly (the stumps of earlier thinnings have already been similarly treated).

The debris left after clear felling (tree-tops, side-branches) is either burned or left where it is. The way is now clear for planting the second crop of trees. These will be again planted in a 2 m x 2 m arrangement, placing the plants in between the rotting stumps.

24.4 The Planting/Thinning Strategy

Trees are planted at 2 m x 2 m spacing mainly for two reasons. Firstly, dense planting allows a high degree of *selection* among the trees (i.e. the better trees grow well at the expense of the poorer trees). When this process is enhanced by thinning, the final stand trees are usually of *very good size and quality*.

Secondly, dense planting causes trees to grow tall and straight as they compete for light. This suppresses side-branch development and hence knots. Best quality timber and best yield of saw-log (construction) timber is obtained from trees which are *long, straight, free of knots and with minimum taper*.

The thinning schedule shown in *Table 24.3* is a generalized one, but the principles involved have been developed as a result of much experience and experimentation by foresters.

Exercises

Exercise 56. Examination of species, planting patterns and drainage in a forest

Materials needed
1. Access to commercial forest
2. Spade

Procedure
1. Identify sitka spruce, lodgepole pine and any other tree species planted in the forest.
2. When you are familiar with the appearance of sitka spruce and lodgepole pine, find a vantage point which gives a view of a large expanse of forest. Estimate by eye the relative proportions of the two species.
3. Check, by pacing out, that the spacing of young (< 10 years old) trees is 2 m x 2 m.
4. Identify the mechanism of planting. Is it *mound-planting, plough ribbon-planting*, or *slit-planting* (planting into undisturbed ground)? Plough ribbon-planting means ploughing ribbons (furrow slices) in parallel lines 2 m apart. Trees are then planted at 2 m spacing on the ribbons.
5. Compare tree distribution in an unthinned and a thinned area of the forest.
6. Measure the distance between of the open drains, by pacing out.
7. Clean up the side of an open drain or dig a pit. Identify the soil type.

Results
Record and comment on all measurements and observations made.

Exercise 57. Examination of seedling growth and propagation at a forest nursery

Materials needed
Access to forest nursery

Procedure
1. Observe: (a) seed, (b) young seedlings (before transplanting), (c) "lined-out" (1 year-old seedlings), (d) older plants
2. Find out by questioning what "one plus one" and "two plus two" mean in relation to plants.
3. Examine the soils/growing media used.
4. Find out what use is made of fertilizers, herbicides and pesticides.

Results
Record and comment on all observations.

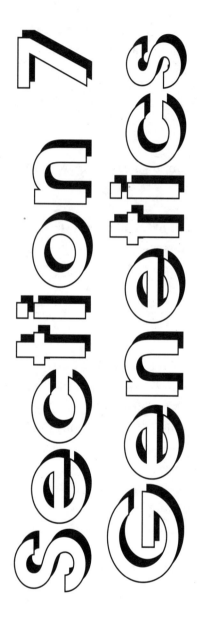

Section 7
Genetics

25 – Principles of Genetics

25.1 Introduction

Gregor Mendel, 1822 – 1884

Genetics is the study of how traits are inherited. Can you roll your tongue? Is your second finger longer than the first? Is your second toe longer than your big toe? Is the hairline on your forehead pointed in the centre (called a "widow's peak") or is it straight? These are all inherited traits in humans.

The basis of modern genetics was research carried out by a monk *Gregor Mendel* who studied the inheritance of different characteristics of peas in the monastery garden at Brno (now in Czechoslovakia). He made his observations between 1857 and 1864 and published them. However, they were completely overlooked until rediscovered at the beginning of this century. In addition to their importance for inheritance studies they were of fundamental importance for evolution theory.

25.2 DNA and Chromosomes

The genetic material is the *DNA* molecules located in *chromosomes* in the cell nucleus. A *gene* is a part of the DNA molecule which *codes for a particular protein or enzyme.* It is the possession or absence of these proteins or enzymes which ultimately results in what we call genetic traits.

A chromosome is a long DNA molecule made up of many genes. In most species of plant and animal, each normal individual has a pair of similar chromosomes, called a homologous pair. This is referred to as the *diploid* condition and often written as "2n". Egg and sperm cells, however, only have half of the number of chromosomes. This is the *haploid* condition and written as "n".

There are two types of cell division: *mitosis* is the usual form of cell division. During mitosis, one cell divides to give two exact copies of itself. *Meiosis* is the type of division involved during the production of sex cells (eggs and sperm) called *gametes.* Gametes produced by meiosis have half the number of chromosomes of the cell from which they are formed. Of each homologous pair, one chromosome ends up in each gamete formed. Meiosis is referred to as reduction division. If it did not occur, the number of chromosomes would double every time fertilization takes place.

The details of mitosis and meiosis are covered in *Chapter 26.* You should read that chapter and then these paragraphs again to really understand the mechanisms involved.

25.3 Genes

A gene is the genetic instructions for the production of a single protein. Since proteins include enzymes and structural proteins, this is the way the genetic information in the chromosomes is ultimately expressed. Each gene occurs at its own particular position or *locus* on the chromosome. Genes can occur in different forms. Different forms of a gene are called *alleles.* As an example we will consider some of the traits of garden peas studied by Mendel.

In peas, the gene coding for plant height occurs in two forms: plants are either *tall* or *dwarf.* Likewise, pea seeds are either *round* or *wrinkled* in shape and *green* or *yellow* in colour. Each of these characteristics is coded for by a single gene which occurs in two variants or alleles.

F₁ hybrid seeds are an example of applied genetics. They will be discussed in *Chapter 27.*

In good seed catalogues, a distinction is drawn between round and wrinkled pea varieties. Wrinkled varieties are the more popular because they produce sweeter peas. Round seeded varieties are hardier and used early in the year. Compare the variety 'Feltham First' with the variety 'Early Onward'. You could investigate this by growing a few plants of each variety and using the sugar measurement methods mentioned on page 90.

Fig 25.1 Seed packets of F₁ hybrids

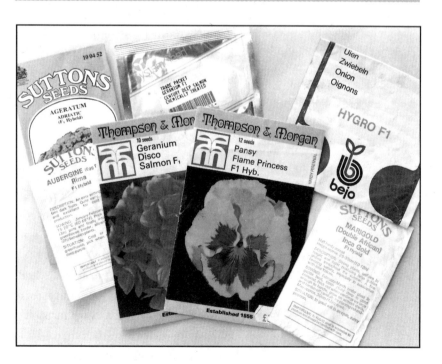

In a diploid individual there can be different alleles present at the same gene locus on each of the homologous chromosomes. For example, at the locus for the gene which codes for height in peas the following combinations of alleles could occur: tall & tall; tall & dwarf; dwarf & tall; and dwarf & dwarf.

25.4 Expression of Genes

When two alleles occur in the same individual which allele is expressed? If an individual has both tall and dwarf alleles present will it be of medium height? Mendel found that that his pea plants were of two heights only - tall and dwarf. Thus when an individual plant possesses two types of allele, one is expressed and the other is not.

When two different alleles occur together the one which is expressed is said to be *dominant*. The allele not expressed is said to be *recessive*. We write dominant alleles using a capital letter and recessive alleles using a lower case letter. In peas, the Tall allele is dominant to the dwarf trait. Thus for the example given above we could write it as: TT, Tt, tT and tt. For the other examples mentioned, Round is dominant to wrinkled seed form, and Yellow is dominant to green in seed colour.

When both alleles coding for a characteristic in an individual are the same we call that condition homozygous. Thus a TT plant is a homozygous dominant or a tt plant is a homozygous recessive. Alternatively, when the two alleles are different, as in a plant with the Tt genotype, we describe it as being heterozygous.

We can now distinguish between the *genotype*, which is the sum of the actual alleles found in an individual, and the *phenotype*, which is how the genotype is actually expressed. Consider two individuals of pea plants. These might have the genotype TT or Tt. Since Tall is dominant over dwarf, both of these individuals will appear tall. Thus they have different genotypes for the height characteristic but they have a similar phenotype. Many of the points covered above can be seen in *Fig. 25.2*.

25.5 Mendel's Experiments

25.5.1 The Monohybrid Cross
The first point to note is that Mendel used *true-breeding* lines to start with. This means that if, for example he was studying the characteristic of seed shape, he chose a line producing all round seeds as his parents of the round seed line, and a line producing all wrinkled seeds as his parents of the wrinkled seed line. This meant that he was using *homozygous* parents as his starting point, even though he did not know it at the time.

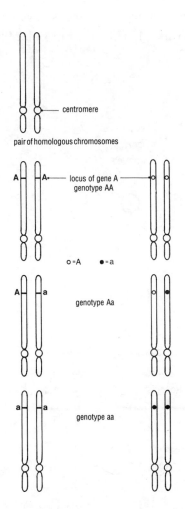

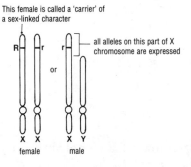

Fig.25.2 Diagrams of chromosomes and genotypes

Mendel crossbred a round-seeded variety and a wrinkled-seeded variety. Pollen from the wrinkled variety was transferred to the round variety and vice versa. The parental cross is called the P_1 generation. He obtained 253 seeds in the next generation called the ("first filial") F_1 generation. All of these seeds were round. He planted them all and allowed them o self-pollinate.

In the next generation, the F_2, he obtained 7,324 seeds of which 5,474 were round and 1,850 were wrinkled. This is a ratio of 2.96 round seeds to 1 wrinkled seed.

Fig. 25.3 Monohybrid cross in peas

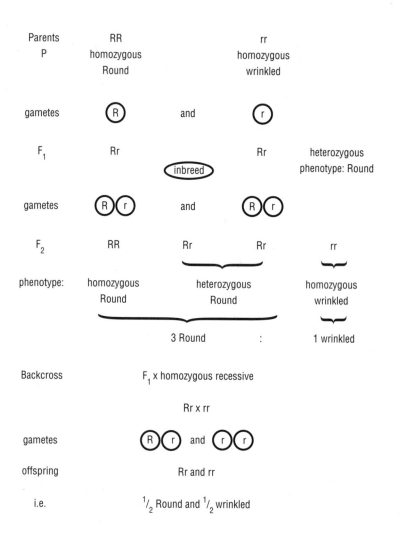

This is an example of what what we now call a monohybrid cross i.e. a cross involving a single characteristic. Today we would write out this cross as in *Fig. 25.3*. Thus we see that we expect a 3:1 ratio in a monohybrid cross.

25.5.2 The Punnett square

A monohybrid cross can also be shown using a *Punnett square*, named after a British geneticist (*Fig. 25.4*).

Fig. 25.4 Monohybrid cross in peas, using a Punnett square

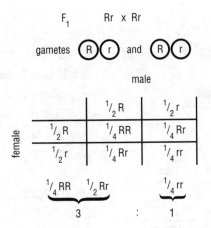

Punnett square of F_1 monohybrid cross:

F_1 Rr x Rr

gametes (R)(r) and (R)(r)

male

	$\frac{1}{2}$ R	$\frac{1}{2}$ r
$\frac{1}{2}$ R	$\frac{1}{4}$ RR	$\frac{1}{4}$ Rr
$\frac{1}{2}$ r	$\frac{1}{4}$ Rr	$\frac{1}{4}$ rr

$\frac{1}{4}$ RR $\frac{1}{2}$ Rr $\frac{1}{4}$ rr

3   :   1

Again we conclude that the expected ratio from a monohybrid cross is 3:1.

25.5.3 Mendel's First Law of Inheritance

One important outcome of this is now referred to as *Mendel's First Law of Inheritance*, also called the Law of Segregation. This states that *when gametes are formed one allele from each pair of alleles is distributed to each gamete.*

Put another way, of the pair of alleles present in the diploid parent cell, only one will be present in the haploid gamete.

25.5.4 Back-crossing

It is possible to verify that the genotype Rr is heterozygous using a *back-cross*. This involves crossing Rr individuals with pure-breeding recessive parents, rr. Can you predict the expected ratio in a back-cross situation?

25.5.5 The Dihybrid cross

Mendel also studied the inheritance of two characters considered together. For this experiment he crossed two pure-breeding lines as follows:

1. plants with round seeds and yellow seed colour and
2. plants with wrinkled seeds and green seed colour.

We can represent the parents in this cross as follows: RRYY and rryy pure-breeding parents.

The possible gametes are RY and ry.

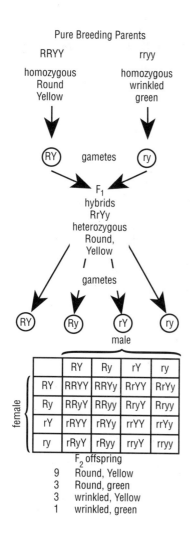

Pure Breeding Parents

RRYY — homozygous Round Yellow

rryy — homozygous wrinkled green

gametes: RY, ry

F_1 hybrids RrYy heterozygous Round, Yellow

gametes

RY, Ry, rY, ry
male

	RY	Ry	rY	ry
RY	RRYY	RRYy	RrYY	RrYy
Ry	RRYy	RRyy	RrYy	Rryy
rY	rRYY	rRYy	rrYY	rrYy
ry	rRyY	rRyy	rryY	rryy

female

F_2 offspring

9 Round, Yellow
3 Round, green
3 wrinkled, Yellow
1 wrinkled, green

Fig 25.5 Punnett square of dihybrid cross in peas

The genotype of the F_1 generation is RrYy. Thus, they are heterozygous for both seed shape and seed colour but they are phenotypically Round and Yellow. If these F_1 individuals are allowed to cross-breed, the resulting F_2 generation can be predicted using a Punnett square *(Fig. 25.5)*.

You should copy this into your copybook and satisfy yourself that the expected ratio of a dihybrid cross is: 9 Round Yellow; 3 Round green; 3 wrinkled Yellow; 1 wrinkled green.

25.5.6 Mendel's Second Law of Inheritance

We now have evidence to state Mendel's Second Law of Inheritance, also called the *Law of Independent Assortment*. This states that *when gametes are formed, each member of a pair of alleles of one gene segregates independently of the alleles of any other gene.*

25.6 Incomplete Dominance

So far, the examples we have studied involve straightforward dominant or recessive characters. However, there are cases where neither gene is fully dominant over the other. This is called *incomplete dominance*. In fowl, neither allele for feather colour, Black (B) and White (W) is dominant. Heterozygous offspring are called "blue". Try to write out the phenotype and genotype of the offspring of a "blue" hen mated with a "blue" cock. Roan coat colour (a mixture of white and red hairs) in shorthorn cattle is another example. The genotype for roan (Rr) shows incomplete dominance between red coat colour (RR) and white coat colour (rr).

25.7 More than Two Genes

Consider a population of organisms. For a moment look at your classmates. Look at their height. There are not just tall and dwarf individuals but a complete range between the shortest and tallest. This is called *continuous variation*. In higher organisms, including all mammals, most characteristics are quantitative, i.e. they do not fall into distinct groups and there is continuous variation between the two extremes.

Quantitative characteristics are coded for by a number of genes interacting with each other. Even though the inheritance principles are exactly as outlined above in the case of one or two genes, it means that it is more difficult to predict the characteristics of the offspring. This is where animal breeding (for example in artificial insemination situations) comes into play. Computers are used to catalogue the desirable characteristics of a particular breeding line.

25.8 Multiple Alleles

Do not confuse multiple alleles with the multiple gene effect just described. *Multiple alleles* refers to the situation where *within the population* there may be more than two alleles of a particular gene. Any one individual will, of course, only have two of these. The best known example of this is the human ABO blood group system. There are three alleles coding for this system. The different combinations of the alleles found in each individual gives four blood groups overall (A,B,AB and O; allele A and allele B are dominant to O).

25.9 Fruit Flies and Genetics

At the beginning of this century, *T.H. Morgan* began using fruit flies for his genetics' investigations. He used the species *Drosophila melanogaster*. Fruit flies are now routinely used throughout the world for genetics' studies. This is so for a number of reasons:

1. fruit flies are easy to culture in small bottles in the laboratory,
2. they produce a new generation every two weeks, so that an investigation going from parents to F_2 can be completed in about a month,
3. they have only four pairs of chromosomes and so are reasonably uncomplicated genetically (humans have 23 pairs of chromosomes),
4. they produce large numbers of offspring allowing for more accurate results,
5. they also have well-documented genetic varieties called *mutants* (*see Exercise 58*).

Female fruit flies have four pairs of homologous chromosomes. Males have three pairs of homologous chromosomes. The remaining two chromosomes are actually different. One is larger than the other and is also found in female fruit flies. It is called the *X chromosome*. The other, smaller, chromosome in male fruit flies is called the *Y chromosome*. Thus sex determination in fruit flies is caused by the presence of a pair of homologous chromosomes, XX in females or by the presence of a pair of different chromosomes, XY in males.

We should distinguish between the chromosomes responsible for sex determination, called the *sex chromosomes* and the other chromosomes, called *autosomes*. Although there are other forms of sex determination in the animal kingdom, the XY chromosome form of determination as found in fruit flies is very common and is found in humans.

25.10 Sex Linkage

Morgan also discovered *sex linkage*. This is where the gene coding for a certain characteristic is carried on the sex chromosome, or X chromosome. Remember that males have one X chromosome and one Y chromosome. This means that the characteristic is always expressed in a male since even if it is a recessive character there is no other allele on a homologous chromosome to mask its expression. Since females have a pair of X chromosomes a recessive character will only be expressed if it is present on both X chromosomes. Morgan documented the first-known example of sex linkage - the *white eye* character in fruit flies. Let us examine a cross involving this character *(Fig. 25.6)*.

Sex-linked characters are only common in males (think about how a sex-linked character might occur in females?). The character tends to jump from one generation to the second next - that is from grandfather to grandson. In humans, two well-documented examples of sex-linked inheritance are *red-green colour blindness* and *haemophilia*. The inheritance of these characters is similar to that outlined for the inheritance of the white eye character in fruit flies. A useful exercise would be to write out the genetic crosses for these characters.

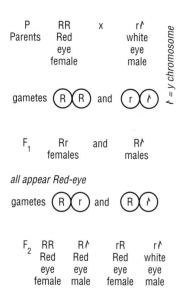

Note: the white eye character skips one generation

Fig. 25.6 Sex linkage in fruit flies

25.11 Linkage of Genes

It was soon discovered that Mendel's studies did not explain all the results observed where the inheritance of multiple genes was being studied. Mendel's results did not cover the situation where the genes concerned were *located on the same chromosome*. These genes are inherited together as a package - genes which occur on the same chromosome are said to be "linked". We should realize by now that each chromosome has genes coding for many characters. Linkage covers the situation where these characteristics are inherited together. These genes are only separated by "crossing over" which sometimes occurs during meiosis, and is described in the next chapter.

Mendel was "lucky" in that the characters he studied, seed shape and seed colour in peas, happened to be coded for by genes located on different chromosomes. Remember that around 1860 nothing was known about chromosomes, or genes, and very little was understood about genetic inheritance. This makes Mendel's studies and results all the more remarkable. Today our knowledge of chromosomes and the role of DNA is much wider.

25.12 Fruit Flies for Genetics

About 20 species of *Drosophila* are found in Ireland. The species used for genetics is rare in the wild here. *Drosophila* larvae feed on the yeasts in rotting fruit. They are cultured on a food medium which is similar to porridge with yeasts added. They should be maintained at warm room temperatures, i.e. 20-25°C. A domestic hot press is ideal. *Drosophila* generations are completed in about 12 days, depending on the temperature.

Adults are anaesthetized with ether *(see Exercise 58)* for examination. Use *Fig. 25.7* to see the differences between the sexes. The most critical stage in a genetics investigation with *Drosophila* is setting up the parental cross as the parents must not have mated beforehand. To ensure this, the cultures used to breed the parents are cleared of all adults. The crosses are set up 12 hours later using adults newly emerged from the cleared cultures (fruitflies do not mate until they are about 1 day old).

A common mutant used for monohybrid crosses is *vestigial* which has the wings reduced to stumps. Sex-linked investigations usually involve *red eye* (dominant) and *white eye* (sex-linked).

Fig. 25.7 Male and female fruit flies

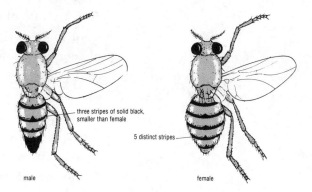

Exercises

Exercise 58. Simple genetics investigations

Materials needed
1. Paper soaked in PTC (see reagents' appendix)
2. Some mutant strains of *Drosophila*, ideally one where a cross has been set up
3. Grow some commercially produced genetic strains of seeds, e.g. tomato

Procedure
1. Examine the distribution of some genetic traits of humans such as the ability to taste PTC (TT and Tt are tasters; tt are not). Place paper soaked in PTC on the tongue. PTC is unpleasant to tasters. It occurs naturally in cabbage and cucumber. Draw bar charts to represent tasters and non-tasters in your class.
2. Examine the *Drosophila* cultures. Maintain cultures at about 25°C (but not above 28°C). If a cross has been set up, allow the F_1 adults to emerge. Observe them and write down their phenotype. Now place about 6 adults in a fresh culture bottle and maintain for 12-14 days. In the meantime, you should see larvae in the food and eventually pupae on the sides of the bottle. When the F_2 adults emerge, proceed as follows: transfer the flies to a dry conical flask by removing the plug of cotton wool and allowing them to walk upwards into the flask. When all (or most) of the adults are in the flask plug it with cotton wool soaked with ether. Sort the adults into the different phenotypes about 10 minutes after they stop moving. Further adults should emerge in the culture tube the following day and you can repeat this procedure. Write out the cross involved and see how your results compare to the expected ratios.
3. Follow the instructions to grow the genetic seeds. Write out the crosses involved. When the seeds grow, count the different phenotypes observed and explain your results.

26 – Cell Division

As already mentioned briefly in *Chapter 7,* there are two kinds of cell division, mitosis and meiosis. In this chapter we will study cell division in more detail.

26.1 Mitosis

Mitosis is the form of cell division which results in two identical cells from one parent cell. We will now consider the main stages in cell division.

Before a cell starts to divide it is at the interphase stage. Most of the normal activities of cells take place at this stage, e.g. production of more DNA and proteins, division of mitochondria and other cell organelles.

It is possible to study the stages of mitosis under a microscope. The material used must come from a site where active growth is taking place. A squash preparation of an onion root tip is used in Exercise 59. When a root tip is examined, cells will be found with all of the stages overleaf.

Fig 26.1 Stages in mitosis

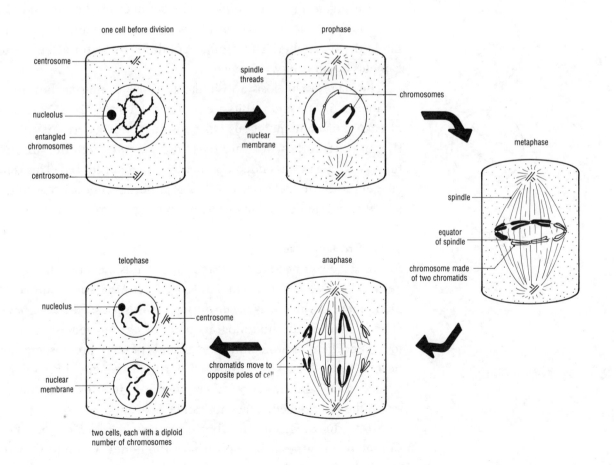

26.1.2 Stages in mitosis

It is usual to define four main stages in mitosis. You should refer to *Fig. 26.1*.

1. *Prophase:* During prophase the chromosomes become shorter and thicker.
2. *Metaphase:* The membrane of the nucleus breaks down. Each chromosome can now be seen to consist of two chromatids joined together by a centromere. Each centromere becomes attached by fibrils to a spindle at each end of the cell.
3. *Anaphase:* The centromere of each chromosome divides and the chromatids move towards the spindles.
4. *Telophase:* The chromatids arrive at the opposite poles of the cell. New nuclear membranes form.

Finally, the cytoplasm divides and what was one cell is now two complete cells.

26.2 Meiosis

Remember that mitosis produces daughter cells which are an exact replica of the cell which formed them. Meiosis gives rise to cells with half the number of chromosomes.

Most organisms have a diploid *(2n)* number of chromosomes in their nuclei. Meiosis results in the production of gametes with the haploid *(n)* number. The diploid condition is restored once the gametes fuse during *fertilization*.

The stages of meiosis are similar to those of mitosis, but more complicated. The end results are summarized in *Fig. 26.2*. Note that of each pair of homologous chromosomes which were present in the parent cells when meiosis began, one member of the homologous pair has ended up in each gamete produced. This is in keeping with Mendel's Second Law of Inheritance which has to do with this segregation of characteristics during meiosis.

26.2.1 Crossing Over

At this stage you need to be clear about what is meant by linkage of genes. This was covered in *Chapter 25.11*. One very important phenomenon which may occur during meiosis is called *crossing over*. During meiosis the homologous pairs of chromosomes lie close together. These entwine and short strands of one chromosome can be transferred back and forward between the members of the homologous pair. This is called crossing over. It is the main way by which the linkage between genes can be broken.

Study the diagrams showing crossing over in *Fig. 26.3*. For simplicity, imagine a situation where the genes A, B and C, with

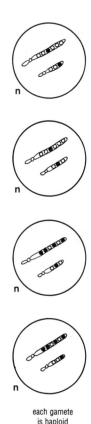

1. Before meiosis. Simplified cell with two pairs of homologous chromosomes.

2n diploid

Let o and ● represent alleles of different genes.

2. After meiosis. Four kinds of gametes.

n

n

n

n

each gamete is haploid

Fig. 26.2 Gamete formation

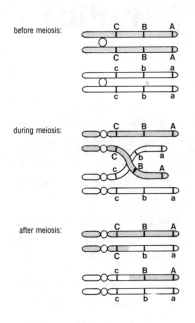

before meiosis:

during meiosis:

after meiosis:

Fig. 26.3 Crossing over

Fig. 26.4 Photomicrograph of onion root tip. Note various stages of cell division

alleles a, b and c occur on the same chromosome. Notice that crossing over is more likely the further genes are apart on a chromosome and that when two genes occur very close together on a chromosome they are rarely separated by crossing over. The important effect of crossing over is that new combinations of genes appear. In turn these are acted upon by natural selection (in evolution) or selected for by animal or plant breeders (see Chapter 27).

Exercises

Exercise 59. Mitosis in an onion root tip

Material needed
Prepared microscopic mount of onion root tip

Procedure
Examine the prepared microscopic mount and identify the various stages of mitosis observed. Use as high a magnification power as possible. Draw the stages found in a number of neighbouring cells (Fig. 26.4)

27 – Applied Genetics

27.1 Genes and Mutations

Chromosomes consist of long strands of genes. Each gene consists of a length of the chemical DNA (deoxyribonucleic acid). This DNA produces another chemical called RNA (ribonucleic acid) which in turn produces proteins and enzymes. It is these proteins and enzymes that eventually express the genetic characteristics which we have been discussing.

The important part of the structure of DNA is called the *"genetic code"*. This consists of various combinations of four bases called adenine, guanine, cytosine and thymine (here we will refer to them by their first letter). These bases code for the production of RNA which in turn codes for the production of strings of amino acids. Triplets of bases code for an individual amino acid. Thus AAA codes for the amino acid lysine, CCC for proline and GCA for alanine. There are 64 possible combinations and there are only 20 amino acids. *(Refer to DNA structure, Fig. 7.6.)*

Remember that proteins consist of long chains of amino acids. Thus the function of the genes is to line up amino acids in the correct order so that proteins can be formed. Occasionally, very occasionally in nature, one of the bases gets changed. A mistake occurs. Thus, for example, in the GCA triplet mentioned above which codes for alanine, the guanine may be replaced by alanine, giving a different triplet ACA. This codes for another amino acid called threonine. Thus the protein formed from this new combination will have the amino acid threonine where alanine formerly occurred. This phenomenon is called a *mutation.*

27.2 Natural Selection and Artificial Selection

A new protein formed by a mutation may function in exactly the same way as the previous protein. It may be better or it may be worse and in the extreme it may be lethal. In nature, mutations are one source of the variety of life. The new combinations produced by crossing over add further variety. In nature, these differences between organisms are subjected to evolutionary pressure through the process of natural selection. This is the mechanism for evolution proposed by *Darwin* and *Wallace* around 1850.

Natural selection takes millions of years to act. Modern agriculture has to speed things up. This is done by *artificial selection* used by animal and plant breeders. Mutations can be induced using chemicals, e.g. colchicine. Another way of increasing the rate of mutation is to use radiation. This is mainly used to help in the production of new breeds and varieties. These have to be fully tested before release. Most of them are rejected but the occasional new variety makes this form of breeding worthwhile.

Since all our varieties ultimately come from wild species, this underlines the importance of retaining as many wild species as possible - if only as a reservoir of genetic material for use in the future for breeding new varieties. Every now and again it is possible to search in the original species for characteristics which are not included in the genotype of the varieties now used in agriculture. This is called the *gene pool* which can be defined as the sum total of all the alleles in a breeding population.

27.3 Clones

Clones are individuals produced by vegetative or asexual reproduction. Cloned individuals are *exact genotypic copies of each other.*

Plant breeders produce new varieties of plants using sexual reproduction. For example, to produce a new variety of apple one sows the seeds (pips) of an apple. One has to wait until it crops to see if it is a worthwhile variety. Most plants produced in that way do not offer any advantage over existing varieties. Occasionally plant breeders find a new young plant which is worth developing as a new variety. Today these can be patented, and breeders' rights are available to the breeder. This new variety is reproduced asexually or vegetatively (see *Chapter 12* for more details on this).

Modern methods of micro-propagation allow rapid multiplication of new varieties. Each plant sold to the public is a member of a clone of the plant originally obtained as a result of breeding by sexual reproduction. To return to the apple seed example, many apple varieties are centuries old. Many bear their discoverer's name, e.g. Cox's Orange Pippin, Bramley's Seedling. Young apple trees are produced by grafting a short piece of a clone of the original seedling (the "scion") onto a rootstock.

27.4 Breeding - Farm Animals

Inbreeding can be used to concentrate "desirable" genes in a group of close relatives. For example, a bull may be mated to its own daughters, or a brother to its sisters. Inbreeding was used to establish uniform breeds with distinctive traits. However, inbreeding can concentrate undesirable as well as desirable traits. Today, inbreeding in cattle is rare, but it may be used to produce contrasting families which are then used for crossbreeding or outbreeding.

> **Discuss the genetic differences between a purebred and a mongrel dog.**

Crossbreeding in its most extreme form, can involve mating what are considered to be two separate species, e.g. European cattle with tropical cattle. This is done to try to introduce new traits into the genes of the European cattle. However, crossbreeding more commonly involves the interbreeding of two breeds. This leads to the production of "half breds", e.g. in sheep *(see page 356)* and in cattle.

Breeding can be of major importance to agriculture. For example a single bull at an AI (artificial insemination) station can act as sire to many cows. The two main methods used to rate bulls are:

1. performance testing, and
2. progeny testing.

Performance testing refers to keeping records of the animal's individual performance - growth rate, efficiency at converting feed - and comparing them with the records of other animals kept under similar conditions.

Progeny testing refers to comparing records of an animal's offspring with the offspring of other animals kept under similar conditions.

27.5 Artificial Insemination (A.I.)

This allows the sperm from a superior bull to fertilize a large number of cows. This is done by collecting sperm in an artificial vagina. The sperm is then diluted using an extender medium such as milk and egg yolk mixed with a buffer. It is then stored in small vials. Artificial insemination involves introducing this stored sperm into the cow's uterus.

27.6 Embryo Transplantation

This technique depends on the fact that the cells of newly formed embryos can be split up. Each cell can produce a new individual. This means that a clone can be formed. Splitting the embryos to form a clone can now be done completely in the laboratory - this is called *in vitro* to distinguish it from the natural or *in vivo* situation. *In vitro* cattle-embryos are now becoming available commercially.

The principle is to produce progeny by a superior bull, whose progeny have been tested, and a superior cow whose performance is known. The cow may be treated with hormones to increase egg production. The eggs can be removed, fertilized *in vitro*, and cloned as described above. This yields embryos which can be transplanted to "ordinary" cows who act as *surrogate* mothers. Embryos can be tested for gender before being transplanted. The result is superior calves.

27.7 Breeding - Plants

Similar principles are involved in plant-breeding. Inbreeding involves the production of seeds by mating close relatives. The offspring produced are highly homozygous and are phenotypically uniform. These are often sold as cultivated varieties or *cultivars,e.g.* many of the varieties in a seed catalogue. Outbreeding, on the other hand, involves the production of seed from unrelated parents. The offspring are highly heterozygous and phenotypically variable. Wild populations are usually outbreeders.

Plant breeders record the ancestry of an individual. This is the *pedigree*. All the plants descended from a common ancestor are said to form a *family*. *Open-pollinated* plants are those pollinated in the field. To produce specific crosses, pollination has to be controlled. This is often carried out by removing the stamens from the flowers. All of these practices are involved in the production of F_1 seed varieties, described below. New varieties are tested by a process of *trialling*.

27.8 F_1 Seed Varieties

Nowadays, seed catalogues have many examples of what the seedsmen call *F_1 hybrids (refer back to Fig. 25.1)*. These are special varieties with desirable characteristics, often uniform in performance. For example F_1 hybrid cabbage varieties are bred to crop together over a short time- span. This can be very useful for a farmer who wishes to market the crop quickly. It can be less useful for a household gardener who may want to harvest over a longer period. Compare the characteristics of the cabbage varieties 'Greyhound' and 'Hispi'.

F_1 varieties are the offspring of parents which the company producing that seed hold and do not release. Seed produced from these F_1 plants will not produce the same desirable characteristics. Briefly, the way in which F_1 hybrids are produced is as follows *(see Fig. 27.1)*:

1. Plant breeders grow parent populations in the field and produce offspring from these by open pollination.
2. Desirable individuals are chosen and inbred families are produced from these.
3. Eventually two highly inbred lines are produced. These will be homozygous for most characteristics and uniform.
4. These two inbred lines are crossed to produce the F_1 hybrid seeds which are sold to the public.

The parents of the F_1 hybrids are retained by the plant breeder and not released to the public. If F_1 hybrids are allowed to set seed

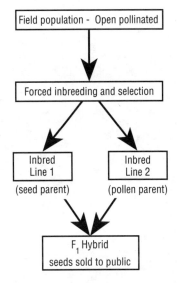

Fig 27.1 The production of F_1 hybrids

they produce highly variable offspring. Hence, the only way to obtain the desirable F_1 hybrid characteristics is to purchase more F_1 hybrid seeds. Because of the more expensive breeding techniques involved, F_1 hybrids are always more expensive. The farmer must evaluate their true value in each particular situation.

27.9 Polyploidy

Polyploidy describes the situation where cells contain *multiple copies of chromosomes*. It is common in plants, especially in cultivated varieties used in agriculture. Wild populations are usually diploid. Imagine a situation where mitosis goes wrong. That is, if cell division does not take place. The result is a *tetraploid*. *Triploids* can be produced by crossing a tetraploid and a diploid. Sometimes the production of polyploids can be induced by the chemical *colchicine* which disrupts mitosis.

Polyploid varieties are often sterile. However, this can be an advantage to a grower. Instead, varieties are propagated by asexual techniques. Wild potatoes are diploids. Cultivated potatoes are *tetraploid*. Cultivated strawberries are *octaploid*.

Section 8
Animal Science

28 – Living Organisms
2. The Invertebrates

In this chapter we will introduce the invertebrate animals which are important to agriculture either directly or indirectly. The term invertebrate is a general term which means without a backbone. Vertebrate animals such as birds and mammals are introduced in the next chapter.

28.1 Principles of Classification

Most estimates put the number of animal species in the world at between one and two million. Obviously, we need some way to classify these so that we can keep track of the different species. This is called classification. We have to consider two things: firstly how do we define a species and secondly how are they named?

One working definition of a species is that it is a group of *"actually or potentially interbreeding individuals"*. Members of different species do not usually interbreed and produce fertile offspring. If the individuals we are studying are actually interbreeding then they obviously belong to the same species. But sometimes they cannot interbreed for some good reason, e.g. they could be prevented from doing so by inhabiting two countries separated by sea. Then the second part of the definition, "potentially interbreeding", comes into play. A common example found on Irish farms is relevant here. The horse belongs to the species *Equus caballus*. The donkey is *Equus asinus*. They can produce offspring called mules and ginnets. However the offspring cannot themselves reproduce since they are sterile. This is evidence that horses and donkeys are separate species. They do not interbreed in the wild.

Today we name species using a system first proposed by the Swedish biologist Carl von Linné (or *Linnaeus* in Latin) around the year 1750. He proposed what is called a binomial system of naming species. Each species is given a unique name: in the case of the horse it is *caballus*. Related species are grouped into a genus, which, in the case of the horse is *Equus*. Thus the full name of the horse is *Equus caballus*, and other members of the same genus are *Equus asinus* and *Equus zebra*. Note that the correct way to write a species' name is with a capital letter for the genus, a small letter for the species and print it in italics or underline it: either *Equus caballus* or <u>Equus caballus</u>. Human beings belong to the species *Homo sapiens* or <u>Homo sapiens</u>.

In turn, related genera (the plural of genus) are placed in families; related families are grouped into orders, orders into classes and finally related classes into a phylum (plural phyla). There are about thirty phyla in the Animal Kingdom. Many phyla are only common in the sea and are not important in agriculture. We will study examples from seven phyla which have a direct bearing on agriculture.

Quite often, common species are referred to by using the generic name only, i.e. the first name. For example, you will find the names *Babesia*, *Drosophila*, etc. throughout this book. This is acceptable so long as confusion is not possible.

28.2 Phylum Protozoa

This phylum consists of single-celled animals. Many of them are free-living in both the sea and freshwater. They are all microscopic or at most barely visible to the naked eye.

The Protozoa are classified according to how they move. One group has extensions called pseudopodia ("false feet"), e.g. *Amoeba*. Others have cilia or a whip-like tail for movement. The fourth group has spores as part of its life cycle and we will consider them in more detail.

The spore-producing Protozoa are of major importance to humans as the cause of diseases in both humans and domestic animals. One of them causes redwater fever in cattle. Related organisms with similar life cycles include the parasite which causes human malaria and organisms which cause major diseases in horses and poultry.

Redwater fever affects 100 000 cattle every year. It is transmitted by bites of a blood-sucking tick *(see 28.7.1)*. Redwater fever is caused by a protozoan of the genus *Babesia*. The life cycle is summarized in *Fig. 28.1.*

*Fig. 28.1 The life cycle of **Babesia***

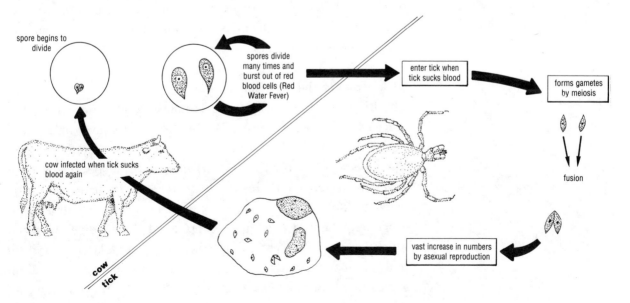

Babesia is transmitted by the sheep tick, *Ixodes ricinus*. *Babesia* sporozoites in blood sucked by a tick undergo the sexual reproductive part of the cycle in the tick. The sporozoites form gametes which fuse to form a zygote. This is the only diploid stage in the life cycle. After meiosis, or reduction division, many spores are formed in the tick by asexual reproduction. These are transmitted to another cow during the tick's next blood meal. Within the cow, the spores form sporozoites which enter the red blood cells. These multiply at a great rate and infect other red blood cells. While bursting out they cause the breakdown of the cell wall. This releases haemoglobin which is passed in the urine. Hence the name of the disease, redwater fever.

Redwater fever can be transmitted to people but only if their spleen has been removed. Removal of the spleen is rare but those individuals without a spleen should avoid tick bites as the disease can be life threatening.

28.3 Phylum Platyhelminthes

The name of this phylum, *platy* = flat and *helminthes* = worms, gives us the main characteristic of the phylum. They are all bilaterally symmetrical which means they have a front end and a rear end. They are triploblastic which means they have the three cell layers found in most animal groups (ectoderm, endoderm and mesoderm). These two characteristics are shared by all the animal groups which follow. In addition, the platyhelminths are all flattened from top to bottom, or *dorsoventrally*. They have a rudimentary brain and nerve system. They are *hermaphrodites* (both sexes in the one individual). They do not have a body cavity unlike the remaining phyla. There are three classes in the phylum. One of these consists of the free living flatworms which are very common in Irish freshwater and marine habitats. The other two groups are parasites and are the flukes and tapeworms.

28.3.1 *Fasciola,* the liver fluke

The flukes belong to the Class Trematoda. The most important species for Irish agriculture is *Fasciola hepatica,* the liver fluke. Adult flukes occur in the liver and liver ducts of both sheep and cattle. They feed on blood and liver cells and have a specialized outer covering called a cuticle which protects them from the host's defences. Refer to Fig. 28.2. They have an oral and ventral sucker which help them to attach to the host. Flukes have a digestive system which has two lobes, each with many branches. A large part of the body is taken up with testes, which produce sperm and vitelline glands which produce the covering of the eggs. A single ovary lies around the middle. Fertilized eggs are stored in the uterus until released.

Fig. 28.2 Diagram of **Fasciola hepatica**

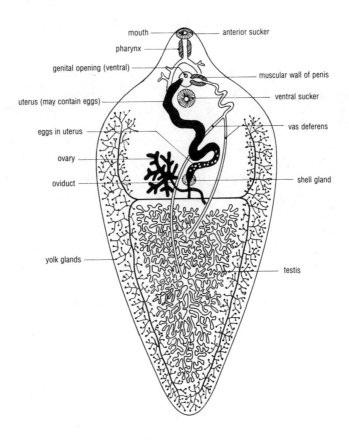

The adult liver fluke lies in the ducts of the liver. It is a hermaphrodite. When many flukes occur in the same host, they usually cross-fertilize each other. However, being a hermaphrodite, a single fluke can produce fertilized eggs on its own if necessary. The eggs pass down the bile ducts into the intestine and leave the host in the faeces. They hatch in about two weeks in water into a ciliated larva called a *miracidium*. The miracidium enters the foot of a mud snail using enzymes secreted by a special penetration gland.

The species of snail is called *Lymnaea truncatula*. It is a small snail (about 6 mm) which feeds on the green algal slime found on the surface of mud near pools in wet fields. It is an amphibious snail, i.e. it is able to live both on land and in the water. (Snails found permanently in water tend to be other species not associated with the liver fluke.) This snail is called the *"secondary"* host of the liver fluke. The *"primary"* host is the host in which it becomes sexually mature, namely the sheep or cow.

Once in the snail, the miracidium undergoes a number of larval stages which produce vast numbers of infective flukes by asexual reproduction. Refer to *Fig. 28.3* for the life cycle of the liver fluke.

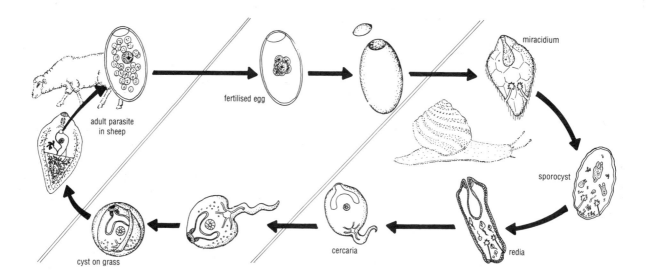

adult parasite in sheep

fertilised egg

miracidium

sporocyst

redia

cercaria

cyst on grass

Fig 28.3 The life cycle of **Fasciola hepatica**

The first stage in the life cycle of the fluke in the snail is called a *redia*. Each redia can produce more rediae within it by asexual reproduction. Eventually the rediae produce the next stage, the *cercaria*. The cercaria is shaped like a miniature frog tadpole with a tail for swimming. It leaves the snail and forms a cyst on waterside vegetation. Cysts can survive short periods of drying. Once eaten by the final host, the young fluke is released. It bores into the host's abdominal cavity and enters its liver from there.

Livers from animals infected with fluke are easy to pick out in the abattoir as they have a mottled white appearance. This is because the ducts containing the flukes develop thick, white walls and are often calcified and gritty when cut. This greatly inhibits the functioning of the liver and results in emaciated appearance and loss of weight of the host *(Fig. 28.4)*.

Fig. 28.4 Cow suffering from liverfluke infection

Control of fluke can be by (a) dosing with anti-helminth chemicals which control the flukes in the host or (b) attempts to control the snail populations. The latter includes drainage to remove sites where the snails might live and the use of snail-killing chemicals ("molluscicides"), which have not been very successful.

28.3.2 Tapeworms

Tapeworms are platyhelminths belonging to the Class *Cestoda*. They are not important in Irish farm animals now - with the exception of some hill sheep and horses not regularly dosed for worms. Adult tapeworms lie in the intestine of the host and absorb their nutrients from the food of the host. They do not have their own digestive system. They have an outer covering, called a cuticle, which protects them from the host's digestive system and yet allows them to absorb all their nutritional requirements.

28.4 Phylum Nematoda

This is a vast phylum of animals. Some are free-living in the soil and are referred to as nematodes. The remainder are parasites of either plants or animals. Plant nematodes are called *eelworms* and animal nematodes are called *roundworms*, or sometimes hookworms, threadworms, lungworms or hairworms. Many Irish schoolchildren have "worms" at some time - the most common are hairworm infections.

All nematodes are round in cross-section ("roundworms"), they are elongate, but are not segmented (compare to the earthworm, below). They are pointed at either end. They have a body cavity called a *pseudocoelome*. The sexes are separate. In size, they range from a few millimetres to 15 cm in the pig roundworm.

Most nematode infections of animals have a similar life cycle. Eggs are passed in the faeces of the host. Outside the host they hatch into a larva which can withstand desiccation and live for a long time. They gain access to the host by being eaten with vegetation. Inside the host, the larva hatches into the adult infective stage. If you are examining preserved nematodes, you may notice small differences at the end which show the difference between male and female.

Important examples of nematodes are:

Dictyocaulus, a lungworm which causes hoose. The adults are 5 — 10 cm in length and inhabit the bronchial tubes of cattle. The life cycle is given in *Fig 28.5.*

Cooperia which causes severe infections in calves. Other nematodes which infect cattle include *Ostertagia* and *Nematodirus.*

The potato eelworm, *Heterodera,* is an example of a nematode which causes damage to an important agricultural crop.

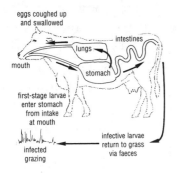

larvae migrate through stomach wall to blood system to lungs. They mature to egg laying stage.

eggs coughed up and swallowed

intestines

lungs

mouth

stomach

first-stage larvae enter stomach from intake at mouth

infective larvae return to grass via faeces

infected grazing

Fig. 28.5 Life cycle of hoose.

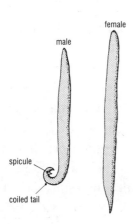

female

male

spicule

coiled tail

Fig. 28.6 Diagram of nematodes

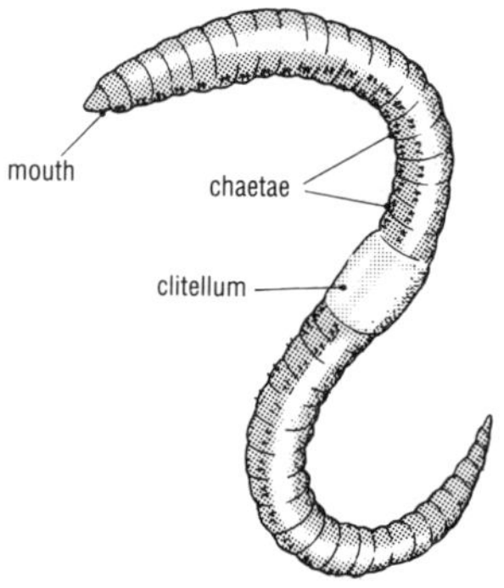

28.5 Phylum Annelida

This phylum includes the familiar earthworm, *Lumbricus terrestris (Fig. 28.7)*, and also leeches, found in freshwater and marine habitats, and the marine worms.

Earthworms are round in cross-section *(Fig. 28.8)*, segmented, have four pairs of bristles (called *chaetae*) on each segment, and have a body cavity called a *coelome*. The bristles enables the earthworm to anchor itself in position, e.g. to prevent it being pulled out of its burrow by a predator, or when crawling along the ground it pushes forward and anchors itself to the substrate also with its bristles. About one-third way along an adult earthworm is a shiny area called the saddle, or *clitellum*. This has a function during mating.

Earthworms are bulk feeders. They injest large quantities of soil. Their intestine includes a muscular gizzard used for grinding. They live on some of the organic matter in the soil and pass the remainder as "worm casts" - coils of soil found on the surface near the entrance of the burrow. This habit of burrowing and moving of soil which makes earthworms important in soil aeration and turnover was first pointed out by *Charles Darwin*, the British naturalist better known for his contribution to our knowledge of evolution.

Earthworms are hermaphrodites. However, they cross-fertilize each other when they mate. Two worms lie together and the clitellum of each secretes mucus. Eggs and sperm are laid into this mucus and when the earthworms withdraw, the eggs remain in a purse-shaped cocoon. These can be found in the soil during spring.

28.6 Phylum Mollusca

This phylum is a diverse group including bivalves (e.g. mussels and clams), octopus, squid, and also slugs and snails. Slugs and snails belong to the Class Gastropoda of the phylum Mollusca.

The main characteristic of the members of the phylum Mollusca is the possession of a foot. This secretes a slimy mucus used for crawling. They also have a specialized tongue with rasp-like teeth, called a *radula*. This is used for eating vegetation. The main difference between slugs and snails is that the snails have a shell. Slugs tend to be pests in gardens and horticultural situations. Their numbers can be reduced by keeping decaying debris to a minimum. Young slugs hatch in early summer and grow in size over the summer months. Slugs are more common in household gardens. This is the reason why maincrop potatoes are rarely worthwhile in small gardens.

One very important mollusc, from the agricultural viewpoint, is the secondary host of liver fluke, *Lymnaea truncatula (see Fig. 28.3)*.

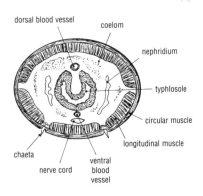

Fig. 28.7 External structure of earthworm

Fig. 28.8 Cross section of earthworm

28.7 Phylum Arthropoda

The arthropods are a vast phylum including about 90% of all species in the Animal Kingdom. In addition to the groups we will consider, they also include scorpions, lobsters, crabs, woodlice, millipedes, centipedes and spiders. A variety of arthropods are shown in *Fig. 28.9.*

Fig. 28.9 Various arthropods

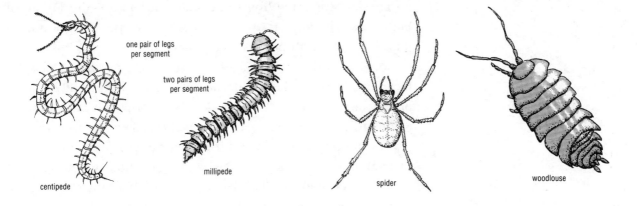

one pair of legs per segment

two pairs of legs per segment

centipede

millipede

spider

woodlouse

Members of phylum Arthropoda have jointed appendages and an external skeleton. Throughout their life, they have regular moults, called *ecdyses*, which allow them to grow rapidly before the new skeleton hardens.

Members of two classes are important to Irish agriculture, class Arachnida and class Insecta.

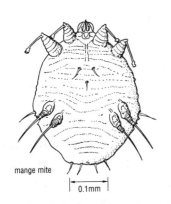

mange mite

0.1mm

mange mite burrowing in the skin

sucking mouth parts

sheep tick

1mm

Fig. 28.10 Ticks and mites (notice difference in scale)

28.7.1 Class Arachnida

Arachnids have *two main body segments*, a head-cum-thorax, called a *cephalothorax*, and an abdomen. They have *four pairs* of legs. Examples include spiders, mites and ticks. Mites are mostly less than a millimetre in size, many are free-living. Mange, or scabies, is caused by the mange mite *Sarcoptes scabei* which is passed from an infected animal by close contact. The female mite bores into the skin and lays eggs. These hatch and also burrow into the skin. This causes intense itching. Itching can lead to open sores and secondary infection. *(See Fig. 28.10.)*

Ticks are blood-sucking ectoparasites of sheep and cattle. They were mentioned in the section on Protozoa as transmitters of redwater fever in cattle. The only tick commonly found in Ireland is the sheep tick, *Ixodes ricinus.* It is found on all farm animals, on dogs and even humans. It has specialized ridges on its mouthparts to enable it to cling on while sucking blood.

28.7.2 Class Insecta

Insects have *three main body parts*, head, thorax and abdomen. They have *three pairs of legs* and usually *two pairs of wings* on the thorax.

Examples include lice, fleas, aphids (or greenfly), cranefly and butterfly. The life cycle of many insects can be summarized as follows:

egg —> larva —> pupa —> adult

This type of life cycle is referred to as *"complete metamorphosis"*.

The larva is a feeding stage. Caterpillars are the larvae of butterflies. The pupa is a resting stage. Many insects overwinter as pupae. The butterfly pupa is called a chrysalis.

Sometimes the larval stages of insects can be pests. Examples include the larva of the clickbeetle, called a wireworm, and the larva of the cranefly, called a leatherjacket. Wireworms can cause damage to potato crops. Some species of leatherjackets eat the roots of grasses and cereals and heavy infestations can be a problem.

Examine preserved specimens of caterpillar, wireworm and leatherjacket. Refer to the diagrams in *Fig. 28.11* for help. Notice that caterpillars have false legs, called *prolegs*, on the abdominal segments. If you watch a living caterpillar while it is walking you will see how it uses the prolegs. The caterpillar of the cabbage butterfly is a typical example. Wireworms only have three thoracic legs and have no prolegs. Leatherjackets do not have legs, they are softer, and some species have appendages near the end which act as gills (for gaseous exchange). *(See Exercise 62.)*

Aphids, e.g. the greenfly on roses, have syringe-like sucking mouthparts. These can cause damage to plants in a few ways. Firstly, there is the primary damage caused by the loss of sap to the plant. Secondly, plant viruses are transmitted by aphids as they fly from plant to plant. Examples include virus transmission in sugar beet, cereals, strawberries and potatoes. For most of the year the aphids present are all females which produce live young without fertilization. Winged and wingless forms occur. Winged aphids fly to new host plants. In late autumn, males and females are produced. These mate and the females lay eggs which are the overwintering stage for many species of aphid.

Young aphids look just like their mother - they are miniature aphids. They feed by sucking plant sap almost immediately. When the young of insects look like adults we call them "nymphs". Nymphs moult regularly as they grow until they are adults. This type of life cycle is called *"incomplete metamorphosis"*. Contrast it with the complete metamorphosis life cycle where there were distinct stages - larva and pupa, which do not look like the adult.

As an exercise, look for a group of aphids on the underside of sycamore or oak leaves in spring or on the soft tips of rose bushes later in the year. Find examples of winged and wingless females. Can

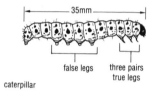

caterpillar

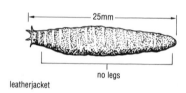

leatherjacket

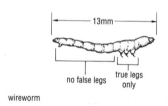

wireworm

Fig 28.11 Three insect larvae

you observe an aphid birth? Can you find different sized nymphs? Use the diagrams in *Fig. 28.12* for reference.

Fig. 28.12 The life cycle of aphids

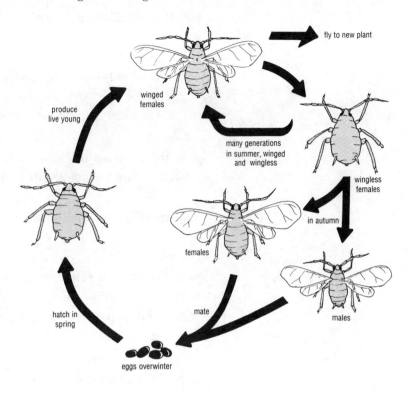

28.8 Parasites

Many of the animals studied in this chapter are *parasites*. Parasites are *species that live at the expense of other organisms*. We have already studied parasites of plants such as potato blight. As you study the examples, pay attention to how they are adapted for a parasitic way of life.

Parasitic animals can be *ectoparasites* (living on the outside of their host) or *endoparasites* (living inside their host). Ectoparasites often have claws to cling onto their host (lice, fleas). They may have sucking mouthparts for sucking blood or plant sap. They may cause secondary damage by transmitting other organisms (ticks and redwater fever, aphids and plant viruses).

Endoparasites often have a special outer covering (called a cuticle in flukes) which protects them from the host's defences. The tapeworm cuticle protects it from digestion by the host but allows absorption of nutrients. Endoparasites have to survive in an environment (the gut of a mammal) where oxygen is scarce. They tend to be hermaphrodites. They produce large numbers of eggs. Many have some means of asexual reproduction to vastly increase the numbers of offspring (e.g. the liver fluke). These characteristics increase their chances of reproducing their species - finding a new host can be risky for a parasite.

Exercises

Exercise 60. Examination of *Fasciola hepatica*

Materials needed
1. Preserved liver flukes and/or prepared microscopic mounts
2. Microscope

Procedure
Use the diagram in *Fig. 28.2* to study the structure of adult liver flukes. Produce a labelled diagram of what you see.

Exercise 61. Examination of various worms

Materials needed
1. Preserved specimens e.g. roundworms, tapeworms
2. Living earthworms
3. Prepared microscopic mount of a cross-section of an earthworm
4. Hand lens or microscope
5. Packaging from various worm treatments

Procedure
1. Examine and draw preserved specimens. Note their sizes. Note which kinds of worms are segmented and which are not. You might be able to sex them by referring to *Fig. 28.5* for the differences.
2. Study packages of worm treatments. List the species mentioned. Enquire about the incidence of the different species in your locality.
3. Observe a living earthworm. Refer to the diagram in *Fig. 28.7*. Observe how it moves. Study a cross section of an earthworm. Refer to *Fig. 28.8*.

Exercise 62. Examination of various arthropods

Materials needed
1. Preserved material of various arthropods including ticks, louse, flea, butterfly and larvae, caterpillar, leatherjacket and wireworm.
2. Hand lens

Procedure
Examine and make your own drawings of the material. You can use the diagrams in the text to help you identify the various structures.

29 – Living Organisms
3. Vertebrates

In this chapter we will introduce the major groups of vertebrates which are important in agriculture. These are the birds and the mammals. We will then study some mammalian structures such as bone, skeleton and dental arrangements. The remaining chapters in this section *(chapters 30 to 35)* cover other aspects of mammalian biology in more detail.

29.1 Phylum Chordata

Backboned animals all belong to the phylum Chordata. Examples of chordates include fish, amphibians (e.g. frogs), birds and mammals. The main characteristic shared by these animals is the backbone or vertebrae. Hence, they are called *vertebrates*. Two groups are important in agriculture, birds in Class Aves, and mammals in Class Mammalia.

29.2 Temperature Regulation

The birds and the mammals are the only two groups of animals in the Animal Kingdom that are *warm-blooded* or *homoiothermic*. This means that they regulate their body temperatures independently, and often much higher, than their surroundings. This has allowed birds and mammals to live in tropical and arctic conditions. Being warm-blooded is expensive in terms of the energy required to maintain the body temperature *(see page 276)*. All other animals which mainly adopt the temperature of their surroundings are said to be *cold-blooded* or *poikilothermic*.

29.3 Birds - Class Aves

Birds are winged vertebrates. Their basic characteristic is that they have *feathers*. Many of their characteristics are associated with flight. For example they have specially lightened bones. They do not have teeth; instead they have a horny beak with which they peck at food. Different species of birds have different kinds of beaks often associated with their particular kind of feeding. Birds do not have a bladder. They produce semi-solid urine: the white on top of bird droppings consists of uric acid. Birds reproduce by means of eggs with hard shells. The basic organization of membranes within the egg is quite similar to that in mammalian reproduction. Many of these topics will be expanded in the chapters which follow.

29.4 Mammals - Class Mammalia

The characteristics of mammals are as follows:

Mammals have *hair.* Most mammals produce *live young.* Before birth, the young are nourished in a womb via a *placenta.* Later the mother feeds her offspring with *milk* secreted by mammary glands (*mamma* is the Latin for breast, hence the name of the class).

Domestic animals include members of the order Carnivora (dogs and cats), and the hooved animals or *ungulates.* Hooved mammals are classified according to whether they have an odd or even number of toes. *Odd-toed ungulates* include the horse and examples of *even-toed ungulates* include pigs, sheep, goats and cows. The latter three belong to a group with a specialized type of stomach and are called *ruminants* which will be covered in detail in *chapter 30.*

29.5 The Mammalian Skeleton

Fig 29.1 Rabbit skeleton

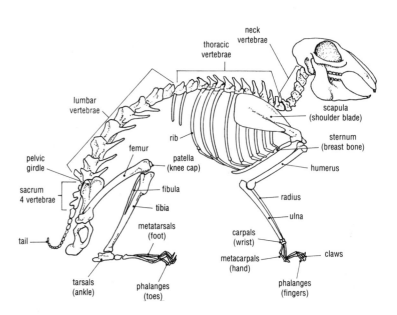

The main bones of the mammalian skeleton are shown in *Fig. 29.1.* The rabbit is a typical mammal with a basic skeleton structure. You should be able to name the main bones of the skeleton. Probably the most important domesticated mammals are the hooved mammals e.g. horses, cows, pigs and sheep. Hooved mammals have evolved a very specialized arrangement of their legs. This is shown in *Fig. 29.2.* Note that the front foot of the horse is basically the same structure as the middle finger of humans. The horse hoof is basically the same structure as the fingernail. The bones of the horse's leg are greatly elongated bones from the wrist down. Hooved animals are collectively called ungulates. The horse is an odd-toed ungulate since it has only one toe. Pigs, sheep and cattle have two large hooves on each foot; this makes them even-toed ungulates.

Fig. 29.2 The bones of horse legs. Compare these with those of the rabbit

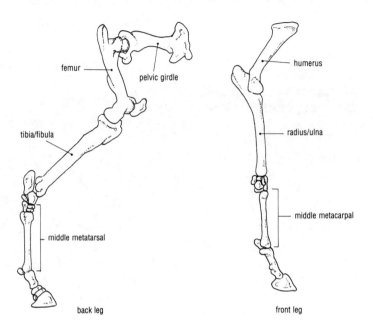

29.6 Mammalian Teeth

Mammals use a variety of feeding techniques. These include grazing herbivores, omnivores (or generalists) and flesh eaters. These have different dental arrangements. Remember the names of the teeth in mammals: (from the front) *incisors, canines, premolars* and *molars*.

Incisors are used for biting and nibbling. Canines, as their name implies, are prominent in the dog family. Lions and tigers use their canines for killing. Canine teeth are often missing or greatly reduced in grazing animals. Grazers usually have a space between the incisors and the grinding premolars and molars. A sheep can make horizontal, circular movements with its lower jaw. Premolars and molars are for grinding. They are at their most advanced in grazers. Try to examine, at least, some teeth from a cow or a horse. Notice also the prominent muscles for chewing in grazers. These are called masseter muscles.

One way of studying these is to use a *dental formula*. A pig has three incisors, one canine, four premolars and three molars in each half of both its upper and its lower set of teeth. This can be written as:

$$\frac{3\ 1\ 4\ 3}{3\ 1\ 4\ 3}$$ giving a total of 44 teeth.

A dog has a very similar arrangement except it has only two molars in its upper half-jaw:

$$\frac{3\ 1\ 4\ 2}{3\ 1\ 4\ 3}$$ giving a total of 42 teeth.

When you examine a fox or dog skull, notice how the molars have surfaces which slide past each other. This is for cutting flesh. Compare this to the grinding molars of grazing animals.

Fig. 29.3 Skulls and teeth of dog, sheep and rabbit. Arrows show the movement of the lower jaw

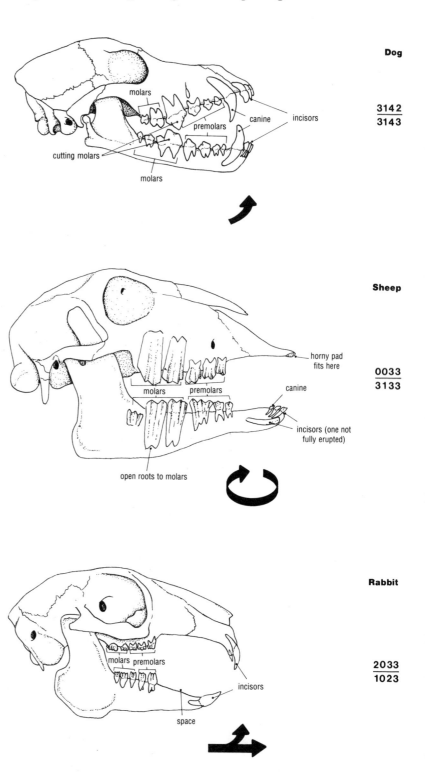

Refer to the diagrams of dental arrangements in *Fig. 29.3*. In a sheep, the incisors of the lower jaw bite against a horny pad in the upper jaw. The dental formulae for sheep and rabbit are:

$$\text{sheep } \frac{0\ 0\ 3\ 3}{3\ 1\ 3\ 3} \qquad \text{rabbit } \frac{2\ 0\ 3\ 3}{1\ 0\ 2\ 3}$$

Consider how dentition varies according to the animal's diet. If we were to use one word to describe the feeding mechanism of these three species, then sheep are grinders, dogs are choppers and rabbits are nibblers.

29.7 Animal Tissues and Organs

The basic structure of an animal cell was introduced in *Chapter 7*. In higher animals we usually observe the functions of groups of specialized cells called tissues. *Tissues are cells which cooperate with each other to perform a group function*. Here we will quickly review the various kinds of tissues found in animals.

The following types of tissues are found in vertebrates: epithelium, connective, blood, muscle and nervous. The last three will be covered separately in their own chapters *(31 and 35)*.

29.7.1 Epithelium
This tissue lines all the cavities in the body. Thus, epithelium is involved in the secretion of enzymes, absorption of digested materials and other chemicals. Epithelium lines the cavities of the lung passages. It secretes mucus to trap dust particles and is involved in the exchange of gases. Epithelium also forms the skin or *epidermis* which covers an animal's body. This provides protection. Epithelial cells are constantly rubbed off from their outer surface and renewed from their inner layers.

Depending on their position, epithelial cells can have a number of forms: two kinds frequently found include *pavement* epithelium, where the cells are flattened and joined along their edges. The epidermis of animals are of this sort. Another common sort is *columnar* epithelium, where the cells are taller than long. This type of epithelium lines the intestine and is involved in secreting enzymes and absorption of nutrients.

29.7.2 Connective
Several kinds of connective tissue occur. Supporting connective tissue includes both cartilage and bone. Binding connective tissue includes tendons and ligaments. Fibrous connective tissue occurs throughout the body where it is used for packing and providing a pathway for blood vessels and nervous tissue. A special type of fibrous connective tissue is *adipose* tissue whose cells are used for

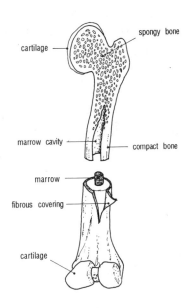

Fig. 29.4 A split mammalian bone

Fig. 29.5 Photomicrograph of bone

storing fat. Suet from the butcher's shop is a good example of adipose tissue.

The supporting connective tissues are also called *skeletal* tissues. *Cartilage* consists of an organic matrix containing cartilage cells. The matrix is secreted by the cartilage cells. A common name for cartilage is gristle. Bone is much harder than cartilage. *Bone* is an organic matrix hardened with calcium salts, mainly calcium phosphate. Mammalian bones have bone marrow in the centre. Note also the arrangement of ball and socket joints in the skeleton (*see Fig. 29.4*).

The calcium salts are secreted by special bone cells called *osteoblasts*. The structure of bone in cross-section is shown in *Fig. 29.5*. Running the length of the bone are canals called Haversian canals which contain blood vessels and nerves. Around the canals are rings of osteoblasts which secrete the bone.

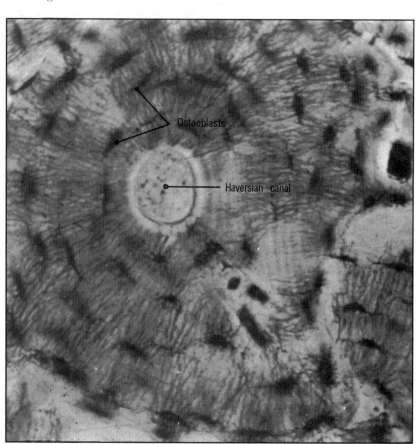

29.8 Organs

An organ usually consists of one or more types of epithelial tissue together with one or more connective tissues. Together, they perform specialized functions in the body. The heart, lungs and liver are all organs.

Exercises

Exercise 63. Structure of the mammalian skeleton

Materials needed
1. Skeleton of a mammal, e.g. rabbit (various identified bones are very useful if a full skeleton is not available)
2. Partial skeleton or drawings of hooved mammal, e.g. horse leg

Procedure
Examine and identify the major bones of the skeleton. Produce labelled drawings. Use *Figs. 29.1* and *29.2* to help you identify the bones.

Exercise 64. Mammalian tooth arrangements

Materials needed
Various skulls of mammals (good diagrams or charts are useful if you do not have skulls) e.g. sheep and rabbit

Procedure
1. Skulls of domestic animals are often found fully cleared of flesh. These should be scrubbed clean and treated with dilute domestic bleach. Wear rubber gloves when doing this. Then allow to dry. Although not necessary, the skull may be coated with varnish.
2. Examine and draw the skulls. Refer to the dental formulae given in the text. As you examine each skull try to explain the function of the dental arrangement.
3. Write out your own dental formula. Either use a cleaned finger or your tongue to count the teeth. Adult humans (should!) have

$$\frac{2\ 1\ 2\ 3}{2\ 1\ 2\ 3}$$ giving a total of 32.

Exercise 65. Bones: composition and structure

Materials needed
1. Bones, e.g. chicken bone, part of long bone from butcher's: ask to have it split lengthwise
2. Prepared transverse section of bone
3. Dilute hydrochloric acid

Procedure
1. Soak the chicken bone in dilute hydrochloric acid for at least 24 hours. Observe the production of gas (which gas?). Remove using a forceps and wash off. Explain what has happened.
2. Examine the split bone section. Refer to Fig. *29.4*. Draw what you see in your specimen.
3. Examine the T.S. of bone under the low power of the microscope (refer to *Exercise 20* for microscopic technique, if necessary). *Use Fig. 29.5* to identify the structures and draw what you see.

30 – Digestive Systems

30.1 Foods

Chemicals found in foods include carbohydrates, fats, proteins, vitamins, minerals and water. Their basic structure and characteristics were covered in *Chapter 7*. Food tests were covered on *page 90*. In *Exercise 66* you will apply those techniques to test a number of foods for their constituents.

During digestion foodstuffs are broken down sufficiently to allow them to be absorbed. Starch is broken down to monosaccharide sugars. Subsequently they may be converted back to a storage polysaccharide - usually glycogen stored in the liver of mammals. Proteins are broken down to the individual amino acids. These are absorbed and are then available to form new and different proteins. Fats are broken down to fatty acids and glycerol.

The other chemicals in the diet are vitamins and minerals. Vitamins were also covered in *Chapter 7*. Mineral nutrition of plants was investigated in *Exercise 32*. Many of the concepts covered in that *Exercise* are relevant in animals also. Trace elements will be mentioned in the chapters which follow. Two can be mentioned here: iodine is necessary for the hormone thyroxine and cobalt is necessary for vitamin B_{12}.

30.2 A Digestive System

A digestive system includes the intake of food, called *ingestion*, the breakdown of food or *digestion*, the absorption of the products of digestion and the elimination of the remaining portion of the food by *egestion*.

30.3 Ingestion

The organs used for feeding in mammals include the lips, tongue and teeth. Animals are specially adapted for the food they eat. The dental arrangements of a number of domestic animals were covered in *Chapter 29*. These are often related to the type of feeding used by the animal. Birds have a horny beak and no teeth. They use this for pecking at food.

The smell and sight of food, and also the presence of food in the mouth, cause the secretion of *saliva* from three pairs of salivary glands located in the lower part of the mouth. Saliva includes mucus, a slimy material used for lubrication, and an enzyme called salivary amylase which begins the breakdown of starch. Since most mammals do not keep food in their mouth for very long it is probably not very important for digestion - except in herbivores.

The food ingested is thoroughly mixed with saliva and chewed. It is now called a *bolus*. The process of chewing and mixing it with saliva to form a bolus is called *mastication*. The large muscles at the side of the head used for chewing are called the *masseter* muscles.

30.4 The Oesophagus

The bolus passes to the stomach through a tube called the oesophagus. Rhythmical contractions, called *peristalis*, propel the bolus along.

In mammals, the oesophagus is a simple tube connecting the mouth and the stomach. Birds (including the domestic fowl) have a specialized storage area called the *crop* at the base of the oesophagus. One benefit of the crop is that birds can continue to digest their meal during the night. When preparing a bird such as a pheasant for cooking, it is often possible to identify the crop contents.

30.5 The Stomach

Here we study the stomach of the fowl, rabbit, pig and ruminant. Refer to *Fig. 30.1* overleaf.

30.5.1 Fowl

The stomach of the fowl consists of two parts: the *proventriculus* is the first part. It secretes digestive enzymes. The second part is unique to birds: it is the *gizzard*. Birds swallow grit and pass it to the gizzard. The highly muscular gizzard and grit are used to grind hard foods such as cereal grains. *(See Exercise 67.)*

30.5.2 Rabbit and pig stomachs

The rabbit and pig have what is called a "monogastric stomach". This means that it consists of a single chamber in which digestion occurs. Gastric juice is secreted by cells in the walls of the stomach. The juice consists of hydrochloric acid, pepsinogen and rennin. The acid is very strong and results in a pH of 2. The pepsinogen forms the proteinase pepsin in the presence of the acid. Another proteinase, rennin is very important in young mammals as it allows the digestion of the milk protein, casein. The presence of food in the stomach stimulates the stomach wall to produce a hormone called gastrin. This circulates with the blood and causes the stomach to continue producing gastric juice.

Food enters and leaves the stomach through valves called sphincters. Food enters through the cardiac sphincter and exits through the pyloric sphincter.

30.5.3 Digesting cellulose

Remember that cellulose constitutes a huge source of organic matter - it is very valuable as a food source if it can be digested. Generally, higher animals are not able to digest cellulose. However, a few groups of animals have solved this problem by culturing micro-organisms to do the digestion for them. In the tropics, termites are insects that specialize in this source of food. Grazing mammals such as rabbits, horses and cows have found a solution to this problem also.

Broadly speaking, there are two different solutions to the digestion of cellulose in mammals. One group of animals have the normal type of stomach, with long intestines and micro-organisms in the hind gut. These are called *hind-gut fermenters* e.g. the rabbit and horse. The second group, including the cow and sheep, have a specialized type of stomach with four chambers. Animals from this group are collectively called *ruminants*. Other mammals, such as pigs and humans, cannot digest cellulose. However, in this group cellulose is called *roughage* and is important for the normal production of faeces.

Fig 30.1 Fowl, pig and ruminant digestive systems

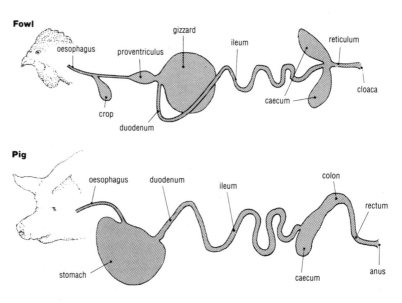

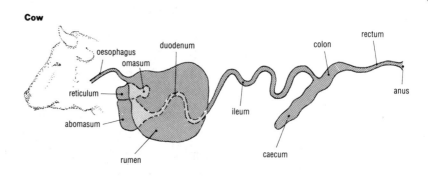

Rabbits, horses and humans have monogastric stomachs *(Fig. 30.1)*. In herbivores with monogastric stomachs, the large intestine and appendix are very important as sites where micro-organisms are present to ferment the food passing through. This fermentation digests cellulose. Herbivores also have a much longer gut than flesh eaters (carnivores). A sheep's intestine is about 30 metres long whereas a lion's is only about 6 metres long (suggest why?). Rabbits have an interesting habit which effectively doubles the length of their intestine: they eat their own faeces - this is called coprophagy.

> *"Whatsoever parteth the hoof, and is clovenfooted, and cheweth the cud among the beasts, that shall ye eat".* Leviticus XI, 3

Chewing the cud has been recognized for a long time!

30.5.4 The ruminant stomach *(Fig. 30.2)*

Cattle, sheep and their close relatives are called ruminants. This is because they have a stomach which is specialized for the digestion of cellulose. Their stomach consists of four chambers. The first part is called the *rumen* or paunch. The rumen holds a huge culture of many species of anaerobic bacteria and protozoa which can digest cellulose. In addition to absorbing the products of microbial activity, ruminants also digest some of their microbial culture. This provides ruminants with microbial protein to supplement their predominantly cellulose diet.

Fig 30.2 The ruminant stomach

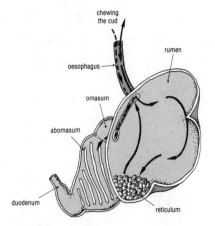

Digestion is continued in the *reticulum* (called the honeycomb stomach after the pattern on its wall). From the reticulum, food is passed back to the mouth for further mastication - *"chewing the cud"*. This gives a thorough grinding to the plant material. The cud is then reswallowed and passed to the third stomach chamber, the *omasum* (called "manyplies" after the layers or lamellae on its wall).

Ask at a butcher's about tripe, drisheen, skirts and lights.

In the omasum the food is squeezed; water is absorbed and the solid part passes to the fourth chamber, the *abomasum*. This final chamber acts like the "normal" stomach of mammals with a monogastric stomach. The usual processes of secretion of gastric juices and digestion take place here. Calves whose diet consist of milk sénd the milk directly to the abomasum where it is acted upon by the enzyme rennin. This is why the abomasum is also called the rennet stomach. Rennet is impure rennin. It is used in cheese manufacture, although today, most of the rennin used is microbial in origin.

30.5.5 Digestion and diet

The various approaches to digestion in domestic animals have obvious implications for farmers. Fowl can digest whole grain but need to be given grit if they are not free-range. Ruminants can digest bulky cellulose but are not efficient at digesting foods with sugars such as root crops and potatoes. Ruminants simply add everything to their culture of micro-organisms and absorb the products later. Finally, hind-gut digesters (rabbits and horses) are not as efficient as ruminants at digesting cellulose but absorb sugars from root crops without further digestion. Further information on the importance of this relationship between digestion and diet is given in *Section 9.1*.

30.6 The Small Intestine

The partially digested food now leaves the stomach via the pyloric sphincter and enters the *small intestine*. The first part of the small intestine is the *duodenum*. Two important secretions are added at this stage: bile and pancreatic juice.

Bile is coloured green by the breakdown products of haemoglobin. Bile is formed in the liver and stored temporarily in the gall bladder. It contains sodium hydrogencarbonate which gives it a pH between 7 and 8. It neutralizes the acid material coming from the stomach. Bile also contains bile salts which give the look and feel of washing-up liquid. Bile acts like washing-up liquid. It *emulsifies* lipids - this means the lipids are broken down into small droplets giving them a greatly increased surface area for the action of enzymes (which enzymes act on lipids?). There are no enzymes in bile.

Pancreatic juice consists of four enzymes: pancreatic amylase (acts on starch), pancreatic lipase (acts on lipids), and trypsinogen and chymotrypsinogen. The last two are enzyme precursors - soon after release they form the proteinases trypsin and chymotrypsin.

Just as in the case of the stomach and the production of the hormone gastrin, mentioned above, the presence of food in the small intestine causes the production of hormones which stimulate the continued secretion of both bile and pancreatic juice.

Intestinal juice is the third source of enzymes. It includes a battery of enzymes which perform the final digestion of many food items. These include sucrase, which breaks down the disaccharide sucrose to glucose and fructose, and lactase which breaks lactose into glucose and galactose (both monosaccharides). Other enzymes (peptidases) complete the job of digesting protein fragments (peptides) into their component amino acids.

30.6.1 Absorption

The internal surface area of the small intestine *(ileum)* is greatly increased by structures called *villi (Fig. 30.4)*. Each villus is a microscopic, fingerlike extension into the gut cavity. It is richly supplied with blood capillaries and lacteals which are capillaries of the lymphatic system *(see Chapter 31)*.

Fig 30.3 A photomicrograph of the small intestine

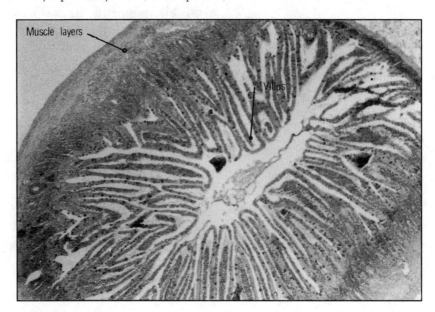

Monosaccharide sugars and amino acids as well as vitamins, salts and water are absorbed into the capillaries in the villi. This absorption is often by simple diffusion but sometimes active transport may be involved. For example, glucose is absorbed even when it is present at concentrations less than in circulating blood (0.1%). Fatty acids are mainly absorbed into the lacteals. These are the smallest vessels of the lymphatic system. The fatty acids are quickly reconverted into lipids which is why the lymph in the lacteals appears white or milky - *lac* is the Latin for milk.

30.7 Large Intestine

The importance of the large intestine for the digestion of cellulose in hind-gut fermenters has already been explained. Hind-gut fermenters use micro-organisms in their caecum to ferment and digest cellulose. Compare the length of the caecum in the diagrams provided. The other major part of the large intestine is the colon. The colon is important for reabsorbing water. If this is not functioning properly, as in the case of diarrhoea, dehydration can occur. There can also be secondary problems due to loss of ions which in humans with diarrhoea can be corrected by drinking water containing properly balanced salt mixtures. The opposite to diarrhoea is constipation.

30.8 Egestion

Any material not absorbed is eliminated as *faeces* coloured mainly by the bile pigments.. It is stored temporarily in the *rectum* prior to defecation through the anus.

Exercises

Exercise 66. Composition of food items

Materials needed
1. Various food items: cereals, potato, various fruits, grass, roots such as beet
2. Sunflower seeds
3. Mortar and pestle
4. Pocket refractometer
5. Materials as on *page 90*

Procedure
1. Using the methods on *page 90,* investigate the chemicals present in the foods tested. It will be best to grind the material first with a mortar and pestle. Test sunflower seeds for the presence of lipid.
2. When sugars are detected, their levels can be measured using the pocket refractometer *(see page 91)*.

Exercise 67. The gizzard of fowl

Materials needed
1. Gizzard of fowl (enclosed as giblets in chickens sold for roasting)
2. Dissecting kit

Procedure
1. Examine the gizzard and observe how muscular it is. Sometimes small pebbles are present. Birds use this grit for grinding grain.
2. Draw. *(See Fig. 30.1.)*

Exercise 68. The rabbit digestive system

Materials needed
1. Rabbit prepared for dissection. The use of fresh material is not advised.
2. Dissecting board
3. Dissecting kit

Procedure
1. Lay out the rabbit on its back on the dissecting board and peg it out using dissecting awls.
2. Open the digestive cavity by making the cuts shown in *Fig. 30.4.*
3. Display the digestive system as in *Fig. 30.5.* Examine and produce a labelled drawing.
4. The dissection is continued in *Exercise 71.*

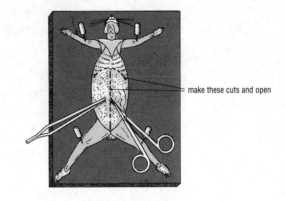

Fig. 30.4 Laying out a rabbit on a dissecting board

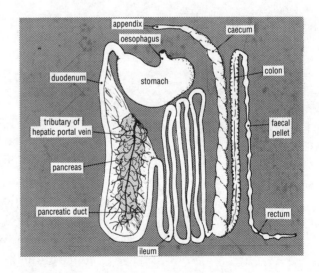

Fig.30.5 Dissection of the rabbit alimentary canal

31 – Circulation, Transport and Storage

This chapter deals with the circulation of body fluids and the way in which the body transports and stores the various chemicals vital for living. We will consider the blood and lymphatic systems.

31.1 Blood System

Mammals have a *four chambered* heart. The heart is a pumping organ. Blood vessels which deliver blood to the heart are called *veins* and those which carry it away from the heart are called *arteries*. The blood vessels near the heart are very large. However, in the organs where the exchange of materials takes place (e.g. absorption in the digestive system, gaseous exchange in the lungs,), the blood vessels are at their smallest. These are *capillaries*. Capillaries are just large enough to permit the passage of red blood cells in single file. Sometimes we refer to capillaries as either arterioles or venules depending on whether they are on the arterial or venous side of the system.

Arteries have more muscular walls than veins. Thus when we examine microscopic transverse sections, arteries are easier to see as they retain their round profile. The walls of arteries and veins are elastic. Veins are equipped with valves, essentially folds of skin, which prevent blood from flowing in the wrong direction. *(See Fig. 30.1.)*

31.2 Pathway of Circulation

The general plan of mammalian circulation is as follows: blood reaches the right auricle (note that the auricles are also called atria, singular atrium) via the main veins or *venae cavae*. From here the blood passes through the *tricuspid valve* (this valve looks like three yacht sails and acts to prevent the back flow of blood) into the *right ventricle*. From here the blood travels to the lungs in the pulmonary arteries. After oxygenation in the lungs the blood returns to the *left auricle* of the heart via the pulmonary veins. From here it passes via the *bicuspid valve* to the *left ventricle*. The left ventricle is the main pump of the body and it pumps blood into the coronary system and into the general, or *systemic*, system.

The *coronary system* is a series of relatively small but vitally important arteries which supply the muscles of the heart itself. When dissecting a sheep's heart, you can find the exit of the coronary arteries just outside the semilunar valves of the dorsal aorta. Push a blunt seeker into these and you can trace these arteries part of the way. It is the blockage of the *coronary arteries* by lipid material which results in a "coronary thrombosis", or heart attack, or the less severe *"angina pectoris"* or chest pains.

The *systemic system* includes the blood supply to the head via the carotid arteries, and to the hind part of the body via the dorsal aorta. The arterial system delivers blood directly to the alimentary canal. However, note that there is a very important difference between the arterial and venous system which serves the alimentary canal. This is called the *hepatic portal system.*

31.3 Hepatic Portal System

The alimentary canal delivers the products of digestion (sugars, amino acids, etc.) to the blood capillaries of the small intestine. (This is covered in detail in *Chapter 30.*) However, instead of travelling directly to the heart for distribution to the body, the veins from the intestine travel to the liver. This is called the hepatic portal system. The main vein is the *hepatic portal vein.* In the liver, the various concentration levels are checked and regulated. Consult the separate box, overleaf, on the vital functions of the liver. In summary, the digestive system delivers varying quantities of nutrients to the liver. The liver regulates their level, stores them and releases them as required. Venous blood travels from the liver to the heart in the *hepatic vein* (note the difference in the name).

Fig. 31.1 General plan of the circulation system in a mammal

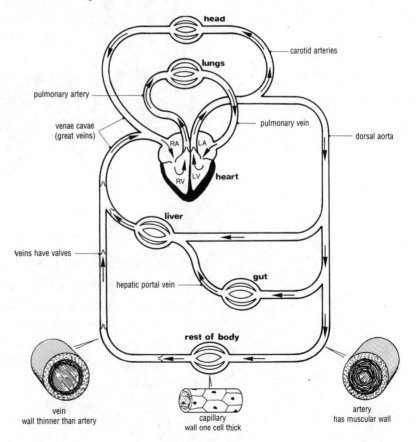

—275—

Functions of the Liver

Essentially, the liver is the buffer between the intestine and the rest of the body. It performs the following functions:

1. The level of circulating glucose is regulated by the liver acting in conjunction with the hormone insulin. If the glucose level drops, then glycogen is broken down to maintain the level. If the glucose level is too high, it is converted to glycogen and stored in the liver cells.

2. Lipid levels are maintained by sending excess lipid to the adipose tissue for storage.

3. It breaks down surplus amino acids which cannot be stored. The amino ($-NH_2$) group is removed. This forms the substance ammonia which is poisonous. These amino groups are converted to urea in mammals. Since ammonia is much more toxic than urea we call this *detoxification*. There is more on this in *Chapter 33*.

4. It produces bile. Bile salts emulsify lipids during digestion. The colour of bile is from the breakdown products of haemoglobin from used red blood cells. This also colours faeces.

5. It is involved in heat production and regulation. The energy released by metabolism is often heat. This is distributed by the circulatory system. This can be regulated by the volume and distribution of blood. The blood vessels of the liver can vary in volume from 300 cm^3 to 1 500 cm^3 (in humans). Thus the liver has a major role in how blood is distributed throughout the body.

6. Formation of red blood corpuscles. This is mainly in the foetus as it is mainly by the bone marrow in the adult.

7. It stores vitamins (A, D and B_{12}) and minerals such as potassium, iron and copper.

Thus the liver is a major regulator of the internal environment of a mammal.

31.4 Blood

Blood is a circulating liquid tissue. The adult human has 5.5 litres of blood. The function of blood is the transport of:

- oxygen and carbon dioxide
- the products of digestion, e.g. glucose and amino acids
- wastes such as urea
- ions such as Na^+, Ca^{++}, Cl^- and HCO_3^-
- hormones
- heat *(see the box above)*

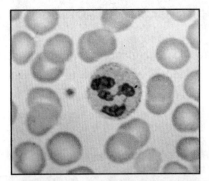

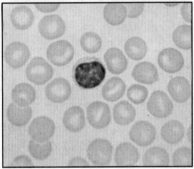

Fig. 31.2 Two kinds of white bloodcell. Note that the cell nucleus is stained. The other cells are red blood cells

31.4.1 Blood cells

Blood consists of three types of cells in a fluid called *plasma*. The most numerous cells are called *red blood cells* (written as rbc for short). They are also called red blood corpuscles or erythrocytes. In mammals, the rbc's are biconcave discs (i.e. shaped like miniature car tyres), they are 7.5 μm in diameter and have no nucleus. They contain the red oxygen-carrying pigment, haemoglobin.

Less numerous, but of vital importance are the *white blood cells* or leucocytes. White blood cells are larger than rbc's. They have no definite shape and they have a nucleus. They play a major role in the body's defense system - the immune response. *(See Fig. 31.2)*

Platelets are minute cell fragments which are important in blood-clotting.

31.4.2 Blood plasma

Plasma consists of a clear liquid called *serum* and a protein called *fibrinogen*. Serum is important for the transport of water-soluble materials throughout the body. These include glucose, amino acids, proteins and enzymes, various salts, hormones and wastes such as urea. Fibrinogen is important for blood-clotting.

31.4.3 Blood-clotting

The basis of blood clotting or coagulation is that the soluble plasma protein *fibrinogen* forms the insoluble protein *fibrin*, which we call a clot. When platelets in the blood are exposed to the air, as in a wound, they set in motion a series of reactions. The reactions involve at least 12 different factors including vitamin K and calcium ions. Eventually, these result in the production of the substance thrombin from its precursor, prothrombin. In the presence of thrombin, fibrinogen is converted to fibrin. Humans with *haemophilia* lack *factor VIII* without which blood cannot clot *(Fig 31.3)*.

When samples of blood are taken for analysis they are put into tubes whose inside walls are coated with an *anticoagulant* called heparin.

Fig. 31.3 Blood-clotting process

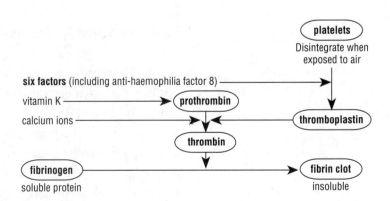

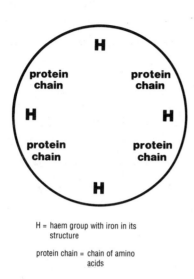

H = haem group with iron in its
structure

protein chain = chain of amino
acids

Fig. 31.4 Diagram of haemoglobin

31.5 Transport of Oxygen and Carbon Dioxide

The red pigment haemoglobin is the vital chemical for the transport of oxygen and carbon dioxide. Each haemoglobin molecule consists of four protein chains and four haem groups. The haem groups have an iron atom in the centre - thus iron is needed for the formation of red blood cells *(see Fig 31.4)*.

In the presence of oxygen, haemoglobin forms oxyhaemoglobin.

$$Hb \quad + \quad 4\,O_2 \quad \longrightarrow \quad HbO_8$$

haemoglobin   oxyhaemoglobin

This is what happens in the lungs. In the body tissues where carbon dioxide is being produced there is a more acid environment. This causes the reverse reaction to take place - i.e. oxygen is unloaded for use in the tissues. In the tissues, the haemoglobin forms another compound with carbon dioxide and this is released in the lungs when it arrives there.

Anaemia is *a reduction in the quantity of haemoglobin*. There are a number of causes of anaemia. A common cause is a deficiency of iron in the diet. Another possible cause is a deficiency of vitamin B_{12} which is necessary for production of haemoglobin. Vitamin B_{12} is supplied to mammals by the micro-organisms present in their large intestine.

31.6 White Blood Cells

One type of white cell, *lymphocytes*, are very important in the *immune response* of mammals. If foreign proteins enter the body they can act as antigens. Antigens stimulate the production of antibodies. If the body is invaded by the same protein again these antibodies can attack and neutralize it. Lymphocytes are produced by the bone marrow and also in lymph nodes. In humans these are located in the groin, neck and armpits. If we are fighting an infection these sites can become inflamed and swollen.

31.7 Immune Response

The immune response is the way in which our bodies become sensitive (i.e. produce antibodies) to foreign proteins such as grass pollen and fungal spores. Mosquitoes and midges are blood sucking flies. They inject enzymes into us to begin digestion of their blood meal. These enzymes are foreign proteins and our bodies produce *antibodies* to combat them. Once sensitised, our bodies react if subjected to these proteins again. This can result in a typical itchy bump in the case of the biting fly or watery eyes in hayfever. Hayfever symptoms, watery eyes and runny noses, are brought about by a chemical called histamine and can be suppressed temporarily by anti-histamine ointments or tablets. Farm animals react in a similar manner to blood sucking arthropods. *Sweet itch* in horses is caused by biting midges. Often the itch causes scratching which exposes sites which are invaded by other organisms such as bacteria.

Extreme immune responses are called *allergies*. The causes of allergies should be identified professionally .

31.7.1 Active and passive immunity

Immunity can be of two sorts. *Active* immunity is what has just been described - i.e. where the body manufactures its own antibodies to a particular antigen. *Passive* immunity is the situation in mammals whereby immunity is passed from mother to foetus across the placenta. Passive immunity can also be acquired by the offspring when it feeds on colostrum. Colostrum (or beestings) is the milk formed during the first few days after birth.

Vaccination is *active artificial immunity*. Various forms of vaccines are now available. Sometimes they involve a virus which has been killed, or a *strain* of a disease-causing microbe which itself does not cause the disease. In this way, the body can be prepared and stimulated to produce antibodies so that the real disease-causing microbe is attacked when it tries to invade the body.

31.8 The Lymphatic System

Blood, when it arrives in the capillaries, is under pressure. This causes fluid to leave the capillaries and to lie around the body's tissues. This is called interstitial fluid and it is very similar to blood plasma but without the protein - since proteins do not pass through the walls of the capillaries.

This fluid returns to the general body circulation via the lymphatic system. This is a system of canals through the body. The smallest lymph vessels are the lymph capillaries, called *lacteals*. Lacteals are blind-ended and there is one to each villus. They are important for the uptake and transport of lipids in the digestive system. The lymph vessels flow into ever-increasing vessels. These vessels do not have a pump but the lymph is moved along by general muscular movement. Along the way there are frequent valves to prevent back-flow and *lymph nodes* which produce lymphocytes (*see the section on immunity above*). The larger lymph vessels open into the veins near the heart and they discharge their contents into these veins.

Exercises

Exercise 69. Dissection of a sheep's heart

Materials needed
1. Sheep's heart, preferably one with the lungs and trachea still attached. However hearts sold for consumption are adequate. Hearts from pigs and cattle are also suitable.
2. Dissecting board and dissecting kit.

Procedure
1. Use the diagram in *Fig. 31.1* to identify the parts. Identify the auricles and ventricles externally. Draw.
2. Use a scalpel to cut open the auricles and the outer walls of the ventricles. Leave the central septum intact. This allows you to open each chamber of the heart and examine the inside. You may have to remove congealed blood. Note the relative thickness of the muscular walls of the left and right ventricles. Can you explain this?
3. Try to locate all the structures labelled in *Fig. 31.5*. As an exercise, follow the pathway of blood through the heart using a blunt seeker. Examine the bicuspid and tricuspid valves. Try to locate the coronary arteries - they leave the dorsal aorta just outside the semi-lunar valves. Insert a blunt seeker into them and trace their course along the outer surface of the heart.

Fig. 31.5 Sheep's heart

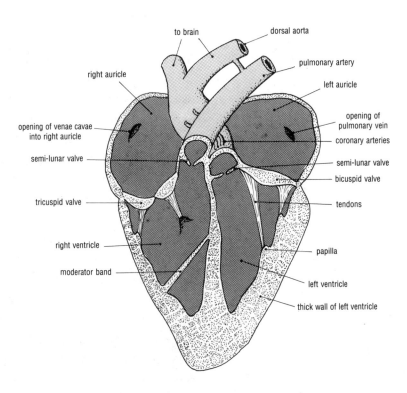

32 – Breathing Air

32.1 Lungs

Mammals have two large lungs in the chest cavity or thorax. When covering the circulation system we saw how blood is delivered to the lungs and that gaseous exchange takes place. We must now study the pathway of air in a mammal *(Fig. 32.1)*.

Fig. 32.1 Trachea and lungs

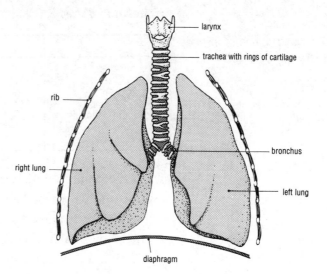

Air enters a mammal through either the mouth or nose. The *glottis* is the opening into the trachea at the back of the mouth. If a mammal is swallowing, a flap of cartilaginous tissue called the *epiglottis* closes off this opening. The trachea are held open by rings of cartilage. You can feel this on your own throat, or perhaps examine a specimen from an abattoir. At the top of the trachea is the voice box or *larynx*.

The trachea splits into two *bronchi* (singular bronchus) at the base. Each bronchus enters a lung. In turn, each bronchus splits repeatedly into *bronchioles*. The bronchi and larger bronchioles are also held open with cartilage rings. Eventually each bronchiole ends in a sac called the air-sac or *alveolus*. The alveolus is the site where the actual exchange of gases occurs. The alveoli greatly increase the surface area available for gaseous exchange. Humans have 300 million alveoli in their two lungs, giving a total surface area of 70 to 80 m^2. (Compare this to the surface area of the skin of about 2 m^2). The alveoli come into contact with an extensive system of capillary blood vessels. The capillaries and alveoli are in close, intimate contact so that the distance of air to blood is only 0.3 μm. This means there is very little resistance to the diffusion of gases.

The thoracic cavity is separated from the abdominal cavity by a muscle called the *diaphragm*. The thorax is surrounded by the rib cage. The ribs can be moved by special muscles called the intercostal muscles. When breathing in, the rib cage is lifted upwards and outwards. The diaphragm contracts under the control of the phrenic nerves and pulls the lungs downwards towards the abdomen. As a result, air is drawn in via the trachea, bronchi and bronchioles. When the rib cage muscles and diaphragm are relaxed air is expelled from the lungs. Breathing-in is called inspiration and breathing-out is expiration.

A comparison of the composition of inspired and expired air is shown in *Table 32.1*

Table 32.1 *Composition of inspired (atmospheric) and expired air*

	Inspired %	Expired %
nitrogen	78.6	74.9
oxygen	20.9	15.3
carbon dioxide	0.03	3.6
water vapour	0.5	6.2

One point to note is that all gaseous exchanges in the lungs take place in what is called an aqueous medium. This means that gaseous oxygen, for example, must first be dissolved in the moisture film which lines each alveolus. From there the exchange proceeds by diffusion. Likewise for the removal of carbon dioxide from the body, the actual exchange takes place through a water medium. This means that anything that reduces the surface area of the alveoli causes a gaseous exchange problem. Pneumonia is an example. Lung epithelium secretes mucus to trap dust particles. This is called phlegm.

The rate of breathing or ventilation rate is controlled by the respiratory centre in the hind brain. This centre has receptors which are very sensitive to the level of carbon dioxide in circulating blood. When this level rises, the ventilation rate is increased.

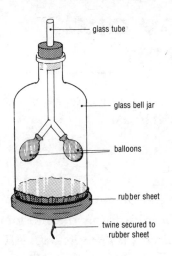

glass tube

glass bell jar

balloons

rubber sheet

twine secured to
rubber sheet

Fig. 32.2 A model of the lungs

Exercises

Exercise 70. Pathway of air in a mammal

Materials needed
1. Sheep's lungs with trachea
2. Clean glass tube
3. Belljar and rubber bung with single bore
4. Polythene and rubber band
5. Plastic Y junction
6. Two balloons

Procedure
1. Observe the breathing of a mammal. Observe your own breathing cycle in front of a mirror. List the sequence of events in breathing.
2. Set up the apparatus in *Fig. 32.2*. Can you explain how each part represents a part of the breathing system of a mammal? Can you use the apparatus to demonstrate a breathing cycle?
3. Examine the lungs of a sheep. Identify the various parts. Use *Fig. 32.1* to help you. Why are the lungs so soft? Explain the colour. Using a clean glass tube you can blow into the lungs causing them to expand.

Precaution
Wash your hands after handling this material.

33 – The Kidney and Urine Production

The kidneys are specialized organs for the production of urine. As we shall see, they have other important roles also.

33.1 De-amination

When amino acids are broken down, the amino group ($-NH_2$) is removed. This is called *de-amination*. This forms the substance ammonia which is poisonous. In the liver it is *detoxified (refer back to the box on the liver on page 276)*. This means that it is converted to relatively harmless chemicals. In mammals this is *urea* which is soluble in water. and is excreted in urine. This is achieved by a special chain of reactions which can be summarized as follows:

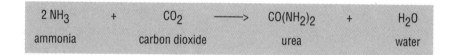

$$2\,NH_3 \quad + \quad CO_2 \quad \longrightarrow \quad CO(NH_2)_2 \quad + \quad H_2O$$

ammonia   carbon dioxide   urea   water

Birds form a related chemical called *uric acid*. This is insoluble and so water is not needed to eliminate it from the body. The white material on top of bird droppings is the uric acid. Birds do not have a bladder. They pass their "urine" and faeces in a single mass.

During the first half of this century *bird guano*, or droppings, were exported from Peru for use as fertilizers. The guano came from major seabird colonies. Since world war II guano has been replaced by fertilizers produced industrially. Try to find out what nutrients occur in manure from domestic fowl - it has high levels of some elements but needs balancing for best use.

33.2 Position of Kidneys

Observe the position and shape of the kidneys in the rabbit dissection. Note that they are oval-shaped and embedded in the muscles of the back wall. The right kidney is located more anteriorly than the left one. Blood arrives in the kidney via the *renal artery*. and leaves via the *renal vein*. Urine formed in the kidney is delivered to the bladder in the *ureter*. The *bladder* is simply for storage - in humans it is about 0.4 litres in volume. Urine is passed to the outside via the *urethra* which passes through the penis in males.

When a kidney is cut open notice a dark band around the outside (called the cortex) and a paler region (the medulla) inside. A microscopic section shows us the reason for the two differently coloured regions.

Fig. 33.1 Kidney structure

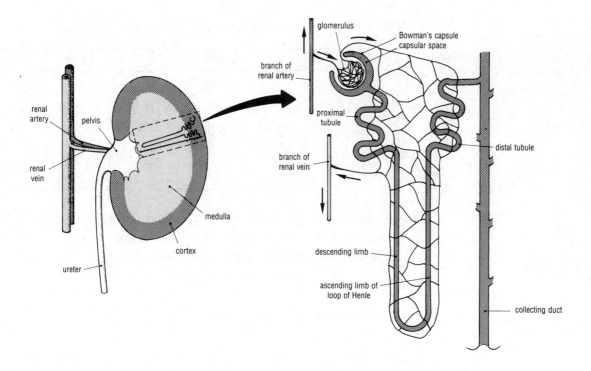

33.3 Structure of the Kidney

The *nephron* is the basic unit of the kidney *(Fig. 33.1)*. Each human kidney has between one and two million nephrons. Examine the drawing of the nephron. At the top of each nephron is a *Bowman's capsule*. Imagine this as being shaped like a microscopic wine glass. The goblet part is the Bowman's capsule. There is a knot of capillary blood vessels called a *glomerulus* in each capsule. The Bowman's capsules are mainly located in the outer part of the kidney and this concentration of glomeruli causes this region of the kidney to be darker in colour.

33.4 How the Kidney Functions

Blood arriving in the glomerulus is filtered under pressure into the internal space of the Bowman's capsule. From there it passes *(follow the diagram)* down the *proximal tubule*, through the *loop of Henle*, into the *distal* tubule and empties into the *collecting duct*.

The general principle of how urine is formed is that many chemicals, including useful ones and water, are transferred into the space of the Bowman's capsule. The nephron acts to reabsorb those chemicals it needs to retain. Anything not reabsorbed is passed as urine. The kidney also concentrates the urine so as to conserve water.

The materials reabsorbed in the kidney include all the glucose, some or all of the salts and some of the water. This is selective re-absorption. The remaining fluid is urine *(Table 33.1)*.

Table 33.1 Percent composition of blood (plasma) and urine

	Blood%	Urine%
Urea	0.03	1.8
Uric acid	0.004	0.05
Glucose	0.10	none
Amino acids	0.05	none
Proteins	8.0	none

Humans produce 180 litres of glomerular filtrate per day. This contains 145 g of glucose and 1.1 kg of sodium chloride (salt). Obviously we cannot sustain such a loss and it is the function of the nephrons to re-absorb the useful materials.

33.5 Formation of Urine

Urine is formed as follows: note the position of the loops of Henle in the inner medulla region. The collecting ducts also pass through this region. The fluid surrounding the loops of Henle develop a high concentration of sodium (Na^+) ions. The walls of the loop of Henle are not permeable to water. However the walls of the collecting ducts are permeable to water in the presence of a hormone called ADH (anti-diuretic hormone). When this hormone is present, water is reabsorbed from the collecting ducts back into the blood capillaries. This results in a reduced volume of urine which is more concentrated. Diuresis is the passing of copious watery urine. Now, what does "anti-diuretic hormone" mean?

The secretion of ADH is controlled by osmoreceptors, or blood-concentration detectors, in the brain. If the blood is too concentrated ADH is released. This could happen if an animal becomes dehydrated or if it eats a meal with high salt content. The presence of ADH results in a reduced volume of a more concentrated urine. Once the blood returns to its normal concentration, the production of ADH is stopped.

33.6 The Role of the Kidney

To sum up, the functions of the mammalian kidney are
- to contribute to the normal balance of the body
- to help eliminate harmful compounds
- to expel salts above certain levels, and
- to remove excess water.

Thus they function in both excretion and osmoregulation.

Exercises

Exercise 71. Mammalian kidneys

Materials needed
1. Rabbit dissection *(continued from Exercise 68)*
2. Kidneys from butcher's shop
3. Dissecting board and kit

Fig 33.2 Urine system of a rabbit

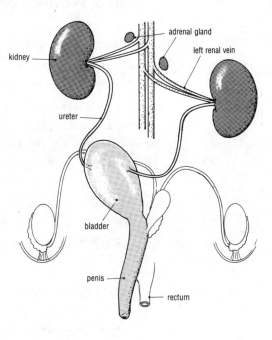

Procedure
1. When the dissection of the alimentary canal is completed, remove it completely by cutting the oesophagus near the stomach and the rectum.
2. Use the diagram in *Fig. 33.2* to identify the following items: left and right kidneys *(note right kidney is more anterior than the left)*; left and right renal veins and arteries. Identify the ureters and follow them to where they enter the bladder. Note also the adrenal glands.
3. Examine the kidneys from the butcher's. Cut and compare what you see to the diagram in *Fig. 33.1*. Draw.

34 – Reproduction in Mammals

34.1 Primary and Secondary Sex Characteristics

The term *"gonads"* is a general term for both testes and ovaries. The gonads and genitals are the *primary sex characteristics* of each individual - i.e. what makes them male or female. *Secondary sex characteristics* are other ways of distinguishing between males and females and are often brought about by the action of hormones. In humans the pitch of voice, the regions where fat is stored, development of facial hair and male baldness are examples of secondary sex characteristics. The different statures of cows and bulls, combs and spurs on the legs in male domestic fowl are other secondary sex characteristics.

34.2 Production of Sperm

Sperm is produced in the seminiferous tubules in the testis. This involves reduction division or meiosis. Consequently sperm is haploid. Sperm is stored and matured in the *epididymus*. From there, it is transported in the *vas deferens* to the *prostate gland* where secretions are added. These include the sugar fructose which supplies energy for the swimming of sperm. The resulting fluid, sperm plus fluid, is called *semen*. Semen is released into the vagina of the female by *ejaculation* during *copulation*. Sperm cells have a whip-like tail or flagellum used for movement *(Fig. 34.1)*.

34.3 Male Hormones

Hormones are covered in more detail in *Chapter 35* under the endochrine system. For now we can consider them as chemical messengers in the body: they are produced in one part of the body and cause a response in another part. Many of the hormones mentioned are produced by the anterior pituitary gland which is a located below the brain.

Luteinizing hormone *(LH)* and follicle-stimulating hormone *(FSH)* are produced by the anterior pituitary. These hormones stimulate the development of the testis and sperm production. The testis produces testosterone which is the main hormone controlling the secondary sex characteristics of males. (Note that LH and FSH used to be given other names in males. Now they are recognized as being the same hormones as in females but with different function in males.)

Fig. 34.1 Diagram of sperm

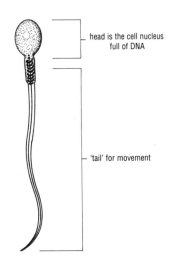

head is the cell nucleus full of DNA

'tail' for movement

34.4 Female Hormones

Depending on the species, one or more egg cells (*ova*, singular ovum) develop in the ovaries in *Graafian follicles*. In humans, usually only one develops in alternate ovaries during each menstrual cycle. In species which produce many offspring, each ovary produces about the same number of ova each time. Development of the Graafian follicle is stimulated by FSH from the anterior pituitary. The developing follicle produces oestrogen which stops the production of FSH. The anterior pituitary also produces LH. *Ovulation* is probably stimulated by a short pulse of LH.

Meiosis takes place just before ovulation. Thus the egg is also haploid. If copulation has occurred, sperm swims up the *Fallopian tube* where fertilization usually occurs. We must now consider two possible courses of events: what happens if fertilization takes place and what happens if fertilization does not take place.

34.4.1 Luteal phase

After ovulation takes place, the cycle moves into the *"luteal phase"*. This means that the follicle from which the ovum was released develops into the *corpus luteum*. The corpus luteum produces another hormone called *progesterone*. The function of progesterone is to build up the wall of the uterus to prepare it for implantation of the developing young, or *foetus*.

If fertilization does *not* occur, the corpus luteum degenerates. This removes the source of progesterone. The wall of the womb which had been built up for implantation now breaks down. This blood/mucus mixture is passed as *menses*. This occurs in regular cycles in humans and is called the *menstrual cycle*. Other mammals have one or more similar cycles each year. This is called the *oestrous cycle*.

If fertilization occurs, other hormones from a membrane of the developing foetus (the *chorion*) maintain the corpus luteum. Consequently, progesterone continues to be produced and the wall of the uterus continues to develop. Implantation occurs. (Later in pregnancy other sources of progesterone take over.) The foetus develops.

34.4.2 Development of the embryo

The developing embryo is contained within embryonic membranes. The embryo is surrounded by the *amnion*. The other important membrane is the *allantois*. All of this is surrounded by the chorion. The allantois develops an *umbilical cord* which connects the foetus to *villi*. These villi match with villi which develop at the maternal side. The intimate contact allows the exchange of nutrients, oxygen and

> **Try not to mix up these hormones**
> How about oestrogen and progesterone appear in alphabetical order? Or the ovum (really the follicle) produces oestrogen - o and o.

antibodies. This connection remains throughout *gestation*, the period it takes for the foetus to develop prior to birth. Gestation periods of different domestic animals are given in their relevant sections.

Fig. 34.2 Membranes and placental arrangements in mammals. Maternal and foetal systems are fully separated by the chorion.

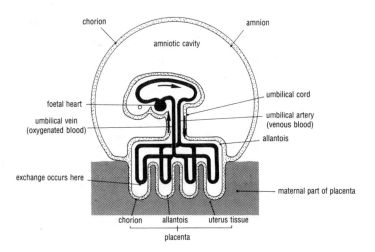

The various membranes are shown in *Fig. 34.2*. This appears complicated but can be clarified by drawing a foetus and adding in each membrane in a different colour. The relationships are then obvious.

34.4.3 Birth

At birth, a number of hormones come into play. One is *oxytocin* which causes contractions in the uterus wall. *Prolactin* stimulates the production of milk and the role of oxytocin in the "let down" of milk is explained on *page 296*. Prolactin may also prevent further ovulation until lactation has been completed.

34.5 Reproductive Hormones and Farming

Modern farming practices often use reproductive hormones to control the breeding of farm animals. Their use is covered in their relevant chapters. We can mention here the use of progestogen impregnated sponges placed in the ewe's vagina to synchronize oestrus in sheep. Another hormone, PMSG (pregnant mare's serum gonadotrophin) is often injected at the same time to increase the fertility and ensure a good response – an increase in litter size.

Exercises

Exercise 72 Reproductive system of rabbit

Materials needed
1. Male and female rabbits *(continued from Exercise 71)*
2. Dissecting boards and kit

Procedure
1. **Male.**

   Find the spermatic cord. This is the spermatic vein, spermatic artery and spermatic nerve running together towards the testis. The spermatic cord leaves the region of the main aorta about 2 cm posterior to the branch to the left renal artery and vein. Trace the spermatic cord to the testis. Using a scalpel cut open the scrotal sac. You should now be able to see the male reproductive organs. Locate the penis outside. It is not easy to trace this fully back to the bladder because the pelvic bone obscures it. Identify the parts of your dissection by referring to *Fig. 34.3.*

Fig. 34.3 Rabbit male (left) and female reproductive systems

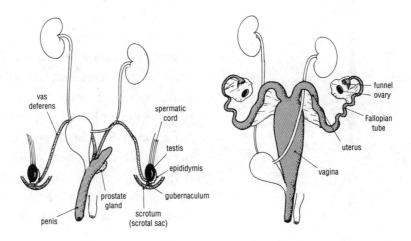

2. **Female.**

   At about the same position as the spermatic cord occurs in the male, the female has ovarian veins and arteries. This is an easy way to find the ovaries as the blood vessels lead to them directly. Now locate the ovary at each side; almost surrounding it is the opening to the Fallopian tube which leads to the more defined uterus. Technically, rabbits are considered to have two wombs, one at each side and both attached to the vagina. Because of the pelvic bone, it is not easy to trace the vagina to the outside. Again identify the parts shown in *Fig. 34.3.*

35 – The Nervous System and Effectors

35.1 Introduction

The nervous system allows an animal to detect what is going on in the world around it. It also provides another service which normally takes place in the unconscious background: constant monitoring and control of physiological events in the body. Once a stimulus has been received, effectors can act on the information. In mammals the most important effectors are muscles and glands. The nervous system consists of two main parts:

1. the central nervous system,
2. the peripheral nervous system.

35.2 Central Nervous System (CNS)

The central nervous system consists of the brain and the spinal cord.

35.2.1 The brain

Fig. 35.1 shows the main parts of a rabbit's brain. The brain can be divided into the fore-brain, mid-brain and hind-brain. Notice the size of the *cerebral hemispheres*. These are much larger in mammals than in other vertebrates, and much larger in primates (including humans) than in rabbits. The cerebral hemispheres are associated with intelligent behaviour; we have named ourselves *Homo sapien*s or "wise man". The brain receives input from twelve pairs of cranial nerves. Two are named in *Fig. 35.1* - the olfactory and optic. These deliver messages to the brain from the organs of smell (nose) and sight (eyes), respectively. Notice also the position of the pituitary gland as it is very important in connection with hormonal control.

35.2.2 Spinal cord

The spinal cord is really a spinal tube as it is hollow and contains cerebrospinal fluid. It is surrounded by the vertebrae, or back bone. It is easy to understand this arrangement by studying a vertebra. The main function of the spinal cord is to connect the peripheral nervous system to the brain.

35.3 Peripheral Nervous System (PNS)

There are two parts to the peripheral nervous system:

1. the sensory part,
2. the autonomic system.

Fig. 35.1 Rabbit brain, dorsal and ventral aspects

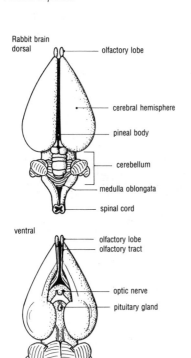

Rabbit brain
dorsal
— olfactory lobe

— cerebral hemisphere

— pineal body

— cerebellum

— medulla oblongata

— spinal cord

ventral
— olfactory lobe
— olfactory tract

— optic nerve

— pituitary gland

— various cranial nerves enter brain

The *sensory* part of the PNS includes the twelve pairs of cranial nerves, already mentioned above, and also spinal nerves which enter the spinal cord. These nerves are responsible for all the conscious awareness of a mammal. They include the gathering of information from organs of smell, sight, sound, touch, taste. This information comes from specialized organs which have specialized cells called receptors. For example, the organs of sight, the eyes, include specialized cells which are stimulated by the presence of light. Many species have colour filters associated with some of these light receptors making colour vision possible in those species.

The *autonomic* nervous system runs in the background. Normally the animal is not "aware" that it is functioning. This system monitors and controls the animal's internal organs such as the heart and intestine.

35.4 Nerve Cells

Fig. 35.2 Diagram of a neurone

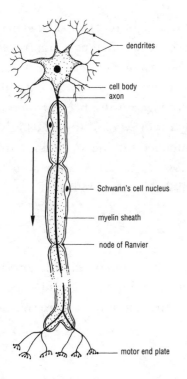

The basic unit of nerve tissue is the *neurone*. This cell has long drawn-out protoplasmic processes. The shorter processes which conduct impulses to the cell body are called *dendrites*. The long process which conducts the impulse away from the cell body is called the axon. The axon is surrounded by *Schwann cells* which have a fatty sheath. A nerve impulse is an electrical event and the fatty sheath provides insulation. Notice that the axon is exposed at the *nodes of Ranvier.*

35.5 Nerve Impulse

When an impulse passes along an axon it jumps from one node of Ranvier to the next and this greatly speeds up transmission of the impulse. Eventually the impulse arrives at the motor end-plates. The gap between the motor end-plates of one neurone and the dendrites of the next neurone is called a *synapse.* The impulse is transmitted across the synapse by a chemical transmitter. *Acetylcholine* is an example of a chemical transmitter found in mammals.

An important point to note about all nerve impulses is called the *"all or none"* principle, i.e the only information contained in a nerve impulse is that a receptor has been stimulated. For example, if we perceive a bright light, the brain receives numerous impulses. The status of each impulse is that a receptor has been stimulated. The brain interprets the number and duration of the impulses and we become conscious that a bright light exists. The same principle applies to all nervous impulses.

35.6 Receptors

Depending on how they are stimulated, we can group receptors into photoreceptors, mechanoreceptors, heat receptors and chemoreceptors. Photoreceptors are present in the sensory part of the eye. They are specialized cells allowing both black and white or colour vision. Mechanoreceptors include touch receptors distributed on the skin, and hearing and balance receptors in the inner ear of mammals. Heat receptors are distributed on the skin. Chemoreceptors include the olfactory (smell) receptors in the nose and the taste receptors on the tongue. We should be aware that humans perceive the world around them differently to other animals. For example, the human ear can respond to sounds up to about 20 000 hertz but dogs can hear much higher frequencies, up to 30 000 hertz. (One hertz corresponds to one wavelength per second; Hz is the proper abbreviation.) Pollinating insects can see patterns on flowers which are only visable in ultraviolet light.

35.6.1 The mammalian eye

The mammalian eye is an example of a light receptor. The general structure is shown in *Fig. 35.5*. The cornea is the tough, transparent front of the eye. Inside this is liquid or *aqueous humour*. The iris can be expanded or contracted to allow more or less light to enter the eye chamber. The lens focuses the image on the back of the eye. Inside the lens, the eye cavity is filled with *vitreous humour*. This is a clear jelly-like material. The eye is supplied with nerve endings from the optic nerve. These carry messages to the brain when the photoreceptors located at the rear of the eye are stimulated.

35.7 Effectors

If a mammal needs to act, consciously or unconsciously, on the information received from the nervous system it does this by means of effectors. In mammals the most important effectors are muscles and hormone-producing glands .

35.7.1 Muscles

There are three types of muscle cell:

1. *Cardiac* muscles are found in the heart. They contract rhythmically without fatigue. The contractions do not have to be initiated by a nerve impulse - this means that each heart beat begins in the cardiac muscle. (As an exercise calculate how many times a heart beats during its life. Allow about 70 beats per minute.)

2. *Smooth* muscle lines the hollow organs of the body such as the

intestine, blood vessels, bladder and uterus. A mammal cannot consciously control this muscle so it is called involuntary muscle.

3. *Striated* muscle or skeletal muscle. As we shall see, this muscle is characterized by the presence of striations or stripes under the microscope. It is voluntary. Another characteristic is that it contracts and fatigues.

Striated muscle

Under a light microscope it is possible to see that this type of muscle has striations. Using the electron microscope it is now possible to understand how muscle contracts.

Fig. 35.3 Diagram of sliding filament hypothesis

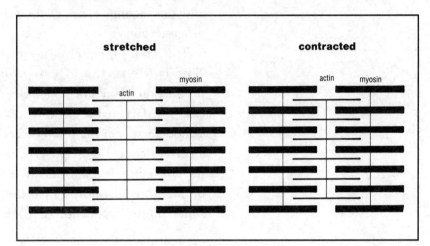

Muscle cells contain two proteins *actin* and *myosin*. All that is needed to make these proteins contract in a test-tube (i.e. *in vitro*) is energy supplied by ATP. *Fig. 35.3* shows a modern interpretation of the arrangement of actin and myosin filaments in a muscle cell. This is a diagram of a view of the filaments from the side. Imagine looking through the stacks of filaments and you can see how the dark and light striations, visable under the light microscope, are formed. It is now thought that when a muscle is stimulated by a nerve impulse, the actin-myosin filaments slide in on each other. This is called the *"sliding filament hypothesis"*. This reaction needs energy from ATP. The ATP is formed in mitochondria which are abundant in muscle tissue. Muscles contain a special pigment called myoglobin which acts, similarly to haemoglobin in blood, as a reservoir of oxygen in muscles. The oxygen is needed to release the energy (respiration) to form ATP.

35.7.2 The endocrine system

The endocrine system refers to the hormone system in the body. *Hormones* are chemicals produced in minute quantities by living cells. They are transported to a different part of the body in the circulatory system where they can cause major effects on a so-called *"target organ"*. Hormones are blood-borne messengers that co-ordinate and regulate the actions of different parts of an organism.

We have already encountered examples of hormones: gastrin in the digestive system and ADH which controls water reabsorption in the kidney. We will now consider hormones of the pituitary, thyroid, parathyroid, thymus, pancreas, adrenals and gonads.

It can be useful to broadly classify hormones into two groups. The first group are peptides (chains of amino acids shorter than proteins). This group bring about their effect within minutes and they are short-lived. Examples are ADH and insulin. The other group are the steroids. These are the opposite. They are long-lived and slow acting. Many of them have names ending in "-one", e.g. progesterone.

Hormones themselves are often controlled by *"feedback control"*. This is where the effect produced by the hormone causes production of the hormone to be "switched off". Consider again the case of ADH in the production of urine. ADH is secreted when osmodetectors in the brain detect that blood concentration is above a certain critical level. ADH allows the reabsorption of water from the collecting ducts in the kidney. This results in a lowering of the blood concentration. Once the osmoreceptors detect this, they switch off the production of ADH. This is feedback control.

Pituitary hormones

The hypothalamus is part of the fore-brain. Located just below it is the pituitary gland. The hypothalamus exercises major control over the functions of the pituitary gland. The pituitary consists of two parts, the anterior and posterior lobes.

The anterior pituitary produces two hormones: ADH, which should be familiar by now and oxytocin.

Oxytocin causes contractions of the uterus wall during birth and is also involved in milk "let-down". When a young mammal suckles from its mother, nerve impulses are sent to the hypothalamus in the brain. This causes the anterior pituitary to release oxytocin into the blood stream. The oxytocin causes contraction of the milk ducts. This is called the "let down" of milk. Milk continues to be released until the ducts are empty or until the suckling stops. Milk production itself is stimulated by the hormones of reproduction, progesterone and oestrogen, and also prolactin - which is mentioned below as an example of a hormone secreted by the posterior pituitary.

The posterior pituitary produces a number of important hormones. These include hormones which control the adrenal and thyroid glands. Two others are follicle-stimulating hormone, FSH and luteinizing hormone, LH which we encountered in the

Fig. 35.4 Milk let-down and production

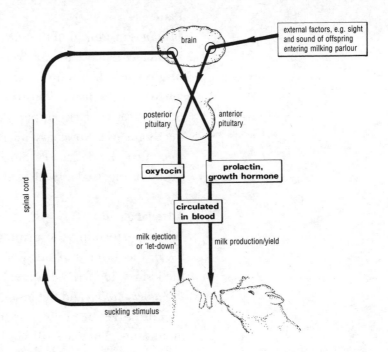

reproduction section *(Chapter 34)*. Another two are prolactin and growth hormone. Prolactin stimulates and maintains lactation. Growth hormone controls growth.

Thyroid glands

These glands lie on either side of the trachea. The main hormone produced is thyroxine. Iodine is part of the molecule of thyroxine. The thyroid hormones are involved in the control of growth and development in mammals. A deficiency in the hormone can result in cretinism in humans - children suffering from this disease can be physically deformed and mentally retarded. If iodine is lacking in the diet, production of thyroid hormones can be affected. The thyroids react by greatly enlarging themselves in an effort to produce more thyroid hormone. This condition is called *goitre* in humans.

Parathyroid glands

These are small glands located near the thyroids. They produce two hormones, parathormone and calcitonin, which are involved in the control of calcium, magnesium and phosphate levels between bone, tissues and body fluids.

Thymus

This is a small gland found in the neck. It varies in size between species - it is easy to see lying just over the auricles in the rabbit thorax. In rats, it is important for the production of lymphocytes, which are important for the immune response *(see page 278)*.

Pancreas

Insulin is produced in the *islets of Langerhans* in the pancreas. Insulin stimulates glucose uptake by cells and prevents excessive breakdown of glycogen. If insulin is lacking, one outcome is the excretion of glucose in the urine. This is called *diabetes mellitus.* In the extreme, this can cause black-out periods or coma in diabetics since the brain needs glucose. Nowadays, microbial insulin is available commercially to control the deficiency. Since it is a protein it must be injected; it would be digested if swallowed.

Adrenal glands

When performing the urino-genital dissection of the rabbit *(Fig. 34.3),* the adrenal glands were noted as two pea-sized organs near the kidney. In fact, the adrenal gland is two glands! The outer part is the *adrenal cortex* and the inner is the *adrenal medulla.*

The adrenal cortex produces over fifty different steroid hormones. They are all vital for life. If the adrenal glands are removed from an animal it eventually dies. Hydrocortisone is an example. It is involved in maintaining blood pressure and preventing blood loss from an injury by controlling the dilation of arterioles.

The adrenal medulla secretes *adrenalin* during stress. Its action has been summarized as "fright, fight and flight". If an animal is frightened, adrenalin acts by redirecting blood to the brain, increasing the heartbeat. This can cause humans to "go white with anger" or cause the hairs on the back of the neck to stand erect (commonly seen in dogs). Another hormone, noradrenalin, switches off this effect.

Gonads

The gonads are the testes and ovaries. The hormones involved in reproduction are covered in *Chapter 34.*

Gland	Hormone	Main function	Problems
Pituitary, anterior		Important hormones which control adrenal and thyroid glands	
	Prolactin	Milk let-down	
	Growth	normal growth	Dwarfism
	FSH	Stimulates follicles in ovaries	
	LH	Stimulates testes in male, corpus luteum in female	
Pituitary, posterior	At least five	Water (ADH), blood pressure, kidney function	
Thyroid	Thyroxine	Respiration	Cretinism, goitre
Parathyroid	Parathormone, calcitonin	Calcium metabolism	Bone problems
Adrenal cortex	Steroid hormones	Metabolism of water, minerals, carbohydrates	
Adrenaml medulla	Adrenaline	Alarm	
Pancreas	Insulin	Glucose –> glycogen conversion	Diabetes
Testis	Testosterone	Male sex characteristics	
Ovary, corpus luteum	Progesterone	Uterus growth during pregnancy	

Table 35.1

Fig. 35.5 Dissection of a cow's eye

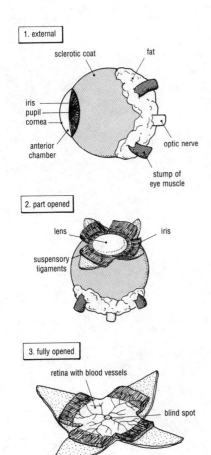

1. external

sclerotic coat
fat
iris
pupil
cornea
anterior chamber
optic nerve
stump of eye muscle

2. part opened

lens
iris
suspensory ligaments

3. fully opened

retina with blood vessels
blind spot

Exercises

Exercise 73 The eye: an example of a receptor

Materials needed

1. Cattle or sheep's eyes from an abattoir
2. Dissecting board and kit

Procedure

1. Examine the external structure. Use *Fig. 35.5* to identify the parts you observe.
2. Make a small cross-cut in the cornea using a sharp scalpel. This releases the aqueous humour. Cut away the rest of the cornea. Examine the iris.
3. Cut all round the circumference of the eye. Note how hard it is to cut. Try to exert as little pressure as possible. Examine the vitreous humour (clear jelly). Examine the retina. Remove the lens, ideally attached to some ligaments so that it can be held up using a tweezers. Now look through the lens and observe what you see. Produce drawings of your dissection.

Section 9 Animal Production

36 – Animal Feedstuffs

Table 36.1 (above) *Categories of animal feedstuffs*

Table 36.2 (below) *Nutrient characteristics of some common feedstuffs*

36.1 Feedstuff Composition

The food types and their function have been dealt with in *Chapter 7*. It is important that these be fed to farm animals in correct amounts so that growth and production are maintained at optimum levels.

Category	Description	Examples
1. Bulky feeds	Feeds relatively high in water and/or fibre content	Fresh grass, silage, hay, root crops, straw, forage crops (kale, rape, etc.)
2. Concentrates	Feeds low in water and fibre content	Cereal grains, cereal grain by-products, fats, oils, molasses, beet pulp, oilseed by-products, legume seeds, animal products, feed supplements

Feedstuff	DM content %	Nutrient content of the dry matter		
		Crude protein (CP), %	Crude fibre (CF), %	Metabolisable energy (ME), MJkg^{-1}
Fresh grass				
Ryegrass ley, young leafy	18.0	18.6	21.2	13.1
Permanent pasture, set-stocked	20.0	15.5	23.0	10.0
Silage, hay				
Silage, good quality	20.0	17.0	30.5	10.3
Hay, good quality	85.0	10.1	33.0	9.0
Root crops				
Fodder beet	22.0	6.8	5.9	12.2
Turnips	12.0	10.8	10.0	12.8
Straw				
Barley straw	86.0	3.8	45.0	6.5
Forage crops				
Kale	14.0	16.0	17.9	11.0
Rape	14.0	20.1	25.0	9.5
Cereal grains				
Barley	86.0	10.8	5.3	13.0
Wheat	86.0	12.4	2.6	13.5
Oats	86.0	10.9	12.1	12.0
Cereal grain by-products				
Bran	88.0	17.0	11.4	10.1
Fats and oils				
Sunflower oil	98.0	0.0	0.0	32.0
Molasses, beet pulp				
Molasses	25.0	9.0	0.0	12.5
Beet pulp, dried	90.0	9.9	20.3	12.7
Oilseed by-products				
Soya bean meal	90.0	50.3	5.8	12.3
Legume seeds				
Spring field beans	86.0	31.4	8.0	12.8
Animal products				
Meat and bone meal	90.0	59.7	0.0	7.9
Fish meal	90.0	70.1	0.0	11.1
Dried skim milk	95.0	37.2	0.0	14.1
Feed supplements				
Mineral / vitamin supplement	100.0	0.0	0.0	0.0

Animal feedstuffs may be classified as shown in *Table 36.1*. The nutritive value of some of these is shown in *Table 36.2*. The meanings of the terms used in *Table 36.2* are:

Dry matter (DM): All feeds are composed of water, organic matter and ash. Organic matter and ash together comprise the DM of a feed. The nutrients are contained in the DM. DM percentage is determined as follows:

1. Weigh a sample of feed - A g
2. Dry sample at 80°C to constant weight and reweigh - B g
3. Calculate DM content: DM content, % = 100 B /A

Crude Protein (CP): This is an estimate of the protein content of a feed. Nitrogen content is determined by the Kjeldahl technique. Then, on the assumption that all proteins contain 16% nitrogen, CP is calculated as follows:

$$\% \text{ CP} = \% \text{ N} \times (100/16) = \% \text{ N} \times 6.25$$

Crude fibre (CF): This contains cellulose, hemicelluloses and lignins. It is determined by treating a feedstuff with a succession of boiling acid and alkali solutions. The organic residue is dried and expressed as % CF

Metabolisable energy (ME): Energy in feeds is derived from a range of organic compounds, including sugars, starches, fats and oils. Energy may be categorised as follows:

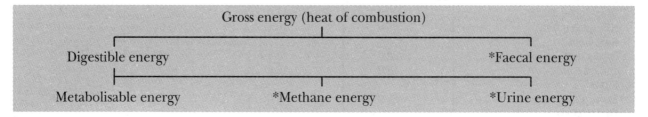

The forms of energy marked by an asterisk (*) are not converted into saleable products (meat, milk, etc.). The residual form, ME is so converted; therefore ME values are of great practical use. ME is determined by a variety of techniques, the best of which involves dietary study of live animals. This is very expensive, however, and cheaper laboratory methods are used routinely. ME is expressed in terms of energy per unit mass, megajoules per kilogram (MJ kg^{-1}).

36.1.1 Bulky feeds

(A) Fresh grass: Fresh grass is the most widely used feed for ruminant animals. It is, however, a feed of variable nutritive value. If adequately fertilized, ryegrass-dominant pastures grazed rotationally provide a fully balanced complete feed capable of supporting high levels of animal production *(see Chapter 19)*. Pastures made up of other grasses and not grazed rotationally, can, on the other hand, be of low nutritional value, especially in autumn or winter *(see Table 36.2)*.

(B) Silage, hay: These are forms of conserved grass, usually, and are widely used as winter feed. Stage of growth at cutting and method of conservation strongly influence their nutritive values. In general, however, it can be said that silage is always of higher feeding value than hay and the data in *Table 36.2* illustrate this.

(C) Root crops: These are feeds whose energy content compares favourably with grass, fresh or conserved, but which are low in protein. The high labour content in their cultivation and feeding has limited their use, except for turnips which are fed *in situ* to sheep in some areas.

(D) Straw: Straw is of low nutritive value *(Table 36.2)* and is generally used for feed purposes only in emergency situations. One such situation arises when all available silage and hay have been fed by a farmer and the cost of buying silage or hay is prohibitive.

(E) Forage crops: The nutritive value of kale and rape compares favourably with that of fresh grass and silage. It is recommended, however, that the intake of these crops is limited to 30% of an animal's total dry matter intake. This is because of chemical agents in the vegetation which interfere with iodine utilisation and cause blood disorders if eaten in excess.

36.1.2 Concentrates

(A) Cereal grains: Cereal grains are very extensively used as sources of energy in compounding feeds for all types of farm animals. In addition to barley, wheat and oats, maize and other imported cereals and cereal products are used in varying amounts.

If cereal grains are fed whole they are not fully digested. This is because the highly digestible starchy interior is protected against digestive juices by the fibrous outer coat. This is especially true in the case of barley and oats which have higher C.F. content than wheat *(Table 36.2)* and which, if fed whole, pass through the digestive system almost unaltered. The treatments used to improve the digestibility of cereal grains are rolling (which flattens the grain and shatters the fibrous coat), and grinding (into a coarse flour). *Exercise 77* examines this problem.

(B) *Cereal grain by-products:* The principal cereal grain by-products used as animal feeds are bran and pollard which are by-products of flour production from wheat. Others used in smaller amounts are oat husks (a by-product of porridge meal and muesli production) and brewers and distillers grains (by-products of beer and whiskey production).

(C) Fats, oils: The only material of this kind used in Ireland is dried sunflower oil which is a constituent of milk-replacer powders used in calf-feeding. The other ingredient in milk replacers is skim milk, the oil replacing the butter-fat in the final product.

(D) Molasses, beet pulp: Molasses is considered to be a concentrate feed, despite its high water content. Its principal use is as a "binder" in pelleting of animal feed compounds. Its sweetness also increases the palatability of the ration. This is important for young animals such as calves, lambs and bonhams.

Beet pulp is comparable in CP and ME to barley *(Table 36.2)* and can be substituted for it in formulating feeds for ruminants. On account of its high CF content, it is unsuitable for pigs or poultry.

(E) Oilseed by-products: Oilseed plant species are grown for the purpose of extracting oil from the seed for use in the manufacture of cooking oils, margarine, lubricants and detergents. The residues after oil extraction are rich in protein and are used as protein sources in feed-compounding.

The principal oilseed by-product used in Ireland is soya bean meal which contains 50% protein. Others used, together with their protein contents are: groundnut meal : 55% protein, cottonseed cake: 46 % protein, linseed meal : 40% protein. All of these oilseed by-products are imported.

(F) Legume seeds: There has been very little use of legume seeds as animal feed components up to now. In recent years, however, small amounts of field spring beans are being grown in the tillage areas on a trial basis. This is an attempt to produce cheaper sources of protein than the traditional imported ones.

(G) Animal products: Mean and bone meal is composed of dried, processed meat factory waste materials. Fish meal is composed of dried, processed fish. Both of these feeds contain very large amounts of protein *(Table 36.2)*. More importantly, they contain protein which is of *high quality*, containing large amounts of *essential amino acids (see page 92)*.

For proper growth of pigs and poultry, certain minimum levels of specific essential amino acids are required in the diet. These are provided by small quantities of meat and bone meal or fish meal. These feeds are, therefore, solely used to remedy deficiencies in the essential amino acid composition of the rest of the feedstuff.

This approach is not necessary with feeds for ruminants because of the ability of the rumen micro-organisms to synthesise all the essential amino acids.

Dried skim milk can be used for the same purposes as meat and bone meal and fish meal. Its main use in Ireland, however, is in the manufacture of milk replacer powders.

(H) Feed supplements: These are materials whose use ensures adequate levels of minerals and vitamins in animals' diets. They generally contain these nutrients in balanced amounts and may be supplied to the animals in one of two ways.

They can be added in small amounts to the other ingredients of feedstuffs during the manufacturing process. Alternatively, they can be made available as mineral/vitamin licks or feeding blocks. The animal is encouraged to ingest the supplement by the inclusion of an ingredient which makes the lick palatable to it (usually salt or molasses).

36.2 Nutrient Requirements

The nutrient requirements of all types of farm animals have been studied for many years and a lot of accurate information is now available. Animals have requirements for *maintenance* and *production.*

36.2.1 Requirements for maintenance
If animals are given no food they use body reserves to supply the nutrients to keep themselves alive. As a result, they lose weight. Maintenance requirements are the amount of nutrients which allows animals to maintain body weight and composition constant.

36.2.2 Requirements for production
Any nutrients fed in excess of the maintenance requirement level are used for production of some kind. Thus, the exact amounts of nutrients required to produce, e.g., 1 kg of liveweight gain (LWG), 1 l of milk, 1 kg of wool or 1 egg are known and utilised in calculating feeding schemes for livestock.

Nutrient requirements are always expressed in one of two ways - either as *daily requirements (in g per animal)* or as a *proportion of the diet (in %).* The second method assumes a certain level of food intake.

36.3 Ration Formulation

The primary aim in formulating a ration is to satisfy the animal's requirements for the nutrients necessary for it to achieve the farmer's production targets. Three pieces of information are required for ration formulation. These are: the *animal's nutrient requirements,* the *nutrient analysis of the feedstuffs* available and the animal's *potential dry matter intake* (appetite).

36.3.1 Animal nutrient requirements
Some examples of the nutrient requirement levels associated with dairying are shown in *Table 36.3.* Corresponding information on nutrient requirements of beef cattle, sheep, pigs and other farm animals is available.

36.3.2 Nutrient analysis of feedstuffs
The data shown earlier in *Table 36.2* are those required for ration

Breed	Liveweight (Kg)	CP (g)	ME (MJ)
(a) Daily requirements for maintenance			
Friesian	550.0	575.0	63.0
Jersey	350.0	375.0	40.0
(b) Daily requirements for production (per kg milk)			
Friesian	–	80.0	4.9
Jersey	–	105.0	6.0

Table 36.3 *Nutrient requirements of dairy cows (five months after calving)*

formulation for most purposes. In formulating rations for non-ruminants (pigs and poultry), additional information on specific amino acid content of foodstuffs is required. This is because the diet of these animals is not based on grass and grass products which are well-balanced with regard to amino acids.

36.3.3 Potential dry matter intake (appetite)

It is important to know the average potential daily DM intake of the animal being fed. Such knowledge enables one to match the levels of nutrients in each component of the diet with the animal's daily nutrient requirements *in a ration which can be consumed* by the animal (i.e. does not exceed his appetite).

36.3.4 Formulation procedure

The example chosen to illustrate the procedure of ration formulation involves the feeding of a dairy cow.

A 550 kg Friesian cow producing 12 kg of milk in mid-lactation (5 months after calving) requires 575 g of crude protein and 63 MJ of metabolisable energy daily for maintenance *(Table 36.3)*. In addition, she has further requirements for milk production. The total requirements are calculated as follows:

Requirements:	CP(g)	ME(MJ)
Maintenance:	575	63.0
Production (12 kg): 12 x 80 =	960	12 x 4.9 = 58.8
Total :	1 535	121.8

To decide how much feed to give, the above requirements are divided by the feed's CP and ME content respectively. This indicates how much dry matter of that food is required. The dry matter is then converted to fresh food.

If the feed is silage of good quality it will contain 170 g kg^{-1} of CP and 10.3 MJ kg^{-1} of ME *(see Table 36.2)*. The amount needed to provide 121.8 MJ of ME is:

$$\frac{121.8}{10.3} = 11.8 \text{ kg of silage DM}$$

$$= \frac{11.8 \times 100}{20} = 59 \text{ kg of silage}$$

The amount of silage needed to provide 1 535 g of CP is:

$$\frac{1\,535}{170} = 9.02 \text{ kg of silage DM}$$

$$= \frac{9.02 \times 100}{20} = 45.1 \text{ kg of silage}$$

Thus, if the 59 kg of silage were fed, it would provide the ME but excess CP. If the 45.1 kg of silage were fed, this would provide the CP but not enough ME. There are two choices which can be made. Either feed the 59 kg of silage and accept the waste of protein or feed the 45.1 kg of silage and make up the lack of ME with another food.

The amount of ME in 45.1 kg of silage is:

$$\frac{45.1 \times 20}{100} = 9.02 \text{ of DM}$$

$$9.02 \times 10.3 = 92.9 \text{ MJ of ME}$$

Another form of energy, low in protein, could be used to supply the lack of ME. The deficit is 121.8 MJ - 92.9 MJ = 28.9 MJ of ME. If barley straw (*for analysis see Table 36.2*) were fed, the amount required would be:

$$\frac{28.9}{6.5} = 4.45 \text{ kg of straw DM}$$

$$= \frac{4.45 \times 100}{86} = 5.2 \text{ kg of straw}$$

The amounts of DM fed in these approaches is:
(a) Silage only : 11.8 kg DM
(b) Silage and straw : 9.02 + 4.45 = 13.47 kg DM.

Both amounts are well under the potential DM intake of a 550 kg Friesian cow in mid-lactation, which is 17 kg DM day^{-1}. Thus, either ration can be consumed by the cow.

Exercises

Exercise 76. Examination of animal feedstuffs

Materials needed
Samples of animal feedstuffs: (a) silage, (b) hay, (c) barley straw, (d) rolled barley, (e) ground barley, (f) ground wheat, (g) soya bean meal, (h) mineral/vitamin supplement, (i) molasses (treacle), (j) beet pulp, (k) dairy nuts, (l) calf nuts

Procedure
1. Examine all the feedstuffs provided. When examining each feedstuff, read the description of it in *section 36.1.1* or *36.1.2*.
2. Compare ground barley and ground wheat. **Note** the greater amount of fibre in ground barley.
3. Pelleted feedstuffs (nuts) are made by first mixing rolled or ground cereal grains, protein-rich concentrates and mineral/vitamin supplement. The mixture is then heated, molasses added under pressure and the mixture compacted and extruded into pellets. Moisten some pellets and break them up: see if the constituents can be identified.

Precautions

Do not taste any of the feedstuffs.

Exercise 77. Determination of the digestibility of rolled *vs* whole barley in the cow.

Materials needed
1. Whole barley grain (500 g)
2. Rolled barley (500 g)
3. Cows, 2

Procedure
1. Obtain facilities for closely confining two cows separately indoors for a period of time. (Most farms have such facilities, which are used at calving time.)
2. Clean the areas around where the cows are to be confined.
3. Feed one cow 500 g of whole barley grain. Feed the other 500 g of rolled barley.
4. Leave the cows loose for one hour.
5. Confine the cows for 12 hours (overnight).
6. After 12 hours collect all the dung passed by the cows, keeping it in two separate containers.
7. Examine the dung from the cow fed whole barley grain for the presence of grains. If grains are found, clean them and cut them open and examine the endosperm.
8. Examine the dung from the cow fed rolled barley for the presence of rolled grains. **Note:** Running water and a 2 mm sieve (soil sieve) may be helpful in steps 7 and 8.

Results

Record your results and comment on them. It is expected that whole grains will be found in step 7; but little evidence of rolled grains will be found in step 8.

37 – Animal Health

37.1 Conditions which Favour Good Health

The most important factors influencing animal health are *diet* and *living environment*. These are either largely or wholly within the farmer's control.

37.1.1 Diet

An animal which is fed a diet containing amounts of the essential food types adequate for its needs is more likely to experience good health than one which is badly fed. A badly fed animal will not grow and develop properly. This makes his system less well able to cope with infectious agents, nutrient and other disorders and parasite attack.

The importance of proper nutrition begins as early as the pre-natal period. If the dam is underfed, especially in late pregnancy, the newly born animal will be small, weak and subject to infection. Feeding colostrum *(see page 325)* in the first days of life provides the young animal with antibodies necessary for early disease resistance.

Thereafter, proper nutrition at all stages of growth, development and production optimises the animal's chances of good health.

37.1.2 Living environment

Animals are often exposed to disease by having to live in *unhygienic conditions.* In the case of housed animals, commonly found instances of bad hygiene include dirty houses, especially feeding troughs, buckets, etc.; bad ventilation; presence of vermin; failure to disinfect footwear of visitors from other farms; failure to isolate newly purchased animals for a time before integrating them with other stock.

With animals kept outdoors, the main problems include infected water supplies; dirty, infected pastures; presence of disease- bearing vermin; failure to isolate sick animals promptly; failure to remove carcases, dead foetuses, afterbirths etc. promptly.

Poor husbandry often causes ill-health. If animals are kept in cold, wet conditions (housed *or* outdoors), the stress caused lowers their resistance to disease. Other instances of poor husbandry include failure to recognise disease symptoms quickly; failure to inoculate or vaccinate animals against high-risk diseases; underfeeding or feeding an unbalanced diet.

Appearance/activity	Sign of good health	Sign of illness	Comment
General appearance	Animal is alert and active.	Animal is quiet and stays on its own.	–
Head	Animal has clear, bright eyes Nose and mouth are free from discharges.	Dull eyes. Discharges from eyes, nose or mouth.	– Caused by colds, chills and mouth infections
Coat/skin	Clean and sleek	Dull	–
Hindquarters	Clean	Dirty with faeces	Caused by diarrhoea
Eating	Normal appetite and eating habits	Loss of appetite. Animal eats soil, tree-bark, etc.	– May be due to a mineral deficiency
Walking	Walks normally	Limps	–
Breathing	Normal	Rapid breathing Laboured breathing Coughing	Caused by high temperature Caused by high temperature –
Sexual/reproductive activity	Normal oestrous activity Normal pregnancy	Lack of oestrus Failure to conceive Abortion	– – –
Production	Normal levels of production	Lowered levels of production (of milk, meat, etc)	Keeping records of milk production, weight gains, etc., is of importance

Table 37.1 Signs of good health and illness in farm animals

37.2 Animal Condition .

37.2.1 Signs of good health, illness

Early detection and treatment of sick animals are important in order to maintain overall stock health and productivity. Signs of good health and illness are listed in *Table 37.1*.

37.2.2 Condition-scoring

The condition of animals in terms of lean and fat is of practical importance to the farmer. Optimum production levels are not achieved by excessively thin or fat animals.

Animal condition is of most importance in the case of breeding females. Normal oestrous activity, conception rate and pregnancy are related to body condition. *Condition-scoring schemes* have been devised for cows, ewes and sows. All are based on examining the animal by hand to assess the amount of fat cover on various parts of the body, e.g. backbone, loin, tailhead.

Condition scores range between 0-5 for cows, 0-5 for ewes and 0-9 for sows. In each case, 0 represents extreme thinness and the highest score (5 or 9) represents highest excessive fatness. Scores in the middle of the range are usually considered most desirable. Details of the scoring scheme for cows are shown in *Exercise 79*.

37.3 Animal Diseases

The principal categories of diseases are listed and discussed below. For each category, the general *modes of action* of the organisms involved, *preventive practices* (i.e. those designed to prevent occurrence of disease) and *treatment practices* are described. Specific diseases of cattle, sheep and pigs are dealt with in later chapters.

37.3.1 Diseases caused by micro-organisms

The principal *pathogens* (organisms causing disease) in this category are bacteria. Others include viruses, fungi and protozoa. They enter the animal body by one of the pathways shown in *Table 37.2.*

Table 37.2 Systems and areas invaded by pathogenic micro-organisms

System/area invaded	Entry point
Digestive system	Mouth
Respiratory system	Mouth or nose
Urinogenital system	Vagina or penis
Abdominal cavity	Navel
Skin and muscle tissue	Cuts, wounds, parasite bites
Circulatory and nervous systems	Parasite bites

Modes of action: When *pathogens* invade body tissues, they reproduce rapidly and can cause irritation, inflammation, fever and loss of condition. Toxins (poisons) are produced in many cases. These lead to blood-poisoning, severe illness and possibly death. Dehydration caused by diarrhoea or fever, if untreated, leads to an increase in the concentration of blood salts and heart failure. In all cases, animal productivity is reduced.

Preventive practices: Disease prevention is greatly helped by paying attention to diet and living environment as outlined earlier.

When disease occurs on a farm, it is important that affected animals are *immediately isolated* to prevent spread of the disease. An isolation house with internal drains is an important feature of well-run farms. Bedding, discharges from diseased animals and other sources of infection should be burned or otherwise disposed of hygienically. Isolation houses should be cleaned and sterilized after use.

Treatment practices: Treatment with drugs may be necessary when animals contract disease. In the case of mild infections, the animal's natural defence mechanism may succeed in overcoming the infection. Animals showing disease symptoms should be isolated and observed to see if this occurs; if the symptoms worsen, then a veterinary surgeon should decide whether or not to use drugs.

Choice of drugs, method of administration and dosage rates are best decided on by a veterinary surgeon. There are regulations governing the use of all drugs and he or she is familiar with these. The use of *antibiotics* to treat diseases caused by bacteria has to be handled with special care. This is because of the risk of encouraging the production of resistant strains of bacteria which may later infect humans.

37.3.2 Diseases caused by parasites

The main parasites causing disease of farm animals are listed below:

Internal parasites	External parasites
Stomach and intestinal worms	Ticks
Tapeworms of the small intestine	Mites
Lungworms	Lice
Liver fluke	Flies

Internal parasites have life cycles involving periods outside the host. Entry to complete the life cycle is always through the mouth. *External parasites* complete their life cycles externally.

Modes of action: Internal parasites take nutrition away from the animal host, thereby limiting the growth of the animal. They damage the tissues of the body and can cause irritation and inflammation. Stomach and intestinal worms can cause diarrhoea, while lungworm infection can lead to pneumonia. The minimal result of infection by internal parasites is loss of condition while severe infections of young animals can cause death.

External parasites cause ill-health through three main effects. Firstly, their biting and/or sucking action irritates the animal. This affects its eating behaviour and lowers its productivity. Secondly, animal tissues can be damaged; examples are skin wounds and anaemia caused by blood-loss. Untreated skin wounds can allow the entry of secondary infections which may have more serious effects than the parasite. Thirdly, some external parasites act as vectors of diseases caused by micro-organisms.

Preventive practices: Detailed knowledge of parasite life cycles is needed in order to make decisions on preventive practices. The life cycles of stomach and intestinal worms and liver fluke have been dealt with in *Chapter 28.* In the case of the former parasite, it is known that eggs passed by the host animal in faeces hatch and develop to the infective larvae stage in 10-14 days.

Thus, removal of stock to fresh clean pasture before this stage is reached (i.e. 10 days after beginning to graze the pasture) reduces the risk of re-infection. The "leader-follower" system of grazing *(see page 327)* utilizes this principle. Young animals, who have little resistance to worm attacks are regularly moved ahead of older animals on pasture. The older animals, who have acquired resistance, then graze down the vegetation left behind by the younger stock.

In the case of liver fluke, since the parasite spends part of its life cycle in the gut of the mud-snail, elimination of snails by draining wet land prevents the occurrence of the disease.

Corresponding preventive practices can be used for the other parasites. Animals can also be *vaccinated* against some parasitic diseases.

Treatment practices: A range of drugs is available for use against internal and external parasites. For the reasons outlined earlier, decisions on the selection and use of these drugs are best made by veterinary surgeons.

37.3.3 Nutritional diseases

Nutritional diseases consist of deficiency diseases, diseases caused by intake of poisons and metabolic disorders.

Deficiency diseases occur when an animal's diet is deficient in some dietary constituent, most commonly a vitamin or trace element. A range of symptoms can result, including rickets, growth-check and anaemia. Deficiency diseases are rarely encountered nowadays, however. Ruminants can synthesise many vitamins in the rumen and the rations fed to pigs and poultry are usually carefully balanced for all constituents. The main incidence of such diseases is found in animals grazing pasture on soils deficient in a trace element.

Intake of poisons is more widespread. Some weeds of pasture (e.g. *ragwort* and *bracken*) are poisonous to some stock. While such weeds may be avoided by stock during grazing, they are eaten freely if present in silage. Other sources of poisoning are contaminated feedstuffs, lead in painted surfaces and carelessly handled farm chemicals, such as herbicides and pesticides.

Metabolic disorders are sometimes referred to as "production diseases" because they are associated with high levels of production. Animals operating under such conditions (e.g. a cow in early lactation or a ewe bearing twins) may draw on body reserves of energy, protein or minerals in order to maintain production. This leads to a temporary reduction in blood levels of these constituents. This can disrupt normal metabolic processes and lead to disease.

Modes of action: The modes of action of nutritional diseases are varied. All, however, result in disruption of the normal processes of nutrition and nutrient absorption and assimilation. Symptoms include growth-check, anaemia, disorientation, paralysis and death.

Preventive practices: Preventive practices are largely self-evident.

They include

1. Treating soils known to be deficient in a trace element with an appropriate fertilizer material.
2. Feeding properly balanced rations to all housed animals.
3. Elimination of poisonous weeds and chemicals from animals' living environment.
4. Careful nutrition of animals operating at high levels of production.

Treatment practices: Again, practices are largely self-evident and include:

1. Administration of vitamins or minerals to animals showing deficiency symptoms. These are normally administered orally or by injection under veterinary supervision.
2. Veterinary treatment of animals showing symptoms of poisoning.
3. Veterinary treatment of animals showing symptoms of metabolic disorders.

37.3.4 Notifiable diseases

These are diseases whose highly contagious nature makes them a serious national animal health risk. Owners or persons in charge of farm animals suspected of having a notifiable disease are required to report such suspicions immediately to their local District Veterinary Office so that appropriate control measures can be taken. Failure to report such diseases is a criminal offence.

Herds containing confirmed cases of notifiable diseases are immediately isolated and the animals quarantined or slaughtered. Some notifiable diseases are listed in *Table 37.3*.

Table 37.3 Notifiable diseases and types of animals affected

Disease	Animals affected
Foot-and-mouth disease	Cattle, sheep, pigs
Brucellosis	Cattle
Tuberculosis (T.B.)	Cattle
Anthrax	Cattle, sheep, pigs
Bovine spongeform encephalopathy	Cattle
Rabies	Cattle, sheep, pigs
Sheep scab	Sheep
Swine fever	Pigs
Aujeszky's disease	Pigs
Newcastle disease	Poultry

37.3.5 Zoonoses

These are diseases which can be transmitted from animals to humans. Extra care should be taken when handling animals suffering from these diseases. Some of them are notifiable. They are listed, together with mode of disease transmission to humans, in *Table 37.4*.

Table 37.4 *Zoonoses and their modes of transmission to humans*

Animal disease	Human disease	Mode of transmission
Brucellosis (cattle)	Undulant fever	Consumption of infected milk and meat
Tuberculosis (cattle)	Tuberculosis	Consumption of infected milk and meat
Salmonellosis (pigs and poultry)	Salmonella food poisoning	Consumption of infected meat
Ringworm (cattle)	Ringworm	Handling infected animals
Orf (sheep)	Orf	Handling infected animals
Leptospirosis (cattle)	Infectious jaundice	Handling infected animals, contact with contaminated water, etc.

Exercises

Exercise 78. Examining calves/weanlings for signs of health

Materials needed
1. Calves/weanlings
2. Clinical thermometer

Procedure

Note: This exercise can conveniently be carried out with young calves in March/April or with weanlings in October/ November/December.
1. Confine the animals in a house or collecting pen.
2. Examine them for signs of good health or illness, using the appearances/activities listed in *Table 37.1*. If there is agreement that one or more animal is ill, enquire from the owner/manager of the stock whether he agrees with you.
4. Ask the owner/manager to take the temperature of the animal suspected to be ill. Note its respiration rate. The normal temperatures and respiration rates are: calves, 38.6 °C; 30 – 60 breaths min^{-1}, weanlings, 38.6°C; 30 – 50 breaths min^{-1}.

Results
Record observations and measurements recorded. Comment on the accuracy of your suspicions in relation to ill- health.

Precautions
Be very careful in the vicinity of animals. Do not handle them without experienced help.

Exercise 79. Assessing condition score of cows.

Materials needed
Cows of varying body condition

Procedure
1. Confine the cows in a cattle crush and race.
2. Examine them in the loin and tailhead areas for degree of fat cover under the skin. Refer to the descriptions given in *Table 37.5*.
3. Score the animals on the scale 0-5, including half-scores (i.e. an 11-point scale).

Results
1. Record all results carefully.
2. Record final scores.
3. Comment on the implications of the condition scores of the cows selected.

Precautions
1. Keep a safe distance from cows which are not confined to avoid the possibility of being kicked.
2. Be careful when examining cows by hand through the bars of a cattle crush or race. Sudden movement of cows can cause injury to the hand or arm.

Table 37.5 Condition scoring of cows

Score 0 (very poor)

Tailhead area: Deep cavity under tail and around tailhead. Skin drawn tight over pelvis with no fat in between.

Loin area: No fat detectable. Shape of transverse processes clearly visible.

Score 1 (poor)

Tailhead area: Cavity present around tailhead. No fatty tissue felt between skin and pelvis, skin is not drawn tight but supple.

Loin area: End of transverse processes sharp to touch and upper surfaces are easily felt. Deep depression in loin.

Score 2 (moderate)

Tailhead area: Shallow cavity lined with fatty tissue felt at base of tail. Some fatty tissue felt under skin. Pelvis easily felt.

Loin area: End of transverse processes feel rounded, but upper surfaces felt only with pressure. Depression in loin visible.

Score 3 (good)

Tailhead area: Fat easily felt over the whole area. Skin appears smooth but pelvis can be felt.

Loin area: Ends of transverse processes can be felt with pressure, with thick layers of fat on top. Slight depression visible in loin.

Score 4 (fat)

Tailhead area: Folds of soft fat present. Patches of fat apparent under skin. Pelvis felt only with firm pressure.

Loin area: Transverse processes cannot be felt. No depression in loin.

Score 5 (grossly fat)

Tailhead area: Base of tail buried in fat. Skin distended. No part of pelvis felt even with firm pressure.

Loin area: Folds of fat over transverse processes. Bone structure cannot be felt.

38 – The Principles and Importance of Dairying

38.1 National Importance

Dairying and beef production together account for 73% of all agricultural production in Ireland. They are closely related industries, the dairy herd producing both milk and beef animals. The national importance of dairying is shown in *Table 38.1*.

Table 38.1 Importance of dairying in Irish agriculture

	1970	1980	1990
Value of milk and dairy products (IR£million)	80	540	1 192
Percentage of total agricultural output	23	32	38
Percentage of total agricultural exports	19	24	27

There are 1.4 million dairy cows in the country and they produce six billion litres of milk per annum. About 10% of this is sold throughout the country for direct consumption (liquid milk). The remaining 90% is processed in creameries and other manufacturing plants into butter, cheese, milk powder and a range of other products.

Dairying is practised in all counties but the greatest concentration of dairy herds is found in the south of the country with almost 70% of milk being produced in Munster.

38.2 Breeds in the Dairy Herd

Cattle breeds are of three types: dairy, beef and dual-purpose. Some examples of these types are shown in *Table 38.2*. The principal breed in the Irish dairy herd is the Friesian which makes up more than 90% of the herd. The remainder is composed of small numbers of Jerseys, Dairy shorthorns, Holsteins and Ayrshires.

Table 38.2 Classification of the principal cattle breeds in Ireland

Dairy breeds produce milk only	Dual-purpose breeds produce milk and beef animals	Beef breeds produce beef animals only
Holstein Jersey Ayreshire	Friesian Dairy shorthorn	*British* Hereford Aberdeen angus *Continental* Charolais Limousin Simmental

The Friesian breed suits the Irish dairy industry very well because, in addition to its high milk yields, it supplies calves which

Fig. 38.1 A Friesian cow

are of use to the very important beef industry. A Friesian cow is shown in *Fig. 38.1*.

38.3 Principles of Dairying

38.3.1 Birth, growth rates, puberty
A female calf, destined for a place in a dairy herd, weighs about 40 kg at birth. If reared properly, she will reach puberty at about one year old. She usually weighs about 250 kg at this stage.

38.3.2 Oestrous cycle, gestation period
The length of the oestrous cycle is 21 days and the average duration of oestrus is 18 hours. The gestation period is 283 days (9.5 months).

38.3.3 Lactation
A cow commences to milk immediately after calving. If the cow is suckled and does not become pregnant she will continue to milk for up to 2 years. If she becomes pregnant (in-calf), she goes dry about 2 months before calving as her system prepares for calving.

In commercial milk production, the aim is to have cows calving once per year at as near as possible to the same date each year. This means that cows milk for about 10 months of the year. Milk yield records kept for assessing and comparing cows' production potential are based on a standard lactation of *305 days*.

38.3.4 Lactation yield
Average lactation (305 days) yields for five breeds of cow are shown in *Table 38.3*. Lactation yields achieved by individual Friesian cows in Ireland vary from 2 000 kg to 13 000 kg. The mean lactation yield for the country has increased from 2 500 kg twenty years ago to 4 000 kg at present and many of the better farmers are achieving average herd yields of 5 500 kg and greater. These improvements are achieved by *selection* within the breed. Lactation yield varies with a cow's age as shown in *Table 38.4*.

Table 38.3 *Average lactation yields for 5 dairy breeds*

Breed	Yield (kg)
Holstein	5 800
Jersey	3 400
Ayreshire	4 000
Friesian	5 000
Dairy shorthorn	4 000

Table 38.4 *Lactation yield vs age and lactation number*

Age (yr)	Lactation no.	Lactation yield as % of maximum
2	1	75
3	2	85
4	3	90
5	4	95
6	5	100

While cows normally produce their first calf at 2 years old they do not reach their maximum yield until their fifth lactation. From this age onwards lactation yield decreases.

38.3.5 Frequency of milking, milking interval

Milking empties the udder and stimulates the milk-secreting alveoli to commence further secretion. Frequently milked cows have the highest daily and lactation yields. Thus cows milked four times daily give more milk than those milked three times, and so on. In practice, however, the yield-increases obtained by milking more often than twice per day are uneconomic and so twice-daily milking is the normal procedure.

With twice-daily milking, the milking interval should ideally be 12 hours. This puts least stress on the cow's system and gives the best chance of maximising yield. As this interval makes for a very long working day, many farmers use 14/10 or 13/11 hour intervals.

38.3.6 Milk composition and utilisation

Average milk composition is as shown in *Fig. 38.2*. Milk for sale to the consumer *(liquid milk)* must, by law, have at least 3.6% cream and 8.5% SNF.

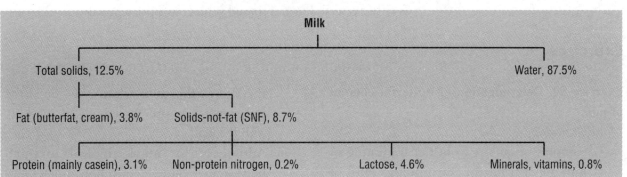

Fig 38.2 Average composition of milk

In *processed* milk, the use made of the different milk components

Table 38.5 Milk products and their raw materials

Product	Milk component used
Butter	Fat (butterfat)
Butter oil	Fat (butterfat)
Cheese	Whole *or* skim milk
Yogurt	Skim milk
Ice cream	Whole milk
Chocolate crumb	Whole milk
Whole milk powder	Whole milk
Skim milk powder	Skim milk
Milk replacer	Skim milk
Cream	Fat (cream)
Cream liqueurs	Fat (cream)
Casein	Casein

is as shown in *Table 38.5*.

Depending on the use planned for it, milk may be purchased by creameries and factories at either (i) a flat price rate per kg or (ii) a price per kg based on percentage fat, casein, protein or some other component.

Milk composition varies with breed, Jersey milk having the highest amounts of fat and total solids. Milk from old cows and from early lactation milkings tend to have slightly lower fat content.

Fat content varies considerably during milking. The first milk removed from the udder can have as little as 1% fat while "strippings" (the last milk) may have as much as 8-10% fat.

38.3.7 Hygienic quality of milk

Milk containing dirt, bacteria or antibiotics causes problems during treatment and processing. Dirty milk is the result of using unhygienic milking machinery and defective milk filters. High bacterial content results from dirty milk, improper cooling of the milk or a combination of these factors. Antibiotics in milk are usually the residues of medical treatment for mastitis, milk having been sold too soon after treatment.

When milk fails to pass the quality tests imposed by creameries, it is either rejected or purchased subject to a price penalty.

Exercises

Exercise 80. Determination of butterfat content of milk

Materials needed

1. Samples of milk A from the beginning of milking B from the "strippings" (end of milking)
2. Gerber apparatus
3. Sulphuric acid, conc. (density, 1.815)
4. Amyl alcohol

Procedure

1. Mix each of the milk samples thoroughly (but do not shake vigorously).
2. Bring the temperature of the samples to 20°C $\pm$ 2°C. If flakes of cream or butter are present, warm the sample(s) to 40-45°C to liquify the fat and then mix thoroughly.
3. Add 10 mls of sulphuric acid to each of 4 butyrometers.
4. Deliver a sample of milk A to each of two butyrometers. Use a 38.8 ml pipette. Allow the milk to flow gently down the side of the butyrometer to prevent mixing of the milk with the acid.
5. Add 1 ml of amyl alcohol to each butyrometer. Stopper each butyrometer and shake and invert several times until all the curdy material has dissolved.
6. Transfer the butyrometers to the centrifuge while they are still hot. Mark the positions of the butyrometers to identify the samples.
7. Repeat steps 4, 5 and 6, using milk B.
8. Make sure that the rotor of the centrifuge is balanced by placing the butyrometers symmetrically.
9. Centrifuge for 3 min at 1 100-1 300 rpm. The total time of centrifugation is 5 min as it takes about 2 min to bring the speed up to 1 100 rpm.
10. Remove the samples and transfer to a water bath heated to 65°C, graduated necks

upwards, (make sure you can still identify which sample is which). The water should cover the fat columns.

11. After 2 min at 65°C, read the percentage fat from the graduations. The fat column can be adjusted by regulating the position of the test-bottle stoppers.

Results

1. Obtain mean fat percentages for milk A and milk B.
2. Compare the mean values.
3. Comment on the practical significance of the difference between the fat contents of milk A and milk B.

Precautions

Handle the sulphuric acid with care. Use a pipette with a pipette filler.

Exercise 81. Assessment of hygienic quality of milk (Resazurin test)

Materials needed

1. Samples of milk: (i) fresh, unpasteurized, (ii) stale (24 hrs old), unpasteurized, (iii) pasteurized
2. Resazurin solution
3. Clean (preferably sterile) test-tubes, 3
4. Marker
5. Stoppers for test-tubes (clean or sterile), 3

Procedure

1. Place the test-tubes in a test-tube rack. Label A, B, C.
2. Pour 10 mls of fresh unpasteurized milk into test-tube A, 10 mls of stale unpasteurized into test-tube B and 10 mls of pasteurized into test-tube C.
3. Add 1 ml of resazurin solution to each test tube.
4. Stopper and incubate at about 37 °C for 10 minutes in warm water
5. Place the test tubes back in the rack and examine the colour of each milk sample.

Note: Hygienic quality is indicated as follows:

Blue —> Mauve —> Pink -> White

Best quality   Poorest quality

Results:

1. Record the results.
2. Comment on them.

39 – Dairy Herd Management

39.1 Management of Milking Cows

39.1.1 Planning production

Milk production in Ireland is a low-cost system, based on producing milk from *summer grass*. For this reason, 80% of all calvings occur in spring, usually in January and February. Autumn calvings are found mostly in herds near Dublin, Cork and other large cities to cater for the demand for liquid milk, which is a 12-month demand.

There are two main items of planning in managing spring-calving dairy herds.

1. *Plan calving dates.* It is of prime importance that all or nearly all cows calve during the January/February period, so that full use is made of summer grass, the cheapest food. This involves very close attention to oestrus detection, as described below.

2. *Balance grazing and grass conservation.* The amount of land allocated to summer grazing and that allocated to conservation for winter feed must be carefully and accurately calculated. It must match herd needs. If feed shortages occur in summer, milk production will fall unless expensive concentrate rations are purchased and fed. Purchase of such rations greatly reduces profitability.

   If shortages of silage for winter feed occur, they may occur at the end of the winter when cows are calving and beginning to milk. This again will lead to high feed purchase bills.

39.1.2 Calving

The period of calving in January and February is the most critical in the dairy farmer's year. The sale of calves accounts for up to 30% of the annual income of dairy farmers. For this reason, care of the cow immediately before and during calving, together with care of the calf at birth and for the first 24 hours of life, is of great importance.

A recent Teagasc survey showed that 6% of all calves die at birth each year and a further 3% die during the first week of life. Most of these deaths are avoidable.

Mismanagement at calving can also cause death of the cow or injury or illness leading to loss of milk production, infertility or other problems.

The three rules for successful calving management are:

1. *Isolate the cow before calving.* It is important to keep careful breeding records so that the calving date is known. An experienced person should then regularly examine the cow

approaching this date, looking for signs of the onset of calving. The cow should be removed to a calving box (a small, disinfected house designed for calving purposes) 1-2 days before calving.

2. *Have an experienced person present at calving.* The isolated cow should be regularly inspected day and night to ensure that the calving process can be supervised by an experienced person.

3. *Obtain veterinary assistance if needed.* Once the cow goes into labour, an experienced person can handle a normal delivery with a helper. If the birth is delayed or abnormal in any way, it is advisable to obtain veterinary assistance *immediately.* Many deaths are caused by delay in calling for such assistance.

39.1.3 Management in early lactation

After calving, the cow produces *colostrum*, a type of milk needed for feeding the calf for the first 3-4 days of its life. This milk will not be accepted by the creamery, so the cow does not participate fully in the herd until this period is over.

Fig. 39.1 Lactation curve for a cow producing 5 000 kg of milk

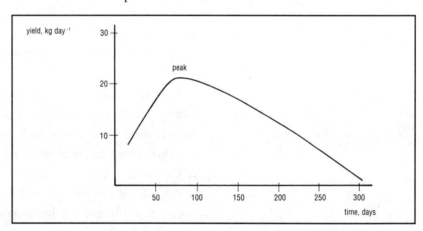

The daily milk yield varies over the lactation period in the manner shown in the typical *lactation curve* of *Fig. 39.1*. It is very important that the cow be fed sufficient nutrients to ensure that she achieves her full potential in the period up to and including the *lactation peak*. The reason for this is that the amount of milk produced at the peak governs total lactation yield as follows:

Total lactation yield (kg) = Daily yield at peak (kg) x 200 (for average management) or

Total lactation yield (kg) = Daily yield at peak (kg) x 220 (for high level of management).

Thus, if the cow's potential peak yield is not achieved, her potential lactation yield cannot be achieved.

The cow is fed for maintenance and production during this period. With older cows, whose past record of milk production is known, the amount of feeding can be accurately calculated. With first-lactation heifers, on the other hand, it is advisable to feed at a higher level than their milk production suggests. This is done in order to *ensure* that they achieve their potential peak yield.

Concentrate rations always have to be fed in addition to silage in early lactation. While it may appear an expensive practice, it should be remembered that these concentrates determine peak yield and therefore lactation yield potential. The bulk of this potential is, however, produced by grass, the cheapest feed. Concentrate feeding can thus be regarded as an essential prerequisite for efficient utilization of grass.

Cows are "turned out" onto grass as soon as there is enough available for them. Time of turning out depends on spring weather, geographical location and fertilizer use. It can vary from early March to early May.

If grass is scarce at first, concentrate feeding should be continued to prevent milk yield falling. Once grass is growing normally, concentrate feeding is reduced and quickly stopped altogether, except for cows with very high yields. Grass is utilised by one of the grazing systems outlined in *Chapter 21*, usually paddock or block-grazing. If farmers have not taken preventive measures against grass tetany *(see page 332)*, they should observe cows closely during their first days on grass in case they show symptoms of this disease.

39.1.4 Calving interval, heat detection and servicing

Efficient heat (oestrus) detection and servicing are essential if the cow's calving interval is to be kept regularly at 12 months duration.

Cows normally come into heat 3-8 weeks after calving and every 21 days thereafter. Allowing 9.5 months for gestation, cows should be got in calf not later than 2.5 months (10 weeks) after calving to ensure that the calving interval does not exceed 12 months. Since cows do not always conceive at first service, it is essential that no early heat periods are missed. The ideal sequence of events is shown in *Fig. 39.2*, in which day 56 should be the target date for service. This leaves a 26-day "safety valve" in case cows require a repeat service.

Fig. 39.2 Procedure used to obtain a 12-month calving interval

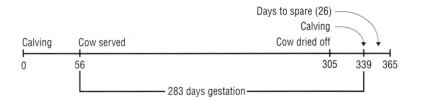

When cows are in heat they attempt to mount other cows and other cows attempt to mount them. The best way to detect this is to inspect the herd 4-5 times daily, especially late in the evening and early in the morning. "Tail-painting" is a helpful technique in heat detection.

Fig. 39.3 "Tail-painted" cow

'tail painted' strip

A strip, 5 cm wide by 25-30 cm long, is painted along the cow's back as shown in *Fig. 39.3*, using flat (emulsion) paint. If the cow has been mounted since the observer's last inspection, the strip of paint will be noticeably damaged or broken up.

The vast majority of servicing of dairy cows is carried out by artificial insemination (AI). As soon as a cow is detected as being on heat the AI company should be informed. When they have accurate information on the time of commencement of heat, they can plan the time of service so that there is the greatest chance of conception occurring.

39.1.5 Management in mid- and late lactation and before calving

Two-thirds of the lactation yield are supplied in the first half of the lactation period. Therefore, from mid-lactation onwards, cows are easily able to maintain themselves and produce milk from well-managed grassland. In late lactation, daily yield of milk becomes so small that cows are milked once a day only. At this stage, cows may be treated with medication, injected into the teat canal, to minimise the risk of disease during the "drying- off" process.

Cows are dry for about 2 months before calving. During this period, the size of the calf in the cow's womb increases rapidly. Cows must be fed on an increasing plane of nutrition to allow proper development of the calf, e.g.when cows are fed silage of average/good quality *ad lib*, they should be fed a ration containing 15% crude protein. It should be given at a rate of 2 kg day^{-1} 10 weeks before calving, increasing to 6 kg day^{-1} at calving.

39.2 Calf-rearing

Calves can be reared naturally by suckling the cow or artificially away from the cow. In dairy-farming, all calf-rearing is done artificially. The cow's milking routine and production of saleable milk would be seriously disturbed by allowing a calf to suckle her, even for limited periods.

Calves reared may be either heifer calves being reared as replacements for cows in the herd or bull or heifer calves for sale as weanlings or to be fattened for beef production. Whatever the purpose, the principles of rearing are the same.

39.2.1 Feeding colostrum

The differences between colostrum and milk, together with the reasons for them, are shown in *Table 39.1*. Colostrum is a more concentrated material and contains large amounts of highly digestible nutrients.

Its most important attribute, however, is its increased protein

Constituent	% in milk	% in colostrum	Function of increased amount in colostrum
Fat	3.8	4.0	Slight laxative effect
Protein	3.1	15.2	Provides disease resistance (antibodies) Provides protein and energy for growth Slight laxative effect
Non-protein nitrogen	0.2	0.2	–
Lactose	4.6	1.4	–
Minerals & vitamins	0.8	1.2	Improves disease resistance Stimulates growth
Water	87.5	78.0	–

Table 39.1 Composition of milk; composition and functions of colostrum

level, much of which is made up of *immunoglobulins*. These substances are also known as antibodies. They can be absorbed intact by the young calf, giving it resistance to a number of diseases.

Since the calf is born without antibodies in its system, it is vitally important that it obtains them quickly. The calf's ability to absorb antibodies is greatest in the first 3-12 hours of life. It is recommended that it consume 2 – 3 kg of colostrum during this period. If the calf is weak and cannot suckle the mother properly, it should be hand-fed.

After 24 hours, the calf's ability to absorb antibodies has ceased but colostrum should still be fed as long as it is available (usually 3-4 days) due to its high nutritive value. Excess colostrum can be diluted and fed to older calves.

The importance of feeding colostrum to calves cannot be over-emphasized. Research has shown that the majority of deaths, illnesses and failure to grow properly during the first three months are caused by inadequate intake of colostrum. Where a cow dies at birth or fails to produce colostrum for any other reason, colostrum from another recently calved cow may be fed to her calf. Excess colostrum can be frozen and stored for this purpose. A substitute can also be prepared using milk, fresh eggs, cod liver oil and castor oil.

39.2.2 Feeding milk and milk replacer

Milk is the food ideally suited to the calf's digestive system. It is, however, far more costly than alternative feeds as is shown in *Table 39.2.*

The calf is unable to digest concentrate ration at a very early age because its rumen is not fully developed. The normal procedure, therefore, is to feed the calf the following sequence of feeds:

(i) Colostrum, (ii) Milk, (iii) Milk replacer, (iv) Concentrate ration. For cost reasons, the more quickly the calf can be weaned onto concentrate ration the better. In practice, however, this cannot be achieved until the calf is at least 5-6 weeks old.

Table 39.2 Relative costs (per unit of food value) of possible calf diets

Diet	Relative cost
Milk	100
Milk replacer	60
Concentrate ration	20-25

The digestive system of the calf is very sensitive and easily upset. It is only in recent years that the successful use of milk replacer for calf rearing has been perfected. Milk replacer is made by mixing milk replacer powder and water in the proportions, 125 g powder : 1 l water. It must be introduced to the young calf gradually: this is done by gradually replacing whole milk with milk replacer over a period of 4-5 days.

Bucket-fed calves are given 2 l of milk replacer twice daily at body temperature. Milk replacer can also be fed to calves using an automatic feeder; with this system, calves feed themselves as often as they wish. The cost is justified only when large numbers of calves are being reared.

39.2.3 Weaning onto hay and concentrates (meals)

Hay, concentrates and water should be made available to calves from the time they stop drinking colostrum. At first they will eat very little hay or concentrates but their consumption increases as they grow older. Both of these feeds, but particularly the hay, supply micro-organisms which help to develop the calf's rumen flora and enable it to digest fibrous materials.

By the time the calf is 4 weeks old, he should be eating 300- 400 g of concentrates daily. His consumption continues to increase with time and when it reaches 500 g day $^{-1}$, the calf can be weaned from milk replacer. From this time until he is allowed out onto grass, the calf is fed concentrates, hay and water.

39.2.4 The calf on grass

Calves should not be allowed onto grass until the weather is warm. The change from warm housing to cold outdoor conditions can cause a shock to their system and a setback in growth. Meal- feeding should be continued on grass for at least 2-3 weeks. This helps calves to maintain growth while they are adjusting to their new diet.

Calves are selective grazers. In order to keep them growing satisfactorily, they should be kept on fresh, palatable grass and not required to graze pastures bare. They should graze in a "leader-follower" system, i.e. they should always graze in advance of older cattle, which can later graze down the grass the calves have left behind. A second reason for employing this system is to minimise levels of infestation of parasitic stomach- and lung-worms *(see pages 349, 350)*.

At the end of the grazing season, when grass becomes scarce, concentrates should again be fed for 2-3 weeks. When calves are housed for the winter on November 1st they should weigh 200 kg. Calves which have not reached this weight should be housed in a separate group and fed extra meals until they have caught up with the remainder of the calves. At housing, calves should also be checked for lice and treated if necessary.

39.3 Replacement Heifers

Cows need to be replaced in the dairy herd at a rate of about 20% per year. There are several reasons for replacing cows, some of which are:

(a) Milk production declining with age

(b) Infertility problems

(c) Disease

(d) Injuries to udders, feet, etc.

(e) "Grading-up"

Grading-up refers to the practice of replacing low-yielding cows with heifers from the higher-yielding cows in the herd with the objective of increasing average milk yield per cow.

Replacement heifer calves should be reared in the manner already described. The target weights for calves born in January/February are as follows:

April 15 : 72.5 kg

November 1: 200 kg

The calves should be fed good quality silage and some meals over the winter to ensure that they achieve their next target weight, which is *300 kg* on May 1 (i.e. at 1 year, 3 months old).

Heifers reach puberty and come into heat at 8-12 months old but they should not be got in calf until they are *at least 15 months old and 300 kg in weight.* Otherwise, they will be very small at calving. As a result, they may have calving difficulties and will never achieve their full size and milking potential. If heifers are got in calf about May 1 of their second year, they will calve in mid-February at just two years old. This is the objective of most farmers.

Replacement heifers calving at two years old should weigh *450 kg on November 1* and *500-525 kg before calving.* Such animals are not fully grown and care should be taken to feed them for *growth* as well as for maintenance and milk production during their first lactation. Otherwise they will fail to reach their full size, weight and milking potential.

39.4 Milking and Milking Hygiene

The essential parts and layout of a milking machine and dairy are shown in *Fig. 39.4.* The functions of the parts are:

Vacuum pump: This creates a partial vacuum which is used (a) to perform the milking process, (b) transport the milk to the receiving vessel and (c) transport the detergent solution through the milk line during the washing process.

Vacuum line: This transmits the vacuum to the milking clusters and to the milk line.

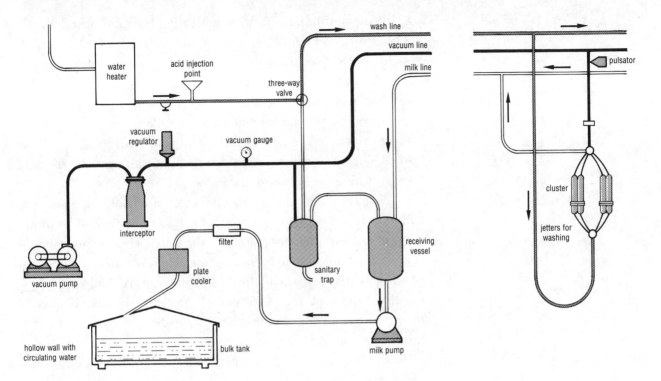

Fig. 39.4 Layout of a milking machine and dairy. Arrows show direction of flow of milk and detergent solution

Vacuum regulator: This maintains the vacuum at a constant value.

Pulsator: This interrupts the vacuum in the outside of the teat cup with periods of atmospheric pressure *(Fig. 39.5)*. This squeezes in the rubber *teat-cup liner* and performs the milking action.

Cluster: The cluster of teat cups is attached to the cow's udder during milking.

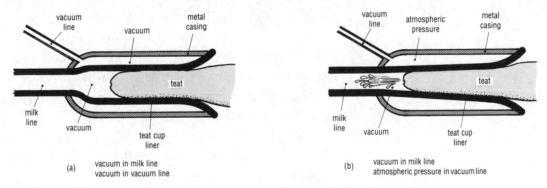

Fig. 39.5 Action of teat-cup during milking

Milk line: The milk is transported along the milk line by the partial vacuum there. There may be *recording jars* on the line through which the milk passes before it reaches the *receiving vessel*.

Milk pump: This pumps the milk from the receiving vessel to the dairy.

Cooler: When it enters the dairy, the milk passes through the cooler, which lowers its temperature from 30°C to about 12°C.

Bulk tank: The milk is stored here before transport to the creamery. It is further cooled in the bulk tank to 4°C.

Wash line: Detergent solution is flushed through the cluster, milk line and cooler during the washing procedure.

Milk is maintained in a hygienically clean condition by (1) keeping dirt and contamination of all kinds out of milk and (2) cooling milk quickly after milking. *Contamination* of milk is prevented by the following measures:

(a) Washing cows' udders and teats before milking

(b) Checking all teats for mastitis at all milkings

(c) Regular washing of the clusters, milk line and cooler

(d) Using a *filter* to remove any dirt particles which get into the milk

(e) Washing the bulk tank regularly.

Cooling is carried out in two stages. A plate cooler uses water at ambient temperature to lower the temperature of the milk to within a few degrees of the temperature of the water. This initial cooling is very important as it prevents bacterial development. The final cooling is performed in the bulk tank, where water at 1°C is circulated through the hollow wall of the tank. The milk is agitated in the tank and the temperature is slowly lowered to 4°C. It is thermostatically maintained at that temperature.

In the creamery or milk factory, milk is subjected to a number of tests for hygienic quality. These are the *litmus* and the *delvo* tests. They are designed to detect milk which has not been cooled properly.

39.5 Diseases of Cows and Calves

39.5.1 Diseases of cows

1. **Tuberculosis (TB):** This is a disease of both cows and beef cattle. It affects bulls, cows, bullocks (steers), heifers and calves and is a zoonose. It is caused by the bacterium *Mycobacterium bovis*. TB is *highly infectious* and can spread quickly throughout a herd. Man can be infected by close contact with infected animals or by drinking unpasteurised milk from infected cows.

   Symptoms: The early symptoms are failure of animals to thrive, sweating and bad appearance (dull coat). In advanced cases, emaciation occurs and coughing and fever lead to death.

   Prevention: There is no way of preventing the occurrence of TB in cattle, but some practices help to prevent its entry onto individual farms. These include: (a) not buying in stock (rear all herd replacements), (b) maintenance of good farm fencing to prevent mixing of stock, and (c) using clean water sources (avoid slow moving streams and stagnant water).

   Treatment: Veterinary treatment of infected animals is slow and often unsuccessful. On account of this fact, together with the risk to human health and the lack of a market for infected cattle, a government scheme for the eradication of TB has been in existence for the past 30 years. This involves regular

TB testing of herds (inoculating animals with the disease organism and testing three days later for a positive reaction). Animals showing a positive test ("reactors") are slaughtered and farmers are compensated for losses incurred.

2. **Contagious abortion:** This disease is caused by the bacterium *Brucella abortis*. If infected animals are pregnant, they abort their calves. This usually occurs between the fifth and seventh month of pregnancy. Non-pregnant animals can act as carriers of the disease.

   The disease is *highly infectious* and can spread quickly throughout a herd. It is spread by contact with: (a) infected cows, (b) carriers, (c) discharges from infected cows, (d) cattle marts, (e) boots and clothing, (f) contaminated water. It is a zoonose, causing undulent fever (brucellosis) in humans.

   Symptoms: Abortion between the fifth and seventh months of pregnancy.

   Prevention: There are some preventive measures which can be used by farmers to keep down the level of infection in their herds. These include: (a) vaccination of heifer calves. This is not always successful but is tried by some farmers, (b) making sure that foetuses aborted between the fifth and seventh months of pregnancy are tested for the disease organism. The suspect cows should be isolated until test results are known, (c) maintaining good farm hygiene (good fencing; disinfecting visitors' boots), (d) rearing all replacement heifers (bought-in heifers can be infected).

   Treatment: On account of the highly infectious nature of the disease and the human health risk, contagious abortion is being tackled nationally on an eradication basis on the same lines as the TB eradication scheme. Herds are tested and "reactors" are slaughtered and farmers compensated.

3. **Mastitis:** This is a bacterial disease of the udder. Infection occurs via the teat canal and is the result of *bad hygiene.* It exists in two forms, sub-clinical (which is detectable only by bacterial examination of the milk) and clinical (i.e. displaying more obvious symptoms). Infection is due to a variety of bacteria, possibly up to 20, including *Streptococcus, Staphylococcus, Escherischia* and *Pseudomonas.*

   Symptoms: Sub-clinical mastitis is diagnosed by bacterial contamination of milk and reduced milk yield (up to 10% reduction). Symptoms of clinical mastitis include swelling and pain in the udder, clots in the milk and general ill-health.

   Prevention: The main preventive measures are: (a) maintain hygienic housing conditions, (b) keep milking machine spotlessly clean, (c) use teat dips (antiseptic dipping of teats after milking), (d) clean teat cups between cows with hot running water, (e) Wash teats before milking with running water. Injuries and sores on the teats and udder (especially if near teat tips) are a predisposing cause of infection. They should be carefully treated and cured.

Treatment: Clinical mastitis is treated with antibiotics injected hygienically into the teat canal. Milk from cows undergoing treatment must be discarded for several milkings. There are penalties for supplying antibiotic-contaminated milk for sale.

4. **Milk fever (parturient hypocalcaemia):** This is a metabolic disorder caused by subnormal levels of blood calcium in cows. It is caused by the sudden onset of lactation, with the production of milk rich in calcium. The disorder usually occurs within 24-48 hours of calving, so cows should be observed carefully during this period. The readily available body reserves of calcium are used up in milk production and the bonemarrow cannot make up the deficit quickly enough.

Symptoms: Nervousness, excitability, spasmodic hind-leg movements, inability to stand up, followed quickly by coma and death if untreated.

Prevention/treatment: As there is *no reliable prevention*, careful observation of newly calved cows and *prompt treatment* are the best approach. Treatment involves the injection of soluble calcium intravenously, and is usually successful if carried out in time.

5. **Grass tetany or grass staggers (Hypomagnesaemia):** This is a metabolic disorder caused by subnormal levels of magnesium in the blood. It affects beef animals and calves as well as cows. In England it is known as Hereford disease because of its prevalence in Herefordshire due to soil conditions there being a predisposing cause.

Hypomagnesaemia can occur at any time of the year if magnesium levels in the diet are low. Its most common occurrence in an acute form, however, is when lactating cows are put out in spring onto *lush, heavily fertilized grass.* Such grass is often deficient in magnesium. This can be aggravated by the stress of recent calving or by cold spring conditions.

Symptoms: These include nervousness, muscle tremors, twitching eyeballs, followed quickly by muscle spasms, coma and death. Often, the discovery of dead cows in the field in the morning is the first sign.

Prevention: Hypomagnesaemia can be prevented by feeding "calcined magnesite" (MgO) in the diet at a rate of 60 g head^{-1} day^{-1} for 2-3 weeks before turning out to grass. This additive is available in dairy and other rations from most feed compounders. It should continue to be fed for a while after turnout.

Treatment: Prompt intravenous injection of soluble magnesium under veterinary supervision.

6. **Lameness:** This is a common problem with cows wintered on concrete yards. Lameness begins with wear and injuries to the hoof (wear from concrete; injuries from loose stones, etc.). It is aggravated by bacterial infection of the damaged hoof.
Symptoms: Lameness in one or more leg(s).
Prevention: Lameness may be prevented by careful hoof care. Teagasc provides training courses for farmers in this area.
Treatment: This involves repair of injuries, shoeing of hooves and treatment with antibiotics.

7. **Lice:** Lice affect all cattle, including cows, calves and beef cattle. In adult cattle their presence causes animals to thrive badly. As their effect on calves is of most importance, the disease is described later. *(see page 335).*

8. **Redwater (Babesiasis):** This is a parasitic disease caused by the organism *Babesia bovis* whose lifecycle has already been described *(see page 249).* The organism is transmitted by the common tick and destroys red blood cells. Animals reared in redwater districts (i.e. where the disease is very prevalent) usually do not show serious symptoms as they gradually acquire immunity. The greatest risk is to adult cattle brought in from redwater-free districts.
Symptoms: The first symptom of disease is the passing of reddish brown urine. The colour is caused by the presence of broken-down blood cells. This is quickly followed by listlessness, lack of appetite, fever and death if not treated.
Prevention: This involves mainly the removal of the tick from the environment of cattle. Old, poorly grazed pastures are favoured by the tick. Heavy grazing, topping and reseeding are all practices which lower tick populations. Ticks can also be removed from cattle by hand or by chemical treatment.
Treatment: Treatment is by injection of specific drugs under veterinary supervision. It is only successful if carried out in the early stages of the disease. Therefore, cattle should be regularly inspected for symptoms when the disease is prevalent (May/June and October).

9. **Other diseases of cows:** Other diseases of cows of lesser importance generally than those already covered are listed and commented on in *Table 39.3.*

39.5.2. Diseases of calves

1. **Scour (diarrhoea):** This is the most important disease of calves, causing the greatest number of deaths among young calves. There are two types of scour, nutritional and bacterial,

Disease	Comment
1. Foot-and-mouth disease	This is a highly infectious, notifiable disease. Infected cattle must be slaughtered. There has not been an outbreak in Ireland since 1941.
2. Liver fluke	This is an important parasitic disease on farms with areas of wet land which harbour the mud snail, a vector of the liver fluke organism. Drainage prevents the disease.
3. Bloat	This is caused by an accumulation of gas in the rumen. Acute cases can cause respiratory or heart failure. It is usually caused by lush spring grass.
4. Ringworm	This is a fungal infection of the skin and hair. It causes hair loss, itching and failure to thrive.

Table 39.3 Some other diseases of cows

the latter being *highly contagious*. Scour is caused by bad feeding management, unhygienic housing conditions or a combination of these factors. Inadequate intake of colostrum is often a contributory factor.

Symptoms: In both types of scour, diarrhoea is the first symptom, followed quickly by listlessness, dehydration and death if untreated.

(A) Nutritional scour is caused by the calf ingesting too much milk or milk replacer in one feed. A "milk-ball" is formed in the calf's stomach. This is a ball of partially digested milk or milk replacer which becomes larger each time the animal is fed. The digestive processes are upset and diarrhoea and dehydration result.

Prevention: The disease is prevented by feeding at regular intervals. Overfeeding should be avoided.

Treatment: The calf is fed water or a fluid replacement solution for a period of 24 hours until the milk-ball has dissolved. It is then gradually weaned back onto milk or milk replacer. A fluid replacement solution is a dilute solution of sugars and salts. It is designed to combat the effects of dehydration on blood composition.

(B) Bacterial scour is more serious. It is caused by unhygienic housing conditions, principally dirty buckets used for feeding calves. High levels of *E.coli* and other bacteria in the stomach upset the digestive processes and scour develops. The infected calf should be immediately isolated to protect other calves from infection.

Prevention: Strict attention to hygiene should be observed at all times.

Treatment: Veterinary assistance is required to identify the bacterium responsible and treat the calf with the appropriate antibiotic. During treatment the calf should be fed a fluid replacement solution. After the scour has disappeared, the calf is gradually weaned back onto its normal diet.

2. **Virus pneumonia:** This is a highly infectious, mild virus disease which commonly becomes more serious due to secondary infection of the lungs by bacteria.

Spread of infection is encouraged by poor ventilation in calf houses. Old, modified buildings used by some farmers for rearing calves are often very unsuitable because of poor ventilation. Research by Teagasc has shown that adequate ventilation is far more important than warmth. Calves can be satisfactorily reared in open sheds or outdoors provided they are sheltered from breezes and draughts.

Symptoms: These can vary from barely noticeable coughing to fever and sudden death.

Prevention: This involves (1) providing well-ventilated, draught-free housing and (2) good husbandry to ensure early detection and treatment of the disease.

Treatment: Infected animals should be isolated. The viruses causing the initial infection do not respond to medication. Treatment, therefore, concentrates on the bacterial invaders. Antibiotics should be used under veterinary supervision. Recovery is often slow and animals may fail to grow normally and be subject to further lung disease for the remainder of their lives.

3. **Navel-ill or joint-ill:** This is a disease caused by bacteria, usually *E.coli,* entering the calf's system via the unhealed navel. It is the result of bad hygiene in the calving area and failure to treat the navel properly after birth. It should be dipped in iodine and tied with iodine-soaked string or sterile tape.

*Symptoms***:** These vary greatly and include swollen, painful navel; swollen joints; abscesses in the liver and other organs; septicaemia (blood-poisoning) and sudden death.

Prevention: Ensure good hygiene at calving.

Treatment: This usually involves the use of antibiotics and, to be successful, should begin early.

4. **Lice:** Lice are of two kinds; biting lice and sucking lice. Both are parasites of calves. They cause irritation of the skin and this leads to restlessness, with animals scratching, rubbing and licking themselves. Such animals do not thrive properly. Calves heavily infested with sucking lice may develop anaemia which can cause death.

Symptoms: See above.

Prevention: There are no effective preventative practices.

Treatment: Calves should be treated with a suitable insecticide, either externally or by injection. Since eggs cannot be killed, treatment should be repeated after 14 days. By this time all eggs will have hatched, but no lice will have reached adult, egg- laying age.

5. **Lead-poisoning:** Calves are highly susceptible to poisoning by substances containing lead. These include lead-bearing

paints, car batteries, roofing felt, used engine oil, linoleum and putty. Calves are inquisitive animals and will lick and chew any or all of these objects. For housed calves, flaking paint is the most common source of poison. Calves at grass should be kept in clean fields well away from dumped or discarded objects.

Symptoms: These include staggering, convulsions and frothing at the mouth.

Prevention: Removal of all sources of lead from the calves' environment.

Treatment: The disease is almost always fatal as there is no effective treatment.

39.6 Buildings used in dairying

Fig. 39.6 Cow cubicle house

1. *Cow cubicle house:* This is the commonest type of winter housing used on dairy farms. It consists of rows of cubicles backing onto a central dunging passage *(Fig. 39.6).* The cubicles are raised above the level of the dunging passage. This is done to ensure that the cows dung and urinate onto the passage (cows will not reverse into a raised cubicle). Cubicle dimensions are:

   length - 2.0 m

   width - 0.8 m

   height above dunging passage - 8 cm

   The dunging passage is constructed wide enough for a tractor to remove the dung and urine daily.

2. *Dungstead:* This is an open pit into which the dung and urine removed from the cubicle house are put. It is comprised of a concrete floor and four concrete walls. It should be sufficiently large to store all the dung and urine, together with washing water, produced over a winter period.

3. *Milking parlour, dairy and assembly area:* The *milking parlour* contains the milking machine, the cows being milked and a pit in which the milker works. The type of parlour most commonly found in Ireland is the herringbone. The *dairy* houses the pump, cooler and bulk milk tank.

   The *assembly area* is an area in which the cows gather before milking. They enter the milking parlour from this area in an orderly manner, being encouraged to do so by the *backing gate.* A 20 stall, 10-unit herringbone milking parlour, together with dairy and assembly area are shown in *Fig. 39.7.* The arrows indicate the direction of movement of the cows.

4. *Calf-rearing house:* Young calves can be reared separately or in groups. The first method is the better of the two because it lessens the risk of spread of disease. It involves greater

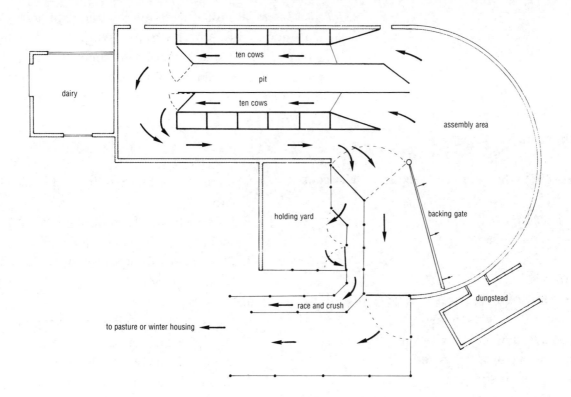

Fig. 39.7 20-stall, 10 unit milking parlour, with dairy and assembly area

financial outlay on buildings, however. A compromise made by many farmers is to rear calves separately for the first 2-3 weeks (when disease risk is highest) and in groups thereafter. Good ventilation is of great importance in calf-housing in order to prevent the occurrence and spread of virus pneumonia. A calf- rearing unit is shown in *Fig. 39.8.*

Fig. 39.8 Purpose-built calf rearing unit

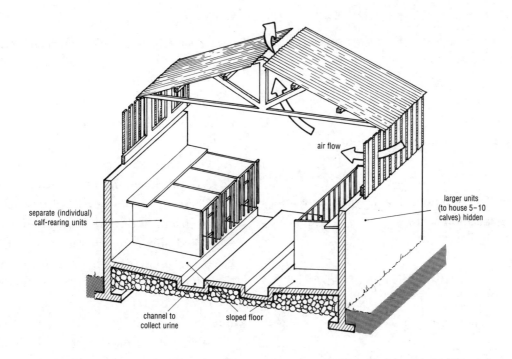

5. *Isolation house:* This is a small house used to temporarily keep sick animals while their disease symptoms are being investigated. The isolation house is specially designed to prevent spread of infection and the most important feature is the presence of an *internal* system of drains for disposal of dung, urine, etc.

Exercises

Exercise 82. Observation of milking of dairy cows

Materials needed
Access to milking unit

Procedure
Observe the procedures involved in milking, making sure to see the following:
1. Collecting yard and backing gate
2. Washing of the cows udder
3. Use of the strip-cup
4. Milking (examine cluster, teat cups, milk line, vacuum line, recording jars, pulsator)
5. Teat-dipping
6. Plate cooler
7. Bulk tank and bulk tank cooling system
8. Hygiene features of parlour and dairy
9. Washing of the system (teat cups, milk-line, plate cooler etc. after milking).

Results
Keep a record of all the procedures seen, using sketches if necessary.

Precautions
1. Keep a safe-distance from cows to avoid the possibility of being kicked.
2. Keep a safe distance from motors, pulley belts etc. in the dairy.

Exercise 83. Examination of milk yield data and drawing of a lactation curve

Materials needed
1. Weekly records of milk yields of individual cows
2. Graph paper

Procedure
1. Arrange the axes of a graph so that time is on the horizontal axis. It should range from 0 to 45 (weeks).
2. Have daily milk yield on the vertical axis. It should range from 0 to 30 kg.
3. Plot the records of daily milk yield *vs* time.
4. Draw the curves.

Results
1. Calculate the lactation yield (area under the curve) for one cow.
2. Determine the peak daily yield.
3. Calculate the ratio of lactation yield to peak daily yield. It should be in the region of 200:1.
4. What does this ratio tell you about the management skills of the farmer (*see page 323*).
5. Obtain other peak daily and lactation yield figures and examine the degree of variability between cows.

Exercise 84. Observation of artificial insemination of a cow.

Materials needed
Cow ready to be inseminated.

Procedures
1. Observe the insemination procedure.
2. Ask the inseminator questions about: (a) Correct time after onset of oestrus at which to inseminate. (b) Storage of semen (c) Breed and other characteristics of the bull being used (d) Why is this particular bull being used? (ask the farmer this) (e) signs of oestrus.

Results:
1. Write a description of the insemination.
2. Record the answers to the questions asked.

40 – The Principles and Importance of Beef Production

40.1 National Importance

The beef production industry is the largest sector of the Irish agricultural economy. Its national importance is shown in *Table 40.1*.

Table 40.1 Importance of beef production in Irish agriculture

	1970	1980	1990
Value of beef and beef products (IR£million)	120	594	1 311
Percentage of total agricultural output	35	36	39
Percentage of total agricultural exports	48	44	50

There are 4.5 million beef animals in the country, producing about 0.5 million tons of beef per annum, 80% of which is exported. Beef animals are slaughtered and exported by meat companies which have factories throughout the country. The principal export markets for Irish beef are the UK, Germany, and a number of countries outside the EC, including Egypt, Libya and Iran.

There is a strong tradition of beef-farming in Ireland and most farmers keep some beef animals. Most of the calves for beef production come from the dairy herd. Since dairying is located mainly in Munster, there is a lot of movement of calves from there to the rest of the country for rearing and fattening. There is also a beef herd of 0.7 million suckler cows.

Beef-farming is mainly based on grassland utilization and income per ha is low by comparison with that of other types of farming *(see Table 40.2)*. Many beef farms are too small to provide a reasonable income and are farmed part-time, their owners having outside employment.

Enterprise	IR£ per ha
Creamery milk	815
Sugar beet	700
Spring lamb	450
Winter wheat	360
Malting barley	360
Feeding barley	312
Beef	275

Table 40.2 Average financial returns per ha from farming enterprises, including beef, 1990

40.2 Breeds of Beef Animals

Most of the animals fattened for beef in Ireland originate in the *dairy herd* and so are either Friesians or Friesian crosses. Dairy farmers tend to use high-quality Friesian bulls from AI on their best cows in the hopes of obtaining heifer calves which can be retained as replacement heifers or sold to other dairy farmers. Bull calves resulting from such matings are used for beef production.

Poorer yielding cows may be crossed with one of the beef breeds listed in *Table 38.2 (see page 317)*, with the intention of selling all calves (male and female) from such crosses to beef farmers. Such calves are more suitable for beef production than Friesians. They

Charolais bull

produce carcases of higher valuè because of the beef characteristics donated by the sire. A comparison of the conformation characteristics of beef and dairy breeds is shown in *Fig. 40.1*.

Fig. 40.1 Conformation characteristics of beef and dairy breeds

	Beef breeds	Dairy breeds
General appearance	Block-like in two dimensions. 1. Topline and underline parallel. 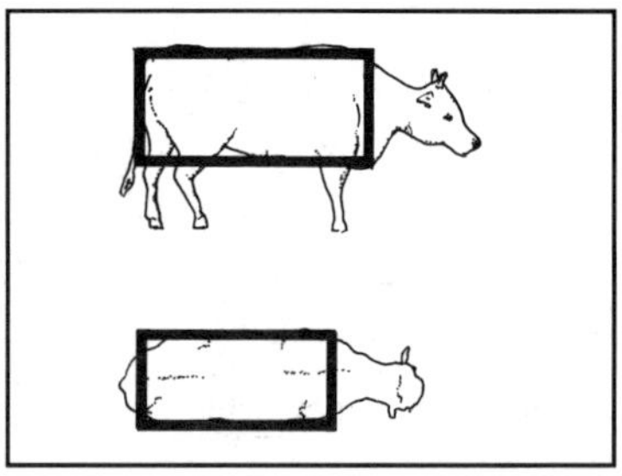 2. Shoulders and hindquarters wide and well fleshed	Wedge-shaped in two dimensions. 1. Topline and underline converge at a point beyond the head. 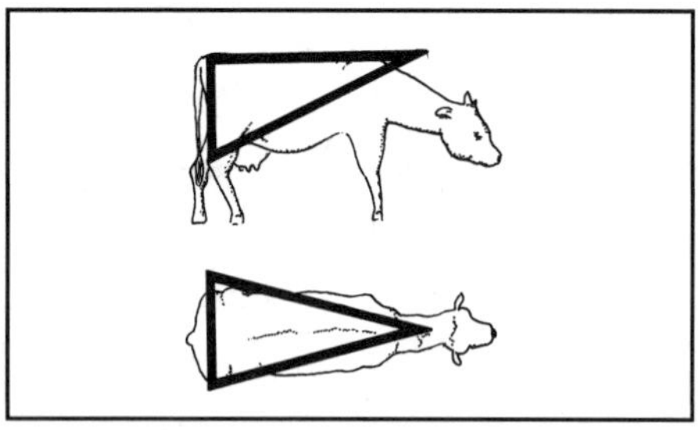 2. Hindquarters wide, shoulders narrow
Head	Head short and wide, neck short and thick	Head long and narrow, neck long and thin
Shoulders	Shoulderblades well apart Shoulders well fleshed	Shoulderblades close together Shoulders strong but not well fleshed
Back	Level. Broad at all points	Level
"Barrel" (chest and abdomen)	Deep from front legs to loin	Depth unimportant Should have good lung capacity
Hindquarters, legs	Long, wide, deep. Evenly fleshed to hocks. Good feet	Long, wide, strong. Not fleshed. Good feet

There is a greater diversity of breeds in the *beef herd*. The breeds most commonly found among cows are Friesian, Hereford x Friesian crosses and Herefords while all bulls are of beef breeds. There are increasing numbers of pure bred beef herds of Continental breed, especially on the better soils in the east, southeast and midlands.

40.3 Principles of Beef Production

40.3.1 Growth rates from birth to slaughter

The growth curve for an animal fed on a high plane of nutrition from birth to slaughter is shown in *Fig. 40.2*.

The age at which the animal reaches maturity and is slaughtered for beef varies. It can be as low as 1 year on all-concentrate systems, such as those practised in parts of the U.S. where animals are housed at all times and fed on a diet composed mainly of maize. For systems based on grass, such as those used in Ireland, the age at maturity varies from 1.5 to 2.0 years, depending on the level of feeding and management. The weight of beef animals at maturity depends on their breed as shown in *Fig. 40. 2*.

Many beef cattle in Ireland are not fed on a uniformly high plane of nutrition. Instead, they are fed only moderate-quality silage or hay for each winter of their lives. Such animals enter a *store period* over

Hereford bull

Fig. 40.2 (a) Growth curve for animals fed on a high plane of nutrition for beef production; (b) Effect of diet on A and effect of breed or cross on B

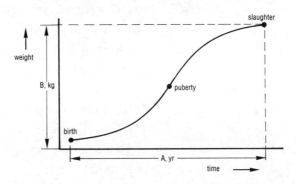

Variation of A			Variation of B	
Diet		A, yr	Breed or cross	B, kg
All concentrates		1.0	Aberdeen Angus	450
			Hereford x Friesian	550
			Friesian	600
Grass, high quality silage + concentrates		1.5	Continental x Friesian	700
			Continental	850
Grass, average quality silage, some concentrates		2.0		

the winter, during which their frame grows but they put on very little flesh. As a result, their winter growth-rates are greatly reduced and their overall growth-curves are as shown in *Fig. 40.3.*

Fig. 40.3 Growth curve of animals fed poorly during the winter for beef production

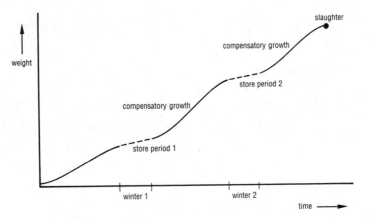

Animals fattened in this manner exhibit *compensatory growth* during the summers following each store period. Compensatory growth is growth which occurs when an animal is fed well after a period of restricted feeding. Growth rates during the compensatory growth period can be higher than those of animals which have been kept continually on a high plane of nutrition.

This system of beef production keeps down winter feed costs and places great emphasis on grazed grass. It is, therefore, a low–cost system. Where animals are housed in winter and summer grazing is abundant and of high quality, this system can be profitable. Very often, however, animals fattened in this way are outwintered (i.e. not housed) and summer grazing is of poor quality. In this situation, production is inefficient and animals can often be three years old or older before they reach slaughter weight.

40.3.2 Tissue development and body composition

The body tissues fat, muscle and bone develop as shown in *Fig. 40.4* in a Hereford x Friesian animal. This is the most commonly found beef animal in Ireland. The most significant feature of *Fig. 40.4* is the sharp increase in fat percentage from 2 years old onwards. Much of this fat is deposited in the abdominal cavity and subcutaneously and is trimmed from the carcase after slaughter. Thus it is bad farming practice to continue to feed animals after fat deposition has begun to increase as the feed converted into fat is wasted.

The age at which fat deposition begins to increase varies with breed: for *early maturing breeds* such as Hereford the age is 1.5-2.0 years, while in *late maturing breeds* such as Charolais it is 2.3-2.5 years. Hereford x Friesian, Friesian and Continental x Friesian animals reach maturity at intermediate ages.

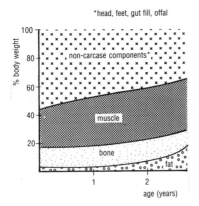

Fig. 40.4 Development of body tissues as affected by age for a Hereford x Friesian animal

40.3.3 Conformation and carcase composition

Conformation refers to the shape of an animal and, in particular, the distribution of muscle on the body. Conformation characteristics of beef animals are shown in *Fig. 40.1* and good conformation means that muscle is concentrated in the parts of the carcase which have most value. These are the hindquarters (which yield round steak and roasting beef) and the back (which yield sirloin roasts and steaks, rib roasts, T-bone steaks).

The main factor influencing conformation is breed. The Continental beef breeds (Charolais, Limousin, Simmental etc.) have the best conformation, followed by the British beef breeds (Hereford, Aberdeen angus), with the dual-purpose breeds (Friesian and Dairy shorthorn) next and dairy breeds worst. Most beef is produced from cross-bred animals using beef bulls and Friesian cows and these have variable conformation characteristics.

Animals are graded at slaughter on the basis of two criteria: conformation and fatness. The price per kg paid to the farmer depends on the grade obtained. The grading categories are shown in *Fig. 40.5*. Conformation grades range from E (best) to P (worst) and fatness grades from 1 (leanest) to 5 (fattest).

Most of the beef slaughtered in Ireland has grades located in area A of *Fig. 40.5*. It is of moderate quality and can be exported only to less-discerning markets at lower prices. If carcases can be moved to area B, then the beef will be of high quality and suitable for export to the more valuable markets such as those of France and Germany.

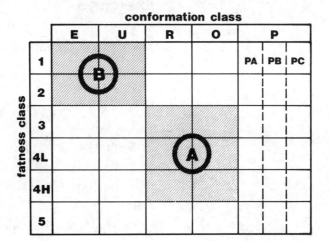

Fig. 40.5 Beef carcase grading scheme

This change can be brought about by greater use of continental breeds and earlier slaughtering (i.e. not allowing animals to become over-fat).

40.3.4 Influence of sex status on growth and development

The types of animals used for beef production are males (bulls), castrated males (steers or bullocks) and females (heifers). Culled cows are also fattened and slaughtered for beef.

Bulls exhibit the fastest rates of growth and development but can be violent. Bull-beef production requires very good fencing and housing for safety reasons. There is little bull-beef production in Ireland.

Steers do not produce testosterone, the male sex hormone, which, as well as controlling sexual development, acts as a growth stimulant. Their growth rates and weights at maturity are consequently lower than those of bulls. Almost all males used for beef in Ireland are castrated. This is so because, production being based on outdoor utilization of grassland, bulls represent a health-risk to farmers handling them. They may also serve heifers or cows on the farm, thus interfering with the farmer's planned breeding programme.

Heifers have lower growth rates and weights at maturity than steers or bulls. Typical slaughter weights and growth rates for bulls, steers and heifers of Hereford x Friesian breed are shown in *Table 40.3.*

Table 40.3 Slaughter weights and growth rates for Hereford X Friesian cattle of different sex status

Sex status	Wt. at slaughter, kg	Average daily liveweight gain (LWG), birth to slaughter, kg.
Bull	750	1.0
Steer	550	0.7
Heifer	450	0.6

Exercises

Exercise 85 Comparison of beef and dairy breeds of cattle

Materials needed
Cattle of the following breeds:
1. Holstein
2. Friesian
3. Charolais or Charolais x Limousin or Limousin x Simmental or Continental x Friesian.

Note:
re: 1. If a Holstein is not available a Friesian of a "milky" strain should be used .
re: 3. Use as many of the breeds/crosses listed as can be found.

Procedure
Compare the breeds using the characteristics outlined in *Fig. 40.1 (see page 340)*.

Results
Record your observations on each breed.

Precautions
Stay well clear of animals at all times to minimise the likelihood of being kicked or knocked down.

41 – Beef Production Systems

41.1 Beef Production from Calves Originating in the Dairy Herd

This type of production accounts for most of the beef produced in Ireland. The calves used are born in the dairying areas and sold to beef farmers, usually *via* dealers, who rear and fatten them. The main features of successful beef production using this system are outlined below.

40.1.1 Calf-rearing

The principles of calf-rearing outlined earlier *(see Section 39.2)* hold, in general, for calves reared for beef. The only difference occurs immediately after purchase when the calf must be very carefully handled and weaned onto his new diet.

When purchasing calves, it is of great value to the buyer to obtain them from a farmer whom he knows and can trust. In that way, he is more likely to obtain calves which have obtained colostrum in the proper manner. In addition, he can receive reliable information on how the calves have been housed and fed up to the time of sale and whether or not they have had any illnesses. All of this information can help the farmer in rearing the calves. Finally, the calves can be transferred from the seller's to the buyer's farm quickly and without stress.

Very often, however, calves are purchased from dealers or in cattle marts and the buyer knows nothing of their background. When purchasing such calves, attention should be paid to the points listed in *Table 41.1.*

Table 41.1 Points to look for when purchasing calves

(a) Conformation	
Shoulders:	wide
Hindquarters:	wide
"Barrell":	deep
(b) Health	
Eyes:	Bright and clear, no discharge
Ears:	"Pricked up"
Nose:	Clean, no discharge
Mouth:	Clean, no dribbling or discharge
Navel:	Clean, fully healed, no swelling
Anus:	No sign of scour (diarrhoea)
General appearance:	Lively and alert

When the purchased calves have been brought back to the farm, they should be housed in dry, draught-free quarters and allowed to rest and recover from the stress and trauma of their transport and sale. They should be fed only water and glucose for the first 24 hours. This is done so that their digestive systems can be cleared of their contents. They should then be weaned gradually onto milk replacer over a period of 3-4 days.

The feeding regime for the first six days after purchase is shown in *Table 41.2*. When the calves reach the point where they are consuming full strength milk replacer, the greatest risk of digestive disorders is over. Their subsequent rearing is as already outlined in *Section 39.2*.

Table 41.2 *Early feeding regime* for purchased calves*

* Meals, water and hay should be fed as outlined in *section 39.2*.

Day after purchase	Glucose (g)	Milk replacer powder (g)	Water (l)
1 PM	100	–	2
2 AM	100	–	2
PM	50	70	2
3 AM	–	70	2
PM	–	125	2
4 AM	–	125	2
PM	–	200	2
5 AM	–	200	2
PM	–	265	2
6 AM	–	265	2
PM	–	265	2

41.1.2 Housing and feeding for the first winter

By November 1, spring-born calves should weigh 200 kg. They are now fully reared, are called *weanlings* and are ready for housing for the winter. Weanlings can be housed in open sheds bedded with straw or in slatted houses. Houses should be well- ventilated but draught-free and should not be over-crowded: animals should have a minimum of 1.4 m^2 of floor space and 7 m^3 of air space per animal.

The key to winter-feeding of weanlings is *silage quality*. If silage is properly made from young leafy grass it has a high DMD value. Feeding it will ensure steady growth over the winter. Silage with 73% DMD gives a daily gain in weight of *0.6 kg* in Hereford x Friesian animals and ensures that they will weigh *280 kg* at the end of the winter. If the quality is poorer than this, the silage must be augmented with meals if this type of animal performance is to be achieved.

41.1.3 Grazing management of yearlings

Yearlings should be grazed rotationally on good quality grass during their second grazing season to ensure continued satisfactory growth rate. They should also be dosed for lice, stomach worms and hoose as required. If they have access to wet areas of land, they may need to be dosed for liver fluke also. The presence of any of these parasites impairs animal performance, which should be *0.8 kg liveweight gain (LWG) per day*, bringing yearlings to a weight of *460 kg* when they are housed on November 1.

41.1.4 Housing and feeding for the second winter

Housing for fattening cattle is basically the same as for weanlings except that the animals, being larger, need 2.0 m^2 of floor space and 10 m^3 of air space per animal.

Feeding is again based on silage. With top quality silage, very little meals are needed to sustain a target growth rate of *0.9 – 1.0 kg LWG*. This rate of growth will have Hereford x Friesian animals ready for slaughter at *550 kg* by *February 1* at the latest.

41.1.5 Summary

The essential features of successful beef production are purchasing good calves, rearing them well, feeding them well for the remainder of their lives and controlling diseases which would impair their growth. These features, together with target weights at different ages and corresponding target performance (LWG) values, are shown in *Table 41.3* for Hereford x Fresian animals.

Table 41.3 *Target weights, LWG rates and management features of successful beef production*

Date		Age (yr, mths)	Target weight (kg)	Approx. daily LWG (kg)	Diet	Diseases to be prevented
Yr. 1	Feb 1	0,0	40			
				0.55	Milk replacer, hay, meals, grass	Scours, pneumonia, lice
	May 1	0,3	90			
				0.60	Rotationally–grazed grass, meals	Stomach–worms, lungworms, lice
	Nov 1	0,9	200			
				0.60	High DMD silage, possibly meals	Lice
Yr. 2	Mar 15	1, 1.5	280			
				0.80	Rotationally–grazed grass	Stomach–worms, lungworms, lice
	Nov 1	1,9	460			
				·1.00	High DMD silage, meals	Lice
	Feb 1	2,0	550			

41.2 Beef Production from the Beef Herd

The beef herd is composed of cows which are not commercially milked but instead suckle their calves for a prolonged period. Thus, it is also commonly referred to as the suckler herd. Beef produced from the beef herd amounts to 25-30% of total production.

41.2.1 Breeding management

Most suckler herds employ a *spring-calving* system, so that best use can be made of cheap summer grass. Since most of the income comes from the sale of fattened progeny, it is essential that each cow produces one or more reared offspring per year. The extent to which this is achieved is measured by the *reproductive efficiency* of the herd.

Reproductive efficiency refers to the number of calves weaned per 100 cows served and suckler beef producers should aim at values of 90-100. The most important factor in achieving high reproductive efficiency is diet. The cows should be well-fed before mating so that their condition scores are high (2.5 or greater) at service. In this way, best conception rates will be achieved.

The second important consideration in breeding management is *calving interval*. It is desirable that this be kept as close as possible to 12 months so that summer grass can be fully utilized. Accurate heat detection is essential. In large suckler herds, where it is economically feasible to keep a bull, heat detection and servicing are reliably carried out by him. It is important, however, to check on the bull's fertility before purchase and during his time on the farm. In smaller herds, AI is normally used and heat detection and servicing are carried out as already described for dairying.

41.2.2 Suckling period, calf performance targets

In beef herds, the cows suckle the calves from birth until weaning in October/November. Feeding the cows is the most expensive part of suckler beef production. Cows can be fed for maintenance only for much of the time but they must be fed on a high plane of nutrition for 6-7 months of each year.

A correct feeding regime, as shown in *Fig. 41.1* ensures good foetal development and strong healthy calves at birth ("A"), good condition scores at mating ("B") and good milk production for 5-6 months of lactation ("C"). Where good grass is available, it can supply all the cow's nutritional needs. Feeding of concentrates is common just before and just after calving.

Fig. 41.1 Level of feeding of suckler cows

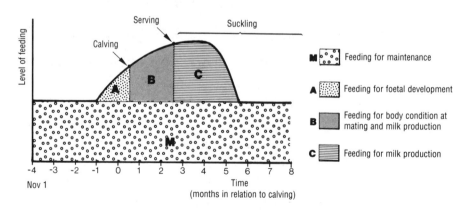

The suckler calf's growth rate is influenced more by milk intake than grazing for the first 4-5 months of life. After this, grazing becomes more important. This is one of the reasons for the drop in level of feeding at +4 – +5 months in *Fig. 41.1.* To maintain high growth rates, it is good farming practice to employ "creep-feeding" from July onwards. This practice involves allowing the calf access, through an entrance too small for the cow, to better quality grazing and/or concentrates.

Calves are weaned on November 1 when being housed for the winter or sold. Their performance targets vary greatly depending on breed as shown in *Table 41.4.*

Table 41.4 *Performance targets for suckler calves*

Breed/cross	Daily LWG (kg)	Wt at weaning (kg)
Continental	1.50	400
Continental X Friesian	1.25	340
Hereford X Friesian	0.8 – 0.9	280

41.2.3 Subsequent management

The management of weaned suckler calves for the remainder of their lives is basically similar to that of calves reared artificially. Features of a well-managed system would, therefore, be winter housing, winter feeding on high-quality silage, provision of good quality summer grazing and careful maintenance of animal health. With proper management, the weight advantage of 80-100 kg which suckled calves possess at weaning over artificially reared calves is maintained subsequently and they reach slaughter weight more quickly.

41.3 Diseases of Beef Cattle

1. **Tuberculosis (TB):** *See page 330*
2. **Stomach and intestinal worms:** This parasitic disease is caused by infestation with nematodes of the genera *Ostertagia* and *Cooperia.* The biology of nematodes has been described in *Chapter 28 (see page 253).* The disease is most serious in young cattle in their first grazing season. Older cattle have acquired resistance to the disease.
   Symptoms: Symptoms include failure to thrive, dull coat and diarrhoea. Heavy infestation in very young animals causes severe growth restriction and sometimes death.
   Prevention: The disease may be prevented by proper grazing management. Young cattle should be moved onto clean (worm-free) pastures regularly. This prevents the build-up of large populations of infective larvae. Older cattle can graze down the pastures after the young animals have moved on: this is the "leader-follower" system.
   Treatment: When disease symptoms occur, animals should be dosed with a suitable nematicide.

3. **Lungworms (hoose, husk):** The nematodes causing this parasitic disease belong to the genus *Dictyocaulus*. The life cycle has been described already *(see page 253)*. The disease is most serious in young cattle, older animals acquiring resistance.

Symptoms: Infected animals have a hoarse husky cough and fail to thrive. They are susceptible to secondary lung infection by bacteria. This disease, *hoose pneumonia*, is often fatal.

Prevention: The practices used are the same as for stomach and intestinal worms, i.e. proper pasture management. Moving young cattle onto clean pastures ahead of older animals prevents the build-up of infective larvae populations. In areas particularly susceptible to lungworm disease, veterinary advice should be sought as a *hoose vaccine* is available and may be of use.

Treatment: Infected animals should be dosed with a suitable nematicide, under veterinary supervision.

4. **Blackleg:** This is a disease caused by the bacterium *Clostridium chauvoei*. Spores of the organism are found in a very persistent form in certain soils and regions of the country. When they are eaten on contaminated pasture, they may in some cases, migrate to muscle tissues and cause severe infection.

The disease progresses very rapidly and is nearly always fatal. Animals usually die within 24 hours of showing symptoms of the disease; very often discovery of a dead animal is the first sign of trouble.

Symptoms: Lameness, swollen limbs with black discolourations, listlessness and high fever.

Prevention: Blackleg is easily prevented as there is a reliable vaccine available. Cattle should be vaccinated every six months, especially in areas known to be susceptible to the disease.

Treatment: There is no reliable treatment for blackleg.

5. **Grass tetany or grass staggers (Hypomagnesaemia):** *See page 332.*
6. **Lice:** *See page 335.*
7. **Redwater (Babesiasis):** *See page 333.*
8. **Other diseases of beef cattle:** There are other diseases of beef cattle which are of lesser general importance than the seven dealt with already. These are listed and commented on in *Table 39.3 (see page 334).*

41.4 Buildings used in Beef Production

1. *Slatted winter housing:* The use of winter housing ensures that cattle continue growing and gaining weight over the winter.

Slatted houses are commonly used for this reason. They consist of separate slatted compartments on either side of a central feeding passage *(Fig. 41.2)*. The dung and urine drop through the slats and are collected in an underground tank, which is usually about 2.5 m deep. The tank should have sufficient storage capacity to last the winter. The floor and feeding-space requirements of the cattle are shown in *Table 41.5*.

Fig. 41.2 Slatted winter housing

Table 41.5 *Floor and feeding space for housed cattle*

	Floor space (m^2)	Feeding space (m)
Weanlings	1.4	0.3
Fattening cattle	2.0	0.4

2. *Isolation house: See page 338.*

Exercises

Exercise 86 Monitoring growth rates in beef cattle

Materials needed
1. Weight data for the following spring-born animals (from birth to 12 months old): (a) suckler heifer from a beef herd, (b) suckler bull/bullock from a beef herd [same breed/cross as (a)], (c) bucket-raised bull/bullock from the dairy herd (Hereford/Friesian cross).
2. Graph paper

Procedure
1. Plot the data for weight *vs* time for animals (a), (b) and (c). Put time on the horizontal axis.
2. Draw curves for (a), (b) and (c).

Results
1. Compare the shapes of curves (a), (b) and (c).
2. Calculate the mean daily liveweight gain (LWG) for animals (a), (b) and (c): (i) for the period birth - 3 months (ii) For the period 3 - 9 months, (iii) for the period 9 - 12 months.
3. Compare the LWG values with those shown in *Table 41.3 (see page 347)*.

42 – The Principles and Importance of Sheep Production

42.1 National Importance

Sheep and wool production account for 6% of total agricultural production in Ireland. The scale and importance of sheep production have increased greatly in recent years *(Table 42.1)*. This has occurred because EC policy to limit production of milk and dairy products has caused many farmers to expand into sheep production in search of an alternative or additional source of income.

Table 42.1 Importance of sheep production in Irish agriculture

	1970	1980	1990
Value of sheepmeat and wool (IR£million)	16	70	200
Percentage of total agricultural output	4.5	4.1	5.9
Percentage of total agricultural exports	1.3	0.9	2.0

At present there are 4.6 million ewes in the country, producing 80 000 tonnes of sheepmeat per annum. Sheep are slaughtered in the same way as beef cattle, in many cases in the same meat factories, at a number of locations throughout the country. Export markets include France, Belgium, Germany and Italy.

Income from the sale of wool accounts for less than 10% of the total income of sheep farmers.

42.2 Nature of Sheep Production

The main product of the sheep industry in Ireland is sheepmeat. Wool, milk and cheese production, which are of some importance elsewhere, are of minor interest here. Sheepmeat consists of *lamb,* which is meat from animals slaughtered at age 3-12 months and *hogget mutton,* meat from animals slaughtered as yearlings. Most of the sheepmeat consumed at home and exported is lamb.

Traditionally, sheep have been associated mostly with hill and mountain areas. They are well-suited to exposed conditions, thriving better there than cattle. This continues to be the case. Breeding stock are produced on mountains and hills and lamb production is located in adjacent lowland areas. The concentration of breeding ewes throughout the country is shown in *Fig. 42.1.*

Mountain and hill sheep production tends to be extensive in nature, utilizing rough grazing and heather. Grazing of shared areas of mountain (commonage) by groups of farmers is widely practised. This tends to reduce individual initiative to improve land and other

Fig. 42.1 Numbers of breeding ewes per 100 ha of agricultural land plus rough grazing, 1990

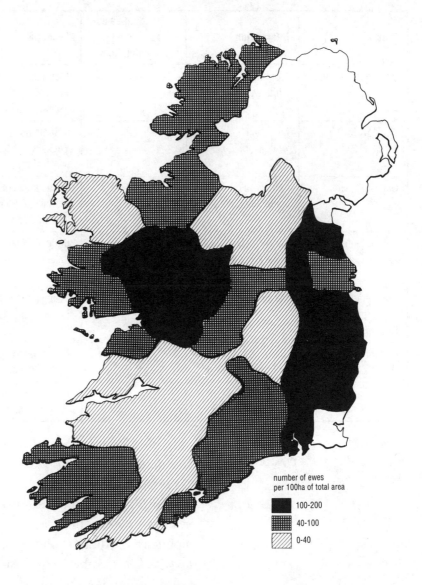

number of ewes
per 100ha of total area

■ 100-200

▨ 40-100

▧ 0-40

conditions. Unless management is good, mortality of lambs and even ewes can be high, particularly in severe winters. Production targets are low, except where farmers have access to lowland. The products are ewes for sale as breeding stock and lambs for fattening on lowlands.

Lowland sheep production is, in contrast, an intensive enterprise with well-defined management practices and high production targets. On good land, farmers aim at stocking rates of 12.5 ewes ha^{-1} (2.5 LU ha^{-1}). Profits per hectare are comparable with those of other enterprises *(see Table 40.2, page 339).*

42.3 Breeds of Sheep

Sheep breeds, in common with breeds of cattle and other farm animals, are very often named after the geographical area in which they originated. Of the 50-60 sheep breeds found in the British Isles,

Breed	Description	Breeding ewes as % of total breeding flock	Location	Products
Blackface mountain	Mountain, white wool, horned	22	Mountains over 350m in Kerry, Galway, Donegal, etc., except Wicklow	Wool, breeding ewes
Wicklow Cheviot	Mountain, white wool, polled	12	Mountains and hills in Wicklow, Carlow, N. Wexford, Kildare	Wool, breeding ewes, lambs for lowland fattening
Galway	Long wool, white wool, polled	28	Plains areas of Galway, E. Mayo, Roscommon, Clare, W. Midlands	Wool, fat lambs, store lambs and hogget mutton, breeding ewes
Border Leicester	Long wool, white wool, polled	2	Carlow, Wexford, Kilkenny, Tipperary	Wool, rams for crossing with mountain breeds, breeding ewes
Crossbreds (Halfbred, Greyface, Brownface)	Mixed features	16	Plains and uplands. Good pasture and tillage land	Wool, fat lambs
Down breeds (Suffolk, Oxford, etc.)	Short wool, white wool, polled	18	Plains, good soils in east of country and midlands	Wool, rams for siring early lamb, breeding ewes
Texel	Long wool white wool, polled	2	Plains, good soils in east of country and midlands	Wool, rams for siring store lamb

Table 42.2 *Description and other characteristics of the principal sheep breeds*

only 10-12 are of practical importance in Ireland. These are listed and described in *Table 42.2*. Some of the more important of these are shown in *Fig. 42.2*.

The Blackface mountain and Wicklow Cheviot are termed *mountain breeds*. They are small, very hardy and able to withstand mountain conditions. All the other breeds in *Table 42.2* are termed *lowland breeds* as they require a less severe living environment. The Galway is the only truly native breed of sheep, the Wicklow Cheviot being an Irish strain of the Cheviot breed. The Down breeds are lowland breeds originating in the downs of southern England. They are noted for their fast growth rate and good carcase quality.

For successful, profitable sheep-farming, a proper breeding strategy must be employed using the breeds and crossbreds listed in *Table 42.2*. Details of breeding strategies used are given in the next section.

42.4 Principles of Sheep Production

42.4.1 Breeding strategy

In *mountain* sheep-farming, breeding strategies are fairly simple. Ewes of the mountain breeds are mated with rams of the same breed. Ewe lambs are either kept for flock replacements or sold to other farmers for breeding purposes. Ram lambs and some ewe

Fig 42.2 Sheep breeds (a) Scottish blackface, (b) Wicklow cheviot, (c) Galway, (d) Suffolk

lambs are either fattened for the Italian market (which requires very small carcases) or sold as stores in the autumn for fattening on lowland.

Ewes in this system do not continue to thrive in the harsh environment for more than four or five years. At that stage they are sold off to hill farmers. Such ewes, when moved to better conditions, have several more years of lambing left. They form an important part of the plans of hill sheep farmers. They are referred to as "culled-for-age", "draft" or "cast" ewes.

In *hill* sheep farming, culled-for-age mountain ewes are mated with rams of a prolific breed (i.e. a breed giving high litter numbers) to give crossbred offspring. Ewe lambs from such matings have good mothering ability, inherited from their mountain dam, and prolificy from their sire. These crossbred ewes are much in demand by lowland sheep farmers for lamb production. The parentage and names of such ewes are given in *Table 42.3*.

Table 42.3 Breeding of crossbred ewes

Parentage		Name
Border Leicester (male) or Belclare Improver (male)	x Blackface mountain (female)	Greyface
Border Leicester (male) or Belclare Improver (male)	x Wicklow Cheviot (female)	Halfbred
Suffolk (male)	x Wicklow Cheviot (female)	Brownface

In *lowland* sheep farming, the emphasis is on the production of lambs for slaughter. Farmers talk of ram breeds and ewe breeds. Ram breeds are always purebred strains and are required to donate fast growth rate and/or carcase quality to their progeny. The most popular ram for early lamb production is the Suffolk, which gives fast-growing lambs of good conformation when mated with any type of ewe. Other popular ram breeds are the Oxford Down, also for early lamb, and the Texel for mid-season lamb of very high carcase quality (i.e. low fat cover).

The best ewe breeds/crosses for lowland lamb production are the Greyface and Halfbred and these are present in large numbers in lowland flocks. Other breeds/crosses found include Brownface, Galway, Suffolk and Suffolk x Galway. Almost any ewe when crossed with a Suffolk ram will produce a lamb of acceptable growth rate and conformation.

Degree of prolificy is, however, a very important consideration and, other things being equal, ewes with litter sizes in the 1.5 – 2.0 range are of most value.

The Belclare Improver is a breed which has been developed in the past 15 years by crossing better strains of Galway with the Finnish Landrace (to improve prolificy) and Llynn (to improve conformation). The end result of this breeding programme has been the Improved Galway ewe, obtained by crossing the Belclare Improver ram with the Galway ewe. This ewe has better conformation and greater litter size (1.80 *vs* 1.45) than the Galway.

42.4.2 Birth, growth rates, puberty

Lambs weigh 3-5 kg at birth. They are slaughtered at weights ranging from 30 to 40 kg, depending on breed and age at slaughter. Ewe lambs being kept for breeding have traditionally not been got in lamb until their second year (i.e. as hogget ewes). Ewe lambs reach puberty at a weight of about 40 kg, however. Thus, lambs born early and reared and fed well can be got in lamb in their first year and there is an increasing tendency to do this.

42.4.3 Oestrous cycle, gestation period

Sheep are seasonally polyoestrous. This means that they come into oestrus repeatedly but only over a certain period or season of the year. This period is from early September to February for most breeds. The length of the oestrous cycle is 17 days and the average duration of oestrus 36 hours. The gestation period is 149 days (5 months).

42.4.4 Synchronised breeding, breeding out of season

Traditionally, ewes are introduced to the ram in early September and left with him for 6-8 weeks. They come into heat and are served at different times over this period. This leads to a protracted lambing period in springtime. Oestrus can be *synchronised* artificially by the farmer, leading to shorter mating and lambing periods. This has advantages in terms of flock management.

Synchronisation of oestrus is carried out by placing progesterone-impregnated sponges in the ewes' vaginas and leaving them there for 12-16 days. The progestogen blocks the oestrous cycle by prolonging the life of the corpus luteum. If the sponges are removed simultaneously, all ewes come into oestrus two days later and are then mated together. The ram:ewe ratio must be altered, however, from the normal ratio of 1:40 to 1:10.

Breeding out of season is a technique employed to induce ewes to lamb early enough for the lambs to be ready for the Easter market, when prices are highest. Lambs born from conventional September/October matings are very unlikely to be ready for Easter. Ewes must be brought into oestrus out of season, i.e. in July/August.

The technique used involves placement of intravaginal progesterone-impregnated sponges as already described. However, in this case, a single intramuscular injection of pregnant mare's serum gonadotrophin (PMSG) is administered at the time of sponge removal. PMSG is a hormonal material which further ensures induction of oestrus. As with synchronised breeding, a high ram:ewe ratio (1:10) must be used during mating.

42.4.5 Mixed grazing of cattle and sheep

Research in Ireland and elsewhere has shown that cattle and sheep, when grazed together, show growth rates 10-15% greater than when grazed alone. These findings are dependent on good grassland management and adequate use of fertilizers. The increased growth rates and production are the result of three factors.

Firstly, the close-grazing habit of sheep causes increased tillering, a denser sward and increased DM production. Secondly, the flush of grass surrounding cattle dung pats, which is unpalatable to cattle, is palatable to and efficiently utilised by sheep. Lastly, mixed grazing leads to a more even recycling of nutrients than does cattle grazing. This is due to (a) sheep grazing around cattle dung pats and (b) the nature of sheep dung and urine deposition.

42.4.6 Wool production and quality

Wool fibres are modified epidermal cells. They have solid cores compared with hair fibres which are medullated. Sheep have been selectively bred throughout history for wool quantity and quality. Wool fleece yields vary from 2-4 kg per animal per year. Ewes, hoggets and wethers (castrated males) are shorn whereas lambs destined for slaughter are not. Shearing is carried out in June.

Wool quality is determined by fineness of fibre. The finest wool is obtained from the Merino breed which originated in Spain but is now most numerous and successful in Australia. The ratio of wool:hair and hairlike fibres (kemps) is 25:1 in Merino wool. In most British and Irish wools the ratio is less than 8:1. Merino wool fibres are 15 μ in width compared with a width of 40-50 μ for British and Irish wools.

The standard measure of wool quality is the Bradford Count. This is defined by the International Wool Council as:

> *"The number of hanks of yarn, each 510 m long, that can be spun `from 450 g of wool prepared for spinning."*

The Bradford Counts of wools found in Ireland range from 28-40 for the Scottish Blackface to 54-58 for the Suffolk and Oxford Down. Merino wool has a count of 80+. On a world basis, wools are classed as follows:

Category	Bradford Count
"Merino"	60s and over
"Crossbred"	40s - 58s
"Carpet"	40s and below

Merino wool is made into best quality worsted and woollen materials. Crossbred wool is used for tweeds and lower quality woollen materials. Carpet wool is used for carpets mainly.

Exercises

Exercise 87. Examination of wool quality

Materials needed
1. Samples of wool from:
   (a) Blackface mountain breed, (b) Galway breed, (c) Suffolk breed
2. Hand lens (Magnification x 10)

Procedure
Examine the wool samples using the criteria:
(a) Fineness of fibre and (b) abundance of kemps (kemps are hairlike fibres, which are *whiter* and *more brittle* than wool fibres).
Note: If this Exercise is carried out on a sheep farm, note that there are more kemps at the edges of the fleece, i.e. near the neck, tail and belly.

Results
1. Record your findings.
2. Comment on them. The expected result is that Suffolk wool will be of highest quality. Galway wool will be of intermediate quality and Blackface mountain of poorest quality.

43 – Lowland Lamb Production

43.1 Breeding management

Lowland lamb production is similar to suckler beef production in that most of the farm income comes from the sale of fattened or finished progeny. Thus it is important to ensure that the reproductive efficiency *(see p.348)* of the flock is high. The target should be 200 lambs sold per 100 ewes mated, although this figure is rarely achieved in large flocks.

The factor which has greatest influence on reproductive efficiency is the *prolificy of the ewe flock*. Field research carried out by Teagasc has shown that gross margin per ewe increases by 13-15% for each extra 0.1 lambs sold per ewe mated. Teagasc states that flock prolificy can best be improved by (i) buying in more crossbred ewe lamb replacements, and (ii) more use of Belclare Improver rams. The litter sizes of some breeds and crosses are shown in *Table 43.1*.

Diet of ewes and general flock management also influence reproductive efficiency. Details of these are given below.

Table 43.1 Litter size of some breeds and crosses of sheep in Ireland (source: Teagasc)

Breed/cross	Litter size
Galway	1.45
Wicklow Cheviot	1.60
Halfbred	1.70
Greyface	1.70
Improved Galway	1.80
Border Leicester	2.00
Belclare Improver	2.00

43.2 Ewe and Ram Selection

The breed/cross of ewe and ram has already been dealt with *(see page 355)*. Within the breed/cross, individual ewes and rams should be selected using the criteria listed in *Table 43.2*.

Table 43.2 Selection criteria for breeding ewes and rams

	Criteria
Ewe	Good conformation, good general health, daughter of a prolific mother, free from hereditary defects, good feet
Ram	Good conformation, good general health, performance-tested by Department of Agriculture and Food, very good feet

43.3 Flock Management

The sequence of events in the production cycle for lowland lamb production is shown in *Table 43.3*. Details are given below.

43.3.1 Preparation of flock for mating
Ewes should be in good condition (condition score 3.5-4.0) at the beginning of the mating season. This helps to give high conception rates. A further technique employed is known as *flushing*. This involves having ewes in improving condition during the mating season.

Table 43.3 Management sequence over a 12-month period for lowland lamb production

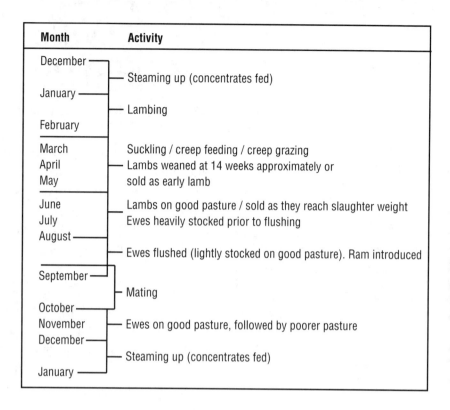

Month	Activity
December	Steaming up (concentrates fed)
January	Lambing
February	
March	Suckling / creep feeding / creep grazing
April	Lambs weaned at 14 weeks approximately or
May	sold as early lamb
June	Lambs on good pasture / sold as they reach slaughter weight
July	Ewes heavily stocked prior to flushing
August	
	Ewes flushed (lightly stocked on good pasture). Ram introduced
September	
	Mating
October	
November	Ewes on good pasture, followed by poorer pasture
December	
	Steaming up (concentrates fed)
January	

The usual practice is to stock ewes heavily (25-30 ha^{-1}) on bare pasture (i.e. feed them on a low plane of nutrition) for some time between weaning and mating. Then, 3-4 weeks before the beginning of the mating season, their nutrition is improved by stocking them less heavily (15-18 ha^{-1} on better pasture). This is continued up to and throughout the mating season.

Flushing leads to: (i) more eggs being released at ovulation (i.e. a greater chance of twins or triplets), (ii) more regular heat periods, (iii) higher conception rates, (iv) better attachment of the embryo(s) to the uterine wall.

Rams should also be in good condition, but not fat, entering the mating period. Their feet should be pared and excess wool around the eyes and sexual organs clipped. Any other defect which might impair their performance during mating should be attended to.

43.3.2 Mating

The ram:ewe ratio for conventional mating is 1:40. Where oestrus is synchronised, the ratio is 1:10. Ram/ewe groups must be kept separate from each other, as rams will fight and injure or kill each other if mixed.

With conventional mating, it is important to keep a reliable record of when each ewe is mated so that her lambing date will be known. The best way to do this is to use a marker dye on the ram's chest so that he marks each ewe as he mounts and serves her. The dye can be used in the form of a raddle attached to a harness *(Fig.*

Fig. 43.1 Ram fitted with a raddling harness

43.1). Alternatively it can be mixed with vegetable oil and smeared on the ram's chest daily.

All ewes should be ear-tagged for identification and then daily inspection for the marker dye enables the farmer to keep his mating records. The colour of the marker dye is changed every 17 days during the mating period so that repeat services can be detected.

Ewes which come back into oestrus repeatedly should be culled from the flock. Where repeat services are widespread, the ram's fertility is suspect and he should be immediately replaced.

The mating season ends when all ewes are in lamb or after 6-8 weeks. A very protracted lambing season is undesirable. The quality of grazing available to the flock during the mating season should be high.

43.3.3 Flock management from mating to lambing

The good quality grazing and moderate stocking rate used during the mating period should be continued with the pregnant ewes for the first 3-4 weeks of pregnancy. This ensures proper embryo development and attachment to the uterine wall. Thereafter in early and mid-pregnancy (weeks 5-15), ewes can be fed on a low/moderate plane of nutrition as they need only to maintain their weight. While grazing is available, it meets the ewe's needs. After growth stops, 1 kg of hay per ewe per day is a suitable diet.

About 75% of foetal growth occurs during the final 6-8 weeks of pregnancy. The ewe's nutritional requirements during this period increase accordingly. Hay or silage supplemented by concentrates containing 15% protein and a balanced mineral/vitamin mix should be used. This practice is known as "steaming up".

The amount of concentrates fed should increase gradually up to a maximum at lambing of 0.5 kg per ewe per day for ewes carrying singles and 0.7 kg per ewe per day for ewes carrying twins. Failure to feed adequate concentrates can cause pregnancy toxaemia *(see page 363)*.

Rams do not graze normally during the mating season and are often thin and in a weakened condition when removed from the ewes. They should be put on good quality pasture and fed concentrates, if necessary, to allow them to recover.

As lambing time approaches, ewes should be housed if they have not been already. This facilitates management and care prior to and at lambing. Lambing outdoors, although widely practised, is not recommended.

43.3.4 Lambing

The records kept during the mating season enable the farmer to accurately estimate the lambing date of each ewe. Lambings are usually normal and trouble-free. They should be observed by the farmer but not interfered with unless there are problems. In such cases, a veterinary surgeon should be called, unless the farmer is very experienced.

Small or weak lambs must be carefully minded for the first week of life. This is of most importance where ewes lamb outdoors. Feeding colostrum, ensuring that the lamb can suckle the mother and maintenance of body temperature are all of great importance. *Colostrum* can be frozen and stored as described already in calf-rearing. In an emergency, *cow's colostrum* can be fed using a *stomach-tube.*

Chilled lambs are revived using an *infrared lamp,* supplemented by *glucose injections* in severe cases. A *fostering crate (Fig. 43.2)* can be used to encourage a ewe to foster an extra lamb (usually one of triplets).

Fig. 43.2 Fostering crate

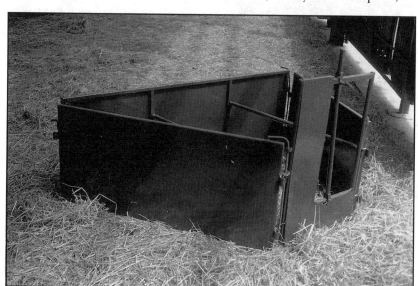

43.3.5 Ewe lactation, growth and sale of early lambs

Growth rate of the lamb(s) being reared by the ewe depends greatly on the amount of milk produced. This, in turn, depends on the ewe's level of nutrition. The high level which pertained before lambing should be continued during early lactation and suckling.

Where lambing occurs early (December-February), ewes must be fed hay or silage and concentrates. This should be continued until spring grass becomes available. In late-lambing flocks (March onwards) grass provides all the nutritional needs of ewes suckling singles. Ewes suckling twins should be given some concentrates.

As the year progresses and lambs graze more, their growth rate becomes less dependent on milk intake. Lambs being produced for the Easter market should be given creep feeding of *both* grass and concentrates. Grass is given by inserting a *creep gate* in the fencing to allow lambs access to an adjoining area of young leafy grass. Concentrates are fed using a *lamb creep-feeder (Fig. 43.3).*

Fig. 43.3 Lamb creep-feeder

Early lambs are sold off as soon as they reach the correct weight for markets for which they have been bred. The requirements are shown in *Table 43.4.*

Table 43.4 *Live and carcase weights required by markets for Irish lamb*

Market	Required weight (kg)	
	Liveweight	Carcase weight
French-North	39-41	19-20
French-Paris	33-38	16-18
French-South	24-27	11-12
Belgium	44-48	21-23
Germany	44-48	21-23
Italy	15-22	7-10
Home (Ireland)	41-52	20-25

43.3.6 Weaning, post-weaning flock management

Lambs sold before June 1 continue to suckle their mothers up to the time of sale. Lambs being kept longer on the farm are weaned in June. Ewes and lambs are separated for a period of 7 days, during which time the ewes go dry. Ewes should be examined during this time for signs of *mastitis.*

When weaning is completed, ewes and lambs can be grazed together, if necessary. The correct management practice, however, is to keep them separate. Lambs are put on good quality grazing to keep them growing well, while the ewes are put on bare pastures. This keeps them from gaining weight and has them ready for flushing prior to mating. Lambs are sold for slaughter for the home market in late summer or autumn.

43.4 Diseases of Sheep

1. **Twin-lamb disease (Pregnancy toxaemia):** This is a nutritional disease caused by *inadequate nutrition* of ewes in late pregnancy. It occurs almost exclusively in ewes bearing twins or triplets. The extra lamb(s) put strain on the ewe's system and she responds by mobilising body fat reserves. Some of this fat is not properly utilized, however, and accumulates in the liver, causing liver malfunction.

   Symptoms: Listlessness and staggering, followed by collapse and death unless the animal is treated, or birth or abortion occurs.

   Prevention: Ewes should be fed concentrates as already described during the final 6-8 weeks of pregnancy. This is necessary, even if the hay or silage being fed contains enough protein and energy. This is because the increasing size of the foetuses can physically restrict the rumen size, thus limiting intake of bulky feeds.

Treatment: Response to treatment is usually very poor and mortality rates can be as high as 90%.

2. **Lambing sickness (Hypocalcaemia):** This disease is equivalent to milk fever in cows. It occurs around lambing time (either shortly before or after lambing). The causes, nature, symptoms, prevention and treatment of the disease are similar to those described already for milk fever in cows *(see page 332)*.

3. **Chill/starvation of lambs:** This is the most common cause of death in young lambs (accounting for about 40% of all deaths). It is caused by insufficient intake of colostrum and/or exposure to severe weather conditions. It is most common in mountain and hill production because of the higher incidence of lambing outdoors.

Symptoms: Weakness and prostration, followed by death if untreated.

Prevention: The occurrence of this disease is minimised by good management practices. These include: (i) feeding the ewe well in late pregnancy to ensure a healthy active lamb and a good milk supply; (ii) supervision of lambing, ensuring that lambs obtain colostrum within one hour of birth; (iii) provision of pens or houses for lambing to make supervision easier.

Treatment: Starved lambs should be fed colostrum from the mother or another ewe. A stomach-tube should be used, if necessary. Cows' colostrum can also be used. Chilled lambs should be *dried, warmed* and *fed.* An infrared lamp may be used to heat a "hot box" (to warm the lamb) to a maximum temperature of 40°C. Severely chilled lambs (i.e. with a body temperature of less than 37°C and more than five hours old) should be given an injection of sterile glucose solution into the body cavity to help to revive them.

4. **Naval ill/joint ill:** This disease is equivalent to naval ill/joint ill of calves *(see page 335)*.

5. **Clostridial diseases:** These diseases are caused by a variety of soil-borne clostridial bacteria. They affect sheep of all ages and types, invading a range of body tissues and organs. Diseases include *lamb dysentery, pulpy kidney, tetanus, braxy, blackleg* and *black disease.* All are serious diseases which are often fatal.

Symptoms: There are many and varied symptoms of clostridial diseases.

Prevention: This is fairly straightforward. An "8-in-1" vaccine is available which is very effective in controlling the diseases. All breeding stock should be vaccinated routinely: this gives them protection. Lambs born to vaccinated ewes acquire some disease resistance from colostrum. Those being fattened as early lamb are safe; those being kept for autumn/winter finishing or breeding should be vaccinated.

Treatment: Treatment of outbreaks of clostridial diseases is difficult and is best carried out by a veterinary surgeon.

6. **Foot rot:** This is a *highly contagious* disease caused by two species of *Fusiformis* bacteria. The tissue between the toes is first affected causing *"scald"*. This should be treated by cleaning the foot and foot-bathing *(see below)*. If this is not done the condition quickly develops into foot rot. Infection spreads onto the sole of the foot and up under the horn, causing the horn to separate from the tissue. This leads to severe lameness.

Foot rot is most commonly found in lowland sheep production, particularly on wet soils or in unhygienic wintering conditions.

Symptoms: These include lameness in one or more feet and loss of condition. Affected animals may graze on their knees or lie down and stop grazing altogether. A rancid, unpleasant odour can be detected coming from the dead tissue.

Prevention: Paring of hooves to expose infected tissue and foot-bathing to kill the disease-organism are the main measures. This procedure should be carried out routinely once per month. A 10% solution of formalin or copper sulphate is used in the foot-bath. Bought-in sheep should be foot-bathed before being mixed with the flock.

A vaccine exists which can be used in very disease-susceptible areas.

Treatment: When an outbreak occurs, infected animals should be isolated and treated individually by careful foot-paring and use of an antibiotic aerosol spray. They should be kept separate from the rest of the flock until cured. Increased preventive use of foot-bathing with the main flock is advisable during this period. All sheep should, if possible, be moved onto clean pasture. This is pasture which has been rested from sheep for at least 14 days (i.e. the life-span of *Fusiformis* in soil).

7. **Orf:** Orf is a virus disease which affects sheep of all ages and types. It is *highly infectious* and up to 90% of a flock can become affected. It causes failure to thrive and, if untreated, can be fatal in some cases.

Orf is *transmissible to humans* (a zoonose) and persons handling infected sheep should wear gloves and protective clothing.

Symptoms: The disease is also known as scabby mouth or "soremouth". Pustules, ulceration and scabs are found mainly on the mouth of ewes and lambs. The udder, feet and genitalia can also be affected.

Secondary infection by bacteria is common unless treatment is prompt. *In man,* pustules and scabs are usually found on the hands from contact with infected animals.

Prevention: A fairly effective vaccine is available. Ewes should be vaccinated 4-6 weeks before lambing and lambs at about four weeks old. As the disease can persist on land for many years, vaccination should be carried out every year.

Treatment: There is no effective treatment. Antibiotic creams or aerosols should be used to prevent secondary bacterial infection.

8. **Stomach and intestinal worms:** This is an internal parasitic disease broadly similar to stomach and intestinal worms in cattle *(see page 349).* Some species have the same type of life cycle as those of cattle while some have longer life cycles.

   Symptoms: Infected animals fail to thrive properly. Diarrhoea is commonly seen, leading to loss of weight, dehydration and possibly death. Soiling of the fleece around the tail, caused by diarrhoea, increases the risk of fly strike *(see below).*

   Prevention: The main preventive method involves keeping lambs on clean pasture. This is not easy since lambs suckle and graze with their mothers and are commonly infected by grazing pasture contaminated by them. Dosing ewes before lambing lessens this risk. Once they are weaned, lambs should be moved onto clean pasture every 2-3 weeks, using the "leader-follower" system *(see page 349).*

   Treatment: When disease symptoms occur, animals should be dosed with a suitable nematicide.

9. **Liver fluke:** This disease is similar to that already described for cows and cattle *(see page 334).*

10. **Fly strike ("Maggots"):** This is an external parasitic disease caused by maggots (larvae) of "green bottle" and "blue bottle" flies. The flies are active from May to September. They are attracted by soiled fleece around the tail and lay eggs there. These hatch and reach maggot stage in a few days. They then begin to feed on the skin and flesh for 2-3 days before dropping off to continue their life cycle on the ground.

    Repeated attacks over the summer cause irritation and pain. Infected animals fail to graze or thrive properly. If they are untreated, the area infected becomes larger and deeper with time and the animals may die from weakness and blood-poisoning.

Symptoms: Infected animals stop grazing and stand still except for nervous twitching and tail-wriggling. If untreated, they become progressively more listless and weak.

Prevention: Preventive measures include: (i) good worm control to prevent diarrhoea, (ii) clipping of the fleece in the region of the tail and hindquarters to reduce the amount of soiling, (iii) dipping with an approved "summer dip" insecticide. This gives 7-14 weeks protection against infection.

Note: Dipping is effective only when care is taken to ensure the following: (i) sheep are immersed for 1 minute, (ii) insecticide is freshly made up each day and replaced when dirty, (iii) insecticide is made up to the correct strength and protected from dilution. Details of sheep-dipping facilities are given in *Section 43.5.*

Treatment: The wool is clipped from the affected area and maggots removed. The area is then treated with an insecticide to kill developing maggots. Sheep with wounds should be treated with an antibiotic cream and housed until the wounds have healed.

11. **Sheep scab:** This is a *highly infectious* external parasitic disease caused by the mange mite *Psoroptes ovis.* It is a disease of major importance because of its potential to spread rapidly and cause large-scale losses. It has been successfully eradicated in many countries and was eradicated in Great Britain and Ireland for some time before reappearing in 1975. It is a *notifiable disease (see page 314).*

The mites remain dormant during the summer and become active in the October to March period. They feed by piercing the skin and sucking lymph fluid. Pustules result and these rupture to form scabs. The wool over the scabs becomes moist and matted and after some time falls out. The scabs and wool-loss quickly become extensive and the animal stops eating, loses condition and dies.

Symptoms: Symptoms develop progressively as follows: nervousness, nibbling and biting at the affected area, scab formation, wool-loss, wasting and death.

Prevention: Sheep scab occurrence has been successfully controlled in recent years by strict enforcement of Government safety regulations. These may be summarised as follows: (i) anyone who owns or is in charge of a sheep suspected to have sheep scab must notify the Gardai without delay; (ii) sheep owners must dip *all* their sheep at least once per year. The dipping must be carried out between September 15 and January 31; (iii) only dips approved by the Department of Agriculture and Food may be used; (iv) animals must be totally immersed except for the head and ears and must remain so immersed for not less than one minute.

Treatment: If an outbreak of sheep scab is suspected, the Gardai should be notified immediately.

12. **Other diseases of sheep:** Other diseases of sheep of lesser importance generally than those already covered are listed and commented on in *Table 43.5.*

Table 43.5 *Other diseases of sheep*

Disease	Comment
Mastitis	This is a bacterial disease of the udder which occurs occasionally in lactating ewes. Inflammation and discolouration of the udder are seen.
Hoose	This disease corresponds to hoose in cattle but occurs less commonly.
Grass tetany (staggers)	This disease corresponds to grass tetany in cows *(see page 332).*
Louping ill	This is a virus disease transmitted by ticks.
Cobalt pine	This is caused by cobalt deficiency in soil and consequently in the diet. Affected animals thrive very badly.
Swayback	Affected animals cannot stand or walk properly. The disease is due to copper deficiency.
Foot-and-mouth disease	*See page 334.*

43.5 Sheep-handling Facilities

Fig. 43.4 Sheep winter housing

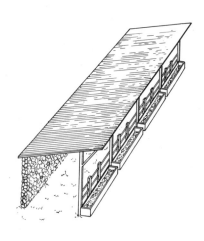

(A) *Winter housing:* The provision of winter housing is an important part of intensive sheep production. In-wintering sheep rests pastures, preventing poaching and encouraging earlier growth of grass in spring. It also facilitates management, especially at lambing time.

Winter housing for sheep is generally fairly simple in design and structure. What is needed is buildings in which animals can be housed in groups and easily fed and handled. A wide range of designs and types is found; one type commonly found is shown in *Fig. 43.4.*

(B) *Sheep-handling unit:* A sheep-handling unit should contain a collecting pen; storage pens; a foot-bath and race; and a dipping unit.

The *collecting pen* is used for the initial collection and sorting of the flock. Animals may then be moved to *storage pens* where they can be shorn, have their feet pared and treated, etc. The *foot-bath and race* is used for foot-bathing and the *dipping unit* for summer and winter dipping. A sheep-handling unit, together with details of the foot-bath and the dipping unit, is shown in *Fig. 43.5.*

Fig. 43.5 (a) Sheep-handling unit; (b) foot-bath; (c) dipping unit

Exercises

Exercise 88. Comparison of sire and dam breeds of sheep

Materials needed
1. Sheep (preferably ram) of Suffolk breed
2. Sheep of the following breeds; Wicklow Cheviot, Galway, Halfbred, Greyface

Procedure
1. Identify all the breeds seen.
2. Compare the Suffolk with the other breeds. Pay attention to (a) size of hindquarters, (b) size of shoulders, (c) depth of torso, (d) broadness of back.

Note: If there are lambs present, note the mixed features they possess. Note how they have inherited some conformation traits from their sire.

Results
1. Record and describe the breeds and crosses seen.
2. Record the major differences between the Suffolk and the other breeds.

Exercise 89 Observation of flock activity during the mating season

Materials needed
Access to a sheep flock during the mating season

Procedure

1. Observe the activity of the flock.
2. Make sure to see: (a) the rams. Identify their breed(s), (b) the raddling or other device used to mark the ewes, (c) the number of ewes bearing the marking fluid on their backs and hindquarters. Note if there has been more than one colour of marking fluid used, (d) A ram serving a ewe, (e) the quality of the grazing available to the flock, (f) the condition of the ewes.
3. Note any signs of illness.

Results

Record and comment on all observations.

Precautions

Stay well-clear of the ram and stay in groups in case he becomes violent.

Exercise 90 Examination of sheep-handling facilities

Materials needed

Access to a yard containing sheep-handling facilities

Procedure

1. Examine the general area.
   Note in particular: (a) the collecting area, (b) the sheep scales, (c) the foot-bath and race (examine the base of the bath. The surface should be corrugated to spread the sheep's claws to allow good contact with the bath fluid.), (d) the dipping tank. Note its dimensions and the manner in which sheep are induced to enter it.
2. Examine any further items on show, e.g. fostering crate, "hot box", implements such as castrators, lambing aids, etc.

Results

Record and describe all the facilities inspected.

44 – The Principles and Importance of Pig Production

44.1 National Importance

The importance of pig production is shown in *Table 44.1*.

Table 44.1 Importance of pig production in Irish agriculture

	1970	1980	1990
Value of pigs, bacon and pork production (IR£)	42	131	168
Percentage of total agricultural output	12.2	7.8	5.0
Percentage of total agricultural exports	7.3	3.2	2.6

Pig production is a highly specialized type of farming. The number of pig producers in Ireland has fallen from 35 000 in 1970 to less than 1 000 at present. The size of pig production units has increased accordingly and Ireland now has the largest average unit size in the EC. Some units fatten 50 – 60 000 pigs per annum.

Pig production has also changed greatly in terms of geographical distribution. Most of it is now located in two regions, Cavan/Monaghan and Cork. This has led to some water pollution problems which are discussed later *(see page 385)*.

44.2 Breeds of Pigs

Two pig breeds, the *Landrace* and *Large White*, dominate the Irish pig industry. Small numbers of purebred animals of these breeds are used to supply the crossbred sows and fattener offspring for the industry.

Fig. 44.1 (A) Landrace boar; (B) Large White boar

The Landrace *(Fig. 44.1)* is a breed of Danish origin whose desirable characteristics are associated with *good conformation.* It has a long body, which yields a lot of valuable back bacon and pork, small shoulders and large hams. The Large White *(Fig. 44.1)* is of British origin and its desirable characteristics are fast growth rate, high prolificy, good food conversion ratio and good meat quality.

44.3 Principles of Pig Production

44.3.1 Breeding strategy

The ideal sow for breeding is the first generation cross between purebred Landrace and Large White. This animal has half of its genes from each breed, hybrid vigour and an excellent combination of desirable characteristics. To have all breeding sows of this type would mean that very large numbers of expensive purebred sows would have to be maintained on each production unit. This is not economically feasible and a cheaper alternative system, known as *criss-cross breeding,* has been developed.

Fig. 44.2 Criss-cross breeding programme

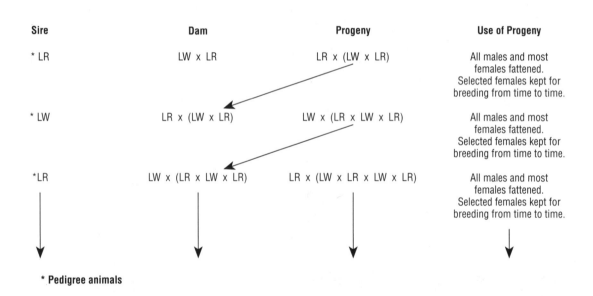

Sire	Dam	Progeny	Use of Progeny
* LR	LW x LR	LR x (LW x LR)	All males and most females fattened. Selected females kept for breeding from time to time.
* LW	LR x (LW x LR)	LW x (LR x LW x LR)	All males and most females fattened. Selected females kept for breeding from time to time.
*LR	LW x (LR x LW x LR)	LR x (LW x LR x LW x LR)	All males and most females fattened. Selected females kept for breeding from time to time.

* Pedigree animals

This system is explained in *Fig. 44.2.* It involves maintaining a small number of pedigree boars of each breed and using them alternately on crossbred sows. A small number of first generation cross-bred gilts (young females) has to be purchased to begin the breeding herd. Expansion can be carried out by adding selected gilts from the progeny as shown.

In this system the balance of genes and associated desirable characteristics in fatteners fluctuates about the 50/50 figure. Some hybrid vigour effect is lost by comparison with that obtained in the ideal system. The animals are nevertheless very suitable for fattening.

Boars have to be replaced every two years to prevent a serious level of inbreeding.

44.3.2 Birth, growth rates, puberty

Bonhams weigh 1.0-1.5 kg at birth. Average litter size is 11. When reared and fattened indoors, as is normal in commercial pig production, bonhams reach bacon slaughter weight (82 kg liveweight) in about 6 months.

Both sexes reach puberty at 5-6 months at about slaughter weight. Males kept for slaughter are not castrated. Mature, fully grown pigs weigh 140-200 kg.

44.3.3 Oestrous cycle, gestation period

The length of the oestrous cycle is 21 days and the average duration 2-3 days. The gestation period is 114 days.

44.3.4 Food conversion ratio

Food conversion ratio (FCR) is the ratio of food consumed to liveweight gained. An FCR of 2.0, for example, means that for every 2.0 kg of food eaten an animal gains 1.0 kg of liveweight. Low FCR values mean *good feed efficiency.*

Almost 80% of the costs of pig production are attributable to feed costs. If feed efficiency is improved (i.e. FCR lowered) profits increase. In practice, FCR is the most important factor affecting profitability of pig production units. Farmers aim at average FCR values of 1.75 for weaners (9-32 kg) and 3.25 for fatteners (33-82 kg).

There are five factors affecting FCR which are influenced by farmers: (i) breed, (ii) health, (iii) management, (iv) housing, (v) diet.

The *breeds and crosses* used in pig production have been arrived at taking FCR into consideration. The ability of boars to confer low FCR values to their offspring is recognised and used to improve herd average FCR. The *health* of pigs depends greatly on the *management* skills of the farmer. Only healthy animals can fully achieve their potential to utilize feed efficiently.

The influence of *housing* on FCR is mainly through reduction of heat loss. Well-insulated houses keep pigs warm so that most of the food consumed is used to put on flesh rather than maintain body temperature. Properly constructed, draught-free houses also help to maintain healthy animals.

Diet is probably the most important factor on a day-to-day basis. A great deal is known about pig nutrition and a range of rations suited to bonhams, weaners and fatteners is available. Rations should have balanced quantities of energy, protein, minerals and vitamins. The amounts of certain essential amino acids, e.g. lysine, are also critical.

44.3.5 Carcase grading of bacon pigs

At present, carcase quality is more stringently assessed for bacon pigs than that for cattle or sheep. Pig production is very competitive and the profit margin per pig sold is small. The extent to which pigs sold achieve the higher carcase quality grades greatly influences profitability. Carcase quality is influenced by breed and diet, principally.

Grades are assessed on the basis of (a) depth of fat over the shoulder, (b) depth of fat over the loin and (c) length of carcase. These are shown in *Fig. 44.3*.

Fig. 44.3 Points of assessment of grading in bacon pigs

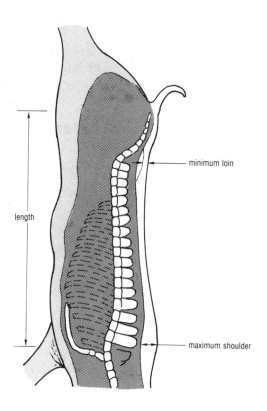

45 – Bacon Pig Production

Pigs produced in Ireland are utilized as shown in *Table 45.1.*

Table 45.1 *Types and usage of pigs*

Type of pig	Live wt., kg	% of total production	Usage
Pork	60-90	58	Fresh meats sold by pork butchers, fresh meats for processing
Bacon	75-100	38	Factory cured: sold as bacon and ham
Heavy	>100	4	Fresh meat used in the manufacture of processed foods

The production of the three types in *Table 45.1* is similar in terms of breeds, housing, feeding and management. Bacon pig production is the most prevalent type and is described below for that reason.

45.1 Types of Production Units

Most of the bacon pigs produced in Ireland come from *integrated pig production units.* These consist of (a) a breeding and rearing unit with its herd of sows with accompanying bonhams and (b) a fattening unit used to bring pigs from weaning to slaughter weights.

Integrated units have the advantage of being self-contained. This lessens the risk of disease entry and eliminates transport stresses on pigs. They demand knowledge and management skills of a high calibre, however, ranging over all aspects of production.

Some producers concentrate on *breeding and rearing* only, rearing the young to weaner stage, at which they sell them to *fatteners* who complete the production cycle. These types of units are scarce and becoming scarcer.

45.2 Sow and Bonham Management

Fig. 45.1 Ideal production year of sow, yielding 2.39 litters

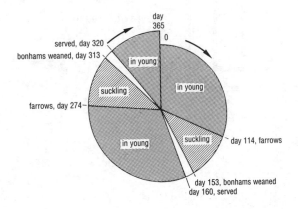

The sow has a central role in pig production. She is expected to produce 2.0-2.25 litters, yielding more than 20 weaners, per year. The "ideal" production year for a sow is shown in *Fig. 45.1*.

45.2.1 In-young sow

The in-young sow is housed in a *dry sow house (Fig. 45.2)*. She is fed once per day, being given about 2.50 kg of meals. In early pregnancy some sows are over-thin after rearing their litter of bonhams. These are given extra feeding to bring them back to their proper weight.

Fig. 45.2 Dry sow house

In the final 3-4 weeks sows are fed an extra 0.5 kg day^{-1} to ensure strong healthy bonhams and good milk production. About a week before the farrowing date, the sow is moved into the farrowing house.

45.2.2 Farrowing

In the farrowing house, the sow is washed, deloused and disinfected and put into a cleaned, disinfected *farrowing unit (Fig. 45.3)*. The house is maintained at a temperature of 20°C. At farrowing, the sow should be observed to ensure that she farrows without difficulty, which she usually does. Veterinary assistance should be obtained if problems arise.

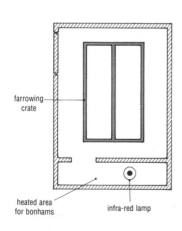

farrowing crate

heated area for bonhams   infra-red lamp

Fig. 45.3 (a) Farrowing unit; (b) farrowing crate

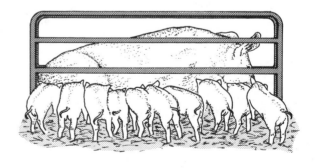

The farrowing crate is designed to allow the sow to farrow with minimum risk to the bonhams. Subsequently it allows her to stand up and lie down without crushing them. It also allows the bonhams easy access both to the sow for suckling and to an infrared lamp.

45.2.3 Suckling period/weaning

Immediately after birth bonhams should have their front teeth broken off to protect the sow's teats from injury. On day 2-3 they should be injected with iron to prevent anaemia *(see below)*.

The sow usually suckles the bonhams for 5-6 weeks. She is fed suckling ration at a rate of 1.8 kg + 0.5 kg per bonham per day. After 5-7 days, creep ration (containing 20% protein) is introduced, being scattered on the floor. Separate supplies of water are available to the sow and bonhams.

Bonhams are weaned abruptly at 5-6 weeks.

45.2.4 Post-weaning sow management

After weaning, the sow is moved back to the dry sow house. She normally comes into oestrus within 5-7 days of weaning. In the dry sow house, a boar is released once per day to detect sows in heat. When detected, sows are removed and served by the appropriate boar *twice within 24 hours*.

Double-serving increases conception rates and litter sizes. If the sow returns to service after 21 days, she is served again as before. If she repeats again she is culled from the herd.

The in-young sow now enters her next production cycle and this cycle is repeated continuously for 5 or more litters. Sows are culled at 4-5 years old when litter size and health begin to decline.

45.3 Management and Feeding of Weaners

Litters being weaned at the same time are mixed for a short period and then groups, made up of pigs of similar weight, are selected. These groups are moved to weaner houses. They are stocked at a sufficiently high density to allow house temperature to be maintained at 24°C by the animals' body heat. Houses have under-floor insulation and low roofs to conserve heat. They are generally similar in shape and design to fattening houses *(see Fig. 45.4)*.

Weaners are fed weaner ration *ad lib.* and water is available. Weaner ration contains 18-20% protein, 13.7 MJ kg^{-1} digestible energy (DE) and 1.15% lysine. Weaner weights increase from 9 kg at weaning to 32 kg before they move to fattening houses. As weaners increase in size they are regrouped from time to time to lower the stocking density so that houses do not become overcrowded.

Fig. 45.4 Solari-type fattening house

45.4 Management and Feeding of Fatteners

When weaners are moved to fattening houses, they are again mixed, arranged into groups of equal-sized pigs, and stocked at the density required to maintain the houses at the correct temperature (22°C). There are many different types of fattening house. The type most commonly found in Ireland is the *Solari (Fig. 45.4)*. Features of this type of house are very good insulation and low roofs.

Fattener ration, containing 15% protein, 12.5 MJ kg^{-1} DE and 0.8% lysine, is fed *ad lib*. Water is available. Many producers restrict feeding for the last few weeks before slaughter in order to restrict fat deposition and improve carcase grades. Mixing and regrouping to lower stocking density is carried out from time to time.

Pigs are sent for slaughter when they reach weights of 80-82 kg or greater and have the degree of "finish" required by the factory. Farmers assess this either visually or with the aid of ultrasonic devices which measure shoulder and back-fat thickness.

45.5 Replacement Gilts

Gilts are female pigs which have not yet had their first litter. As fatteners approach slaughter weight, gilts showing the best general conformation and health are selected as breeding herd replacements. These are housed together for a further 4-6 weeks before being moved to the dry sow house when they weigh 100 kg. After some time there they come into oestrus, are served, and enter the production cycle.

45.6 Diseases of Pigs

Pigs commercially reared and fattened indoors are subject to a much smaller number of diseases than cattle or sheep. The reasons for this are as follows: (i) pigs live in a controlled environment with little or no contact with soil or vegetation, both of which are important sources of disease organisms, (ii) temperature, humidity, hygiene and diet are all controlled and kept at levels optimum for growth and development. This minimises the risk of disease, (iii) most pig production units are self-contained, except for occasional purchases of boars, so there is little risk of "buying in" disease.

On the other hand, the controlled environment of pig units is ideal for the growth and spread of disease organisms. If disease enters a unit, therefore, it can spread very rapidly and cause large losses. For this reason, pig production units pay great attention to hygiene, especially in relation to visitors.

Hygiene barriers are a standard feature of units. These ensure that all vehicles must drive through a disinfectant bath when approaching the unit. Drivers and passengers must then walk through a foot-bath before entering the buildings.

1. **Anaemia of bonhams:** This is the principal nutritional disease of bonhams. Bonhams require iron for proper growth and development. The sow's milk is unable to provide adequate amounts. In outdoor systems this would not be a problem as bonhams would obtain sufficient iron from rooting in the soil.

   Symptoms: Listlessness and poor growth at 2-3 weeks old; rough hair growth; paleness of mouth, eyes and skin. Diarrhoea is commonly found, caused by bacterial infection of the weakened bonham.

   Prevention: The disease is very easily prevented by giving bonhams a single intramuscular injection of a soluble iron compound in the first week of life. This is now standard practice in all pig units.

   Treatment: The need for treatment does not normally arise, because of the preventive methods used.

2. **Coliform scour:** This is a disease caused by *E.coli* bacteria and is similar in nature to bacterial scour in calves. It can affect pigs of any age but is most common in bonhams and weaners up to 8 weeks old. It is usually caused by a combination of poor management and poor hygiene.

   Symptoms: Diarrhoea and dehydration are the common symptoms. In severe cases sudden death may occur.

   Prevention: Strict attention should be paid to hygiene, especially in the farrowing house. Before farrowing, the sow should be washed and disinfected, and the farrowing area thoroughly cleaned and disinfected. Good management is important: this includes the provision of warm, dry well-insulated housing; avoiding sudden changes of diet; avoiding unnecessary stress. A *vaccination* can be given to sows before farrowing to ensure high levels of antibody in their colostrum.

   Treatment: Antibiotics should be used under veterinary supervision. A fluid replacement solution should be fed during treatment to prevent further dehydration.

3. **Virus pneumonia:** This is a virus disease similar to virus pneumonia in calves *(see page 334)*. Poor ventilation encourages the incidence and spread of the disease.

   Symptoms: Coughing is the first symptom, accompanied by lowered growth rate. Secondary invasion of the lungs by bacteria leads to fever and possibly death if untreated.

   Prevention: Good housing, including good ventilation and

temperature control are the main preventive measures. As the disease is most common in weaner and fatteners, special attention should be paid to their houses.

Treatment: There is no treatment for the virus. Secondary infections are treated with antibiotics.

4. **Diseases of breeding stock:** There are some diseases of pigs which affect breeding stock (sows or boars) only. Prevention and treatment of these are performed on a routine basis. These diseases are dealt with in *Table 45.2.*

Table 45.2 *Diseases of breeding pigs*

Disease	Comment
Farrowing fever	This disease includes bacterial infections of the uterus and mammary glands leading to fever and lack of milk. The disease is prevented by good hygiene in the farrowing house. Outbreaks are treated with antibiotics.
SMEDI	This virus disease gives rise to a variety of symptoms which explain its name. These are stillbirth (S), mummification (M) of embryos, embryonic death (ED) and infertility (I). The disease is prevented by routine vaccination of sows. There is no treatment.
Erysipelas	This is a bacterial disease of sows, replacement gilts and boars. It is a serious disease, causing a range of debilitating symptoms, including sudden death. It is highly infectious. It is prevented by annual vaccination. Outbreaks may be treated with antibiotics.
Roundworms, tapeworms, lice	These parasites can infest all types of pigs but routine treatment of breeding stock is sufficient to prevent infection of weaners and fatteners. Sows, replacement gilts and boars should be dosed at least twice a year.

5. **Other diseases of pigs:** Some diseases of less general importance than those already dealt with are listed and discussed in *Table 45.3.*

Table 45.3 *Other diseases of pigs*

Disease	Comment
Atrophic rhinitis	This bacterial disease causes sneezing and sniffling and, in some severe infections, may lead to a distorted snout. Growth rate suffers. *Prevention* is achieved by maintaining a closed herd and buying in breeding stock only from herds certified free of the disease. *Treatment* is difficult and not always fully successful.
Transmissible gastro-enteritis (TGE)	This is a *highly contagious* virus disease of all types of pigs. Greatest losses occur in bonhams. Sudden onset of diarrhoea causes loss of condition in older animals and deaths in bonhams. The disease is *prevented* by strict hygiene in relation to purchases of stock and visiting lorries, persons, etc. There is no effective *treatment.*
Aujeszky's disease	This is a *highly contagious* virus disease of pigs of all ages. It is most serious in bonhams where mortality can be as high as 100%. Early symptoms in young pigs are coughing, trembling and disorientation followed by collapse and death. Older pigs show similar symptoms but fatalities are less common. Pregnant sows abort. *Preventation* and *treatment* are the same as for TGE.

45.7 Buildings used in Pig Production

Buildings used in pig production units in Ireland are almost all *purpose-built.* Great attention is paid to insulation and ventilation. All construction utilizes knowledge of the environmental needs of pigs gained from research in Ireland and elsewhere.

The buildings are usually built close to each other so that an *integrated slurry system* can be used. This is arranged as follows: (i) a portion of each house contains slats overlying a shallow *slurry channel*, (ii) the slurry flows by gravity from each house out into a *collector channel*, (iii) The collector channel conveys the slurry by gravity to a *slurry pit* for storage.

1. *Farrowing house:* The farrowing house is a house containing a number of farrowing units. The number varies according to herd size. The house is maintained at a temperature of 20°C. A farrowing unit is shown in *Fig. 45.3 (page 376).*

2. *Weaner house; fattener house:* These houses are basically similar in design *(see Fig. 45.4, page 378).* They are maintained at temperatures of 24°C and 22°C respectively by the animals' body heat as described already.

3. *Dry sow house:* The dry sow house *(see Fig. 45.2, page 376)* contains the dry sows and the boars. The space allowed per sow is $1.05m^2$ (1.5m x 0.7m). The temperature is maintained at 20°C and some heating is usually required.

4. *Other buildings and structures:* Other buildings and structures found on a standard pig production unit include an office, meal store, meal storage bins, loose houses (for occasional use by breeding stock) and an isolation house. There are no special features or temperature requirements of the houses, except for the isolation house which has already been described *(see page 338).*

Exercises

Exercise 91. Examination of an integrated pig production unit

Materials needed
Access to an integrated pig production unit

Procedure
Tour and inspect the unit. Be sure to see all the sections and animals.

(a) *Dry sow unit:* Inspect sows and boars. Observe system of dung and urine disposal. **Note** the water supply to sows.

(b) *Farrowing house:* Observe the farrowing crates, infrared lamps, suckling, creep-feeding. **Note** the degree of variability in bonham size.

(c) *Weaning house/fattening house:* Examine the shape and design of the house. Observe dung and urine removal. Count pig numbers in different houses and note how this varies.

(d) *Meal storage facilities*

(e) *Slurry flow* from individual units to the central storage pit.

(f) *Isolation house*

Results
Record and describe all the houses, animals and facilities seen.

46 – Poultry

Poultry are kept for *meat* and *egg* production. The poultry industry has become highly specialised and intensive in recent years and can be accurately described as *factory farming*. Consumption of chicken has increased by almost 30% and turkey by 35-40% in the last 25 years. Egg consumption has increased also. At present, almost all poultry production is for home consumption, as there are little or no exports.

46.1 Broiler Chicken Production

A broiler chicken is a young bird of either sex, slaughtered and sold at a liveweight of 1.5-2.75 kg (0.9-1.9 kg carcase weight). A broiler production unit is comprised of:

1. *Broiler breeder unit:* This contains breeding stock (cocks and hens) and the product is *fertilized eggs.*
2. *Hatchery:* Fertilized eggs are incubated here for 21 days at 38.5°C. They are rotated automatically to prevent the developing embryo (chick) sticking to the inside of the shell (in natural conditions the hen does this task herself). The chicks hatch from the eggs on day 18.
3. *Rearing and fattening unit:* The "day-old chicks" are reared and fattened here in *controlled-environment housing*. Infrared lamps are used for the first week. Thereafter, temperature, lighting, ventilation and humidity are fully controlled. The birds reach slaughter weight at 6-8 weeks old.
4. *Slaughter and processing unit:* Birds are slaughtered, plucked and prepared as whole carcases, portions, or cooked products here.

In some cases, all of these sub-units are located and managed together. In others, some activities are subcontracted. For example, individual farmers may receive batches of day-old chicks and rear and fatten them on contract.

Broilers are a poultry strain specially bred for high meat:bone ratio. They have an overall (birth to slaughter) *food conversion ratio* of about 2:1.

Diet is highly specialised and rations fed are meticulously prepared and balanced. Use is made of detailed knowledge of requirements for protein, energy and range and amount of amino acids, vitamins and minerals.

Disease control is very important in broiler units. Birds are commonly inoculated against a range of diseases and are observed carefully for disease occurrence.

46.2 Turkey Production

The peak demand for fresh turkeys is at Christmas and, to a lesser extent, Easter. There is a steady demand for frozen turkeys for the remainder of the year.

Turkey production is similar to broiler production in most respects. Thus, there are meat strains of bird; production units are similarly subdivided into breeding units, hatcheries and so on; housing, diet and disease control are similar. Whereas broilers are slaughtered at about 2 kg liveweight, turkeys are slaughtered at 7-12 kg liveweight.

46.3 Egg Production

Eggs are produced by laying strains of bird. These have low meat:bone ratio and poor conformation but achieve high levels of egg production.

Almost all eggs are produced under the *battery cage system*, where the birds are kept in individual cages for all of their productive life. They are fed and watered automatically. Diet and disease control are approached in the same way as with broilers and turkeys, except that birds are fed for production of eggs, not meat. An example of a battery cage unit is shown in *Fig. 46.1*.

Hens begin to lay at 18-20 weeks old (*pullet stage*) and produce about 250 eggs each per year. Control of daylength is used to manipulate egg production. In nature, most wild birds begin laying in spring, when daylength is increasing. They may continue up to mid-summer.

With laying hens, daylength is increased artificially from 8 hours at 20 weeks to a maximum of 17 hours at 38 weeks. This is achieved by weekly increases of 30 minutes. Daylength is then held at this level until the completion of laying.

After this, the hens are replaced by pullets who begin a new production cycle. The culled hens are sold for slaughter. Their meat is used for processed poultry products, mainly soups.

Fig. 46.1 Stepped-cage laying unit

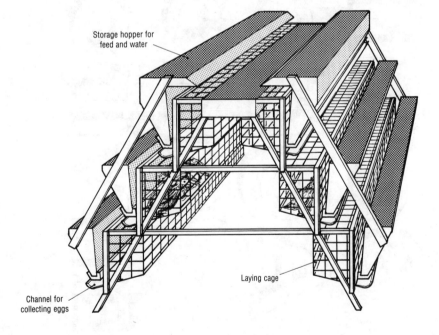

Storage hopper for feed and water

Laying cage

Channel for collecting eggs

Section 10
Agriculture and the Environment

47 Agriculture and the Environment

Agriculture and the environment

By its very nature, agriculture involves an intimate relationship with the environment. Every farmer needs to appreciate the effect, called the environmental impact, of farming practices on the environment. There are two additional reasons for this: consumers are increasingly demanding cleaner and "greener" produce and are willing to pay premium prices for "organic" products, and, secondly, the law is being tightened up to enforce the regulations.

In this chapter we raise some of the issues involved. We hope that each class will discuss and debate some of these issues. Sometimes we ask questions. There may be no single correct answer. We believe that awareness will help.

47.1 Organic wastes

47.1.1 Fish kills

The common cause of fish kills in rivers is that the fish die due to a lack of oxygen. This situation arises as follows.

Oxygen is only sparingly soluble in water. It is more soluble at low temperature than at higher temperatures (observe the gas bubbles when you boil a kettle of water). Sometimes low water conditions combined with high summer temperatures cause such low oxygen levels as to cause a "natural" fish kill. It is more usual that other factors come into play.

When organic matter is released into a stream, aerobic bacteria and other organisms act to break it down. These organisms use oxygen and exert what is called a *biochemical oxygen demand* (B.O.D.) on the system. B.O.D. is a measure of the amount of oxygen required (expressed in mg/litre) by 1 litre of organic pollutant. The higher the B.O.D. the more oxygen is used up. Some farm wastes have a very high B.O.D. *(Table 47.1)*.

It is easy to see how discharge of organic wastes such as those listed in Table 47.1 can exert a major B.O.D. This is especially important at vulnerable times such as in summer with high temperatures and low water levels. These factors can combine to cause a fish ill. Notice the high B.O.D. value of dairy washings: even very dilute washings (0.1% milk) can be as polluting as domestic sewage.

Effluent	B.O.D. (mg/l)
Domestic sewage	300
Cattle slurry	12 000
Pig slurry	30 000
Silage effluent	54 000
Poultry slurry	65 000
Dairy washings	15 000
Whole milk	100 000

Table 47.1 B.O.D. values of farm wastes

47.1.2 Other effects

To summarise, the effects of pollution by organic matter are as follows:

Deoxygenation (see above, 47.1.1)

Artificial enrichment. This causes "algal blooms" - green slime, and often called eutrophication.

Toxicity. Certain levels can be poisonous to aquatic life.

Spread of bacterial and viral diseases.

Sound agricultural practice requires the proper collection, treatment and storage of farm wastes. They can often be spread safely on land when it is safe to do so. Many suggestions are made throughout this book for the proper treatment of farm wastes.

47.2 The effect of fertilizers

Properly used, artificial fertilizers have added greatly to the yields of Irish agriculture. Increasingly abroad there is worry at the increase of nitrate levels in groundwater. Groundwater is the source of water in wells and it is the ultimate source of our drinking water. Although much lower than in other countries, e.g. the Netherlands, nitrate levels are rising in Ireland and farmers need to be aware of this. Run-off of artificial fertilizers is also wasteful for the farmer. Run-off can be minimised by ensuring that:

- the fertilizers are applied at the proper rate
- the correct fertilizer is used
- it is applied during periods of rapid grass growth
- it is not applied during a drought period.

47.3 Pesticides

Consider the following chain of event: a leaf of a plant is eaten by a snail, which in turn is eaten by a song thrush, which in turn is eaten by a sparrowhawk. This everyday event is called a food chain. More often in nature we find, not food chains, but complicated interlinked food chains called food webs. Now introduce a pesticide by spraying the plant. Even though the actual level sprayed on the crop may be very low it is finally concentrated in the snail, concentrated further in the songthrush and finally the top predator in the chain, the sparrowhawk, gets the most concentrated remains of the pesticide.

The magnification of pesticides (especially the insecticide DDT, no longer used) in the food chain caused a major decline in birds of prey such as hawks and falcons. Humans are also at the end of a food chain and have to take note of this effect. The bird populations are recovering again with the more enlightened use of pesticides of recent years.

AGRICULTURE AND THE ENVIRONMENT

Farmers should also be aware that the consumer is increasingly willing to pay premium prices for organic produce - that is, food produced without pesticides. This calls for the development of alternative controls for pests and diseases. A number of methods of biological control are now becoming available: white fly in glasshouse crops of cucumbers and tomatoes can be controlled using a parasitic wasp, the Formosan wasp.

These techniques are likely to be more important in the future.

47.4 Other issues

47.4.1 Hedgerow removal

Hedgerows in Ireland are important as remnants of broadleaved woodland. They provide very important sites for many species of wildlife. Each species is necessary to maintain the complex food chains mentioned above. For example, large stretches of prairie are now the scene in Canada. Lucerne is grown as a fodder crop. Lucerne needs bees for its pollination to set seed. These bees now have to be reared artificially for this purpose. In Ireland, another legume, red clover is important as a fodder crop. The main pollinators of red clover are bumblebees with long tongues - red clover has a floret too long for the tongue of honeybees. These bumblebees depend on hedges for their nesting sites.

Many other pieces of evidence could be given for the importance of hedges. Perhaps as a project you could gather some of this evidence. You could also try to chart the removal of hedges as follows: various editions of Ordnance Survey maps are available since about 1830. You could investigate the extent of hedges in a small part of your home area by using, for example, maps from 1830, early 1900's and present day (by walking).

47.5 Conclusion

Since human beings first began their earliest forms of agriculture about 10 000 years ago farmers have been working together with the environment to produce their food crops. Modern farming techniques allow much higher yields but have the danger of having a high impact on the environment. Farmers need to be aware of this and take it into consideration in their practices. Farmers, and everyone else, need the environment to continue their existence.

B

Biological control is the control of one organism by the deliberate use of another organism.

Biological oxygen demand (B.O.D.) is the amount of oxygen required (expressed in mg l^{-1}) to oxidise fully, by biological means, the organic matter in one litre of organic pollutant or water sample.

Biomass is the amount of living matter in a given area.

Bradford count is the number of hanks of yarn, each 510 m long, that can be spun from 450 g of wool prepared for spinning.

C

Carbohydrate refers to chemicals containing carbon, hydrogen and oxygen according to the general formula $(CH_2O)n$ where n can be a number between 1 and many thousands. Examples include sugars, cellulose, starch and glycogen.

Cation exchange capacity is the total amount of exchangeable cations that a soil or a clay can adsorb.

Chipboard is a form of board made by gluing together dried chips of wood and then pressing and curing them to a given thickness.

Chloroplast is a sub-cellular unit, or organelle, containing the green pigment chorophyll, where photosynthesis takes place in green plants.

Chromosomes are the structures in the nucleus which contain the genes.

Citrate insoluble means insoluble in neutral ammonium citrate solution. *See Citrate soluble.*

Citrate soluble (in relation to phosphorus fertilizers) means soluble in neutral ammoniuim citrate. This is considered to be equivalent to soluble in average soil conditions.

Clone refers to the descendants of one individual produced by asexual ("vegetative") reproduction. Members of a clone are identical genetically.

Cotyledon refers to the seed leaf (either one or two) forming part of the embryo in seeds. Cotyledons are simpler than normal leaves. Monocots have one and dicots have two.

Crude fibre is a constituent of animal feedstuffs comprising mainly cellulose, hemicelluloses and lignin.

Crude protein is an approximate assessment of the protein content of animal feedstuffs, usually calculated as 6.5 x %N.

Cytoplasm is all the protoplasm outside the nucleus. *See also Protoplasm.*

D

Denitrification is the biological reduction of nitrates to nitrites, nitrous oxide or nitrogen gas.

Diffusion is the movement of molecules from a region of higher concentration to a region of comparatively lower concentration. *See also Osmosis.*

Digestible energy is that part of the energy of a feedstuff that is available to the animal after digestion.

Diploid refers to the (usual) condition in the cell nucleus where the chromosomes occur in pairs. *See also Haploid.*

DNA stands for deoxyribonucleic acid, the chemical of the genetic code. *See also RNA.*

Dry matter is the material remaining when water has been removed by oven-drying to constant weight.

Dry matter digestibility is the proportion (expressed as a percentage) of the dry matter of a feedstuff which is retained in the animal's system following digestion.

E

Essential elements are those chemical elements required for the normal growth of plants and animals. They are divided into two groups. Macronutrients are required in relatively large amounts; they are carbon, hydrogen, oxygen, nitrogen, phosphorus, potassium, calcium, magnesium and sulphur. Micronutrients (also called trace elements) are used in relatively small amounts; they are iron, manganese, boron, molybdenum, copper, zinc, chlorine and cobalt.

F

F_1 (first filial generation) refers to the first generation offspring from an experimental crossing of plants or animals.

Fibre board is a type of board made by gluing together dried wood fibres and then pressing and curing them to a given thickness.

Fluid replacement solution is a dilute solution of sugars and salts fed to animals suffering from dehydration.

Flushing involves feeding female animals on a low plane of nutrition, followed immediately by a high plane of nutrition to increase their fertility and conception rate.

Fruit is the ripened ovary of a flower which includes the seeds.

Fumigant (pesticide) is a material which, when volatilized in an enclosed space, kills pests.

G

Glabrous means smooth and hairless.

Great soil group is a group of soils having the same kind, arrangement and degree of expression of horizons in the soil profile.

Gross margin is the gross profit from an enterprise. It is calculated by subtracting all the variable costs (e.g. feedstuffs, fertilizers, veterinary fees, seeds, sprays, casual labour) associated with the enterprise from the income resulting from the enterprise. It is usually expressed on a "per hectare" basis.

H

Haploid refers to the condition where cells contain half the usual number of chromosomes, as in gametes during sexual reproduction. *See also Diploid.*

Hygroscopic (in relation to fertilizers) is a tendency to absorb water vapour from the atmosphere.

Hygroscopic water (in soil) is adsorbed water, i.e. water held very tightly in the soil by the attraction of soil particles, mainly clay and silt.

L

Livestock unit is the amount of farm livestock which consumes a quantity of food equivalent to that consumed by a mature (550 kg liveweight), productive cow.

Lodging (of cereals) refers to the collapse of all or part of the crop. It is usually caused by the straw being too tall, too weak or diseased, or the crop being too heavily fertilized with nitrogen fertilizer. Stormy weather aggravates the problem.

M

Macronutrients. *See Essential elements.*

Magma is the fluid rock material found under the earth's solid crust.

Malting is the process by which barley grain is prepared for brewing or distilling.

Malting barley is barley used for brewing or distilling.

Medullated means containing a hollow cellular central portion surrounded by an outer layer or cortex.

Meiosis is the kind of cell division by which a diploid cell forms daughter cells which are haploid. It usually occurs during sexual reproduction. *See also Diploid, Haploid and Mitosis.*

Metabolisable energy is the energy of a feedstuff less the energy of faeces, urine and methane.

Micronutrients *See Essential elements.*

Mitosis is the kind of cell division which forms daughter cells identical to their parent cells. This is the usual kind of cell division. *See also Meiosis.*

Mulch is material (such as straw, leaves, plastic film, etc.) spread on the soil surface to protect the soil from excessively high or low temperatures.

N

Nitrification is the biological oxidation of ammonium salts to nitrites and the further oxidation of nitrites to nitrates.

Nitrogen fixation is the conversion of atmospheric nitrogen from gaseous form to organic forms which can eventually be used by plants.

O

Osmosis is a special kind of diffusion which involves a semi-permeable membrane (i.e. water molecules can pass through it but larger molecules such as sugars cannot). Osmosis refers to the passage of water molecules through a semi-permeable membrane so as to equalize the concentration of water molecules at each side of the membrane.

P

Pallet wood refers to boards used for the construction of pallets (for use with forklift trucks).

Pasteurization is a heat treatment, mainly of milk, to kill disease causing organisms such as TB. Milk is pasteurized by heating to 72 °C for 15 seconds and then cooling rapidly.

Permanent wilting point is the moisture content of soil at which plants wilt permanently and will not recover unless watered immediately.

Photoperiod literally means day length. In agriculture its use refers to the response of many plants and animals to a critical day length. Some plants respond to a lengthening day, some to a shortening day.

Placenta in mammals, refers to an organ consisting of embryonic and maternal tissues by which the developing embryo is nourished. The embryo is connected to the placenta by the umbilical cord.

Protoplasm refers to the living part of a cell, including the cell membrane, the nucleus and the cytoplasm. *See also Cytoplasm.*

R

Rhizome is a swollen underground stem which roots at the nodes. (Examples: scutch grass and yellow flag iris.)

RNA stands for ribonucleic acid. It is related to DNA (see also) but is found mainly outside of the nucleus. DNA makes RNA and RNA makes protein.

Runner is a form of vegetative reproduction where an overground shoot creeps over the soil surface rooting and forming new plants at nodes. (Examples: strawberry and creeping buttercup.) *See also Stolon.*

S

Soil horizon is a layer of soil, approximately parallel to the soil surface which differs from adjacent layers in physical, chemical or biological properties.

Soil profile is a vertical section of the soil showing all its horizons, extending into the parent material.

Species is the smallest unit used to classify organisms and refers to actually or potentially interbreeding individuals.

Stolon is a form of vegetative reproduction when a branch of parent material bends over until it contacts the soil. It then roots and forms a new plant. (Example: blackberry.) *See also Runner.*

Swath is a ridge or line of grass lying on the ground after being cut by the mower.

Systemic (in relation to herbicides, pesticides) refers to chemicals transported throughout the plant's system and consequently affecting all its parts.

T

Threshold temperature is the temperature (usually air temperature) at or above which plant growth occurs.

Top dressing (of fertilizers) means applied onto the land (crop and soil) surface.

Trace elements. *See Essential elements.*

Translocation is the movement of soluble organic food materials through the tissues of plants, e.g. from the leaves to the storage organs. *See also Transpiration.*

Translocated (in relation to herbicides, pesticides). *See Systemic.*

Transpiration is the loss of water vapour by plants.

Tropism is the response to a stimulus by plants e.g. response to light is phototropism.

Tuber is a swollen underground stem tip or root which acts as a form of vegetative reproduction. (Example: potato.)

V

Vitamin is an organic chemical which is necessary for the normal function of the mammalian system but which cannot be formed by the mammal's own system.

W

Ware potatoes refers to potatoes sold for human consumption in an unprocessed condition.

Z

Zoonose is an animal disease which can be transmitted to humans.

Appendix

Reagents and resources Here we list "recipes" for many of the chemicals listed in the text and sources for some of the required materials.

A

Alcohol: *See Industrial methylated spirits.*

Alkaline pyrogallol: First make up sodium hydroxide (2M) by dissolving 4 g sodium hydroxide in 100 cm^3 distilled water. Just before use add 10 cm^3 2M sodium hydroxide to 1.0 g pyrogallol crystals. The mixture is useful for about one hour.

Aluminium chloride (0.02M): Dissolve 4.82 g aluminium chloride, $AlCl_3.6H_2O$ (note the chemical formula) in distilled water and make up to 1 litre.

Ammonia, dilute solution: Purchase ammonia solution specific gravity 0.88. Use a 10% solution. Dilute 10 cm^3 to 100 cm^3 using distilled water in a fume cupboard.

Ammonium molybdate solution: Dissolve 5 g ammonium molybdate in 50 cm^3 distilled water. Pour into 50 cm^3 concentrated nitric acid. Add 100 cm^3 distilled water. Carry out these procedures carefully in a fume cupboard.

Ammonium oxalate: Dissolve 20 g ammonium oxalate in distilled water and make up to 1 litre.

B

Barfoed's solution: Purchase from suppliers.

Barium chloride solution: Dissolve 122 g barium chloride in distilled water and make up to 1 litre.

Benedict's solution: Purchase from suppliers.

C

Calcium chloride (0.05M): Dissolve 10.95 g calcium chloride, $CaCl_2.6H_2O$ (note the chemical formula) in distilled water and make up to 1 litre.

Copper sulphate, 1%: Add 1 g copper sulphate to 100 cm^3 distilled water.

D

DCPIP: Follow the instructions on the pack.

Diphenylamine (0.2%): Dissolve 0.2 g of diphenylamine in 100 cm^3 concentrated sulphuric acid. Perform this operation with care in a fume cupboard. Note: handle this reagent with great care during use in class as it is highly corrosive.

Dissection: Obtain proper dissecting boards made from obeiche wood. Some drawing boards are suitable. Purchase dissecting kits from suppliers. Note that prepared/preserved material is generally safer for use over a few days. If preserved in formaldehyde specimens can be stored in water, or merely covered with a damp cloth for a few days. You must ensure that the material does not dry out. The use of unpreserved wild rabbits is not recommended. When using fresh material, including abattoir material, ensure that hands are well washed afterwards. Experience has shown that abattoir material (hearts, lungs, kidneys) can be deep frozen before use. Allow sufficient time for defrosting. However eyes for dissection cannot be frozen satisfactorily and must be used fresh. They can be stored for two days in a domestic fridge.

Drosophila: Purchase from suppliers or contact Dr J. Breen, Chemical & Life Sciences Dept., University of Limerick.

E

Ethanol: *See Industrial methylated spirits.*

F

Fehling's solution: Purchase from suppliers.

Feulgen's stain: Used to stain for DNA in root tip preparations. Purchase from suppliers.

Formalin, (1%): This is purchased as 40% formaldehyde. Treat this as 100% formalin. To make 1% formalin dilute formaldehyde 1:100. Note that 10% formalin is a useful preservative for specimens. Dilute the 40% formaldehyde 1:10. Against its use is the pungent smell and it has also been listed as a possible carcinogen.

FAA, formal acetic alcohol: Used for preserving plant material e.g. potato leaves with blight, maize stems for cutting transverse sections. Mix together 4 cm^3 formaldehyde, 60 cm^3 industrial methylated spirits, 4 cm^3 acetic acid and 40 cm^3 distilled water.

Formaldehyde. *See Formalin.*

Fruit flies. *See Drosophila.*

H

Hydrochloric acid (0.1M): In a fume cupboard, carefully add 8.6 cm^3 concentrated hydrochloric acid to distilled water and make up to 1 litre.

Hydrochloric acid (1%) Carefully add 10 cm^3 concentrated hydrochloric acid to 100 cm^3 distilled water. Do this in a fume cupboard and with care. Make up to 1 litre.

Hydrochloric acid, dilute: This is a 1M solution. In a fume cupboard, carefully add 86 cm^3 concentrated hydrochloric acid to distilled water and make up to 1 litre.

I

Industrial methylated spirits: This is the cheapest form of "alcohol" available for laboratory use. It can be used as ethanol for most investigations. Note that it is poisonous. Note also that generally a licence is required from the Revenue Commissioners but that school suppliers are now authorised to sell useful small quantities to schools. Diluted to 70% IMS can be used to fix and preserve biological specimens.

Iodine: Purchase from suppliers. Alternatively, prepare a saturated aqueous solution of potassium iodide. Now add crystals of iodine to this solution until no more will dissolve. Filter. Dilute with distilled water to a pale brown colour.

L

Limewater: Prepare a saturated solution of calcium hydroxide in water. Allow to settle and filter.

M

Methylene blue: Add 1 g methylene blue to 100 cm^3 distilled water.

P

Potassium chloride (1%): Dissolve 1 g of potassium chloride in distilled water and make up to 100 cm^3.

PTC: Purchase as phenylthiourea. Prepare a solution of 1.3 g PTC per litre in water. Soak clean absorbent paper (e.g. filter paper). Air dry. Cut up into 1 cm squares.

R

Resazurin solution: Follow manufacturer's instructions.

S

Silver nitrate solution: Dissolve 17 g silver nitrate in distilled water and make up to 1 litre. Store in a brown bottle away from light as it is light sensitive.

Sodium chloride (0.1M): Dissolve 5.85 g sodium chloride in distilled water and make up to 1 litre.

Sodium cobaltinitrite: Dissolve 5 g colbalt nitrate in 25 cm^3 distilled water. Dissolve 30 g sodium nitrite in 50 cm^3 distilled water. Mix the two solutions. Acidify with 2.5 cm^3 acetic acid. Cover with a clock glass and stand in the dark for 24 hours. Filter and make up to 100 cm^3 with distilled water.

Sodium hydroxide, dilute: This is 0.1M sodium hydroxide. Dilute 4 g sodium hydroxide and make up to 1 litre with distilled water.

Starch: Mix 1 g soluble starch into a paste with cold water. Stir into 100 cm^3 boiling water. Cool. Make up fresh as required - daily if necessary.

Sucrose: Use a 10% solution. Dissolve 10g sucrose (shop sugar OK) in 100 cm^3 distilled water.

T

Tomato genetic strains: A number of strains are available. The xanthophyll mutants are most useful for monohybrid investigations. These mutants show chlorosis; i.e. they are yellowish and easily distinguishable. The other mutants available involve stem colour. These are less easy to use as intense lighting conditions are required.